Laughter in the Amen Corner

❧ Laughter in

The Life of Evangelist Sam Jones

Kathleen Minnix

the Amen Corner

The University of Georgia Press   Athens & London

© 1993 by the

University of Georgia Press

Athens, Georgia 30602

All rights reserved

Designed by Richard Hendel

Set in Bodoni Book

by Tseng Information Systems

Printed and bound by Maple-Vail Book Manufacturing Group

The paper in this book meets the guidelines for

permanence and durability of the Committee on

Production Guidelines for Book Longevity of the

Council on Library Resources.

Printed in the United States of America

97   96   95   94   93   C   5   4   3   2   1

Library of Congress Cataloging in Publication Data

Minnix, Kathleen.

Laughter in the amen corner : the life of evangelist

Sam Jones / Kathleen Minnix.

p.   cm.

Includes bibliographical references and index.

ISBN 0–8203–1539–7 (alk. paper)

1. Jones, Sam P. (Sam Porter), 1847–1906.

2. Evangelists—United States—Biography. I. Title.

BV3785.J6M56 1993

269′.2′092—dc20

[B]   92–37645

CIP

British Library Cataloging in Publication Data available

Photograph of Sam Jones on title-page spread taken in

April 1906. Courtesy of Howell Jones.

To my husband, Larry,

another of God's comedians

Contents

Preface

This is a biography of Sam Jones, an evangelist who influenced modern evangelism and American history. At his death in 1906, it was said that Sam Jones had spoken to more Americans than anyone who ever lived. He was considered the most widely quoted man of the nineteenth century; he had a way of coining epigrams, of expressing the ordinary in an extraordinary way. Some of his expressions are sunk deep in the language—for example, "The road to hell is paved with good intentions." Frequently infuriating, Sam Jones was always interesting, a sanctified circus in full swing. A natural comedian burdened with an emotional imbalance that drove him first to alcohol and then to bouts of euphoric energy and leaden depression, Jones's life has all the elements of low comedy and high tragedy.

Not only was Sam Jones one of the nation's most popular evangelists, he was a political activist and a newspaper columnist. He advocated rights for women at a time when most men favored keeping ladies on the pedestal and out of politics, yet he followed the South in its drift toward malignant racism. An idealist who envisioned a dry utopia where children would not cry for bread and all men would be redeemed, he was capable of both common sense and crass compromise. He praised Catholics in an age that feared the "Romish heresy," and he embraced Jews as fellow children of God in an era that saw them as Christ killers. Yet he was shrill in his insistence that America was "being harassed by the influx of lower and alien elements" and must restrict immigration in order to "become and remain American." A family man who spent only a few months at home every year, an egotist who exalted God, Jones was a man who blended baffling contradictions without apology or analysis.

Christians will find the problems Jones faced familiar: the debate about the authority of Scripture, the dispute over whether the "star system" of evangelism helps or hurts the church, the question of whether God calls women to preach. We in the twentieth century face the dilemma over whether individual liberties should be upheld when the public is endangered by drug abuse or disease; nineteenth-century Americans struggled with the right of the individual to drink versus the need for a society to protect itself from the ravages of alcohol. Then, as now, conservative Christians like Sam Jones valued the safety of society over the rights of the individual, while liberals upheld personal liberty. Then, as now, conservatives relied on law, while liberals relied on reason and education.

The modern Christian bemoans the advance of "secular humanism"; the nineteenth-century believer lamented the encroachments of "worldliness." Both fretted over denominational infighting, spiritual apathy, the worship of materialism, the collapse of the traditional family structure, and the breakdown of public and personal morality. For a large number of believers the answer of a century ago is the answer of today: the entry of committed Christians into the political process as an informed and organized lobby, ready to reward friends and punish enemies.

This book is divided into ten chapters and a conclusion. In Chapter 1 the reader is set down in the midst of a Sam Jones revival, the Nashville meeting that catapulted Jones to national prominence. Chapter 2 discusses his childhood and the circumstances of his conversion, and Chapter 3 his early ministry and influences on his style and theology. Chapter 4 deals with the Orphan Home and Jones's rise to fame; Chapter 5 discusses his role as spokesman of the New South and reconciler of the sections. Chapter 6 looks at Jones's role as enemy of the "isms" (Darwinism, agnosticism, materialism, spiritualism, biblical criticism), and attempts to place him among the Social Gospelers and prefundamentalists who were spawned by the social conditions and theological disputes at the end of the century. Chapter 7 deals with the twin controversies of holiness and professional evangelism that shattered the Methodist church and cost Jones his credentials. Chapter 8 covers prohibition, and Chapter 9 examines Jones's views on race and politics. Chapter 10 deals with the erosion of Jones's popularity as an evangelist, his struggle with illness, and the disappointments and pleasures of his family life. Finally, in the Conclusion, I try to assess the particular contributions of this peculiar man to American social and religious history.

Acknowledgments

This work has had several incarnations: first a term paper, then a thesis, next a dissertation, and finally a book. Any project with that many lives has had several parents; *Laughter in the Amen Corner* is no exception. I would like to express my thanks to four professors at Georgia State University who guided the dissertation: Drs. John Matthews, Neil Gillespie, Tim Crimmins, and Gary Fink. Thanks also to those in the Interlibrary Loan Department at the Pullen Library of Georgia State University who scoured the country for microfilm of obsolete newspapers. I was graciously assisted as well by archivists at the Archives of the State of

Georgia, Special Collections at Emory University, the Document Center at the University of Georgia, and the Sam Jones Museum in Cartersville. Any author is indebted to their editor and copyeditor; Nancy Holmes and Ellen Harris have been sources of encouragement and humor.

I would also like to thank those members of the Jones family who have allowed me to pore over their letters and manuscripts. The late Lucy Cunyus Mulcahy, a great-grandniece, generously allowed me access to her records. Howell Jones, a great-grandson who inherited many of the family documents, was extraordinarily obliging with the photographs he has in his possession. The late Paul Jones, Jr., a grandson, and Dorothy Roth, a great-grandniece, were kind enough to give me several interviews that allowed me to clarify family relationships. It is difficult to grant a stranger access to a family's past, but Sam Jones's descendants were more than gracious to me.

My family has also been wonderful. My father, Don Wright, my sister, Rosalind Wright, and my brother, Lawrence Wright, are all published authors. It has been therapeutic to be able to talk with them about how terrible it is to write, and how wonderful to have written. My mother, who "only writes letters," as she says, has the essential role of encourager. My parents-in-law, Frances and Lawrence Minnix, have been equally supportive. Many weekends and evenings they provided loving care for my children and made me grateful that when I married my husband, I married his family. My children, John and David, have been understanding, as well, of times when "Mama was writing."

It is traditional at this point to give a bow to the spouse who "made it all possible." My husband, Larry, who supported me emotionally and financially through this work, gave up his Saturdays to the project and even took up his red pen to edit when the book grew beyond manageable proportions.

Perhaps it is appropriate for me to share my views on Sam Jones and his theology. Jones was not a perfected saint, but one does not need to read far into the Scriptures to find that God can use people who are not perfect. Jones may have suffered from manic depression, and skeptics may use this speculation to dismiss him as a man driven by religious delusions. I do not. I am convinced that Sam Jones tried to live out God's claim on his life. If he brought a handicap into his ministry, others—Saint Paul, for example— have also. If he was arrogant, coarse, encumbered with cultural assumptions, others—Saint Paul, for example—have been also. The story of Sam Jones is one of transformation, not of one transformed.

 Laughter in the Amen Corner

The Lord's hand was with them, and a great number

of people believed and turned to the Lord.—Acts 11:21

The law then is meant to drive the sinner to Christ by

showing him his exceeding sinfulness and helplessness. It is

the burning heat that drives the weary traveler to the shadow

of a great rock in a desert land.—J. D. Williams

1
❧ That Memorable Meeting

It was Sunday afternoon, May 10, 1885. The great Nashville revival was about to begin. For hours carriages had been pulling up before the huge tent, and mule-drawn streetcars were burdened with human cargo headed to hear the eccentric evangelist Sam Jones. Thousands were walking, drawn to the corner of Eighth and Broad like filings to a great magnet. By the time the first preacher got up to pray, ten thousand people, one out of every five in that Tennessee town, had turned up at the tent. All the planks were packed; the sawdust aisles were clogged with people. Though parents took children on their laps and preachers crowded cross-legged on the platform, twenty-five hundred people were turned away.

Those seeing Sam Jones for the first time were often impressed with how physically unimpressive he was, expecting all that energy to be grounded in flesh. "Sam Jones is a very insignificant looking person," one reporter remarked. "He is a small, thin, wiry-looking man with a firm jaw, pinched face, sallow complexion, a small black mustache, coal-black hair brushed high off a rather narrow forehead, finely lined eyebrows, and hands as small and delicate as a woman's." Jones was aware of the effect his appearance had on people and used it for comic effect: "I weigh 135 pounds, but 132½ of that are solid backbone," Jones would boast, "and I don't want but 2½ pounds of surplus."[1]

An individual in all things, Jones did not wear the funereal frock coat favored by ministers, nor did he wear robes or a clerical collar. "No man shall say I ever hid behind my ministerial robes," Jones explained defiantly. "I have never dressed like a preacher and I never talked like one." In the early years of his ministry, his outfits were combinations of stripes and plaids, or alpaca suits, accessorized by a limp tie and a wilted felt hat. As he became more prosperous his attire improved, and he began to look like "a well-to-do country merchant" or a "railroad engineer." He never wore cuffs, however; "he hated starch of all kinds."[2]

His unclerical appearance had advantages. It ensured his anonymity with folks he met on trains and in lobbies—people who were taken aback when they realized they had been talking in an uncensored way with a famous evangelist. It refuted rumors that he was amassing a fortune evangelizing, and it demonstrated his contempt for a society that judged a man by the cut of his clothes rather than the size of his heart. Also, his rumpled folksiness set him apart from the starched clerics who encircled him, identifying him more closely with the men in the pew than with the men on the platform.[3]

Thus, in Nashville when Sam Jones ambled across the platform, tossed his overcoat on the back of the chair and settled into a slump, amazement accompanied the sight of a man who "staggered about looking as little like a preacher as the next man." He made it clear that his originality extended to his approach to the Almighty. He asked God not to convict a single sinner at that service: "The company in the Church ain't good enough for them yet." It had gotten so the poor heathens could not sit down at a card table or sidle up to a bar without being crowded out by Christians, Jones lamented. And "if you will go round one night and look," he said, shooting a look at the ministers, "you'll ketch 'em." No wonder the churches were in poor shape when men spent all their time and all their money on the world; "some people are actually ashamed to let the right hand know how stingy the left hand is."[4]

A speaker given to seismic shifts in mood, Jones understood the visceral response of his audience to the "Lost Cause" in that era of voluptuous sentimentality. Few in Nashville had forgotten the terrible battle of Christmas 1864 when the ragged, raw-footed Confederates, making their way through a blizzard to occupied Nashville, fought a skirmish near Franklin, Tennessee, that ended in an "unparalleled slaughter of officers." It was the last offensive of the southern army. Thus, when Sam Jones ended the meeting that first night with an incident from the Tennessee campaign he described as "not historical but in many respects true," he tapped a rich vein of emotion.[5]

General John Bell Hood was watching with anguish as the Union forces, entrenched in a fort near a locust grove, rained fire upon the faltering Confederates. Twice General Hood sent his adjutant to generals in the field, presenting his compliments and asking for the fort; twice he was told that the officers had fallen. The third time Hood instructed the adjutant to present his *love* to General Cockrell and ask for the fort in the locust grove. "General Cockrell straightened himself on the saddle, cast his bright eye down the line, and said: 'First Missouri Brigade, Attention!' and dropped his finger on the fort. And they charged with a fearful loss on that fort, and captured it and silenced the guns," Jones said in a choked voice. "Brethren of Nashville, at this hour, as adjutant-general of the Lord Jesus Christ, I point my finger at the citadel of sin in Nashville, and tell you that my Lord and Saviour presents you all His love, and He asks at your hands this fort that is desolating so many hearts." When he called upon all to stand who wanted God to have that victory, "the people rose to their feet, with tears streaming down their faces."[6]

Suddenly brusque, Jones announced 6 A.M. services every morning at McKendree Methodist Church in addition to the 10:00 and 7:30 meetings in the tent. Though the sunrise services had been popular elsewhere, Jones suspected that "there's many a good Methodist, Baptist and Presbyterian in the city who wouldn't turn over in his bed to save Nashville from hell." Aiming his final shot, Jones commanded every preacher in Nashville to be there, "Dr. Barbee thrown in."[7]

This jab was directed at the Reverend J. D. Barbee, pastor of "the first pulpit in Methodism," McKendree Methodist Church. The sparring match between the preachers had started several months before when Jones had dumbfounded Nashville clergymen by demanding a three-thousand-dollar tent. Although Jones was a celebrity in his home state of Georgia and had created a sensation in Memphis the year before, his boast that no church in Nashville—"the city of churches"—could contain his crowds was greeted with derision. Prove it, the exasperated Protestant Ministers Association shot back.[8]

Never one to dodge a dare, Jones had come, preaching three times in the largest churches Nashville could offer, denouncing the "whiskey sellers, drunkards, gamblers and theatre-goers" who populated the pews. Jones had made a particular enemy of Barbee when he announced that if Barbee "drew the line" where God draws the line, McKendree would have one hundred members instead of one thousand. These comments inflamed interest, and as word spread of the incendiary evangelist over Sunday dinners and during Sabbath strolls, the mini-revival gained such momentum that hundreds were turned away at the evening service. The following day, Jones preached three times at the Tulip Street Methodist Church, kicking off a revival that resulted in 150 conversions and 111 additions to that church. Tuesday he left the city, still insisting that no tent meant no revival. All existing buildings were inadequate because it was "impossible to manipulate a crowd inside one of them."[9]

Nashville's ministers were repulsed by his "vulgarisms"—his advice to girls to marry a mulatto before a gambler, a drunkard, or a "spider-legged dude" was particularly distressing to those not inclined to erase the color line. It seemed the invitation would be withdrawn when Dr. John B. McFerrin, the seventy-eight-year-old patriarch of the Tennessee Conference, stood up. A towering man with a jagged brow and imposing intellect, McFerrin was known for his "sanctified pugnacity." Though almost blind and deaf, McFerrin dominated any discussion he entered. Admitting he had heard "some things which would be better unsaid," McFerrin insisted he had also heard "some wonderful things which went direct to the heart." The association surrendered: better a revival with the unsavory evangelist than no revival at all. They voted to buy the tent, only the aggrieved Dr. Barbee dissenting.[10]

Not everyone was won over, however. Nashville was fond of thinking of itself as the embodiment of the ideals of the Old South, a place where people had exhibited grace under the pressure of a three-year occupation by Yankee vandals. Surely a city whose gentility had withstood the humiliation of defeat and the poverty of Reconstruction would not fall before this barbarian who insulted his social betters. The editor of the *Daily Union* professed himself amazed "beyond expression" that the ministers' association would sponsor a man whose sermons were replete with "coarseness, vulgarity, slang and positive misrepresentations." The citizens of the "Athens of the South," the editor warned the absent evangelist, "are past the age of being ridiculed or abused into religion."[11]

"Brother Jones has developed into an epidemic," a reporter noted ruefully as columns filled with emphatic opinions on the evangelist. Barbee suggested with startling insight and unctuous charity that the evangelist's tendency to be "extravagant in his utterances" was due to a biochemical imbalance. Even the infidels got in on the act, publishing a circular advertising the "Great Show and Circus" at which "the laughable farce, Christianity, will be expounded by the great clown, Sam Jones." Though tickets are free, managers "Humbug" and "Ignorance" explained, "don't forget the missionary box, for you know that the action of the clergy is no money, no preach."[12]

Sam Jones was thrilled by the criticism. The greater the controversy the larger the crowd, for "when a feller barks there's a hundred will have to come see what he's treed." He kept in mind that "some of you talking about me are like the skunk telling a 'possum his breath is bad." Jones estimated that twenty thousand people in twenty states were praying for the revival: with such a multitude interceding on behalf of the sinners of Nashville, "there will be a great victory for God."[13]

Southern Methodists had been beseeching God for a revival for two years, ever since Bishop George Pierce had voiced the prevailing sense of spiritual deadness in the midst of fabulous growth. While there were religious revivals aplenty, what was needed was a "revival of religion," Pierce had proclaimed, "a sin-killing, sin-hating, sin-forsaking, debt-paying, God-serving, man-loving religion." In chorus, the columns of Methodist newspapers from Maryland to Texas had filled with jeremiads bemoaning the worldliness of the church. "I have almost heard the voice of lamentation in the land," the Atlanta minister W. F. Glenn wrote. Fingers were pointed. Glenn blamed the decline in spiritual power on demonic interference, an unwholesome dependence upon itinerant evangelists, and the divisive debate over the authority of Scripture. One anonymous contributor traced the declension to the church's neglect of the Negro. The very people who were groaning to God for an awakening were grieving the Spirit, this angry critic contended, "but if the word of God is not a fable, and Christianity a farce, they will never obtain a revival until they change their ways."[14]

Though the Lord tarried, southern Methodists had an almost messianic expectation of an awakening. Each report of revival from an obscure corner of the Kingdom was greeted as the first gleanings of the future harvest. Hopes were especially high in Nashville, home of Vanderbilt University, the publishing house, the mission boards, and the most important paper of the connection, the *Christian Advocate*. The editor of that paper, Dr. O. P. Fitzgerald, described the swelling spirit of revival: "The need is felt, the desire is expressed, the pastors are moving and praying men and women are calling upon God for power on high." The tide of religious feeling in Nashville, already at flood stage when Jones made his whirlwind visit in March, spilled over into a dozen churches during the six-week hiatus. "These are good times for Nashville Methodism," one preacher rejoiced at the beginning of May 1885. "The best is yet to come." That faith was shared by thousands, and those gathering at the first meeting of the revival that balmy afternoon in May came with the expectation that harvest time was at hand. The gay reaper had appeared, God's comedian, cracking jokes and cracking hearts, slashing away at pretense and binding up the bruised reed. Sam Jones had come to town.[15]

The enthusiasm of the first meeting hardly prepared the city's pastors for the one thousand people who showed up for the sunrise service. Half of them were men, surprising since in Nashville's churches, as in most Protestant churches of the time, women not only outnumbered men but were far more likely to have the pitch of piety that would pull them out of bed before dawn. After Jones's musical director, Professor R. M. McIntosh, warmed up the crowd with lively hymns, Jones preached briefly on the shortcomings of a church so slow "the devil can travel a mile while we are putting on our boots." Jones then threw the meeting open for testimonials and prayer requests. Though several men stood up, the women held back until the evangelist exclaimed, "I am glad to see you good women so thoroughly furnished with grace that you don't need any more," a statement that inspired two women to rise. Jones then called for everyone who would ask God's blessing on the meeting to stand up. The entire audience rose.[16]

By 3:30 the tent had turned into a "sweatbox" and Jones's temper had risen with the temperature. The mellow joking mood of the morning had vanished, and the evangelist spent the afternoon and evening services "jumping the Scribes and the Pharisees." He had no use for Christians who attend dances Saturday night and church Sunday morning; dancing was simply "hugging set to music." An immoral electorate had chosen corrupt officials, Jones charged; the police were in collusion with prostitutes and gamblers, and the preachers were standing idly by, "not stopping the downward course of men they know are going down." However, he believed God would send a revival. "Brethren, in all my experience I have never seen a meeting take up better than this," Jones confided. Lies were being told, but his feelings were not hurt: "This ain't the first fight I was ever in." His attackers may have been able to "shell him out" while he was not present to defend himself, "but I'm in the shelling business myself," he boasted. "Let 'em commence to tackle me now."[17]

Jones customarily divided his audience into two classes: "the outbreaking sinners" and "the goody-goody sinners." When he was after "the goody-goody sinners," church folk who looked righteous on the outside but inside were "whited sepulchres," Jones was abrupt and merciless, his sermons full of slang and sarcasm. "I want to get your hide loosened up," he would explain. "Sometimes the currycomb is worth more than the corn in a hide-bound church." When churches began to come to life, Jones would turn to "the out-breaking sinners," those who were not hypocrites but heathens, and his tone would warm and soften. Thus, on the fourth day of the campaign when Jones stopped scolding the saints, the change in technique was dramatic. "It was evident to all who listened to the Georgia evangelist yesterday, that what has been termed irreverence is disappearing from his preaching," a perceptive reporter noted. "Having gathered his audience and concentrated their attention, he is getting down to serious work."[18]

Jones was contemptuous of "heart religion," that piety which touched the emotions but failed to reform the life. Do not "come to this meeting and blubber around," he ordered at the second sunrise service when emotions threatened to erupt. However, with sinners he often opened floodgates of feeling, as in the sermon "What Must I Do to Be Saved?" He was often weary in this life, the evangelist admitted, but he knew that if he followed the narrow path he would come at last to that bright world where the saints see their Savior's face and walk the golden streets. One day he would be in heaven praising God, and his wife would suddenly be beside him; they would join hands and never be parted again. Then an angel would bring one precious child after another until all had been joyously reunited on that other shore, that blessed place where God's own hand would brush away each tear.

The meeting exploded. "It would be difficult to describe the situation that arose," the reporter from the *Daily American* wrote, picking his words carefully. Some "passed about shaking hands and giving loud expression to their outbursts of emotion." "Violent laughter" and "shouts of 'hallelujah' " ricocheted around the tent while "the evangelist stood smiling and crying out occasionally 'Bless God.' "[19]

Jones was a reformed alcoholic, and he used the same strategy—alternating blasts of sentiment and sarcasm—to persuade tipplers to take the pledge. Sometimes he used stinging humor, inviting his audience to "take those jokes home and crack them, and they would find a hornet in every one." Sometimes his anger seeped through, and he would thunder at the Christians who peddled Beelzebub's brew. "If I ever want to sell whiskey," he growled, "I am going to the town and get a license from those old members of the Church, and I will tell my wife to put my license in the coffin when I die. I will pull out my license and tell the Lord, 'Here's my license, signed by Methodist stewards and Baptist deacons'; and God Almighty will put us all in hell together."[20]

Other times Jones used emotional ammunition, pleading with sinners to remember the home that had nurtured them, the Bible they once revered, and the mothers who waited, wasted with worry and worn out with praying, for their prodigals to return. "Boys, boys, boys, boys. Never let it be said you added a pang to a mother's heart," Jones would say. "There are burdens here on a mother's heart, she can't carry much longer. I tell you, human hearts will carry just so much and then they'll break. There are mothers in this town who, if God don't take 'em to Heaven, will be raving maniacs in twelve months. My mother! my mother!"[21]

This combination of accusation and entreaty were too much for "Steamboatin'" Tom Ryman, a figure of mythic proportions in Nashville. Ryman owned thirty-five steamboats that brought millions of dollars' worth of produce and cotton into Nashville from the small towns and farms along the Cumberland River. Brought up by devout Methodists, he never charged churches for transporting materials, but ships carrying sacred cargo were stocked with old wine and young whiskey, and dancing girls entertained in ornate gambling casinos. As one account has it, Thomas J. Ryman was "a swinging soul who ran floating dens of iniquity" until the night "he and some boys roared into the tent meeting of an evangelist named Sam Jones."[22]

Ryman and "the boys" had come not to acquire eternal life but out of a more earthly concern: to protect their business interests. Informed that some riverboat men had expressed an interest in assault, Jones announced that he welcomed exercise after the service. He then preached a sermon replete with unkind allusions to the Devil's brew and the rascals who served it. After an unrelenting hour and a half, the evangelist ended by extending the right hand of fellowship to any who might care to grasp it. A hard-muscled man with a firm jaw and a determined look stumped forward, leaning heavily on his cane. "I came here for the purpose stated by Mr. Jones," Tom Ryman admitted, "and he has whipped me with the Gospel of Christ."[23]

Ryman gave his heart to God and his allegiance to Sam Jones. To glorify them both he built the Union Gospel Tabernacle, later known as Ryman Auditorium, "the Mother Church of country music" and home of the Grand Ole Opry. He risked his competitive edge in the fierce war against the railroads and transformed the barrooms on his boats into mission halls, turning wine into water. He christened his best steamboat "Sam Jones," converted his saloon on the wharf into the "Sam Jones Hall," and hired a minister and a teacher for the steamboat men, gamblers, and drunkards who washed up on the riverbank. For the next twenty years two wagons were a familiar sight to Nashvillians: one filled with food, medicine and clothing for the poor; and one equipped with its own choir, organ, and pulpit, carrying the Good News into neighborhoods without churches and to Sabbath breakers in the business district.[24]

New legends collected around Ryman. When he died after a carriage wreck in 1904, four thousand people came to the tabernacle on Christmas Day to hear Sam Jones eulogize this "gentle man of child-like faith." Jones considered Ryman the brightest jewel in his heavenly crown, and when asked whether his converts "stuck" he would point to the riverboat captain, saying "there has been no more wonderful convert to God in the nineteenth century than Tom Ryman, of Nashville."[25]

The spectacular conversion of Tom Ryman and hundreds of others won over those who had expressed reservations about "the Georgia Cracker." Editors tripped over themselves extolling the evangelist and analyzing his puzzling power over people. The *Daily Union,* which had deplored Jones's crude witticisms only a few weeks earlier, now rhapsodized over the man who had earned the "well-nigh universal" praise of the city. The *Daily American* marveled that the evangelist's crudeness no longer offended; rather, it made him seem "a bubbling fount fresh from the bosom of the earth; nature's own." Dr. Fitzgerald of the *Christian Advocate* was effusive in his praise of a revival that had exceeded all expectations. "Luxurious men and delicate women who have not seen sunrise for years, leave their beds at dawn and hurry to 'the gospel tent,' working men with their dinner-buckets in their hands stop to see and hear this apostle for the masses." Preachers rejoiced to see a "pentecostal power" of which they had only heard, and "a new and strange fervor in the exhortations, songs and prayers, attest that these are the days of the Son of Man in Nashville."[26]

One week into the revival, Sam Jones threw the morning meeting open to the preachers, asking them to "tell us something of the gladness of their hearts." Jere Witherspoon, the genial pastor of the First Presbyterian Church, spoke first, rejoicing that during the Sunday service "there was a mellowness and earnestness about the congregation I never saw before." Dr. Strickland of First Baptist spoke of the "happy tears" that were being shed, and J. P. McFerrin testified, "We bin up to the bilin' point at Elm Street [Methodist] Church for some time, and on Sunday we boiled over. . . .

I never saw such power in my life." Even Barbee confessed that "the fire is kindled, and my people are awake and alive."[27]

Sam Jones was the most tolerant of intolerant men, and his inclusion of churches outside his own Methodist denomination was typical of his ecumenical inclinations. It was his belief that doctrines deaden and divide: "I despise theology and botany, but I love religion and flowers," Jones would say. In Nashville he rejoiced to see theological disputes set aside for the revival. "The Methodists have come to feed on Presbyterian grass and the Presbyterians are here feeding on Methodist grass," the evangelist exulted, "and Methodists and Presbyterians will just lock arms and go down to the Baptist pond and take a good old drink."[28]

Convinced that the Holy Spirit was at hand, the evangelist again opened the altar, preaching a sermon that displayed his mix of sulphur and sentiment: "What Wait I For?" "I want you to solve this question tonight," the evangelist began. "Let your heart go out toward God. Men reach God heart forward and not head forward." There was no need for delay; nothing on earth could stop salvation, and heaven itself yawned open to receive them. "This revival is not aimed to get God ready to accept your soul, but to get your soul ready to accept God. This much I will tell you—you will never see God's gates wider open than they are now, and if you won't enter through a wide gate, will you trouble to push through a narrow one?"[29]

Someone in the audience is hoping to get better terms, but there are no better terms. God has only two conditions: "Lay down those things that are hurting you and your children here and hereafter and take up those that will help you and your children here and hereafter." Another listener is waiting for the church to get right: "You'll be in hell a million years before that comes." Another is waiting to "feel" religious. "Oh! my brother, when a man feels he ought to quit the wrong and do right, that's all the 'feelin' there is on the subject."[30]

Someone else is trying to get better on their own, but "you won't go fifty feet before the devil will wallow you in a mud hole—you remind me of a feller in a dead drunk tryin' to walk a chalk line." Another is waiting for faith, but "he's like a feller says he's going to be a blacksmith when he gets enough muscle. How do you get faith? By using what you've got, don't you see?" Another is waiting to feel worthy, but

> I tell you, brethren, that is the most ridiculous attitude a man can occupy. A man is starving to death, a friend invites him to eat; he stands off and says he can't eat because he ain't fittin! Offer him soap and water and towel and he will still stand off 'cause he ain't fittin. Ain't that foolish?

Let me tell you the very reason God likes you is because you feel your own unworthiness. . . . You may be frail; yes, but your hope's in God. Your appetite may be like a roaring lion; yes, but your hope's in God. . . . You'll have dark days, that's sure, but this journey ends well. Don't think of the road, but of where it leads. . . . Start tonight. The train's here; the bell's ringing. Step aboard.[31]

The revival settled into a pattern with Jones alternately "hammering the brethren" and soothing sinners. Crowds grew to the point that the "saved" were asked to stay away from the evening service to leave room for "seekers." Railroads capitalized on the two thousand people pouring into Nashville from the countryside by offering reduced rates; streetcars bore signs which read, "Take this car to hear Rev. Sam Jones." The revival eliminated or overshadowed all other activities. "Society has been in sackcloth and ashes all the week," one editor complained. "Fashion and the Georgia Evangelist have decreed that the dainty dears and curled darlings of society shall attend the gospel meetings."[32]

As the revival swelled, Jones used a system he had introduced to the South the year before in Memphis: the "special meeting" targeted at specific groups. He conducted meetings for mothers, laborers, children—he even held one for convicts at the state prison. Reporters loved the spectacle of such occasions. At the meeting "for Negroes only," the correspondent for the *Daily American* gushed that he was witnessing "the most remarkable address ten thousand negroes ever had made to them since the world began." However, it was the meetings for men only—"stag parties" as Jones tagged them—that generated the most print. In an age of byzantine prudishness, Jones spoke with startling bluntness, cataloging the sins masculine flesh was prone to: drinking, gambling, cussing, and lewd women. "There are people by the hundreds who know you are licentious and not faithful to your wife," Jones would say, pointing a skeletal finger at a suspect. "They know you built that house over there that woman is living in. They've seen you hitching up your horse and buggy at the gate and they know you don't get any money for rent."[33]

Some are sowing whiskey, unconcerned because "all their boys are girls." But "first thing you know the devil will pack off a drunken son-in-law on you. . . . My God, I'd rather have my girls buried tonight out of my sight than have them lie in the embraces of a drunken son-in-law." Some were sowing cards and reaping a "spider-legged" gambler who walks around looking "like he's melted and poured into his pants." Some were sowing billiards and reaping fools: "I never knew a first-class billiard player that was worth the powder and lead it would take to kill him." Some were sowing thoroughbreds and reaping damnation: "There's many a man here that's going right straight into hell on a blooded horse. I reckon you think though it's better to go that way than to walk."[34]

These remarks made an impression upon General W. H. Jackson, Civil War hero and owner of the famous Belle Meade horse farm. Though Jackson had converted during one of the revivals that flared along the front lines of the Confederate army, his ardor had ebbed away after the war. Inspired by Sam Jones to reconsecrate his life, the grateful general raised ten thousand dollars to buy the Jones family a house in Nashville.[35]

The evangelist was moved by the gesture and struck by the sense of basing his endeavors in Nashville, a railroad center and home of official southern Methodism. He had paid only one hundred dollars on his house in the little town of Cartersville, Georgia, and owed a thousand more. Also, he had found himself "greatly drawn to this people." However, his wife, Laura, ailing at home after the birth of the couple's seventh child, refused to bring up her children in a city with saloons. General Jackson insisted Jones accept the money anyway. Though the evangelist wanted to use it to build a new house, Laura would not give up her cottage, so Jones used the money to pay off his creditors and begin furnishing his home in the sumptuous Victorian style for which "Roselawn" would become known in the next decade. The debt-free house was dedicated on Christmas Day 1885, with Jones praying that this would be "a place where God can come and feel at home," a place with nothing "to grieve away his holy spirit."[36]

Toward the end of the Nashville revival, a reporter observed that people from neighboring towns and farms were outnumbering natives and speculated that Jones might affect the spiritual life of the entire middle Tennessee valley. As the revival broadened in circumference, it deepened in influence. Jones ate breakfast with Governor Bates and addressed the state legislature. "The appearance of the speaker was one of all but complete physical and mental inertia," one reporter wrote, "but his words were full of fire."[37]

The evangelist's exhaustion and his affection for Nashville were both in evidence during the final sermon of the three-week revival. He confessed to the audience of eight thousand, "I have never felt more thankful in my life than for the privilege of preaching to the people of Nashville." Jones contended that a powerful pulpit depended on a praying pew, and he closed the revival by asking everyone to stand who would intercede for him and his work. The entire congregation stood up. "Thank heaven, the wonderful power ascribed to me has been at last analyzed," Jones said. "You see that wherever I go, I leave behind thousands of good people who continually pray for me." The service concluded, and so many thousands came forward to shake hands that the exhausted evangelist asked people to say goodbye to him "with their hearts." [38]

The next day, fatigue still etched in his face, Jones was interviewed by the *Daily American*. "The sadness of countenance noticeable at all times is intensified on nearer view," the reporter wrote, "except when the features light up" and Jones is "suddenly transformed from a dreary, fagged being to a bundle of active nerves acutely attentive." A certain remoteness was apparent, not attributable to reserve, but rather to his seeming "to think and speak from an inner impulse rather from the dictates of sifted reason." Not satisfied with the explanation Jones had given for the success of the revival, the reporter pressed for a reason that made sense "from a more practical or worldly point of view." The evangelist laughed: "Why, the whole work is inexplicable to him who confines himself only to natural phenomenon and material things. But to him who has the wings of faith and soars into the supernatural it is perfectly clear." [39]

The reporter then asked the question on everyone's mind: What about the spiritual slump predicted after such a peak? "I believe it is of God, and will last forever," Jones answered; then, after a long pause during which he seemed to be listening to that inner voice, he added, "It's normal and healthy for a man who eats heartily today to be hungry again tomorrow." If coldness afflicts the church again, it is "only proof that we need another work that will warm us into renewed life and activity." But his revivals were rarely subject to much backlash. "I have preached right living, feeling or no feeling, and when feeling is gone righteousness, or right living will abide." [40]

The *Daily Union* agreed, predicting that "the permanency of this work" will come from the fact that Jones persuaded people that "social, as well as religious reforms are needed." In fact, Nashville's preachers were so convinced of this they made Nashville into a headquarters for prohibition work in Tennessee and—often with Sam Jones at their head—led repeated assaults against saloons, Sabbath desecration, political corruption, and prostitution. [41]

Six weeks after the final service, Dr. William Leftwich of the Tulip Street Methodist Church estimated that fifteen hundred people had been converted during the revival; everywhere, Leftwich exulted, "godly living" had replaced worldly pleasures. Jones himself thought that two thousand souls had been born during those weeks in Nashville but acknowledged many of those were longtime church members who had made a pretense of piety and who now had a real commitment to Christ. The minister who supervised the Nashville district was even more euphoric, writing six months after the meeting that the revival had brought ten thousand new members into the church within a hundred-mile radius of the city.[42]

Sam Jones was swelling a rising tide, for this was a revival year throughout the entire southern connection. "In no previous year have there been so many conversions reported," Dr. Fitzgerald rejoiced. "The net gain in membership is the largest in history." It was a banner year for Methodism in Nashville, with the district expanding from five to more than six thousand members. Adult baptisms had increased dramatically, a sign of real church growth in a denomination with a tradition of infant baptism. However, in the four Methodist churches most affected by the revival, McKendree, Tulip Street, Foster Street, and Elm Street, more than half the new members had joined during the six-week period between Jones's first visit to the city and the beginning of the tent meeting, a time when the *Banner* reported 552 conversions and 405 accessions in six Methodist churches. This suggests that Jones's most important contribution to church growth was made during his one-day blitz in March, when by the power of his personality he provoked new interest in Christianity among the unchurched, an interest that the Methodist ministers moved quickly to cultivate. The statistics also indicate that, as the evangelist himself recognized, his greatest impact was on hidden heathens already in the church.[43]

The startling discrepancy between the enormous numbers of accessions anticipated at the end of the meeting and the relatively small number who actually joined the churches happened again and again in Jones's urban revivals. A Sam Jones revival put Christianity in the headlines, brought emotional excitement to the faithful, underlined the practical and social applications of spiritual life, transformed plodding preachers into crusaders for righteousness, and fostered brotherhood among bickering denominations. However, with few exceptions, his revivals in urban areas did not contribute significantly to church growth.

For the rest of his life, Sam Jones thought of the Nashville revival as "the most marvelous in grace I ever looked upon in my life—I believe more men were converted, and more people joined the church from that memorable meeting than any work of grace almost in the nineteenth century." Whatever the eternal effects, the meeting made him a national figure. Newspapers from Boston to San Francisco carried reports of what was termed "the most remarkable religious awakening which the country had seen for many years." By the end of the revival he was booked for the next ten months, signed to conduct meetings in small towns in Mississippi, Alabama, Tennessee, Virginia, and South Carolina, as well as in St. Louis, Baltimore, and New Orleans.[44]

All this acclaim made Laura nervous—for the next few years she would fret that she was a moth married to a butterfly—and she wrote of her amazement that her husband was an important man. "Glad you have found it out at last," Jones joked; then, turning serious, he confessed: "No dear wife. I am less in my own eyes than I have ever been in my life. To God be all the Glory."[45]

The Nashville revival thrilled and humbled Sam Jones. To him it was an indication that though men might flinch at his brutal speech, God approved it. More than ever, he coveted criticism. "I don't apologize for my preaching, but glory in it," he would say defiantly. "I don't say anything that isn't true, and I am not going to apologize for the truth." For those offended by attacks made with "malice aforethought," he offered this invitation: "If any man doesn't like what I say, let him come to me after the meeting and say so, and I will—forgive him."[46]

On a train approaching Nashville six weeks after the revival, a "hard case" was overheard anxiously asking: "Is the Sam Jones epidemic over yet?" It was not, and it would not be for a long time to come. Sam Jones had captured the imagination of the American people and for the next twenty years he would occupy so many pulpits and platforms that at his death it would be said that he had spoken to more Americans than anyone who had ever lived. The "epidemic" had only begun.[47]

Wash yourselves; make yourself clean; remove the evil

of your doings from before my eyes; cease to do evil,

learn to do good; seek justice, correct oppression;

defend the fatherless, plead for the widow.

—Isaiah 1:16–17

After being born again a man experiences peace,

but it is a militant peace, a peace maintained

at the point of war.—Oswald Chambers

2

❦ Born and Born Again

If "blood will tell"—and he believed that it would—Sam Jones was predestined to become a Methodist preacher. Born October 16, 1847, in Oak Bowery, Alabama, this second son of John and Queenie Jones was the product of generations of Methodist inbreeding. Though his father chose a career in law and real estate, four of his uncles were Methodist ministers, as was his grandfather, the redoubtable Samuel Gamble Jones.

Orphaned at the age of four, Samuel Gamble Jones was separated from his brothers and sisters and shipped between relatives until he was bound out at the age of sixteen to a tanner in Elbert County, Georgia. Pining for his family in South Carolina, one night Samuel Jones stopped in at a revival being conducted by a band of roving Methodist revivalists and was convicted and converted in the space of an hour. A year later he felt called to follow his dead father into the ministry and made "a new and entire consecration of heart, life, and all to the church." Though he applied for ordination, he was made a class leader instead, charged with shepherding a dozen or so souls, comforting them when they were sick, rebuking them when they were in error. For twenty years he served as the spiritual supervisor of this tiny flock. His perseverance was rewarded in 1843 when the conference licensed him to preach.[1]

And preach he did for the next twenty-eight years, farming during the week to support his wife and his growing brood. A man of raw, jabbing humor, strong will, and robust health, "Grandpa Jones" lived to be ninety years old, the patriarch of a clan that at his death numbered 116 descendants, 9 of them Methodist ministers. As Sam Jones bragged: "None of my family are rich, but they are religious."[2]

Samuel and his wife, Elizabeth, were a staunch-looking couple, he with his inverted smile and bulbous nose, she with her mournful eyes peeking out from the lace handkerchief that encircled her face like a wimple. Like her husband, Elizabeth Jones was renowned for her piety: by the end of her life she had read the Bible through thirty-seven times "on her knees." When moved by the Spirit, Elizabeth Jones would punctuate Samuel's sermons with shouts. As she walked up and down the aisles clapping her hands, her exhortations were often accompanied by a "Holy Ghost baptism."[3]

Elizabeth Jones came by her religious enthusiasm naturally. She was a descendant of the Puritan divine Jonathan Edwards and the daughter of the Reverend Robert L. Edwards, the "Holy Ghost Preacher" of the South Carolina Conference. Edwards's zeal was revealed in a favorite family story of his shouting down "old brother Dunnagen," an exhorter who was addressing himself to the "assize of England." "Give 'em salvation, brother, give 'em salvation," Edwards hollered. "Brother, I don't care anything about the 'assize of England.' These people are sinners, sir, big sinners, on their way to death. And if you won't tell them where they are going, sit down and let me tell them." Brother Dunnagen yielded the floor, and the sobs of the sinners and the shouts of the saved rocked the old Warsaw campground till sunup.[4]

Like his great-grandson Sam Jones, Robert Edwards relied on his tongue and fell back on his fists. Ambushed on the road by an offended sinner,

Edwards pummelled the man to his knees to pray. "Fighting is the first instinct of a bulldog, and the last resort of a gentleman," Edwards would say, "yet you cannot have moral courage without physical courage as a basis." Both Edwards and his famous descendant were "hungry for souls" and would rout them out without apology. While Edwards prowled the tents after camp-meeting services, Sam Jones would buttonhole backsliders on trains and in lobbies, accosting them with the question of where they intended to spend eternity.[5]

Sam Jones was proud of his pedigree: "If there is a drop of infidelity in the blood of my people," he would boast, "I have been unable to trace it up. My grandfather and his father, and my own father and myself, have never doubted the truth of the word of God." Loving memory covered a multitude of sins, for his father was the black sheep in a family of shepherds, choosing law and land speculation because God's people paid too little. Sam's father was not cut from clerical cloth; "such were the habits of his life that it seemed impossible for him to live religiously."[6]

John Jones's law practice flourished, and those who saw him in front of a jury often compared him to his famous cousin James C. Jones, Tennessee's popular stump speaker. As a boy, Sam loved to hang around the courthouse to watch his father's control over a jury. "At one moment he would have an audience angry because of his invective and sarcasm," he remembered, "and at the next moment roaring with laughter."[7]

Sam's mother was "a beautiful woman with clear-cut features and dark wavy hair—who came to church with her little boy hand in hand," a neighbor remembered. Nancy Porter Jones, nicknamed "Queenie" for her regal manner, was from a distinguished Virginia family and valued education. She enrolled Sam at an early age in the academy of Professor W. F. Slayton, later superintendent of the Atlanta public schools.[8]

The professor's curriculum was rigorous, exposing the youngsters to philosophy, Latin, and Greek as well as reading, writing, and arithmetic. As in most southern academies, rhetoric was given special emphasis, with each boy being assigned a speech on Monday to be delivered on Friday. Even at the age of five Sam insisted on making his own selections, and though he delayed his choice until Friday morning, his remarkable memory ensured a flawless presentation that afternoon. Taken by the boy's poise and quick mind, Slayton contrived for his prodigy to create a sensation at the annual recital with a variation on a well-known juvenile oration. The evening dragged as each boy presented his speech, and young Sam fell asleep in his mother's lap. Finally the moment arrived for him to hold forth. Shaking the sleep away, Sam stood up and announced to the amazed assembly:

You'd scarce expect one of my age
To speak in public on the stage.
With thundering peals and Thornton tones
The world shall hear of Sam P. Jones.[9]

When Sam was eight years old, his world shattered. One night in May 1855 Queenie tucked Sam into the trundle bed next to hers and listened to his prayers; the next morning Sam was told that his twenty-nine-year-old mother was dead. The experience gave him a horror of sudden death, a knowledge of how quickly and devastatingly life can change, and the anguished conviction that "eternity can hardly compensate a man for the loss he suffers when he buries his mother." Jones insisted, "God's most precious gift to man is a good mother, and if you were to take preachers, the Bible and prayer meetings and place them on the right and my Christian mother on the left, I would choose my mother. I believe I'd recognize my mother's voice in Heaven, and I haven't heard it since that day when she said 'Now I lay me down to sleep.' " [10]

A year and a half later, Sam's younger sister, Mary Elizabeth, died two days after her seventh birthday. John Jones had no wish to stay where he had buried a wife and daughter. He left Oak Bowery for Cartersville, a small community in the north Georgia hill country. His parents were there, farming the red-chocolate soil of the Etowah River valley, as was his brother R. H. Jones, a Methodist minister with a thriving carriage factory. After moving his sons, Joe, Sam, and Charles, and his surviving daughter, Annie, into his grandparents' big double log cabin, John Jones located in town, intent on establishing a law practice.

Samuel Gamble Jones had lost his parents, a brother, and two sisters within a three-year period when he was young, and he understood the needs of his four grandchildren. For his scrawny, pallid-faced namesake, already afflicted with insomnia and a nervous stomach, Samuel Jones prescribed fresh air and plain food. Taking Sam out of school, he set him to work on light tasks around the farm. The treatment was successful, and for the rest of his life when his "constitution and by-laws" were "out of fix" Sam would go to his wife's farm in Kentucky and play at being a ploughboy again. Although his grandparents insisted on family worship every day and observance of the Sabbath, they saw nothing sinful in a boy spending his Sunday afternoon wading in the creek. His grandparents had several children close to his age, and two more babies were born during his stay. It must have seemed like Peter Pan's paradise with eleven uncles and aunts, visiting cousins, and the eight orphans the couple had adopted.[11]

Early in 1858 John Jones remarried and sent for his children to live with him and his bride, the former Jane Skinner, known to the family as "Jenny." Sam grew to love his stepmother; his children called her "Grandma Jones," and she spent the last years of her life living in his home in Cartersville. Four children were born to the marriage: Eddie, Julius, Louella, and Cornelia. Only the two girls lived past infancy.

Sam's future teacher Rebecca Latimer Felton remembered young Jones as a boy with a "fine physique," a "springy step," and "beautiful bright eyes." At eleven he was "the life of any gathering," an original personality with "an independence of spirit and disregard for conventionalities." Sam's combative nature was also manifesting itself. "When I was a boy there wasn't a boy in my town with legs that would go within 2 inches of my length that could beat me running," Jones remembered. "And if a boy knocked the chip off my hat I would just call him in a minute for that; I just despised a dull time." Fascinated with the trains that cut through Cartersville, Sam trained his mule Dave to stop when he hooted once like a locomotive and go forward at two hoots. A favorite prank was to pile children in the back of his wagon for a tearing ride through town. When Dave skidded to a stop on his master's command, the children would tumble out the back. With a voice that later could reach five thousand people without a microphone, the boy was a menace to the peace of the small community.[12]

The town's tranquillity was soon shattered by something far more serious when the controversy over secession pitted neighbor against neighbor and alienated upland areas from secessionist strongholds in the black belt. Recognizing that the mountain folk were likely to send unionists to the convention on January 2, 1861, Georgia fire-eaters began a campaign to convince highlanders that their interests coincided with those of the large slave owners. Governor Joseph Brown, an upland boy elected on the "plain people" platform, was their spokesman. Brown warned that "so soon as the slaves were at liberty, thousands of them would leave the cotton and rice fields in the low parts of our state and make their way to the healthier climate in the mountain region." "Wealth is timid and wealthy men may cry for peace, and submit for fear they may lose their money," Brown railed, "but the poor honest laborers of Georgia, can never consent to see slavery abolished and submit to all the taxation, vassalage, low wages and downright degradation, which must follow. They will never take the negro's place; God forbid."[13]

The highlanders did not take Brown's bait. All three delegates from Cass County voted against secession, and some mountain folk threatened to seize the federal mint at Dahlonega to keep it out of Confederate hands. The firing on Fort Sumter on April 12 and President Lincoln's subsequent call for seventy-five thousand volunteers changed most minds, however. Suddenly, the Cartersville humorist Bill Arp wrote, the "boys were hurting for a fight," so hot with anger that recruitment officers went down the line with a bucket, taking only those who sizzled when splattered. The county was named for Lewis Cass, the Democratic nominee for president in 1848. When Cass declared for the Union, the county changed its name to Bartow, honoring Colonel Francis S. Bartow of Georgia, who had died five months earlier at Manassas.[14]

R. H. Jones, the oldest of Samuel and Elizabeth's sons, determined to leave his business and his circuit to join the Confederate army, a "field of labor" he believed was as holy as the ministry. "All that is dear in life is now at stake in this conflict," Jones wrote in a letter accepting command of the Twenty-second Georgia Regiment. "Place, power, wealth, honor, happiness, prosperity, home and country are involved, yea even our own existence and identity is at stake."[15]

His brothers agreed, and all of Sam and Elizabeth's sons enlisted in the "Fireside Defenders," making the Twenty-second Georgia the only regiment in the Civil War with six brothers serving. On August 14, 1861, the family gathered at Silver Hill, where the youngest brother, Wesley, accepted the Confederate flag from "the women of the South," one of whom urged the company, "Never lower this flag in servile submission to the ruthless invaders of our homes, our liberties, our most sacred rights!" In reply R. H. Jones pledged that this banner "shall be preserved as pure and inviolate, as it now comes from your fair hands." The flag "of the eleven immortal States, which have thrown off the yoke of tyranny," Jones asserted with no sense of irony, "is indeed the freeman's flag, under which equal rights and equal privileges are meted out to each and every one."[16]

In a family portrait of the new Confederates in their crisp gray uniforms, John Jones sits limply, his expressive black eyes pools of melancholy. It may be that he had little stomach for fighting for the slave South. Jones owned three slaves (a thirty-year-old black female, an eight-year-old black female, and a sixteen-year-old male mulatto); he also employed a thirty-five-year-old black male. One "J. Skinner," likely his wife, is listed in the 1860 slave census as owning eleven slaves under sixteen years of age and employing a manumitted female. This high number of young, unprofitable slaves—thirteen of the fourteen owned between them—together with the presence of two manumitted blacks in the household was highly unusual. But if John Jones was a reluctant warrior for the Confederate cause, it did not impede his rise through the ranks. Made captain when his brother R. H.

became a colonel, a year later he was entrusted with the job of obtaining and distributing supplies. Other brothers became officers as well. William ("Buck") Jones was made chaplain of the regiment, and Wesley rose from private to captain.[17]

In November 1861 the regiment was ordered to Richmond, "a fast city" according to Colonel R. H. Jones, who was "disgusted with the drunkenness and wickedness I see here among the head men in army offices." The Fireside Defenders had enlisted to fight for their homes. "I telegraphed Gov Brown to let us come back to defend our state," Jones wrote his wife, Lizzie, "but can hear nothing from them." In April 1862 the regiment fought at South Mills, North Carolina, and in June they were sent against Union cannons on Malvern Hill during the Seven Days' Battle. This "was not war—it was murder," General D. H. Hill later wrote of the disjointed, disastrous assault. Colonel Jones concurred. "A more reckless and foolish charge was never made," he wrote in disgust to Lizzie. "It is a thousand wonders we were not killed to the last man." Raising his sword, Colonel Jones had told his regiment: "Men, I don't ask you to go where this don't flash." During the charge, however, Jones was wounded in the face and shoulder, and the regiment, no longer able to hear their commander shouting "Forward, my brave boys," fell back in confusion. Nearly half of the regiment were killed or wounded.[18]

After taking six weeks at home to recover, Colonel Jones returned to his brothers in time for the second Manassas campaign in August. On September 17, 1862, the regiment fought at Sharpsburg, Virginia. When every general and field officer was killed or disabled, Colonel Jones became commander of the division. Attempting to inspire courage by deliberately making himself a target, Jones was wounded by Union sharpshooters, first by a bullet that grazed his head, then in the stomach and left lung. Surrounded by friends "risking capture and a northern prison to watch him to the end," Jones regained consciousness in the evening and asked to be taken across the Potomac to the retreating Confederates. The family had been told Colonel Jones died on the field; his arrival in Cartersville seemed "like a miracle, a giving back from the portals of the tomb." Colonel Jones was more fortunate than his brother Wesley, who was wounded seven times and taken prisoner. On October 25, 1862, Wesley Jones died of his grievous wounds at a Union hospital in Baltimore.[19]

By the time of Sharpsburg, the condition of soldiers in Lee's Army of Northern Virginia inspired pity even in their enemies. "It is beyond all wonder how such men as the rebel troops can fight on as they do," one Union officer wrote; that "they should prove such heroes in fight, is past explanation." In November 1862 the desperate condition of the Twenty-second Georgia was made clear in a letter to the *Cartersville Courier* which described a sixty-five-mile march in four days, made in snow by men without tents or shoes and "quite destitute of clothing." General James Longstreet ordered the men to make moccasins out of rawhide; the Fireside Defenders were spared this when Colonel Jones, in Cartersville recovering from his wounds, had shoes made and sent to the Twenty-second.[20]

It was the search for footwear that would lead the Confederates to a little town in Pennsylvania named Gettysburg. Once again, the Twenty-second Georgia suffered enormous casualties when on the second day of fighting— July 2, 1863—they were the only Confederates to break through Union lines on Cemetery Ridge. R. H. Jones had pledged at the flag presentation in 1861 that before their regimental banner "shall be found trailing in the dust, the last man that composes this company shall be found cold in death upon the field of strife; the last man who survives shall make this beautiful banner his winding sheet." Such was very nearly the case. Of the eighty-five men enrolled, only twelve surrendered at Appomattox.[21]

Sam's father, John Jones, did not surrender with his company. He had been cashiered for selling hats, tobacco, soap, and apples to his fellow soldiers. This punishment was severe: most court-martialed soldiers were jailed, branded, attached to a ball and chain, or fined. It was rare to be expelled altogether from an army in need of soldiers. While his regiment went on to Gettysburg and their glorious, senseless charge on Cemetery Ridge, John Jones went home to Cartersville. In October he watched his second baby boy die. He began "drinking very hard every chance" he had, and he descended into a life of drunken brawling, occasionally accompanied by his sons Joe and Sam, or "Josy" and "Buddy" as the family called them. "I tell you if Brother John dont hold a titer reign over his boys they will be ruined for life they are mity near that know," Lizzie wrote her husband, R. H. Jones. "They say Budy Jones has been drinking and got drunk last Saturday knight don't you know that is bad poor Jenie has her hands full."[22]

Young Sam's revelries were interrupted in the spring of 1864, when General William Tecumseh Sherman determined to "make Georgia howl." John Jones reenlisted, going back into the war with his oldest son, Joe. Though sixteen-year-old Sam did not go to war, the war came to him. Sherman's march followed the railroads through Georgia. Cartersville, a stop on the Western and Atlantic between Chattanooga and Atlanta, was given special attention as the home of the mighty Etowah Iron Works, which was producing pig iron for the Confederacy.

Though the mountaineers had been slow to cast their lot with the Confederacy, they displayed fierce heroism defending their homes that bloody spring. In hopeless skirmishes in wild ravines, Rebs rushed toward the invaders with their hats pulled down over their eyes, like men who didn't want to see death's face. Soldiers on both sides were weary veterans by now, and the war had lost its chivalrous sheen. "It is enough to make the whole world start at the awful amount of death and destruction that now stalks abroad," Sherman wrote his wife from just south of Cartersville. "We have devoured the land, all the people retire before us and desolation is behind. To realize what war is one should follow our tracks." [23]

John Jones's family was in the middle of the chaos, some of the "runagees" fleeing the invading army. Jenny Jones sent Sam to take their horses from their livery stable and hide them in the hills. When she heard the army approach, she panicked and fled with the other children, expecting to meet her stepson on the road out of town. Sam slipped into town by a back route, the two missed connections, and he found shelter in the shack of the free black woman who worked for the family, "Mammy" Viney.[24]

Though Sherman's visit to Cartersville was blazingly brief, he left behind some horses and mules in the care of a small army of occupation. Sam set about recruiting these animals for civilian service. Dressed as a Union soldier or a drunken Confederate willing to share his moonshine, Sam would wait until the guards were asleep or in a stupor, then slip around the camp collecting horses and mules. By daybreak he would have five or six animals hidden out in a swamp, ready to be distributed to their former owners. Altogether he returned about a hundred animals to the private sector, and "many a poor man lived to thank him for his reckless gifts." [25]

With battles raging to the south of Cartersville, Sam headed into Union-held territory and ended up in Nashville. Sam's Confederate sympathies were shallow, and he fell in with Captain Webb Owens and Lieutenant Austin Dupuy, members of the Sixth Kentucky Regiment of the Union army on their way to Louisville to be mustered out. Sam tagged along, and at the invitation of his new friend, settled in at the Dupuy family farm.[26]

The people of Eminence, Kentucky, were captivated by Sam's charm and lack of parochial prejudice, and during his nine-month stay he was the talk of the territory. His reputation reached fourteen-year-old Laura McElwain, and she was quite taken with the celebrated Confederate when her older brother brought him home for a weekend in January 1865. Laura and Sam had little time to get to know each other, however, for Sam had established contact with his stepmother and left to join her in Lumpkin, Georgia. On May 21, 1865, his sister Cornelia was born; three days later his father was paroled by the Yankees, and the family made its way home.[27]

The Cartersville they came home to bore little resemblance to the thriving community they had left. General W. T. Wofford, department commander of north Georgia, described Bartow County in the last months of the war as a place where "strolling bands of deserters and robbers" subjected locals to "a reign of terror." Not that there was much left to pillage in the charred stubble that had been Cartersville. The Etowah Iron Works was in ruins; only three businesses and two houses had been spared. The five hundred citizens of Cartersville were a spunky group, however, and they set about rebuilding their town. By 1866 twenty new businesses had appeared; four years later the town boasted eighty commercial firms and a population of twenty-two hundred.[28]

Many found it harder to rebuild, even to survive. The great drought of 1865 was followed the next year by heavy rains in the spring and no rain at all in the fall, leading to such scarcity that a Marietta man complained, "The people of this section have learned to live on what a ground squirrel would starve on." One traveler who followed the route Sherman had taken into Atlanta estimated that the whole region had as much food growing as an average farm. In 1866 the Georgia legislature appropriated two hundred thousand dollars to relieve distress in the northern counties, and public meetings were held in the North to raise money for the prostrate South. The situation had not improved much by the following year, which found John Jones traveling in the border states, soliciting supplies for the residents of the ravaged Southland.[29]

While the residents of Bartow County rebuilt their town, Sam Jones worked at personal reform. The Methodist minister appointed to Cartersville was Clement A. Evans, a Confederate general who in the midst of the carnage at Fredericksburg had been called to preach. An eloquent and forceful man, Evans persuaded young Jones to join the church in hope that conversion would follow a steady application of the means of grace. Meanwhile, "Captain" Jones had met the McElwain family in Kentucky and had liked Laura. With his father's encouragement, Sam began corresponding seriously with that "healthy, consecrated, camp-meeting, country girl." And, after a ten-year vacation, Sam went back to school, to the academy held in the Methodist church. This school, the first coeducational institution opened in Georgia after the war, soon had eighty students ranging from six-year-old children to "youthful Confederate Veterans who kept down fire hazards with their tobacco juice."[30]

The early success of the academy was due to the reputation of its founders, Dr. William H. Felton and his wife, Rebecca Latimer Felton. At the time Sam studied with him, Dr. Felton was a physician, a farmer, a

Methodist minister, and an educator. During the next decade he became the leader of the Georgia Independents, a band of upland upstarts who revolted against the Democrats who had "redeemed" the state from "black Republicans" and cemented their power with dark warnings of "negro domination" and glowing accounts of the white man's industrial future. To reject the Democratic party was "to stand branded as a renegade to race, to country, to God and to Southern Womanhood." To most southerners, Dr. Felton was a traitor and a fool.[31]

Dr. Felton was aided in his insurgency by his wife, the "Madame Roland" of the "Bloody Seventh District," who as editor of a Cartersville paper and political columnist for the *Atlanta Constitution* advocated woman suffrage, prohibition, and an end to the exploitation of convict labor. She favored lynching to preserve racial purity and disfranchisement of blacks to restore political purity. By appointment she became the first female United States senator.[32]

Although it is difficult to gauge the couple's influence on Sam, there is some similarity between his beliefs and those of his mentors. Jones later demonstrated an irreverent attitude toward the Democratic party, was openly skeptical about the need for a solid South, denounced the double standard of sexual conduct, favored equal pay for equal work, and advocated woman suffrage. So untypical of his era and area were Jones's views that they may have been influenced by his forty-year friendship with the amazing Mrs. Felton. Temperamentally, Jones and Rebecca Latimer Felton were alike: both believed ardently and obstreperously; both were fond of a fight and apt to throw their fists blindly. Jones could have been describing himself when he said of "Sister Felton": "She's a good shot and ain't afraid to shoot. But sometimes I think that when her dog is ten feet from the rabbit she wants and is about to pick him up she'll shoot and cripple her dog just to show the crowd she can shoot." Then home she'll go, "without the rabbit, toting her crippled dog."[33]

Mrs. Felton remembered nineteen-year-old Sam as a "wild rattling chap, that nearly everybody had hard words for," especially after he galloped through a church on horseback. As a student Jones was as devilish as he was bright. Quickly finishing his lessons, he would terrorize the smaller boys with well-aimed plugs of tobacco or convulse the class with his mimicry. Mrs. Felton understood that after fending for himself Sam chafed at the constraints of the classroom, and she corrected him with quiet admonitions.[34]

Sam respected the Feltons, and their reprimands subdued him—until something else came at him "funny side foremost." Keenly aware of the ridiculous, utterly without regard for social conventions, and almost uncontrollably inventive, Sam Jones could never pass up a punch line. When he recognized that a reckless remark had caused hurt feelings, however, Sam was conscience-stricken, and as creative in his apologies as he had been in his insults. His brother Charles remembered how unhappy Sam would be after a sibling squabble. Leaving some small treasure in the latch of the gate, Sam would wait for his brother to discover the surprise and then run out, misty-eyed and laughing. Sam was capable of supreme insensitivity and womanish softness; no one who knew him well "failed to understand and appreciate the tenderness of his nature." [35]

The Felton classroom was deprived of Sam's surgical wit and warm heart when he transferred to the nearby Euharlee Academy. Run by Ronald Johnson, a graduate of Edinburgh University, and his brother, the Reverend A. G. Johnson, the school had a reputation for teaching moral principles along with the classics. The brothers Johnson were not able to keep Sam in line, however; once away from home he began drinking again. Afflicted "almost from his cradle" with nervous indigestion and an ulcerlike condition, Jones was advised by a physician to take wine to alleviate his pain. He began to "seek relief in the intoxicating cup." [36]

The turbulence of the times may have contributed to Jones's inner turmoil. He was coming of age in a world that had fallen apart; he was forging his identity in a place that was being forcibly remade by military conquerors determined to impose a new political and labor system. The refusal of southerners to accept civil rights for their former slaves—an intransigence that caused southern legislatures in 1866 to reject the Fourteenth Amendment—prompted Congress to pass the Reconstruction Act of 1867. Two years after Appomattox, southern governments were declared invalid and many former Confederates disfranchised. With the exception of President Andrew Johnson's home state of Tennessee, which was safe in Republican control, the former rebel states were divided into five military districts. The condition of readmission to the Union was a constitution that ratified the Fourteenth Amendment and provided for black male suffrage. As southerners never tired of pointing out, if generally enforced, the suffrage condition would dissolve most states in the Union. [37]

Unmoved by the gospel of southern nationalism during the war, Sam Jones was converted by Congressional Reconstruction. The commencement address he delivered as valedictorian of the Euharlee Academy class of 1867 revealed a bitterness toward the Yankees as occupiers he had not felt toward them as enemies. With "our country ruined, our schools expunged, our names extirpated from the list of humans through the instrumentality of merciless conquerors," southerners must look to divine deliverance. "If we will only rely on that all gracious being who shields the weak from the oppressor, we will have nothing to fear. He will feed our hearts with hope, courage and confidence." [38]

From 1868 to 1871 the piedmont counties of north Georgia were a center of Ku Klux Klan activity as whites terrorized "uppity" blacks intent on exercising their new political and social freedoms. There is no evidence that Jones was connected to the secret society, which in Bartow County consisted mainly of lower-class night riders motivated by moonshine and racial hatred. But at this time in his life, Sam Jones was unreconstructed in more ways than one, and the mixture of Christian chivalry, mystery, and violence in an organization claiming to protect southern womanhood would have acted powerfully upon a man of his temperament. Jones loved the arcane language and fellowship of fraternal societies; in 1876 he joined the Masons, and by the end of his life he was a Knight of Malta with the Knights Templar, a Knight of Honor, and a Mystic Shriner. His advocacy of "controlled" lynching reveals a readiness to dispense "justice" more quickly than the law allows. Further, Jones's friendship with Thomas Dixon, a Southern Baptist preacher who spun stories of knights in bedsheets, and his admiration for Dixon's book *The Clansman* is suggestive. What is known is that Jones never condemned the Klan, and at one time he was willing to subvert the democratic process to preserve the power of the Democratic party. In 1896 Jones admitted that during Reconstruction he had "chewed a few ballots after midnight." [39]

In his valedictory address Sam offered his generation as avengers of the South. "Just give us a collegiate education and we will prove to you that there is Washingtons, Websters, and Clays who will spring as it were, from the very dust of humiliation." In spite of his expressed ardor for education, Sam Jones never went to college, citing either his stomach or his eyes as the afflicted area. Or he would say: "I could have been an educated man but I was like the little boy who told his pa he couldn't get enough sugar." The father bought a barrel of sugar and lowered his son into it. After some time, the father inquired if the boy had gotten enough. "No sir, pa," the boy answered, "but I've gotten down to where it don't taste good." [40]

In truth, Jones's drinking made college impossible. "Believing that it was the only thing that would save his life," Jones drank, though he felt "all the ambitions and vital forces" of his life "were being undermined by the fearful appetite." In a letter to Laura, he fretted over the time he had lost in eighteen months of illness. "When all my school fellows and youthful companions were striking off with eager hope and earnest intent of some one or other of the many paths of busy life I was standing alone 'Idle in the market place,'" Jones lamented.[41]

At his father's request, Jones studied at home for the bar examination. Common law and torts seemed trivial compared to the issues of the day, however, and he wrote Laura that he could think of nothing but politics and felt "as unqualified to write a letter on any [other] subject . . . as I would be to write a commentary on Shakespeare's works." Nonetheless, he expected to be admitted to the bar "if the Supreme Court is extant this fall." "Times are very hard," he explained. "Enterprise and commerce are but names. There never has been such a state of bankruptcy known to the world as now exists in Georgia."[42]

When Laura hesitated about a marriage that promised penury, Sam rushed to assure her that "Father will get enough practice to ensure a good living. You can apprehend no *fear* as to my future prosperity and success." Laura was, in Sam's words, possessed of "an education much beyond anything I ever met with in a woman I ever dared to approach," and when she expressed concern about submerging herself in marriage, Sam abandoned precision in his haste to assure her that union with him would not mean giving up individual ambition. "You must remember that Cleopatra, Elizabeth and Anna held the ranes with more nerves and wielded the scepter with more power than did Caesar Napoleon or even Washington, and why should you know less than they? . . . Has nature decreeded that modern man and woman be less than thoes of old—or that woman should be less than man intellectually?"[43]

Sam took the law examination in October 1868 and passed with such ease the judge told John Jones he had "raised the brightest boy ever admitted to the Georgia bar." Two weeks later Sam went to Kentucky to claim his bride. Rumors of his drinking problem had preceded him, and Laura's father announced that he would not watch his eighteen-year-old daughter marry an impoverished drunkard. When Laura herself balked, her mother overruled her. "Now, Laura," she said, "you've promised to marry Sam Jones, he has come for you and you are going to redeem your promise." The wedding was a subdued occasion, witnessed only by Laura's mother, brothers, and a few relatives and friends.[44]

Laura described herself at the time of her wedding as a "high-spirited Kentucky girl raised in affluence." She was quickly plunged into poverty, however, for her new husband failed to find clients in either Cartersville or Dallas, Georgia, and did his practicing "principally at the bar of the village saloon." In his courtship letters Jones had expressed hope that sexual satisfaction would ease other appetites and give him new direction: "I cannot apply myself to my studies as I should or would if my desires were appeased," he had fretted. Marriage did not end addiction, however; before the wedding he "simply wanted a wife," and after the wedding he "simply wanted everything else." Like the fellow who, "when he was first married, just felt all the time like he wanted to eat his wife up," Jones admitted, after a week "I lost my appetite."[45]

A baby girl named Beulah was born eleven months after the wedding, and Laura and the infant returned to Kentucky while Sam tried his hand at teaching school in Pleasant Gap, Alabama. The effort was unsuccessful. School lasted only from January through March, the pay was poor, and the parents felt Jones was too harsh with the children. The family was reunited in Cartersville, where Jones went to work in the ocher factory, stoking a furnace from late morning until after midnight for seventy-five cents a day. Periodic sprees caused him to lose even that job, and he bumped down the ladder another notch, driving a dray for fifty cents a day. "I can see him in my imagination now as he stood upon his dray, with his feet about three feet apart, thrashing his old horse as he went to the depot for freight," a Cartersville resident remembered a quarter of a century later. Always handy with animals, Jones trained his horse to stop automatically in front of saloons, a trick that caused considerable embarrassment after his conversion.[46]

Periodically Jones would swear off alcohol and remain sober for three or four months, but then "the old craving" would come upon him and he'd go off on a ten-day spree. Jones was never indifferent to God, however. "If I didn't go to church once in twelve months, when I did go, and sat under the influence of a good sermon, I could not help being moved. I may have carried a smooth enough face, but underneath I was a boiling cauldron." A hundred times he almost surrendered, but coming close to conversion only made his road to hell steeper and slicker. "The 'almost' of my life, as a sinner, instead of being a blessing to my life, was a curse to me, because I found I rolled down that hill faster than I could have, and reached a momentum that I couldn't have reached unless I had climbed up to a point where the altitude lifted me and the incline was steeper."[47]

In August 1871 something happened that kept Sam Jones sober for almost a year. His wife, pregnant with their second child and grieving over her husband's alcoholism, had gone to visit Sam's sister in another state. On the day she was expected home, Jones received a telegram that Beulah was ill; he should come immediately. Two or three times on the long trip he dozed, and each time he dreamed the child was in his arms, looking up at him happily. He took this as a sign that the child was out of danger. He learned upon his arrival that she was dead.[48]

Whatever his shortcomings as a husband and provider, Jones was a devoted father: "I have never seen any man so fond of little babies as he," Laura declared. Convinced God had taken Beulah because he was "a wicked, wayward, Godless man," Jones was wracked with guilt. "I remember one day when I started rudely from the fireside, the little child got my finger and looked up so pleadingly," he said tearfully twenty-two years later. "I wrenched my finger from her hand and went rudely off. I have thought of that day many a time, and thought if I ever got to heaven I would beg her pardon for my treatment of her that night."[49]

Two weeks after Beulah died, their daughter Mary was born, and a chastened Jones struggled to stay sober. One day in July, however, friends asked him to ride with them on the new railroad to Rockmart, and when they urged him to have a little wine to christen the occasion, he agreed. He stayed drunk for the next six weeks. Such was his state when he was called to his father's deathbed in August 1872.[50]

John Jones had found religion in the last weeks of his life; in his will he expressed his confidence that his soul "shall return to rest with God who gave it." He told the six children gathered around his bed he was assured of seeing them all again in heaven—all except one. Sam began to sob. "My poor wicked, wayward, reckless boy," his father said, "you have broken the heart of your sweet wife, and brought me down in sorrow to my grave." Overcome, Sam fell across the bed, clutched his father's hand, and vowed "I'll quit! I'll quit! I'll quit!" John Jones then "shouted his way out of this world." "God laid his body across my pathway to hell," Jones insisted. "God never lets a man go down to hell until he has overleaped every obstacle."[51]

Sam's surrender of alcohol led to a week of spiritual and physical agony. In torment, he visited his grandparents and the three spent hours on their knees in prayer. Jones believed he owed them his salvation: "If God helped me to gather a million souls, I would cast them all at my old grandfather's feet and say, 'Grandfather, take them to Christ; you are worthy to bear them in your hands, for it has all come of the fact that I had a grandfather and grandmother that kept me before the mercy-seat, though I went down to the very doors of death and hell.'"[52]

That Sunday, Sam Jones went to his grandfather's service at Felton's Chapel, and Samuel Gamble Jones opened the doors of the church to all who wanted to enter. "I sat back in the audience and listened," Jones remembered, "and fear again came to me that I would not be received, my condition was so apparently hopeless, my life and habits had been so dissolute and well-known. . . . but directly I got a new strength, and I said to myself:

> 'I can but perish if I go;
> I am resolved to try;
> For if I stay away I know
> I must forever die.'

Sam went forward and gave his hand to the old man, saying, "Grandfather, I take this step today, I give myself, my heart, and my life, what is left of it, all to God and to His cause." Samuel Jones pulled his namesake to his heart and said brokenly, "God bless you, my boy, and may you be faithful unto death."[53]

When the evangelist Dwight Moody spoke of his conversion, he talked of how his rapture seemed to light up all of nature. "It seemed to me," Moody would say, "I was in love with all creation." When Sam Jones spoke of his conversion, it was as a prodigal son who simply came to himself, realized he was eating garbage, and decided to go back to his Father's house. "There's a great deal of nonsense and foolishness in the relation of Christian experience, the way some people do it," Jones decided. "The trees don't look any greener to me now than they did thirteen years ago, and the little birds don't warble any sweeter."[54]

Too many sinners were expecting to be saved by "some sudden unexpected, serious radical transformation," like Saul on the road to Damascus. "There is many a fellow waiting around here for God to shoot one of those cannonballs at him," Jones would say. "God never wastes cannonballs on snowbirds. If God were to shoot a ball like that at you he would not leave a greasy spot—you little dunce." Such folks put Jones in mind of a farmer who expected God to do the work, from the first sprout of wheat to the bread steaming on the table. "Religion is a good deal like farming," Jones would tell his country-bred congregations. "There is a divine side and a worldly side to both. The rain and sunshine in farming is the divine side and planting and hoeing and harvesting is the worldly side. The trouble is some old sisters and brothers want to swap sides and let God do all the hoeing."[55]

Jones's theology of conversion was based upon his own conversion experience. Since he gave up his sins before he experienced salvation, he inverted the usual formula: people do not become good by getting religion, they get religion by becoming good. "God never regenerates a man until he reforms himself," Jones would explain. "There is nothing in grace that will make you a sober man with a quart of whiskey in your stomach. . . . You must place yourself so that God can get an underhold of you." He continued:

Let me illustrate my point. You have a jug sitting there on the table full of molasses. And you cry out and say, "Lord, fill this jug with air." He can not do it without a miracle. But if you want that jug filled with air what must you do? If you will throw the molasses out, by the time the molasses is out your jug will be filled with air. If you get the devil out of your soul and God in, then you will fill your soul with belief, as the jug is filled with air. A soul emptied of sin is a center of gravity to Jesus Christ.[56]

Jones was often asked how long it took him to get religion.

Well, I was fooling along at it a whole week, but as soon as I meant business I got it right there. I went along a whole week a-mournin' an' a-cryin' an' a-prayin', but at last I said: "Sam Jones, you'll have to give this thing up; you'll have to do something more than weepin' and prayin'." I had an idea that the more you prayed and the more you cried and the more you moaned, "the more better," as the darky said, "you got it when you did get it." (Laughter.) Well, as I have said, I kept on a whole week. At the end of the week I took a calm, sensible survey of the field, and said, "Sam Jones, you haven't moved an inch. You've turned round instead of going forward." And I just stood right there and gathered up every sin of my life and threw every one of them down in a common pile; and then I crossed the bridge to the other side; and lest I should return, I returned and set fire to the bridge and watched the last spark drop into the water and waited till I saw the pillars topple to the ground, and it was not fifteen minutes till I was in the arms of God, a saved man.[57]

Though folks in Cartersville were happy to hear Sam Jones had gotten religion, they were skeptical about his chances of holding out. "I could have got 10 to 1 when I was converted that I wouldn't stick three months," Jones said twenty-seven years later. "Wasn't anybody in my town believed I would stick three weeks. . . . Everybody who met me in the first two or three weeks after I joined the church took my hand and said: 'I am glad you joined the church; I hope you will stick,'" Jones remembered with disgust. "And I would meet another and another, and they would keep running that stick into me until if it had not been for my religion, I would have had a hundred fights the first week after I joined the church."[58]

Jones had his own doubts, and when he spoke to new Christians who were afraid of going forward and terrified of falling back, his words were wrenched from his own experience: "I want to tell you, brother, just at this point, who are afraid to start out; you are afraid you can't hold out. . . . Brother, never try to live right a year at a time, or a week at a time; but blessed be God, all that is expected of us is a second at a time. Lord, Lord, help me this second. And, brother, second by second, step by step, by and by I will reach my journey's end; I shall have strength to make the trip through; God has promised that I should." [59]

Though Jones was tormented with feelings of guilt and inadequacy, he came to believe this was not chastisement from a loving Father but the lashings of Satan. "For a long while, the devil tried to tempt me by saying even if I did get into heaven, they wouldn't let me come up around the throne, they would keep me back because of my sins," Jones confessed. "But God told me that he would separate me from my sins as far as the east is from the west. He told me he would blot them out from the Book of Life." He was confident: "I have cursed and swore and drunk and done a thousand mean things, but brother, I will walk the golden streets as if I had never done a mean thing in my life." [60]

Jones was convinced that Satan used his "inborn, constitutional hatred for shams" by tempting him to focus on the speck in his neighbor's eye instead of the log in his own. Finally, he decided to stop conducting a silent critique of church members and examine his own conscience. "What if there are hypocrites in the Church?" he decided. "Is it not the place where your good mother died and went to heaven? Is it not better to live in the Church if it has got hypocrites in it, and go to heaven and get rid of them forever, than to stay out and be with them forever in hell?" [61]

This conviction made him impatient with "Christians" who contended church attendance was unnecessary. Approached after a camp-meeting service by a gentleman who claimed to be a Christian but not a church member, Jones pounced with ferocious wit:

"You are the man I have been looking for for many years. I have offered a reward, a large one, for one of your sort. Christians are sort o' scarce in the church, and I didn't know there was one outside the church. I am mighty glad to meet you, and this afternoon, when I call up penitents, I am going to call on you to pray for them." He said, "Oh, no, I cannot pray in public." "Why?" I asked him. "Because I am not a member of the church," he said. . . . "No, sir," I said, "that's not your trouble. Your trouble is, you belong to the devil from hat to heels. And he's making you believe you are on the Lord's side. I wouldn't go to hell, if I were you, believing a lie." [62]

It was when they publicly declared for Christ that God was able to bring sinners from the "almost" into the "altogether," and it was only by joining a church that sinners got on board "God's train for glory."

Brother, if it was absolutely necessary for me to go to Detroit, would the fact that I wanted to go, and the fact that I walked down to the station, and the fact that I looked at the engine and the cars, and the engineer and the conductor, and then stood there like a fool and let the train go off and leave me, have a good deal of comfort for me? . . . Some people think there is virtue in that. They say, "I never threw any rocks at the engine, and I never cursed the conductor, and I am satisfied that I am going to Detroit." "Did you get on the train?" "No, no, no. I haven't been on the train—I don't intend to get on; but I think I will get to Detroit, because I have never said a word against the engineer, and behaved myself all the time I was in the depot." Look here, brother, ain't it possible for you to have as much sense about your soul's salvation as about any other things in this world? . . . It's getting aboard the train that gets people to places. It's not wishing well to the people on the train. It's getting on board; that's it.[63]

If he thanked his grandparents for bringing him to conversion, Jones credited his wife with keeping him there by her insistence that they study the Scriptures. "I believe that had I turned the Bible away from me that night and not read it . . . I would now be a poor, miserable backslider." Beginning with the writings of James and John—"there is meat in them"— Jones soon discovered the anger and solace in Psalms, and it became his favorite book. Though in the writings of Paul he got "lost in the maze of thought," he refused to be discouraged. "I am not here to discuss the mysteries of the Bible," he would inform audiences. "There are things I don't understand. I don't want to understand them. If I understood them, I would know that the man who wrote them was no smarter than I am." There would be "millions of years in heaven" to study "the deep things of God." Meanwhile, he would just believe it, "from lid to lid." The improbability of certain stories bothered him not a bit. "I believe the Bible just as it was written, and I believe the whale swallowed Jonah. I would have believed it just the same if it had said that Jonah had swallowed the whale."[64]

Sam had hoped to practice law after his conversion: "I thought I could make something wallowing among juries, while I could not preaching." But he felt "there were friends to bring back to life," and he experienced "a consuming fire and a desire . . . to rescue the perishing and save the falling." Seeking the advice of three Methodist preachers, he was given a single message: God had called him to preach and he could consent to God's will, be whipped into obedience, or lose his religion. This last argument was the most compelling—"it scared me out of my boots almost"—and without consulting Laura he decided to become a minister.[65]

Even so, Jones was hardly prepared to preach when his grandfather ordered his namesake to the pulpit, saying, "If God is calling you to preach, you can preach." Sam nervously obeyed and read out the text for the night: "I am not ashamed of the Gospel of Christ." Unable to think of anything on that subject, Sam shut his Bible. "Brethren, I can't preach the text," he admitted, "but I can tell my experience in spite of the Devil." His earnest testimonial was sufficient to convince the elder Samuel that his grandson had the gift, for Jones remembered his grandfather slapping him on the back that night and saying, "Go ahead, my boy! God has called you to the work."[66]

Jones spent the next three months exhorting sinners at his grandfather's services and studying with his pastor, George R. Kramer, "a saintly, good man." Formal theological training was not yet required by the Methodist Episcopal Church, South, so Jones simply read the books recommended by the bishops. He was received on probation by the local quarterly conference of the church, which urged the North Georgia Conference to ordain this young man as a "traveling preacher" when it convened in Atlanta on November 27, 1872.[67]

Sam Jones was determined to go to Atlanta to petition for an appointment even over his wife's heated protests. Laura had been astonished by Sam's conversion; he had shared nothing of his spiritual struggle with her, unwilling to raise her hopes after so many broken promises. "I have told you many times that I have reformed my life, but you have a sober husband now," Sam had told her outside Felton's Chapel. "It is now true." Pleased as she was by the change in her husband, Laura informed him she had married a lawyer, not an itinerant preacher. If Sam went to Atlanta, she went to Kentucky. Undaunted, Sam replied that God had called him to preach, and God would remove the obstacles in his path. "In that case," Laura answered in exasperation, "He'll just have to remove me." The night before Sam's planned departure, she became extremely ill, and fearing that God was about to clear Sam's path, Laura promised that if allowed to live, she would be a faithful preacher's wife. The next morning, Sam Jones left for Atlanta with his wife's blessings.[68]

For Christ didn't send me to baptize, but to preach the Gospel; and even my preaching sounds poor, for I do not fill my sermons with profound words and high sounding ideas, for fear of diluting the mighty power there is in the simple message of the cross of Christ.—1 Corinthians 1:17

Rudeness is a sauce to his good wit, which gives men stomach to digest his words with better appetite.
—William Shakespeare

3

❋ Shepherd and Sheepdog

The North Georgia Conference of the Methodist Episcopal Church, South, was convinced of Sam's call. He was appointed to the Van Wert circuit, a group of five churches spread over four counties. His largest church had two hundred members and was located twenty miles south of Cartersville in Rockmart, the scene of his binge four months before. His smallest flock had four members; he was to preach to them on months that had a fifth Sunday. Jones had not expected to be accepted, and his elation was not affected even when his uncle, R. H. Jones, who had served the circuit the year before, told him he had just received the poorest appointment in north Georgia.[1]

Sam refused to be disheartened. He sold his belongings to help pay drinking debts and left for the town of Van Wert with "a wife and one child, a bobtail pony and eight dollars in cash." Ninety years later, Mrs. R. D. Crowe would remember: "When my father moved him into his first parsonage, he said he was the most destitute man he ever saw. He moved everything Mr. Jones had, including his wife and child, in a one-horse wagon." But Sam Jones was not dismayed on that December day, "because the picture drawn in my mind of itinerant life was one of hardships and privations."[2]

Though the life of a Methodist itinerant had never been easy, in the first years after the war the very survival of the Methodist Episcopal Church, South, was in question. The annihilation of the South left in ruins the church born out of slavery in 1844. In an article published in the *New York Christian Advocate*, an eyewitness reported immediately after Appomattox that "so far as we can ascertain, most [southern] conferences are virtually broken up, its circuit system is generally abandoned, its appointments without preachers to a great extent, and its local societies in utter confusion. All," he ended, "has been submerged into the general wreck of the South."[3]

With the defeat of slavery the reason for separation was removed. However, reunion was unthinkable to the Methodists North and South, for they had become tribal in their loyalties. During the two decades of division, the southern church had been the "ecclesiastical standard bearer" of the Old South, while members of the northern church were so identified with antislavery that it was "difficult to distinguish them from a wing of the Republican party." Both churches saw their cause as holy, pulpits on both sides were used as recruiting posts, and preachers by the thousands took off their clerical collars to put on the Gray and the Blue. "Both read the same Bible and pray to the same God," Abraham Lincoln observed sadly a few weeks before his assassination, "and each invoke His aid against the other."[4]

This merging of religious and military loyalties prompted northern Methodists to occupy the churches of their enemy, and they were loath after Appomattox to surrender them, fearing to legitimize the bastard of slavery. Until the southern Methodists "repent before God and the nation in sack cloth and ashes for their offense," one northerner fumed, "we believe them unfit for communion in Christ's church."[5]

Convinced the northerners were making "conditions of discipleship Christ did not impose," southern Methodists went to New Orleans in 1866 determined that the their liturgy would continue to be spoken with a southern accent. "Neither absorption nor disintegration was to be thought of," the bishops announced. "Whatever banner had fallen, that of Southern Methodism was still unfurled; whatever cause had been lost, that of our Church still survived."[6]

Impressed by these brave words and eager to demonstrate loyalty to the vanquished Confederacy, southerners flocked to the churches searching for meaning in the ruin of their hopes. While the churches lost most of their black members because freedmen were unwilling to accept segregation and continued exclusion from church offices, white membership grew exponentially. Soon "a sound of revival was heard from one border to the other." But though the prestige of the clergy soared, pay was poor and uncertain. The average circuit rider was promised $572 and paid $438, mostly in corn, chickens, eggs, and produce. For those appointed to circuits that had been scoured by Sherman, like Jones's in Van Wert, salaries were lower and more irregular.[7]

Sam Jones found the poverty of his people was exceeded by their stinginess. In violation of the *Discipline*, the rule book of the Methodist church, they had not even arranged for a parsonage. Jones discovered that the only house available was an unpainted shack that rented for $120 a year, $55 more than his uncle had been paid. "I would work on a farm when I was not preaching and make a few bales of cotton, carry them to town, sell them, and apply the money on my debts," he remembered with bitterness in later years. "I could hear people say, 'Well I like Jones, but somehow he don't pay his debts,' and they kept at me in this way until I was nearly crazy." Vowing never to owe anybody ever again, Jones concluded that "death is better than debt."[8]

Though Laura was reconciled to being poorer as a preacher's wife than as the wife of a wagon driver, she was appalled when Sam called her to the altar to pray with sinners. She came, though the prayer was hardly audible, which could not be said of the argument that afternoon. Laura told her zealous spouse that if he did not promise he would never embarrass her again, she would go back to being a Baptist. "You can't sit on the fence and be my wife," Jones told her. "I am going to run you either in or out." Laura ran in, but she held to her opinion that it was unfair for a minister's wife to be expected to do more than the average member. Perhaps her husband ultimately agreed, for she never took a visible role in any of his large meetings.[9]

The Methodist Episcopal Church, South, required a four-year probationary period before an applicant could be fully ordained. Sam Jones was ordained in 1876, two years before the southern Methodist church required candidates for the ministry to complete an extensive course of independent study or attend seminary. Thus he was among the last group of fully ordained Methodist ministers innocent of advanced learning, something Sam considered a cause for rejoicing. "I'll tell you what a theological school is," Jones would offer helpfully. "It is a theological dry-kiln, and after a man has been in there about three years, there is no more danger of him shrinking." Not only was a "cemeterian" so dry "you can hear him rattle while he is preaching," he was likely infected with heresy. "We have left the pure Gospel and gone off after the isms and higher culture and sociology and biology and fool-ology," Jones would say with disgust. "The theological cemeteries are past resurrection." [10]

Because he was learning on the job, Jones's first efforts at preaching were crude. He confessed his inadequacy to his congregation the first Sunday: "Brethren, the Conference has sent me here to preach, but I know nothing about preaching. If there are any sinners here, though, who want to be prayed for, if they will come up here to the altar I will pray for them." [11]

Jones had a volume of sermon outlines, but he relied most on his two other books: the Bible and the fifth volume of the sermons of Charles Spurgeon, a British Baptist whom Jones considered the greatest living preacher. "Of course, my Bible was the book of all books to me," Jones reminisced, "but I read and re-read that volume of Spurgeon's sermons, until my soul and nature was stirred up with the spirit of the man. I remember how frequently I read the text of one of his sermons and then read the sermon; then I would read my text and say, 'If Spurgeon treated his text that way, how shall I treat mine?'" Spurgeon's influence is striking in Jones's famous sermon "Satan's Banquet," a harrowing description of how the Devil had fattened Sam up and then starved him out. In "The Call and the Rejection" Jones used eleven of the analogies Spurgeon had given in "Everybody's Sermon." Jones usually introduced this sermon by reminding his audience that "Mr. Spurgeon said once, God calls us in a thousand ways if we would just stop and listen." He then preached Spurgeon's sermon, simply translating lofty English into earthy American. So frequently did Jones refer to Charles Spurgeon that a modern publisher, reading one of Jones's old sermon books, was inspired to investigate the English divine. From that chance exposure the Pilgrim Press went on to reprint hundreds of thousands of volumes of Spurgeon's sermons, sparking a new appreciation of the "prince of preachers." [12]

Borrowing sermons was looked upon more kindly in those days; for a young minister with no formal training and the pressure of preaching several times a week, the practice served as a sort of long-distance apprenticeship. A story about Spurgeon suggests he would have been pleased by Jones's use of him. Once, when Spurgeon complimented the pastor of a small country church on his sermon, the blushing cleric acknowledged that he had simply read one of Spurgeon's sermons. "And it was just what I needed to hear!" the famous man insisted.[13]

Spurgeon's influence on Jones is reflected indirectly in his attitudes. Jones and his English mentor both disliked narrow sectarianism, and while Spurgeon's ecumenicalism was less exuberant than that of his Georgia disciple, he believed that as Christians, "we ought to delight in the advance of every denomination." On his part, Jones frequently condemned the "hypercritical spirit" that caused Christians to envy and abuse each other. "Why if a Newfoundland dog or a greyhound should come to me with a placard with the statement that he had saved souls in New York," Jones said with characteristic exaggeration, "I would take him into my house, let him sleep on my doormat and feed him three times a day, an' I shouldn't care if people saw me in company with him. . . . I like loose-fitting denominational garments." When a reporter predicted two-thirds of the converts from a Savannah revival would wind up in the Baptist church, Jones said the "web foots" were welcome to them. Jones liked the Baptists—he got his wife "out of that pond." "Ah, brother," Jones sighed: "it doesn't make much difference how you're baptized, nor does it make much difference to what church you belong. I am sure if you are a good man, you may be made better by most churches. If you are a bad man, surely any church is good enough for you."[14]

Jones, like Spurgeon, considered mournful believers repellent. "We have disgusted the world with our religion," Jones would say with black eyes snapping; "it's not attractive to the race, because our religion is without joy, gladness, smiles, and songs." Prayer meetings dragged on like dirges. "You come here and sing, 'Hark from the Tombs a Doleful Sound,' some brother talks about his losses and crosses, you all look solemn and you call that growing in grace," Jones snorted. No wonder sinners hesitated to join the church when Christians dragged about looking like "their Father in heaven was dead, and hadn't left them a cent."[15]

Spurgeon and Jones considered most Christians weak-willed and morally flaccid. While Spurgeon called for "the Church militant, the Church armed, the Church warring, the Church conquering," Jones prayed for "a strong, sinewy, muscular religion! Not this little, effeminate, weak, sentimental, sickly, singing and begging sort." In an era that produced the Salvation Army, the embodiment of bellicose evangelicalism, Jones and Spurgeon preached a galvanic Gospel, "a Christianity with a musket and a cartridge belt."[16]

Both preachers believed that worldliness was sapping the strength of the Lord's army. "You take the sacramental cup into your hand and drink its sacred wine," Spurgeon lamented, "but still you live as worldlings live, and are as carnal and covetous as they. Oh, my brother, you are a serious drawback to the Church's increase." Convinced the church was Christ's only instrument of redemption, Jones was merciless in his attempts to expose pretense. "The difficulty in the way of the conquest of the world is not the wickedness of the world," he insisted. "The difficulty in the way of the salvation of man is the hypocrisy of the professed friends of Jesus Christ in the church. . . . Some of you old brethren get down and pray, 'Lord, turn your guns on your enemy,' and he would kill your old worldly wives first thing."[17]

While Spurgeon looked back to the Puritans for his ideal of holiness, in Jones's mind the church had been decaying since birth. "The Church of God reminds me of a schoolboy's copy book," Jones would say. "The little fellow comes up to the desk, and the teacher sets him a copy and the little fellow goes back; and the first line he writes he imitates the teacher's copy. The next line he writes he imitates his own copy, and so on down the page, until the last line is the worst one in the book. And so it is with us, brethren. Each generation has imitated the copy set for it by its predecessor until now we have lost well nigh all trace of the original."[18]

The similarities between Jones and Spurgeon should not obscure the differences between them in style and theology. Charles Spurgeon was unabashedly Calvinistic, impatient with the "pestilent heresies" that infested the Baptist church in the nineteenth century. Spurgeon contended that a careful study of the Scriptures would convince any reasonable person that while man is depraved and deserves damnation, God in his grace predestined the salvation of the elect at the foundation of the world. "God from the beginning chose His people," Spurgeon rhapsodized. "When the unnavigated ether was yet unfanned by the wing of a single angel, when space was shoreless or yet unborn, when universal silence reigned . . . in the beginning He chose them unto eternal life."[19]

Like all Methodists, Sam Jones was an Arminian who believed Christ died for all, not just the elect. The mention of predestination set him to sputtering; he declared that if he owned a book that mentioned the damnable doctrine he would tear out the offending pages. "Here is hardshellism," Jones said, summing up Calvinist theology: "If you seek it, you can't find it; if you find it you don't get it; if you've got it you'll lose it; if you lose it you never had it at all." "Methodism can do more for a man in one hour than Hardshellism can do in sixty years," Jones once exclaimed in a fit of uncharacteristic sectarianism.[20]

Jones abhorred the idea of substitutionary atonement, a doctrine which described Christ as the scapegoat upon which God poured out all his wrath. "Right out of this belief," the evangelist growled, "growed all the infidelity that exists in the world today." It was the sinfulness of man that crucified the Savior, not the anger of God. Nor did Jones subscribe to the notion that humans were born depraved. "Some lay all of this misfortune to Adam," he would say. "Now you don't think that I would be a sinner if my father should happen to die and leave me a saloon, do you?" What counted was what was done *after* the inheritance; "just dwell on that point in your leisure moments."[21]

Though "the tendency of human nature is downward and hellward," this inclination does not paralyze the will or render humans helpless. "I believe in the semi-competence of human nature and the omnicompetence of God," Jones declared. "Humanity is not rotten, just out of harmony." Nor did he have any patience with the man who moans "he is nothing but a poor worm, and his wife is a wormess and his children are wormettes." "I don't like to have Christian people going about singing 'This world's a howling wilderness,' when you're the dogs that are doing the howling." Nor did Jones subscribe to the Baptist notion of "once in grace, always in grace." "You don't say to your wife after a good meal, 'Wife, once full, always full.'" Grace was like manna: it had to be received daily, and if stored, it rotted. To the "saved" person smugly sure they would go to heaven regardless of their behavior, Jones had this to say: "Just keep right on thinking that and you'll wake up in hell and say, 'Once in hell always in hell,' and you'll tell the truth then."[22]

The Baptists in Jones's audience usually took such slurs in stride. Dr. Ralph Burleson, president of Baylor University, went regularly to Jones's meetings in Waco, Texas. Though in a Baptist stronghold, Jones warned of falling from grace. "You may be on your way to heaven," he cautioned, "and just before you are about to be received, you can make one slip that will cause your soul to awake in eternal woe and despair." Dr. Burleson disagreed, "but knowing Mr. Jones was a good man who loved the Lord, continued to attend the meetings." One night Jones was in "the best fiddle" and "walking about Zion." Noticing the president in the audience, he exclaimed: "Here is Dr. Burleson, his hair ripening for the Glory World. It won't be long until you are there. I want to make this request of you. When you get there, I want you to tell them 'Old Sam' is on his way and will not be long getting there."

"Mr. Jones, I cannot do that," the Baptist retorted. "I would carry your message to them and the day before you are to enter, you would sin and be lost. Then I would be turned out of heaven for lying."[23]

On the whole, Jones did not spend much time discussing doctrines. "A creed hasn't legs," he would say, "and I can't follow it. You've got to tote it. Creeds have been carried through rivers of blood. When a preacher hasn't much religion, he's mighty certain to come out strong on the creed." He never asked Christians whether they had been sprinkled or dipped. "The idea of a Methodist getting up and preaching infant baptism while the babies are all asleep and the old folks a goin' to hell," he scoffed. "The idea of a Baptist preachin' baptism when nine-tenths of his church will be in a place in ten years where they couldn't get a drop of water." As for whether depravity is "partial or total or innate or developed," he would not discuss it. "Every man has natural innate depravity enough to damn him, and I don't know what he would want of any more. If he does, he's greedy."[24]

Despite differences in theology, Jones credited Spurgeon with giving his sermons a directness and simplicity that appealed to all ages. Indeed, he made the salvation of the children in his parish a particular concern. Typical of his approach was an instance when he rode into a village on one of his circuits and spotted a gang of boys huddled in the dirt playing marbles. Preacher Jones reined in his horse and asked the youngsters if he would see them at the service that night. Play marbles with us, they answered, and we'll go to church with you. Jones hopped down, tied his horse to the fence, and captured all the marbles in the space of a few minutes. He then "marched the whole crowd of them off to the preaching." Less successful was his effort with a boy in Dallas, Texas. Jones had just arrived at the depot and asked the youngster where he might find his hotel. The boy told him, and Jones peeled off a ticket for the revival that night (there was never a charge for admission, but Jones liked to pack his pocket with tickets to press upon strangers in the street). The evangelist told the boy that if he came, he would tell him how to get to heaven. "How can you tell me how to get to heaven," was the bewildered response, "when you don't even know the way to the hotel?"[25]

At the end of his second year of preaching, Jones overheard a small parishioner say that Brother Jones was "the only preacher I ever listened to that I can understand everything he says." He considered that the greatest compliment he ever received. But unlike that little boy, there were those who were *not* eager to see Jones reappointed, for his "abrupt and intense manner divided every congregation." When J. W. Lee followed Jones on the Van Wert circuit in 1875, he was told that friends and enemies alike believed Jones's abrasiveness would destroy him. "Old heads" would plead with Jones to tone down his preaching, and he would appear "docile and lamblike," but the next time he climbed into the pulpit he was more daring than before. "Finally, it came to be understood that the thing to do was to let Sam Jones alone." He "defied ruin"; "the more thoroughly he destroyed himself in the esteem of the prudent, the more thoroughly he seemed to live and flame and flourish." Clearly, the man was unique. "Human life got served up an entirely new style in Sam Jones," Lee concluded, "for he was an animated, palpitating camp-meeting, combined with a first-class mirth-provoking circus. . . . Going to hear Sam Jones preach was like going to see a giant geyser at play. He never studied, in the academic sense of that word—he simply stood in the presence of the multitudes and let nature caper." [26]

Though Sam Jones got comfortable in the pulpit, he did not preach conventional sermons. "I never could preach," Jones would admit, adding slyly, "but I can talk a little." His easy conversational tone was such a radical departure from the unctuous affectation of nineteenth-century preachers that it created a sensation. The humorist Bill Arp described the amazement attendant upon Jones's addresses to the Almighty: "His prayer was so peculiar and abounded in everyday talk as though he was holding a little confab with an intimate friend that everybody wanted to know who he was and where he came from." [27]

Given to brutal bluntness, Jones was most effective in those early years when he concentrated his plain-speaking powers on increasing contributions. "It doesn't take anything to purchase religion," members were informed, "but it takes a good deal to keep up repairs after you have got it." His sermons on tithing became even more emphatic in the spring of that first year when Laura informed him that they were out of food and money. God would not let a man be starved out for doing his duty, Jones contended. "We'll stay right here and not say a word, and if you and I and the child do starve we'll let 'em think we died of typhoid fever." Within an hour, a brother drove up with a wagon full of provisions. [28]

Parishioners finally understood the toughness of their preacher when a dying member summoned Jones to his bedside. Though the stricken man begged his pastor to pray for his recovery, Jones told him, "I don't see any good reason for asking the Lord to heal you." The man had not given a penny to the church despite his prosperity, so his membership in the earthly congregation was expendable. "I can ask Him to forgive and save you, and take you to heaven," Jones explained, "but there is no reason why I should ask Him to preserve your life; as you are absolutely worthless to the cause."

It was only when the amazed man promised to become a faithful contributor that Jones asked God for a healing. The man recovered and proved true to his word. It is not surprising that at the end of his three years on the circuit, Sam Jones was making six hundred dollars a year and living in a furnished parsonage.[29]

Though the Van Wert circuit was arduous, Jones came to feel the "years I spent in that work were the happiest three years . . . of all my life." Methodist ministers were rarely left in an appointment more than a few years, however, so in 1875 Jones was sent to the DeSoto circuit, nine churches cobbled together in Floyd County. His largest church had 259 members, 70 of whom were black; one had 12 parishioners, another 10, and three churches had 9 members each. The previous pastor had been paid $241 for the year, and no parsonage was provided.[30]

There had been a severe drought the year before; twenty acres produced only a bale of cotton, and the corn crop was one-tenth of expectation. "And the fall came," Jones remembered, "and the merchants pressed them, and I just rode around over the county, preaching righteousness." He knew how it felt to be poor, Jones told his people, "how it cows a man." He, too, was "living at starvation rates," paying his debts off at a couple of dollars a month, "but listen to me. If the sheriff comes on you and takes your house and your stock and your all, let him take them; and then just walk out with your wife and children bareheaded and barefooted, so that you can say, 'We're homeless and breadless, but my integrity is as unstained as the character of God.' " You will not starve: "God Almighty will take care of honest men, if he has to put the angels on half-rations for twelve months."[31]

Such counsel was hard enough to take, but when Jones started preaching against drinking, profanity, and gambling, his people turned against him with such fury he felt "the combined powers of darkness had conspired to overthrow me." Convinced the Devil has no better servant than "a preacher who is laying feather beds for fallen Christians to light on," Jones refused to mitigate his message. Instead, with his courage "screwed up to the sticking point," he kept preaching to the conscience.[32]

Jones had discovered Charles Grandison Finney's *Lectures on Revivals of Religion,* a book that influenced him so greatly he advised young preachers to live on bread and water until they could buy a copy. If Jones got his simplicity of style from Spurgeon, he took his techniques and theology of conversion from Finney, an evangelist who burst onto the American scene in 1828, when he scorched the "burned over district" of upstate New York. So many of the characteristics of a Jones revival—emphasis on action instead of feeling, relentless rooting out of the hypocrites hiding in the church, his wariness toward education, calculated use of controversy, conversational style, and flare for sensationalism—are reminiscent of Charles Grandison Finney.[33]

Emboldened by the words of the man he considered "the most powerful preacher that ever stood before an American audience," Jones began to "preach to my people just as I thought about my people"; in other words, "to skin 'em rabbit fashion. . . . Cut a hole in the back and pull 'em through." Like Finney, he began to speak aloud secret sins. "Why, I had an old brother in my church who used to sit in front and look like a saint ready to step into Heaven," he remembered.

> I pointed at him one day, and said: "You old hypocrite, you set a poor widow to picking blackberries for you and then paid her in spoiled flour for her work." Why, God bless you! I set him on fire at both ends. He got up and went out of the church. His wife went out and his son, too. Afterward I found them outside holding a caucus. They said something about whipping me. I said, "Shucks, I don't care about being whipped. I can whip any old fellow that would cheat a poor widow, and I can whip all his kinfolks, too." The old fellow paid the widow right. Sent her two hundred pounds of flour. Before I left that place I believe I got him started on the road to Heaven.[34]

Some did not appreciate his efforts to correct them; Jones preached for weeks without a conversion and all but one man—"a hero"—refused to support him morally or financially. The stewards stopped collecting Jones's quarterage, the payments in kind and cash a minister received four times a year, and Jones was paid only $104 that year. But if the stewards thought they could starve Jones into submission, they did not know their man. Informed the cupboard was bare, Jones simply packed up his family and went to stay with one of the leading members. The lady of the house, distressed by this unexpected invasion, told the preacher that her husband was not at home. "Well, that's all right," Jones reassured his harried hostess, "as we shall spend a day or two with you; he will return before we leave and we will get to see him. We have decided that as we can not get our grub raw, that we will take it cooked."[35]

Though Jones assumed an attitude of flippant defiance in front of his flock, the fight was harrowing. One day when he was feeling particularly low, a church member asked him to visit a nearby family. Walking over the brow of a hill, Jones came to a little log cabin that sheltered a young woman "in the last stages of dropsy." Giving her his hand, Jones asked how she felt, sure he knew the answer. "O," she said, "just as happy as I can be in the body." Jones noticed there was not a chair, a table, or a utensil in the tiny cabin, and he asked in amazement how she *could* be happy. The woman said that though her two children had recently died of diphtheria and though she and her husband had lost everything, Jones's parishioner had not only allowed them to use his cabin, but had come to pray and sing with them. All she wanted now was to be baptized: "I don't want to go from this world until my name is enrolled upon a church book."[36]

Jones baptized her and gave her the last of his money. "Look-a-here, you have been grumbling lately," he told himself on the way home, "you have been talking about going back to the law and making a competency for your family." But he had a healthy wife and two beautiful children, and they managed three meals a day. "And right there on the spot I said: 'God, just forgive me. Here I have been growling and complaining. I promise you right now and right along, I will clench my teeth together, and never complain another word while I live. I will just praise God for the balance of my life,' and the first thing I know I was hanging on my horse so happy I didn't know whether I was in the body or out." Soon, backsliders and the unconverted began crowding the altar until "old DeSoto circuit was ablaze of glory."[37]

Jones's temper was fast and flammable. Growing up in a culture that prized an honor easily offended, he was quick to throw his fists. "I thought after I was converted and went to preaching, that it was a man's duty to defend himself," he explained, "and I recollect a time or two when I got what I thought to be an insult, and there was a personal fracas." After a couple of fights, though, he felt he had grieved away the Spirit, and feared "the Lord had about turned me loose for good." Desperate, he vowed: "Good Lord, if you take me back I tell you what I'll do. I will never get mad with any man on the face of the earth until they treat me worse than I have treated you." He resolved to "clench my teeth together and not let my tongue run a bit," for he had discovered his "tongue was a sort of revolving fan for the fire." Though he was not always able to achieve his goal of a "temper rightly tempered," he started no more fist fights. He did, however, finish a few.[38]

More disastrous for a young southern Methodist preacher than trouble with his tongue was trouble with his thirst. On the DeSoto circuit Jones became friends with W. H. LaPrade, minister of the First Methodist Church in Rome, Georgia. One morning Sam showed up on the doorstep of LaPrade's parsonage, disheveled, distraught, and drunk. He had disgraced his calling and must quit the ministry, Jones told LaPrade. Believing such action would be a loss to the church and a catastrophe for Jones, LaPrade told Jones's stewards that though their preacher had sinned, he expected them to remember Galatians 6:1—ever after, one of Jones's favorite texts—"Brethren, if a man be overtaken in a fault, ye which are spiritual, restore such an one in the spirit of meekness; considering thyself, lest thou also be tempted."[39]

The stewards took their preacher back, but Jones never lost his fear of relapse. "I think the awfulest experience I ever had was once when I ate too much pork for supper and dreamed that I had stolen something and had been drunk," he confessed in 1893. "I said to myself, 'Sam, you cannot preach any more.' How glad I was when I awoke and realized it was all a lie." He never expected to be beyond the temptation to drink. "I have still the craving. As I am a mortal man, I do not know that I will not fall victim again."[40]

Jones's temptations made him sensitive to the failings of others. "Personally, I don't go a bit on 'falling from grace,'" he liked to say. "We preachers preach 'falling from grace' on Sunday and our people practice it all week." When he did speak of stumbling, he encouraged rather than condemned. "You'll fall many a time," he told backsliders, "but I've fallen so often I'm just like a rubber ball. The harder I fall the higher up I go on the rebound." If a brother falls, "catch him on the first bounce," Jones urged the upright. "It is not your business to criticize or say 'Just look how that man has disgraced Christianity,' but it is your business to go out to him, and rescue him and bring him back to God. There is many a member of the Church strayed off tonight and wandering away from God that would have been good, active members of the Church if you had been a brother, indeed, to them."[41]

Jones felt there were two watersheds in the first four years of his ministry: the first when he was impressed to preach plainly to his people, and the other when he "turned loose of the willows and just floated out on the boundless, bottomless ocean of God's love." He had spent four years being "a near-sighted Christian," focusing only on what was close and visible. But "blessed be God, I've quit looking around me; I am looking up," Jones told his Nashville audience in 1885. "I used to look on that picture of the cross with the Christian clinging to it, but my later experience is being in the arms of God."[42]

In 1876 Jones was reappointed to the DeSoto circuit. Simon Peter Richardson was his presiding elder, the supervisor of all the ministers in the Rome District. Richardson was "the most unique and original member of the body," a minister wrote when "Uncle Simon" retired after fifty-four years in the itineracy, "the youngest old man we ever had." Brought up a Lutheran in South Carolina, after his conversion to Methodism Richardson boasted that he was a better Methodist than John Wesley. Richardson was untainted by higher education and proud of it. Holding forth at the North Georgia

Conference, Richardson was once interrupted by the cultivated Dr. Summers, who protested, "Bishop, s-i-n-c-e never did spell s-e-n-s-e." With the fierce scowl of an Old Testament prophet, Richardson pulled himself up to his considerable height and replied: "Bishop, I never did mind having my grammar or theology criticized, but the Lord deliver me from one of them spelling book fellows." Sam Jones used that retort many times.[43]

Richardson saw the pulpit as a promontory, a favorable position from which to rain down righteousness, and "woe to the man who fell under his withering sarcasm." Threatened regularly with physical violence, he took to wearing a knife. Mischief makers and scoffers were given short shrift at his camp meetings; he would tie them to the arbor posts and preach at them full blast. "The preacher is God's appointed judge, and the pulpit seat where sinners are tried, convicted and condemned for their sins," Richardson wrote. He was one of the dwindling number of Methodist ministers who prosecuted sinners to the full extent of church law. Bill Arp once encountered the colorful cleric returning from a protracted meeting on the Pee Dee River in South Carolina. Arp asked if many had been taken in during the revival. "Take in, take in," exclaimed the preacher. "No, my friend, we never took in nary a one, but we turned seventeen out, thank the Lord! Oh, it was a glorious revival."[44]

"Uncle Simon" loved to preach—"Preaching is my natural gait," he would say—and he claimed the right to shape his sermons without reference to any graven image, whether it be a Methodist bishop or John Wesley himself. This iconoclastic attitude was liberating to Sam Jones, who was chafing at the restrictions of the Methodist system. "I learned more from him than all other preachers I have ever come in contact with," Jones wrote of Richardson. "I first learned from him that the pulpit was not a prison, but a throne; that instead of bars and walls and boundary lines, I might have wings and space as my heritage. To think the thoughts of God is a freeman's right, with as little reverence for the Nicene Creed as for the resolutions of the General Conference or the Baptist Convention, . . . assured of the human origin of both alike."[45]

Richardson taught Jones the way to hold a crowd's attention was to follow the crowd's attention; if the audience seemed bored or confused, drop the text and stick to the crowd. "There is nothing like holding the gun all over the tree," Richardson would say, like the palsied old man who went out squirrel hunting with his son. It was the old fellow's job to shake the tree and make the squirrel run out on a limb; this was easy because "he had but to take hold of the bush and it would shake without any effort." One day after the son had fired several unsuccessful volleys, the old man demanded a turn. The wobbling gun went off, the squirrel fell dead, and as the old man danced a jig, his surly son grumbled: "Anybody could kill a squirrel up a tree who could hold a gun all over it, as you did."[46]

This scatter-gun technique was known as "shelling the woods" in preacher parlance—firing off epithets so thick and fast someone was sure to be hit. It required energy and an arsenal of verbal ammunition, both of which Jones had in excessive amounts. In his meetings the fusillades flew. Thomas E. Watson, the Populist leader and United States senator, remembered the impact of Jones's assault on his hometown of Thomson, Georgia, in 1877. Although "not ravenously fond of sermons," Watson heard that there was an undersized evangelist at the Methodist church "who was knocking the crockery around in a lively style, and who was dusting the jackets of the amen corner brethren, in a way which brought the double grunts out of those fuzzy fossils."

Watson found the evangelist

clad in a little black jump-tail coat, and looking very little like the regulation preacher. He was not in the pulpit. He was right next to his crowd, standing within the railings, and almost in touch of the victims. His head was down, as if he was holding on to his chain of thought by the teeth, but his right hand was going energetically up and down, with all the grace of a pump-handle. And, how he did hammer the brethren. How he did peel the amen corner. How he did smash their peaceful co-partnership with the Almighty, their placid conviction that they were the trustees of the New Jerusalem! After awhile, with solemn, irresistible force he called on those brethren to rise in public, confess their shortcomings, and kneel for Divine grace.

And they knelt. With groans, and sobs, and tears, these old bellweathers of the flock fell on their knees and cried aloud in their distress. Then what? He turned his guns upon us sinners. He raked us fore and aft. He gave us grape and cannister and all the rest. He abused us and ridiculed us; he stormed at us and laughed at us; he called us flop-eared hounds, beer kegs, and whiskey soaks. He plainly said that we were all hypocrites and liars, and he intimated, somewhat broadly, that most of us would steal. Oh, we had a time of it, I assure you. For six weeks the farms and the stores were neglected, and Jones! Jones! Jones! was the whole thing.[47]

Though the Reverend "Sampson" Jones had acquired a nickname and a reputation as a "king of congregations," the Methodist church still saw him as a novice country preacher and appointed him to the Newbern circuit, a collection of five churches in Newton County. Undismayed, Jones fired another revival, reporting near the end of his first year that "prayer-meetings, class-meetings, Sunday-schools are specialties with us. We have learned that no man can be religious without acting religious, and no man can live his religion without being religious."[48]

In 1879 the Reverend W. W. Wadsworth provided Jones with his first crack at a cultivated congregation when he invited the rising revivalist to Madison, Georgia. Madison was a county seat filled with the town homes of planters who loved literature and Greek Revival architecture along with thoroughbred-horse racing and drinking. It was Simon Peter Richardson's opinion that "in all of Georgia, Madison was the most afflicted with atheism and infidelity."[49]

Although skepticism in the South was confined mainly to eccentrics and the occasional scoffer who envisioned himself the afflicter of the faithful, rumors of heresy abroad in the East had made southern ministers brace for an invasion of "isms." Thus in 1882 the *Wesleyan Christian Advocate* ran an article advising the clergy on strategies to defend the faith. It was futile to fight for Scripture by skirmishing over nonessentials, the editor insisted: "The central truth of Christianity is not conditional upon establishing the fact that Sampson burnt up the Philistine's wheat, that the sun stood still at the command of Joshua, or that the whale swallowed Jonah." All such arguments did was provide occasions of merriment to the "radical pamphleteers" and "their empty-pated admirers." What ministers must do is center their defense of Christianity on the person of Christ and what his churches have done for the world.[50]

With untutored instinct, Jones had hit exactly upon this strategy. He refused to argue with skeptics about the authority of Scripture—"God don't want anybody to prove anything that is true." Nor would he wrangle over details like where Cain got his wife—"from his father-in-law," he would say laughingly. "You can't step up to a sick man and tell him to open his mouth wide, and throw the whole medicine case in his throat. You must give him a little dose," he explained to those who accused him of abandoning the Bible. "So with many a poor little 'in-fiddle.' If you chuck the whole Bible full of truths into him at once you will choke him to death. You must give it to him in small doses. I have never seen one take the medicine of the Bible in this way but what he was cured."[51]

The first to admit that Christians had done awful things in the name of Christ, Jones challenged deriders to name a single hospital or orphanage built by an atheist. "I have noticed this much—that infidels love to live under the shadow of churches," Jones would say. "I have found out that infidel men like good Christian women to raise their children for them. I have found out that infidels will not go off in communities and live together. I have found out that infidels love to live in a land of Bibles, preachers, prayers and sacrifices. I have found that out."[52]

His approach was effective in Madison. "Rev. Sam Jones is the young Moody of the South," the editor of the local paper raved, "and is greatly reviving religion in Madison. He tells some they are too good and others they don't work enough . . . and that all have been backsliding." This success in Madison prompted his appointment to the nearby Monticello circuit, where Jones began his last year as a settled pastor in 1880. The year was easy and pleasant; his people were companionable and eager to please a preacher who was fast becoming famous. They increased his salary by 25 percent, painted the parsonage, put up blinds, and put down carpet. So great was the demand for Jones as a revivalist, however, that he was able to spend only half of his time in his own churches. Through word of mouth and articles in regional *Advocates*, the fame of "the Holy Terror" was spreading beyond the borders of Georgia. "The sound of your voice has reached Florida, and echoed throughout the entire state almost," one minister wrote.[53]

While Jones was conducting revivals in Vicksburg, Mississippi, and Shreveport, Louisiana, he fretted about being away from his family. There were now four children at home: Mary, age eight, Annie, age six, and two boys, Paul and Robert, five and four. Laura was pregnant again and frequently ill; her letters were filled with the complaints of a lonely, overburdened woman. In 1880 Sam had written Laura, "I won't go off any more and leave you," but calls came and he went. He settled for the remedies of an absent husband, urging Laura to visit friends, take her bitters, and use phosphate so she wouldn't have bad dreams. "My dear wife—keep cheerful," Jones wrote from Texas. "Your husband's heart is always near you and his prayers go up for you continually." He consoled himself with the thought he was only a train ride away. "If you see I ought to come home telegraph me," he wrote from Macon in 1881. "I cannot neglect my family."[54]

To him it seemed the family's sacrifices were worthwhile, for he estimated that during eight years as a circuit preacher he had been the instrument of salvation for five thousand souls, two thousand of whom came into his own churches. His estimates are not verified by the *Minutes of the North Georgia Conference* for the years 1872–81. When he was appointed to the Van Wert circuit in 1872, there were 430 members in those churches; when he left three years later there were 500 members. He admitted 229 by adult baptism or profession of faith, so 159 members either died or left. His clearest success was on the DeSoto circuit, where he began with 300 and ended with 500 members. It is more difficult to judge his impact upon the Newbern circuit, since it was not listed in the *Minutes* the year before Jones was appointed. During Jones's two years on the circuit, 130 adults joined the church; however, net membership only increased by only 10 persons between 1878 and 1879. The Monticello circuit had 516 members at the time of Jones's appointment; one year later there were only 480, despite the fact that 130 new members had been gathered into the fold. Altogether, 634 new members were admitted to the churches in Jones's charge during that eight-year period, and 490 died or left. Though this was an impressive record, Jones's errors in accounting suggest that later calculations of converts, much less subject to confirmation, should be viewed with skepticism.[55]

Doubtless there was natural attrition, but most of the members who left Jones's churches were probably thrown out. "I believe in standing up squarely to the issue and putting the rotten members out of the church," he would declare. At a time when many Methodist ministers were easing away from strict enforcement of church law, Jones decided not to wait for God to separate the tares from the wheat. "I remember once in one of my churches I could not get my members straight," Jones told an Augusta audience. "Said I one morning 'I have done my best to no avail, and now I am going to open the back door of my church and I want you to come up here and "jine out." And they wouldn't do it. I said 'I won't let you stay in here as you are a disgrace to the church, and if you won't get out I'll put you out,' and I turned about half of 'em out and my church got all right and went right along."[56]

Jones boasted he never had a card-playing or drinking member in his church, because he would denounce them until they quit sinning or left the church. He once ordered a steward to go through the church rolls and hunt out the names of the folks who had not given anything to the church so he could toss them out. "What, turn them out for not paying to the church?" the shocked steward asked. "No, turn them out for lying," Jones replied. "They never got into the church except by promising to support its institutions, and every man that don't do that is a walking liar."[57]

It was one of Jones's more controversial customs to inform his members of their probable eternal destination as he took his leave of them, believing "a preacher knows who is going to heaven and who not." "Let me say right now that if any of you should have a husband, wife or child die who isn't a Christian, I'm the last man you want to get to funeralize him," Jones warned; "I'll tell the truth no matter what it is." Once while conducting a revival in another state, Jones received a telegraph from a wealthy family in his church offering a ticket home and back if Jones would preach the funeral of one of their members. Jones's relationship with this family was not cordial, but they wanted the prestige that a rising revivalist would provide. Jones arrived just before the funeral began, went directly from the train depot to the church, and stepped up to the pulpit. "I know not whether Brother So and So had mended his ways since I last saw him. However, had he not, I can assure you that today he rests in hell with Satan and his minions."[58]

Whatever direction people were moving in, there was activity in all of Jones's churches. No one was allowed to stand still. More a sheepdog than a shepherd, Jones yapped and nipped at the heels of his people, trying to herd them away from hell and into heaven. It is no surprise that his combativeness created problems for him as a pastor. While his attacks on sin were effective in getting people to get religion or get out, they tended to wear Sunday after Sunday. "Repent ye" was his constant theme. "I am like the old preacher who preached on repentance once," Jones admitted. "Next time he preached on repentance, and again on repentance. One of the old stewards took him out and asked him: 'Is that the only sermon you have? You have preached on that the third time.' The preacher asked him: 'Have all the people repented?' 'No, but they want something new.' 'I cannot find any better text so long as they are not all converted.'"[59]

Jones offered no apologies for preaching more on sin than on salvation: he refused to "talk of Christ and His love" to "reprobates" and "uncircumcized Philistines." Nor would he struggle to please a church who wanted a eunuch in a clerical collar to preach "women's and children's religion." Such folk put Jones in mind of the deacons who warned their new preacher not to preach against fashion lest the fashionable members be offended, not to preach against drinking lest the liquor sellers leave, not to preach against covetousness lest he run off the millionaires. "Well, what can I preach about?" the bewildered minister asked. "Mormons," the deacons answered. "Give 'em blazes. There won't be a Mormon to hear you." Sam Jones would not toady to such compromising Christians, he announced obstreperously; if they did not like what he had to say they could whine to the bishop and get rid of him. All he had to do was "pack his blacking-brush and call his dog."[60]

Beyond his announced intention to offend from the pulpit, Jones refused the weekday civilities that endear a minister to members. "I don't believe in 'pastural' visits," he would say flatly. "I'll visit them who are in need of my help and sympathy, but just to run after healthy, fat Methodists, that ain't in my line." Jones was by temperament a midwife, not a mother; he liked to be present for the birth and to administer an occasional spanking thereafter, but he had little interest in the day-to-day growing of Christians. "What do you think of a mother who had thirty babies, the oldest thirty years old and the youngest at the breast?" he would say. "Not one of them had grown any since they were born. Poor woman! Ten babies on the bed, ten on a pallet on the floor, five or six in the crib, four on her lap, and all of them *squalling!* She is to be pitied. But this is the condition of many preachers in this country. A hundred members, and all of them babies. Not one of them able to take care of himself, much less to help his brother."[61]

Jones was no shirker, however; he averaged four hundred sermons a year those first eight years. He had conferred with himself and come to a decision: "'Jones, if you ever succeed, old fellow, you have got to be one of two things. You have got to be a great worker or a great thinker.' Well, I surveyed the field, and I said: 'Jones, old fellow, you may be a great worker, but you haven't sense enough to be a great thinker. . . .' And after all, brethren, we have got more thinkers than we have workers, and there is room enough for one fellow that don't think much but proposes to work."[62]

Jones had worked hard and taken a lot of abuse in the pastorate; he claimed by the time he left the settled ministry, "there was no lie that earth or hell could concoct" that had not been circulated about him, and "they have reported me drunk on a hundred different occasions." He was grateful for being persecuted. "I thank God that the first eight years of my ministry were spent on the poorest circuits in my State and I thank God I was faithful to my work." At the time he had felt like "a wandering star without a purpose," but looking back he could see God's plan at work. "My mental resources broadened," and he built up the immense reserve he would need to contend with principalities and powers, contentious committees, fleas in the sawdust, heat waves, and the rainstorms that topple tabernacles and tear up tents. Evangelism was physically and emotionally demanding, and required enormous authority. "Men know as well when there is more to follow as a horse knows when his driver's afraid, and know it in the same way—by the inherent power of instinct." The circuit had prepared Jones to make the whole country his parish. He had reached thousands during those eight years. Now he was ready to talk to millions.[63]

Woe to you, Pharisees, and you religious leaders! . . .

You try to look like saintly men, but underneath

those pious robes of yours are hearts besmirched

with every sort of hypocrisy and sin.

—Matthew 23:27

To preach long, loud, and Damnation, is the way

to be used up. We love a man that Damns us,

and we run after him to save us.

—John Selden

4

❧ The Holy Terror

Sam Jones's mixture of plain talk and spicy speech put him in great demand, and soon he was traveling so widely that he was able to devote only half his time to his own appointment. In 1880 Bishop Holland McTyeire recommended that he become the agent of the Orphan Home in Decatur, Georgia. Jones was interested; the position would give him more "tether line" than a regular appointment, and the years spent on his grandfather's farm had given him a special feeling for orphans. An incident a few weeks before conference exercised the most influence on him, however.

Returning from Kentucky, Jones noticed a woman in mourning getting on the train with an infant. Struck by the thought that Laura could be widowed and his own children left fatherless, Jones vowed to do everything in his power to help the "poor little orphans." When the bishop suggested the appointment, Jones assumed the Almighty had accepted his offer.[1]

Many women who had lost their husbands in the Civil War found themselves unable to provide for their families and made the agonizing decision to give their children away, either to relatives or to the orphanages that were springing up all over the South to provide for those left fatherless by the war. The Georgia Conference established an orphans' home in Decatur, but it had been bedeviled from the beginning by mismanagement. Economic woes were intensified by rumors that unscrupulous parents sent their children to Decatur when it was inconvenient to have them at home. Most damaging was the scandal that erupted when a girl from the home was unwittingly apprenticed into the world's oldest profession. The board of trustees revised the rules in 1875 to prevent such abuses, but financial support continued to erode, provoking the trustees to insist: "If we ever were, we are not *now* engaged in an experiment. The Conference Orphan Home is a *fact;* and one that is notorious. We cannot, in the eyes of God and man, turn back."[2]

The home was almost twenty thousand dollars in debt when Jones settled his family in Cartersville and set about convincing north Georgia Methodists that "our institution had repented, been converted, and was now a child of God." But people were not easily persuaded, and the work was hard. Uncertain fare and the drudgery of travel in rural Georgia weakened his already frail body, and torrential rains intensified discomfort. "February, still in the mud," he groused, but resolved to go on "until I am up to my chin." His efforts were rewarded; he raised a thousand dollars in three months' time "in spite of mud, gloom and despondency."[3]

Laura begged Sam not to accept the appointment for a second year, but Jones was determined to put the home on a secure basis. Laura ultimately yielded. "You run the Orphan's Home in Decatur," she said, "and I will run your orphan's home here in Cartersville." Soon after, a conflict with the board of trustees almost accomplished what Laura's pleas could not. When Jones accepted the appointment, he had signed a contract agreeing to give all his time to the orphanage and to forfeit claims to a percentage of the offerings. June 1881 found Jones in Waco, Texas, conducting a revival for a transplanted Georgia minister, and indignant trustees insisted he had exceeded the boundaries of his contract.[4]

Jones was touchy about his status as a free man and contemptuous of the "little time-serving, compromising preacher that is afraid to speak his mind, for fear he will lose his job." The trustees could not have made a more impolitic move than a threat of dismissal. "If I have anything more to do with the Home," Jones wrote testily, "I don't intend to have anything more to do with protracted meetings." Realizing which side their agent would choose in this self-made ultimatum, the board hastened to soothe the feelings of the man they believed could deliver them from their creditors.[5]

Despite his protestations Jones confined himself to north Georgia in 1882, reasoning that if he had raised four thousand dollars working part-time the year before, with an all-out effort he could clear the debt, freeing the home and himself. "I will be heard HERE, or HEREAFTER," Jones announced. It was time for the conference to declare itself: either support the home "or say to the world that 65,000 Methodists in North Georgia have not the brains, nor the heart, nor the means to run a benevolent institution to care for the fatherless and motherless of our land."[6]

As fund-raiser for the Orphan Home, Jones perfected his tactics of spiritual intimidation and emotional manipulation, and many people found "there is no getting around him in a collection." Before the plate was passed, Jones spoke of the tragedies he had seen: hungry, hollow-eyed mothers pushing half-starved babies at him; children growing up heathens in a Christian land. Misty-eyed, Jones would wonder whether he and other fathers would see the delight of their dear ones as they opened presents on Christmas morning, or would they be lying in the cold sod, their children orphaned? No wonder that by the time Jones made his plea for funds "there was not a dry eye in the house, and strong men bowed their heads and were not ashamed of the tears that did honor to their manhood."[7]

Jones had an uncanny ability to perceive a crowd's mood, and if he felt the audience was not responding to sentiment, he would shift to a more brutal approach. Ordering the ushers to lock the doors, Jones would matter-of-factly inform his captives that they would not be freed until their quota was collected. Or he would begin the collection with an impressive personal donation and call out the names of wealthy people to match his contribution. To refuse was to risk public humiliation. "You little stingy narrow-hided rascal," Jones would say to a grudging giver, "a fly could sit on the bridge of your nose and paw you in one eye and kick you in the other. You could look through a keyhole with both eyes and not be cross-eyed either." Give according to your means and not your meanness, Jones would urge: "Give till the blood comes."[8]

Approached by a father who was concerned that his money would damn his already dissipated sons, Jones said:

> I will tell you how to dodge that thing. Give me this afternoon twenty thousand dollars apiece of those boys' money for the orphan home out there, and you go home tonight and say to Tom and Harry: "I have given Sam Jones twenty thousand dollars of each of your portions, and the very next time you get drunk I am going to give him forty thousand dollars more; and on your third drunk, I will make him a deed for that orphan's home for every dollar I have got." "And," said I, "you will straighten those boys right out."[9]

Jones induced two wealthy Atlanta businessmen, George Muse of Muse's Department Store and W. A. Gregg, "a prince in the hardware business," to work on the board with R. A. Hemphill, "one of God's bankers." Jones talked railroads out of charging the home for freight, had Sunday school children contribute Christmas presents to the orphanage, and got Atlanta church women to furnish rooms. Fueled by his belief that religion was simply "sanctified business," by 1885 "Mr. Sham," as the orphans called the man whose life-sized portrait hung in the Sam Jones Hall, had cleared the Orphan Home of debt.[10]

By the time Jones was appointed agent, few ministers could compete with him as a crowd-catcher, as A. W. Lamar learned in 1881. Dr. Lamar was conducting a successful meeting in his Baptist church in Macon when his crowd began falling off. On Monday the audience was half the size of Sunday's congregation; the next night only a quarter of those arrived. Wednesday only the deacons showed up. When a dismayed Lamar asked why the revival had declined so disastrously, the deacons were astounded. Did Dr. Lamar not know that Sam Jones was holding a meeting at Mulberry Street Methodist? Their amazement increased when Lamar replied that he was not familiar with that name, having recently moved to Georgia. "Sam Jones is the greatest sensation Georgia ever produced," one deacon told him. "When he is in town there is no use to try to run against him." His curiosity piqued, Dr. Lamar joined the deserters but told Jones after the service that though his people had been captured, they did not seem to be getting converted. "Brother Lamar," Jones answered good-naturedly, "a fellow has got to catch his fish before he strings them. I am just drumming up my crowd, and will string them after a while." For the remainder of the revival Methodist and Baptist trolled together, fellow fishers of men.[11]

A few years later, as minister of Central Baptist Church in Memphis, Dr. Lamar gave Jones the opportunity to hold his first large union meeting.

It had been the custom among the Protestant ministers to conduct an annual citywide revival, inviting well-known evangelists such as Dwight L. Moody and Edward P. Hammond to lead. When the ministers had difficulty settling on an evangelist for 1884, Dr. Lamar suggested Sam Jones as the man who could "come nearer turning the city upside down than any man on this continent." Even the Methodists had not heard of Jones, but they were impressed by Lamar's promise that "the only trouble will be to get a place big enough to hold the audience." [12]

S. A. Steel, pastor of the First Methodist Church, was assigned to investigate this phenomenon. Steel wrote Atticus Haygood, then president of Emory College, to ask if the Memphis ministers should "carry" Jones. Haygood, who as bishop was to force Jones out of the regular ministry, now got him the revival that brought him to the attention of the southern press, led to the Nashville meeting the next year, and ultimately to the northern and midwestern tour of 1885–86 that made Sam Jones the most famous Methodist of the day. "Sam Jones is a rare man; direct, pungent, earnest, full of shrewd common sense—no clap trap," Haygood replied. "His preaching is not sensational, but *he* is a sensation and always makes one." Haygood concluded with a piece of doggerel:

> Sam Jones is a Methodist preacher
> Good and true
> Give him a chance
> And he'll carry you. [13]

Convinced, the Memphis preachers invited Jones to come in January and leased the auditorium, filling it with bleachers and folding chairs. But Jones was unnerved by the prospect of preaching to people who had heard the greatest evangelists of the century, and was uncharacteristically chaste in his early sermons. Two weeks into the revival, Dr. Lamar visited Jones's hotel room and found his friend discouraged that the meeting was not "growing in power." Lamar prevailed upon the unhappy evangelist to take Jesus at his word: if two or more shall decide upon anything and ask it of him, it shall be done. The two men "went to prayer." [14]

Earlier in the century, pioneer Methodists had carved Wolf circuit out of the wild terrain around Memphis and had imposed two requirements on their preacher: "he must not be afraid and he must needs know how to swim." The morning after the prayer session, Sam Jones proved himself equal to that place, letting himself loose upon Memphis armed with righteous indignation and fortified with farmyard analogies. If he had been afraid to offend their urban sensibilities, he now decided that a hog was a hog wherever it was found and a sizeable number of the inhabitants of that southern city were members of the swine species. Informed of their family connections, some of the people of Memphis began to squeal, a reaction that bothered Jones not at all. As he was fond of saying, it is the hit dog—or hog—that hollers. Displeased by Jones's characterization of their parishioners, some preachers denounced the evangelist in print, and the furor put the meeting exactly where Jones wanted it to be: on the front page. The curious crowded in each day, and Dr. Lamar's prediction came true: in spite of constant sleet and rain, the building could not hold the multitude who came to see the pugilistic preacher.[15]

Jones was triumphant. Soon those who had publicly attacked him were sheepishly stealing into his camp, routed by the results. Jones then held a "talking meeting," giving repentant ministers a chance to recant. After several testimonials "Uncle Ben, the faithful old colored sexton," stood up. For years, Ben said, he had begged God to send a man to Memphis to rescue the souls perishing there. "Now he has come," Ben shouted. "Thank God for him! He preaches the gospel so every one can hear it; he feeds me, he feeds the young and the old, the learned and the unlearned." The ministers of Memphis "have been putting the fodder too high. But this man of God scatters the fodder on the ground and we can all reach it."[16]

Even before the Memphis meeting, Jones had been overbooked. Unable to say no to those who crowded around him at preachers' meetings, he made promises he was unable to keep. When Jones canceled a meeting in Eatonton, Georgia, the Reverend M. J. Cofer warned Jones his practice of scheduling two meetings at the same time in different places gave the impression "you don't care for engagements except as they suit your convenience and pay big." Jones went to Eatonton, but after Memphis there was just not enough of him to go around. The Georgian was besieged by invitations from those who had read about him in the secular and religious press, and ministers vied with each other for the evangelist's attention. "Sinners are asking every day when you are coming," a minister from Corinth, Mississippi, wrote. "All will be disappointed if you don't come and stay longer—Come! Come!! Come!!! . . . *We need you here—we pray God to help you come and bless you as you come.*" When Jones wrote that he was too sick to come to Corinth, he was told, "Sick or well—we cannot give you up."[17]

Jones bowed to pressure and went to Corinth in July 1884. Ignoring exhaustion, he preached every day at six, ten, three, and seven o'clock, often in such intense heat that sinners must have wondered if they were getting a foretaste of their future. Driving to the church one evening, Sam told Laura that he felt too weak to stand, but when he stepped up to the pulpit he felt "the power of God" come upon him with such force that he preached for an hour with great energy. The sensation continued that night in his room until he called out: "This is glorious, the breezes of heaven are sweeping in upon my soul." All his life he remembered the intensity of this "baptism of the Holy Spirit," when "for ten minutes or more these waves of blessing passed over [my] spirit, and for three months or more [I] didn't know the sense of fatigue."[18]

Already afflicted with stomach problems and a tendency toward nervous collapse, Jones had contracted malaria in the fall of 1883 and put off the Memphis meeting for two months to rest and drink quinine water. Three months after his mystical experience, Jones again began suffering from malarial sweats. Ignoring his infirmity, he went in the fall of 1884 to Waco, Texas, and preached powerfully there, bringing 250 people to conversion and so completely winning over the local editor that the journalist proclaimed "all honor to the wizened little Georgia corn-cracker." Jones soon became desperately ill, however, his temperature spiking so high his wife was telegraphed to come at once if she wanted to see her husband alive.[19]

Fourteen days into the illness, Jones believed he was visited by the Devil. Sidling up to the sickbed, Satan taunted the evangelist with his weakness, tempting him to give up the work that was killing him. In spite of feebleness, Jones resisted these entreaties and ordered "his Majesty" to "get out of this room! If I had to go over it all again, I would not strike a lick less!"[20]

Belief in a personal Devil had declined dramatically since the days when demons were thought to swim in the air. Increasingly, the old image of a horned, hoofed Satan seemed a silly superstition. To Sam Jones, however, the "prince of demons" was an actual entity, a malignant being who stalked the earth "seeking those whom he may devour." Though he once jokingly described Satan as "lowdown, snaggle-toothed [and] red-headed," Jones considered that cartoon character a satanic trick. "I want to tell you that if you're the man who thinks the devil is a great big fellow with cloven feet and a spiked tail, and sharp ears like a fox terrier, why you ain't fit to go around by yourself." Like God, Satan was a spiritual power, dependent upon human beings to do his work. "The devil can't run his machine without men," Jones insisted. "He doesn't distill whiskey or sell it and I am sure he never drank it. He gets some scoundrel to make whiskey, an infernal scoundrel to sell it, and an infernal fool to drink it, then his work goes on."[21]

Jones believed he understood Beelzebub, his quicksilver cunning, the shrewd way he turned a man's greatest strength into a spiritual snare. "I know him," Jones would say. "Yes, I do, for I chummed with him a good many years." Even after his conversion Satan had afflicted him, trying to disable him with crippling fears. First the emperor of evil tried to ruin his reputation so "you can't take anybody to heaven with you." Then he tried to seduce him with money, and finally he held up the specter of starvation to the emaciated evangelist, knotting his intestines until he could hardly eat a whole meal in an entire day. "His Satanic majesty" also resorted to indirect attacks, interrupting meetings with barking dogs and brawling drunks, pelting tents and tabernacles with rain and hail, making streets impassible with sleet and snow, and jumbling Jones's train schedules. "The devil is a disembodied spirit and that's what he's mad about. He'll go into anything," Jones explained. "I've seen the devil get into a baby and it would squall and break up a whole meeting." When a revival succeeded despite subversion, Satan used the sedative of self-satisfaction or the poison of guilt to counteract divine grace. "The devil persuades [sinners] that they are good enough without religion until the blessed truth comes along and shows them how mean they are, and then the devil persuades them that they are too mean to be religious."[22]

Though it was "considered vulgar now, really vulgar for a man to get up and preach hell to sinners," Jones intended to tell sinners about Lucifer's incandescent kingdom at every opportunity, reasoning, "If I was going to emigrate to a country, I want to know all about it before I go there." No satanic trick, no fear or illness would prevent him. "No, sir; I am in the field," Jones would say, "and will stand with sword in hand and fight the devil till the blade is worn out and drops from my hand, and then I will hit him until I wear my arms out, and kick him until I kick my feet off, and then gnaw him as long as I got a tooth, and when my teeth play out I will gum him until I die."[23]

In Jones's opinion, many who wore clerical collars were the Devil's dogs. This was especially true of the liberals who turned "the devil into the Church and the world over to the devil" and peddled "cut rates to glory." These men even watered down the Ten Commandments: " 'Thou shalt not steal if there's any likelihood of being caught.' 'Thou shalt not covet, but get all you can and keep all you get.' 'Thou shalt not commit adultery, but have more than one wife, if it suits your convenience.' " Jones had no patience with such laxity: when one audacious man strolled up to inform him there was no hell, the exasperated evangelist inquired: "When did you start an exploring party down there and when will they return to report?"[24]

He did not doubt that a great deal of claptrap was preached about hell. "This thing about a firebox and God pushing men in and locking the lid down on them is nonsense," Jones insisted. "You not only generate the brimstone that is to burn you, but you carry enough of it with you to burn not only you, but this whole city." Hell is nothing but a man's selfishness set on fire, Jones said, "and it is a wonder to me that many of the good old deacons in the Church don't catch by natural combustion and go to hell in a sheet of flame."[25]

There were those who claimed a loving Father made hell an impossibility. "Well, neighbor," Jones drawled, "you haven't got sense enough to see all around the truth." God does love you. "He can't do anything but love you, and He loves you even though you go to Hell." But God's love unclaimed cannot save any more than a lifeboat can save a drowning person who refuses to climb into it. "Can love save?" Jones asked. "If love could save, no mother's son would ever pay the penalty of his crime on the gallows again." Only "the blood of Christ," claimed by a confessed sinner, can save. No, God does not send people to hell; they send themselves. When a good man dies, his soul keeps ascending; when a bad man dies, he falls as naturally as a book drops to the floor, for "hell is the centre of gravity of a bad man's heart."[26]

Jones was unapologetic about his "turn or burn" theology. He sensed instinctively what one modern scholar discovered: while terror arouses hostility, "up to an intermediate level of fear, the more fear the message arouses, the more persuasive it will be." If death took a holiday for a century, "I would have to close up shop," Jones admitted. "Then just before the hundred years had expired . . . they would come around again and want to get religion. Death is the only thing that makes religion." Only the timid would fail to use fear to persuade people to convert. "Take and shake a sinner over a coffin and turn him loose," Jones advised ministers, "and he will hit the ground running every time."[27]

Shortly after Satan's sick call in Waco, Jones received a telegram from Dewitt Talmage, the pastor of Central Presbyterian Church in Brooklyn, New York, and a preacher whose sermons were printed across the country. Talmage had come to Memphis two weeks after the Jones meeting and had found the town buzzing with stories of the unfettered evangelist from Georgia. His curiosity aroused, the New York divine went one hundred miles to hear the phenomenon. The elegant Talmage was not offended by Jones's coarse manner. In the midst of esoteric theological disputes, he thought, "it is a luxury to meet some evangelist who can tell us in our common mother tongue of Him who came to seek and save that which was lost." Convinced "the Georgia Cracker" was just the man to "shell out" his congregation, Talmage asked Jones to conduct the annual tabernacle revival starting in January 1885.[28]

Jones did not admire the Brooklyn preacher; Talmage was just "too much of a monkey" he confided to a friend. However, he accepted the invitation to evangelize in one of the most prestigious pulpits in America and started on his first expedition north wearing baggy pants, scuffed shoes, and an old-fashioned fedora hat. "My name ain't the Rev. Samuel Porter Jones," he announced at the first meeting following a flowery introduction by Talmage. "It is just plain Sam Jones." Though he would try to "run the devil out of Brooklyn," he was not very hopeful: "I am afraid there is too much pride in this church for the Lord to do much for us. If you people and Dr. Talmage had as much of the grace of the Lord in your hearts as you have pride you wouldn't need a little sallow-faced Georgia preacher to come and preach to you."[29]

Jones had miscalculated: his studied offensiveness repelled Talmage's well-heeled congregation. "I was shocked, inexpressibly shocked," one woman sniffed. "He used such plain language, and did not qualify his threats." The *Brooklyn Eagle* was also dismissive of the revivalist who "shouted quaint phrases in drawling southern dialect and with considerable offense to grammatical structure." Though Talmage tried to fortify the Georgian by preaching in tandem, a faltering Jones dropped much of the mountain wit that gave his sermons their pungency and punch. When Ira Sankey, Dwight L. Moody's gospel singer, observed the southerner, he pronounced him "an earnest Christian and indefatigable worker, but not an exceptionally brilliant man."[30]

Jones never spoke of the Brooklyn meeting, though he may have referred to it obliquely when he admitted he had once coveted the reputation of a great preacher: "I made a great effort, but I made a great burst, and I shall never talk about it again." The collection for the Orphan Home from Talmage's congregation was a disappointment—"If they didn't get much it didn't cost them much," the home's administrator observed acidly. However, they were generous to the evangelist himself, presenting Jones with a thousand dollars at the end of the four-week campaign. He refused it, saying that he had not given them their money's worth. Talmage pressed the money upon him, however, and Jones yielded, deciding to use the money to buy books on religion and to support his family for the next six months.[31]

Jones followed the Brooklyn disappointment with a triumphant revival in Huntsville, Alabama. Jones has "a way that is absolutely apostolic in its simplicity," a Presbyterian minister exulted. His authority over an audience was astounding; like a trumpet, Jones sounded, "and all at once we were at his feet." One person was alarmed by the evangelist's restless exhaustion, however, and warned Jones that his incessant efforts might end in extinction. "The nervous temperament predominates very largely in your make-up," J. H. Bryson wrote. "Humanly speaking, it is the secret of your great power over a popular audience." But Jones would be consumed by the fire he kindled if he let it blaze unceasingly. "Evangelism requires a hot fire burning fiercely while it lasts—then must at once follow the cooling, the resting process with fair time to recuperate."[32]

The perceptive Mr. Bryson had sensed the emotional instability that would hound Jones for the rest of his life and disable him for long stretches of time during the nineties. It may be that his problems were genetic, for mental illness ran deep and wide in the Jones family. The evangelist's sister, Annie, was a chronically depressed morphine addict whose son, Porter Stocks, murdered a man while in a drunken rage. Sam's younger brother, Charles, was first a Methodist preacher, then a Baptist exhorter, then decided he was unable to serve either church since emotions beyond his control robbed him of the "courage to stand the test." He resolved "to drown my better impulse in the whirlpool of dissipation," and in "hours of gloom," he confessed to Sam, he "tried to curse God and die." With Sam's backing, he supported his wife and nine children as the proprietor of the Etowah River Mills and ran a general store in Cartersville before moving to Stilesboro to become a farmer. Frequently sullen, Charles was embittered by his dependence and complained of the predicament in which "a poor devil is often placed by the more successful *angels* of light." He continued to be subject to such dark depressions that the oldest brother, Joe, worried that the "poor fellow" would "die by his own hand some day."[33]

Joe was sober while Sam was a drunkard and became a drunkard when Sam sobered up. After downing a quart of whiskey one icy night in January 1885, Joe was run over by a locomotive. His life was saved because he had fallen into a stock gap, one of the holes spaced periodically along the line for livestock. His soul was saved when he was told that both his wife in Cartersville and his brother preaching in Brooklyn had been moved to spend that night in prayer for him.[34]

Joe applied for a license to preach from the Methodist church and prepared to assist his brother in revivals. This partnership was prevented by Laura, who wrote Sam that Joe was "in no wise capacitated to preach," and was "by no means a man of consecration." Furthermore, he was unable to leave his family unless Sam undertook their support, "*which you will certainly not do.*" The brothers did work together occasionally, but their style was so similar that collaboration was redundant. Both "abused people wherever they went, finding in each place something more fearful than the last." Joining Sam in Memphis in 1888, Joe asked everyone to stand up who could recite the Ten Commandments and witness that "the Bible is God's last will and testament and Jesus Christ is appointed administrator of the estate." Disgusted when no one stood, Joe groused, "Well, you're the biggest lot of fools I ever saw. No wonder you ain't getting nothing out of the heavenly inheritance. You ain't read the will."[35]

As with Charles, a careful reading of Scriptures led Joe to conclude that baptism should be by complete immersion. With Sam happily observing, Joe was "dunked" and converted to the Baptists. Though he became a popular evangelist in Texas, Arkansas, and Mississippi, Joe continued to be afflicted with emotional problems. "I need a Guardian," he confessed in 1889. "I don't kno what nor how to do about my children." Nine years later, Joe wrote that he was so "crazy with eczema and nervousness" that if he did not get better he would soon be dead. "I can't stand another spree like I had." Joe continued to suffer from "impoverished blood" and "slight touches of paralysis"; he died in 1902 in Sam's arms.[36]

Children who lose a parent, as Joe, Sam, Charles, and Annie did, often battle chronic depression as adults and may turn to alcohol or narcotics for relief. But the large number of emotionally unstable family members suggests something more may have been at work in the Jones family: bipolar disorder, formerly known as manic depression. Such a diagnosis would explain many of the emotional outcroppings of this turbulent family. Many afflicted with this biochemical disorder abuse alcohol or drugs, seeking to even out emotions by dampening the highs and lifting the lows. The euphoria of a manic state is often perceived as a religious experience, and more severe cases may be accompanied by delusions and hallucinations, such as those which sent Jones's uncle, the Reverend William ("Buck") Jones, to an asylum. The spiritual fluctuations of Charles Jones—religious evanescence evaporating into suicidal depression, guilt accompanied by fears of persecution and inferiority—could have been a manifestation of manic depression. Annie Jones Stocks's depression was alternately inert and frenzied, and the "spree" of which Joe Jones wrote might have been one of manic excitement, as drunkenness would have caused public scandal and ended his ministry.[37]

Whatever the source of Sam Jones's frenetic energy, supernatural power, nervous excitability, or manic episodes, he could not light anywhere long, and his constant traveling and his growing fame put a strain on his marriage. Laura vacillated between self-pity and anger, filling her letters with complaints about back pain, headaches, and sick children. "Dear Husband," she wrote in April 1884. "Yours received. Glad to hear from you. The weather is bad. I am not well. Laura [their daughter] is not well either.

All send love. I will write you again tomorrow." It was just as well that his work took him away so much: "I think you would get tired of me before the week was out." Laura especially resented Sam's spending time with friends rather than family during his brief stopovers at home. "It scarcely seems you spoke of enjoying your *visit* home," she wrote with thinly veiled sarcasm, or "that you were here at all—the time was so short and I saw so little of you." [38]

Sam was disturbed by Laura's loneliness. "I know it is a severe trial to dear Mama for Papa to be gone so much," Jones wrote his young daughter Mary in 1886 from Toronto. "I am often troubled myself because of my separation from her—I know she is the best wife almost in the whole world and I am only hapy when she is hapy. And yet this work which keeps me from loved ones so much seems to be *the work* the Good Lord has given me to do." Convinced of his mission, he steeled himself against Laura's pleas to slow down: "Wife, I haven't got a minute to lose," he told her. "I haven't an hour to throw away; I want to finish the course and do the work God wants me to do, and I can't help from believing that man is immortal until his work is done." He was "a restless, nervous mortal"; he might break down, but he would not rust out. "I am in love with my job," he admitted. "It is crowned work this side of heaven. There is not an angel tonight who would not come down here gladly and take my place and give me his place up there." [39]

Several times Jones was forced to slow down because of poor health. In the winter of 1884 A. W. Lamar of Memphis had provided Jones with his first important union revival and thus had helped propel him into spiritual stardom. By the fall of that year, Lamar expressed alarm over the physical price Jones was paying for attempting to answer every call. "I am sorry to hear of your feebleness, yet I am not surprised," Lamar wrote. "You are neither steel nor iron, and yet you have tried to work as if you were. I want you to put the brakes on before it is too late." Eighteen months later, William Leftwich of Nashville made an even more impassioned plea for Jones to "husband [his] strength" and avoid "wearing out," as he was rumored to be doing. "You are in much more danger than you are willing to see, or believe," Leftwich warned. "The moral obligation to preserve your life, health, and vigor, is just as great as the moral obligation to spend that life for the glory of God. . . . My brother, stop. Stop now. STOP NOW." [40]

After Jones fell ill in Baltimore in 1886, doctors advised Laura that her husband was "too delicate to work continuously in preaching the Gospel" and suggested a cycle of two weeks of work and two weeks of rest. Jones never followed this schedule, but once or twice a year he would go to his wife's home in Kentucky or back to Cartersville for a few weeks of rest. He enjoyed these times, playing with the children and grandchildren or taking the buggy around to visit neighbors. Jones loved animals and enjoyed riding his horse, Dexter, or playing with his favorite dog, Gip, a Scottish terrier given to him by an admirer in Texas. Gip was a first-rate rat catcher, and Gip and Jones could often be found in the barn, sitting with a fishing pole baited with cheese, waiting for the vermin to bite.[41]

Since Sam never changed his wandering ways, it is fortunate that something happened to convince Laura that, "outside of his love for God," Sam's love for her "was the greatest thing in the world." In 1887 Sam persuaded Laura to leave the children at home with their two grandmothers and travel with him to Rochester, New York, for a revival. While there, Laura became critically ill, and after five weeks the doctors advised Jones to take her home so she could see her children one last time. An operation was performed, likely a hysterectomy given the modest silence about the nature of the problem and the fact that Laura, who was in her late thirties, bore no more children. Laura continued to worsen until Jones was told on Christmas Eve that she was "beyond the reach of human skill." In anguish, he vowed that if God gave him back his wife, he would never "give her a moment's pain or speak a cross or impatient word to her." Laura immediately began to improve and claimed after her husband's death that he kept that promise.[42]

During the illness Jones had not left Laura's bedside even to sleep. During her recovery he traveled a thousand miles both ways to spend a few hours with her at home. Buoyed up by this display of devotion, Laura's letters became more cheerful, full of affection toward "the best and dearest of men." Though Jones's absence continued to be "the cross" of her life and she still fretted that her loneliness showed she loved "the creature more than the Creator," she took the advice that Jones had so often pressed upon her and began filling her days with activities and friends. She quickly became a leader in the Women's Christian Temperance Society, the Women's Home Missionary Society, and the Epworth League for Methodist youth. Active in civic affairs, she served as chairperson of the Dalton District Library for ten years before resigning in protest because young people were being allowed to check out books that presented "in a profane name, those delicate matters that should first be discussed by their parents at home."[43]

Jones was proud of Laura's talents and encouraged her independence. "My wife has a check-book and signs my name to a check and gets money from the bank in Cartersville for anything she wants to spend it for," he bragged. "I have never asked her what she spends the money for." Backed by Jones's confidence and steady income, Laura invested in real estate and managed the couple's many rental properties. She became known as a benefactress and a "gracious hostess," decorating her home—to the delight of her bumpkin husband—in lush Victorian style. "I wouldn't swap her at all," Jones announced after twenty-five years of marriage. "I said to her the other day, 'Laura, old girl, there are very few women in the world that I think more of than I do you.'"[44]

At the peak of his career in the 1880s, Jones was rarely home for more than a few days between two- to six-week sieges. He did an astonishing amount of work: he estimated that from September 1885 to September 1886, he traveled twenty thousand miles, preached one thousand sermons to three million people, and added seventy thousand to the rolls of the Methodist Episcopal Church, South. Sensing the evangelist was out of control, Dr. Fitzgerald of the *Advocate* was openly disapproving. "The late movements of our evangelist look a little like suicide," Fitzgerald fretted; "no man can hold up at the rate he is going."[45]

Sam Jones kept going, though, and by the end of that remarkable year reporters from across the country were crowded at the foot of the platform, scrambling to telegraph the sermon back to their hometown papers. So extensive was the press coverage at the Chicago revival of March 1886 that Jones guessed every sermon he preached in that city was read by one and a half million people. A prominent newspaperman remarked that "the press has never in the world's history followed any man so closely, be he king, potentate, or preacher." Publishing was a natural extension of his popularity. His first book, *Sermons and Sayings*, sold thirty thousand copies in four months, and excerpts from his sermons were printed in England, Scotland, Sweden, and Australia, prompting invitations to speak all over the world.[46]

In the ten months between Nashville and Chicago, Jones became a national celebrity; a candy, a campground, and a host of babies were named after him. His personal habits were of intense interest: what he ate for breakfast (oatmeal with cream, fruit, coffee, and lemonade); what size his "yaller shoes" were (a tiny size seven); what he liked to read (the Bible and newspapers). His chest, the *St. Louis Republican* reported, was thirty-seven inches in full respiration, thirty-four in full expiration; he had a thirty-inch waist and a pulse rate of seventy-four beats a minute. Rival newspapers vied to offer their readers the best description, noting his "erect figure and quick movements," the "black, feverish eyes" set in a "thin restless face which looks prematurely aged," the "hard, stern mouth" which suddenly smiled. The mustache was of special interest—"a cross between a soup strainer and a horseshoe"—and when queried about why it was so much blacker than his hair, Jones quipped, "It's younger." Bowing to the fad of the day,

Jones was even examined by a celebrated phrenologist, who warned Jones after mapping the bumps and crevices of the famous skull that self-esteem was a dominant characteristic; he must guard against egotism. "The more I mix with you fellows the more I do get stuck on myself," Jones admitted to his audiences. "It's the truth."[47]

Jones reveled in the attentions of the press and was fond of reporters as a rule, regarding them as a sober big brother might a charming but irresponsible sibling. "Boys," he would say with a sharp glance at the press table, "I will have four shots a day at you, while you will only get one nibble a day at me, and if you can stand it I can." However, he frequently complained that reporters seized upon the gristle and ignored the meat in his sermons. "The newspapers do the best they can, but now I preach 9000 words an hour, and they give you only a hundred or two words," Jones cautioned. "You had as well take a photograph of my head, hands and knees and say it is Sam Jones."[48]

Most of the coverage was flattering, a result both of beliefs and shrewd marketing. The modern reader is struck by how deeply the language of Christianity permeated the nineteenth-century press; obituaries were headlined "Passed to Eternity" or "Dust to Dust," while "The Wages of Sin" or "Reaping the Whirlwind" indicated a crime report. Beyond this tacit acceptance of Christian culture, the upsurge in religious interest in the mid-eighties made newspapers realize that revivals sold papers. Dwight Moody noted this happy development in an interview with William Randolph Hearst's San Francisco paper, the *Daily Examiner*. While Moody's revival of 1881 had been virtually ignored by the press, his California campaign eight years later was covered in depth—evidence, Moody thought, that "more attention is paid to religious movements."[49]

Interest in revivals, expanding literacy, and the burgeoning circulation of newspapers in the late nineteenth century helped Jones achieve international prominence in a matter of months, and reporters were quick to point out the evangelist's debt to the press. "Great as his gifts are, they have required the help of the press to make him a success," a California paper observed. "He preaches the Gospel, but the Cincinnati *Enquirer* did more for him than all the patriarchs and prophets and the twelve apostles, for it gave him wide notoriety, which brought crowds to hear him."[50]

Jones, however, resented being tagged the creation of the press. When a St. Louis paper boasted it had "made" him, the evangelist issued this challenge: "Make another." In the *Chicago Tribune*, a paper devoting two pages a day to his meeting, Jones gave a cold-eyed appraisal of why he was the object of press attention. "The newspapers have aided me wonderfully in my work, yet I am satisfied they would not have given me such a reception if it had not been for the vision of dollars they had before them. . . . While great newspapers are a great invention and absolutely indispensable, yet you never saw one in your life but that it was coldly and selfishly mercenary, ready at any and all times to rush along with the popular tide. . . . They follow the boom and are following Jones."[51]

There were some who thought that God, not Sam Jones, should be the focus in newspaper reports of revivals. To those at the Methodist General Conference of 1886 who suggested it was unseemly for a man of the cloth to be a celebrity, Jones said he had no more to do with the attention of the press "than I had with the nails growing on my fingers." In fact, Jones consciously manipulated the newspapers, provoking the press with attacks and innuendoes. Criticism equaled crowds, so Jones excited censure. "If you people don't quit abusing me, we'll get the crowd so big that we will have to go out and hold our meeting in the open air," Jones warned critics in Baltimore. "It's the devil doing my advertising free. If I had to pay for it all, it would break me in a week."[52]

From his earliest days as an evangelist, Jones had used sensationalism to "drum up a crowd." In 1878 when the first meeting of a campaign in West Point, Georgia, attracted only three women and a preacher, Jones decided to rout out the sinners. Calling on the ladies to reconsecrate themselves at the altar, Jones gave them their orders: while he and their pastor would visit the men at their businesses, the ladies were to call on the women, calmly greeting them with this statement when they opened the door: "You are going to hell." The good sisters were instructed not to become enmeshed in explanations as to how they had secured this information but were simply to move on to the next house, that all might be given the news. A goodly portion of the town's population turned out for the evening service, and so many who came to maim stayed to listen that soon even "men who were notoriously opposed to religion were in constant attendance upon the services."[53]

Jones recommended his methods to other ministers. "Rip and snort and tear your clothes, gentlemen," Jones advised. "It brings men and things to the front." Few ministers took Jones's advice, realizing that they lacked his immunity to ruin. "Jones can say whatever he sees fit and belches forth, it seems—no matter how chaste and refined his audience," one reporter wrote in disgust. "Let any local ministers make like expressions and they would be compelled to climb a tree." The truth of that statement was borne out after Jones's death when Walt Holcomb preached the tabernacle services in Cartersville. As Jones had done, Holcomb ordered a woman to get her "fanny" out of the men's meeting. (Jones had said "butt.") Holcomb was charged with obscenity and fined for violating the town's standards of decency.[54]

Others attributed Jones's success to the vividness of his vignettes, the everyday illustrations that made up half of most sermons. "There has always been one great, undeniable fact connected with the work of Sam Jones, and that is that the people are with him," the humorist Bill Nye wrote in 1894. "It is hard to analyze why this is so at first, but when you notice that he does not pull his sermons out of a cyclopedia or concordance you are coming close to the cause of it."[55]

Jones prided himself on the fact that his sermons were drawn from life, so simple that he did not have to rely on notes. Though Presbyterian and Congregationalist clergymen had long read their intricate theological discourses, in the South, especially the rural South, the reading of sermons was seen as an affectation of ministers more eager to show off their learning than reach their people. As he often did, Jones expressed the attitude of rural southern evangelicals with angry wit. "It tickles me," Jones would say with a scowl, "to see a dry, dogmatic preacher dressed in his cold, conventional suit, with his dingy manuscript of a sermon prepared thirty years ago, stand in the pulpit of a $40,000 church and read his soporific message to the slumbering forty." No one should have to sit still and listen to someone read. "A preacher should be like a beer keg—he should run anywhere you tap him."[56]

There were those who claimed it was Jones's theatrical ability that entranced audiences. "I just hated to hear him stop," a girl said after watching Jones in action. "It was better than a theater." The evangelist's imitation of a cringing cleric begging favors from the rich always brought down the house, as did his portrayal of an "egg-sucking dog." For a man who denounced the theater as "the antechamber of hell," Jones was extremely dramatic, mimicking "in high falsetto tones, the shocked expressions of Mrs. Worldliness or Mrs. Fashion at his plain speech."[57]

A minister once recorded "three loud outbursts of laughter each two minutes during the first half of the sermon." But as Jones felt the audience opening to him, his illustrations became more poignant than pungent. One especially moving dramatization was of a pilgrimage to his mother's grave in Alabama. "I must see her again," he would mumble in a dazed monotone, "must look into her eyes and see her sweet form." Taking up an imaginary shovel, he would plunge it into imaginary earth, murmuring with each shovelful, "I must see my mother again." Finally, the grave would seem to open before him. Reaching into the dirt with both hands, he would cry in horror, "Is that my mother? Is that all that is left of my precious mother?" Walking slowly across the darkened stage until he stood under a solitary light, Jones would suddenly shout: "Yes, I shall see my mother again. My mother is transformed into an angel of light, and she hovers over me on loving pendant wings, and beckons me up to her home on high, where I shall see my mother again." Men who had not been home since they were weaned would get misty-eyed during this performance, punctuating his proclamation with the pitiful howl of an adult orphan.[58]

Jones did not invent American religious theater. Henry Ward Beecher had held mock slave auctions in the 1850s, and Jones's contemporary Dwight Moody listed his meetings in the entertainment section of the paper, answering those who criticized him for lowering the dignity of the pulpit that it was "more undignified to preach to empty pews." Nor was Jones's use of slang unheard of, though the orthodox flinched when he described Saint Paul as "the sensational preacher from Sensationville" and labeled Judas Iscariot "a pretty bad egg." Moody's Bible heroes spoke with fractured grammar, and Billy Sunday, an early twentieth-century revivalist influenced by Jones's style, revealed that when David "socked the giant in the coco right between the lamps," Goliath "went down for the count."[59]

But if other preachers could translate the Gospel into street slang and enliven sermons with dramatic portrayals, Jones's comedic abilities were unique in the American pulpit. "His wit is his first great power with the masses," the Reverend D. C. Kelley of Tennessee decided. "People love wit, and will sit, stand, or pay to hear it." Jones was God's comedian; those who heard him compared his drawling delivery to Mark Twain's, and his wry wit to Josh Billings's. After a quick jab to the funnybone, he would join in the laughter, relishing his own joke for a moment, then pull back, waiting for the merriment to crest before he added another witticism that would send the audience back into a gale of laughter. "Sam Jones furnished more fun than two comedians," one reporter raved, "more philosophy than four universities; more gospel than one-half dozen theological seminarians and almost as much common sense as the mother of a big family of country boys."[60]

Critics charged that Sam Jones had turned the revival into a minstrel show, degrading public taste until an ordinary sermon seemed boring. One Missouri minister complained that after the Jones meeting his people developed a "morbid desire to hear nothing that is solid, real, instructive." Marion F. Ham, a Unitarian minister in Chattanooga, denounced Jones as a "traveling religious agitator." Surely, Ham sniffed, "Christianity is at least a sober and a decent thing, if nothing more." The president of the Congregational Club of Boston remarked sadly, "There is a kernel of truth that is good and nutritious in all that he says, but to get it one often has to fill himself with the husks that the swine do eat." A *Washington Post* reporter suggested the evangelist be locked up until he learned the English language, and a Dallas reporter complained that "Sam Jones is flooding the country with more slang than are all the sweet girl graduates of the year. Sammy thinks it smart."[61]

"Sammy" did think it smart. "I think I owe my success as an evangelist to the fact that I have something to say and say it. The plain truth plainly spoken is, I think, the most omnipotent thing in the world." If he was "dirty" it was because he was in the "business of dragging sinners back from hell." He explained, "The preachers who go out with a silk line and artificial flies are after the mountain trout. I am after the suckers and the mullets and they like worms." His encounters with grammarians he compared to "being nibbled to death by minnows," or being "beaten on the head by a rubber balloon; it doesn't hurt any; it's just an annoyance."[62]

Jones was unapologetic about using humor as a drawing card. "You needn't bother about my eccentricities," he would tell his audiences, "I only put them on to get you here." He recognized that "a great many people hang around revivals just for the loaves and fishes," but they might wind up with the bread of life. Nor did it matter that some who came to hear him would as soon turn out for a cockfight or a carnival. What was important was that the spiritually ill were physically present. "I give you what you want first," he would say, "and I give you what you need second."[63]

Jones believed that for the church to compete successfully with sin, it had to appropriate some of the trappings of the theater. "The pulpit ought to draw like mustard plaster," he contended. "It ought to entertain like a fairy tale." The Wednesday night prayer meeting should be the best show in town. "Fix it so they'll love it," Jones would tell preachers. "Delight yourself in the Lord." As for himself, "if I cannot entertain a man, I won't detain him."[64]

If Jones's witty iconoclasm delighted his audiences, his delivery held them spellbound. At times Jones seemed almost lethargic, swimming slowly in the molasses of his drawl. "On the platform he is the very incarnation of repose," the editor of the *Baltimore Baptist* observed. "He speaks with a deliberation that is extraordinary. He will make a remark, then pause, stroke the side of his face and rest awhile before he makes another. His power is largely in his pauses." Jones "never seems to know that he is making any such impression," the Reverend Kelley wrote; "yet, as he stands in the easy, nonchalant attitude, pausing between sentences as he leisurely walks the platform," his power over people is "almost boundless."[65]

At other times Jones demonstrated what Billy Sunday was to discover: an audience could be caught up by rapid, seemingly erratic movement. Sunday enjoyed adding suspense to his sermons by perching with one foot on the pulpit and another on a precariously balanced chair, "bending over backwards like a springy sword blade" as his audience waited for him to tumble onto the sawdust trail. Jones too "was not built for repose," and nervous energy often drove him back and forth across the stage. Prowling around the platform with a pugnacious look, he would suddenly stop to point a skeletal finger at a sinner or glower at a heckler. "First on one side of the platform, then on the other, swinging his arms frantically and swaying to and fro like a ship in a storm," Jones proved he was an itinerant preacher. With his manic movements, Jones manifested that auditory anomaly: a fast southern drawl. "Words come in floods, following one another so fast the hearer is startled," one reporter wrote. "It is simply a succession of pictures, some pretty and idyllic in their simple repose, while others are very grand and almost terrifying." [66]

Jones never lost control of his audience, and nothing seemed to faze him. In Knoxville, when "every light in the monster tabernacle" went out, Jones "didn't stop for a minute," reassuring the crowd that he had "been through a little of everything." "One thing about it," the evangelist drawled, "you're all better lookin' in the dark, anyhow." When a tornado roared through Dallas, Jones ordered folks to stay put: "If you are that afraid to die you had better stick to the meeting." [67]

At times his control was tyrannical; he would not hesitate to humiliate anyone who disrupted his sermon. During the brush-arbor meeting at his hometown in Cartersville, a common tactic was to stop talking when someone got up to leave and say, "Well, I see the Walker family is here tonight." He was impatient with interruptions. "Nothing is the matter except that a few people who ought to have better manners have been getting up and leaving before we have finished," Jones announced after a commotion at his San Francisco meeting. "I hope they won't come here again during the rest of the services. They are not worth saving." [68]

Aristotle observed that "melancholy men of all others are the most witty." Under the crust of Sam Jones's savage wit was a reservoir of melancholy, a gloominess that showed in his dark, sad eyes, in the smile that faded too quickly, in the mournful resonance of his voice. "The voice has a plaintive as well as a penetrating quality," a Baltimore reporter discovered. "It rises and falls, slowly, drawlingly, and with every phrase tipped with a rising inflection and a twang. It is not wearisome; it is soothing, . . . and it might have taken its melancholy color from the loneliness of the mountains."

A Tennessee minister remembered after Jones's death that the evangelist "could speak to more people, covering a larger area, with less effort than anyone we ever saw. And so penetrating was his voice that while talking in a conversational tone he could be heard to the very outskirts of the audience. He said to us once that he picked out the farthest man in the audience and talked to him, and if he could hear, of course everyone between could."[69]

Sam Jones could talk to a vast crowd with the easy intimacy of "one neighbor talking to another," and he could plead with such intensity that his soul seemed to bleed out of his black eyes. For all that, he might have been just another traveling evangelist, dragging his tabernacle from tiny town to tiny town like a turtle carting its own house, except that he embodied the ideal of his age. In the 1880s the minister who was revered was the man who made the masses sway under the power of his oratory, whose speech bristled with the "metaphors of the marketplace." This was the day when personality, even peculiar personality, was prized above administrative abilities, elegance in ritual, intellectual depth. "Truth through Personality is our description of real preaching," Phillips Brooks, himself a prince of the pulpit, insisted. There were those who spoke against a cult of pulpit personality; P. T. Forsyth condemned it as Protestant idolatry. "The Church does not live by its preachers," Forsyth thundered, "but by its Word." In reality, however, crowds who came to hear a pulpit personality often would not listen to a lesser mortal. On one occasion when an assistant announced that the pulpit would be occupied by a local minister because Jones was too sick to speak, three hundred people got up and left, causing such an uproar with their exodus that the choir was forced to sing a hymn while they withdrew.[70]

Few could fill Jones's pulpit. Though his coworkers Sam Small, George Stuart, and Walt Holcomb were fine preachers, when evangelist and assistant held forth at two locations in the same city, the larger crowd was always with Jones. The Reverend R. G. Lee of Memphis was only a child when Jones died, but he remembered his father talking about the great evangelists who had come to that city: Dwight Moody, DeWitt Talmadge, J. Wilbur Chapman, "Gypsy" Smith, and Billy Sunday. "But my daddy said that Sam Jones was the greatest master of an audience he had ever heard." Women were especially attuned to his influence. "His wonderful magnetism broods over the sea of beings under his eye," a woman with the astonishing name Marie Antoinette Meek swooned, "then he is absolute master [and] the intensity of his spirituality glows in his countenance as he speaks." Even some who did not accept the message fell under the spell of the messenger. "I have heard many of America's greatest speakers, including William

Jennings Bryan," an agnostic reminisced, "but I believe that Sam Jones had the greatest power over an audience of any man I ever heard." [71]

Some worried that Jones might use his power like Carry Nation, the hatchet-wielding prohibitionist from the Kansas plains who led wrathful women on righteous debauches, smashing saloons and defacing the nudes that decorated the bars. Jones "is a dangerous man," the chief of police in St. Louis fretted. "One word from him and five thousand men here to-night would form a mob and destroy every saloon in the city, and my officers could not prevent them." In 1886 Jones was accused of inciting violence in Millegeville, Georgia. During a quick stop to excite antisaloon senti-ment before a local option election, Jones advised prohibitionists to carry their pistols to the polls and "feed the buzzards" with any liquor men who "strike the first lick." Weapons were openly in evidence at a debate a few weeks later, and after the rally, a prohibitionist was shot by an antiprohi-bitionist who claimed self-defense. Jones was widely criticized for igniting a flammable situation. Although he insisted he "never made an incendiary speech in my life," in the future he advised the use of fists, not firearms, in "defense of the helpless women and children of this country." [72]

There is no doubt that Jones could exploit emotion, and at times he stoked the fires of religious enthusiasm. At a St. Joseph camp meeting Jones scolded those who belittled religious enthusiasm, saying most churches were so dead that they should call themselves the First Baptist Cemetery or the Wesley Memorial Mausoleum. He scoffed:

> None of you fellows in there believe in excitement; no, of course you don't. Occasionally some antique ghost gets up in his tomb inside the spiritual graveyard and raising the marble slabs that cover him, pokes out his head and says "Be quiet out there; we don't believe in excitement here." No! You don't believe in excitement, or anything else hardly. Do you know what I'd like to do? I'd like to mash that tablet down if I could get your head held in it.

Tearful testimonials followed, and when an elderly woman began shouting about her hope of heaven, Jones exulted: "I never had a meeting where so much feeling was manifested at one time. Let the old lady shout if she wants to. Perhaps the reason you never shouted was because you had nothing to shout about." [73]

While Jones encouraged expressions of emotion among the religiously repressed, far more often he worked to rechannel religious enthusiasm by striking up a hymn such as "Oh, How I Love Jesus," deflecting raw emo-tion into soft sentiment. While he considered an occasional shout a natural expression of supernatural joy, far too often Christians, especially south-erners raised to revel in "heart religion," were content to *feel* and not *act*. To a woman who had "fallen into the falsetto" Jones said with a smile: "Well, sister, I do not object to shouting, but some people when they shout are like a little steamer I know of on the Coosa River, in Alabama. She has a big whistle, but a very small boiler, and everytime she blows her whistle she stops—she can't blow and run at the same time." [74]

As for himself, he was thankful that the day of the howling, jerking, barking convert was over, saying of the "old-fashioned Methodists" that "they ran on their feelings in those days. Seventy-five years ago, people got religion just like darkies get it now, by feeling and nothing else." Jones insisted that "religion is not all 'holler' and 'hallelujah'; it is a big bundle of do good and not feel good." Many a Christian was fueled by feeling, not faith, wanting "a blessing just like a drunkard wants another drink," and for the same reason: "to make him feel real good." [75]

Jones's emphasis on religion as a way of life rather than a way of feel-ing reflected a trend in nineteenth-century revivalism. Following Moody's lead, ministers in the last quarter of the century spoke more of God as a loving Father disappointed by the sins of his children than as an outraged sovereign ready to sentence transgressors to the awful silence of the outer darkness. "The love of God became the predominant theme and the wrath of God was less dwelt upon," Thomas Lindsay noted in a 1905 article on revivalism. "The abstract question of the guilt of sin, though never aban-doned, was placed behind the more practical question of the power of sin over the heart and life." [76]

The emphasis on the ethical effects of sin was accompanied by a change in methods—the conspicuous mourner's bench was replaced by the after-meeting, during which a seeker could find quiet counsel. Conversion be-came less a dramatic act accompanied by sobs and shouts and more a quiet decision signaled by a misty walk up the sawdust trail or a simple signature on a decision card. "The fierce introspection, the wild paroxysms of remorse for sin and rejoicings over heaven found, which were the chief features of the revival which swept over our country just a hundred years ago, will per-haps never be repeated," G. B. Winton, editor of the *Christian Advocate*, wrote without regret in 1903. "Repentance, trust, pardon, adoption—all this is, really a short and simple process." [77]

However, Sam Jones was far less influenced by changing theology than by his own experience. He had not had an emotional conversion; he simply decided to stop sinning and serve God. While he encouraged saints to shout their praises, he tried to restrain wailing sinners, convinced that the most

steadfast were often the least demonstrative. "Our long experience in revival work taught us that much of the crying and sobbing at the altar was
brought about by the sympathy and commiseration of friends, and it lacked
the godly element that we often found in the hearts of the pale, tearless,
apparently emotionless penitent," Jones's coworker George Stuart wrote to
a minister who had criticized Jones for failing to preach proper repentance.
Jones came to accept a simple handshake, even a show of hands if the aisles
were crowded, as signifying agreement to follow Christ. "He felt if men truly
repented," Stuart explained, "they were saved regardless of their external
demonstration." [78]

In the gospel according to Sam Jones, godliness equaled good behavior,
and conversion was a decision to "quit your meanness." It is ironic that
the man who stressed the necessity of drawing the line between the church
and the world dimmed the difference between the committed Christian and
the good citizen by his behavioral litmus test: Christians are people who go
around doing good; this person goes about doing good; therefore this person
is a Christian. "What is a Christian?" Jones asked. He answered without
once mentioning Christ: "He is a man who is known as a religious man in
the community; it is a man who is at peace with God and all mankind; a
man who, in the light of his conscience and innocence of his soul, knows
that he has done right, and that the declaration of his heart and mouth have
been right." [79]

It seemed to be the evangelist's expectation that the man who obeyed the
laws of man and of Moses and treated his neighbor with kindness would
wind up in heaven even if he did not believe such a place existed. Turning
to a man who doubted the divinity of Christ, Jones said that he expected to
see him in heaven if he "loves God and works for righteousness." At those
shocked by his belief Jones flung the Scripture "Little children, let no man
deceive you: He that doeth righteousness is righteous." [80]

Jewish leaders were pleased by this ecumenical evangelist. After observing Jones in Nashville, Rabbi Julius Ochs commended the Georgian to his
people, saying, "There is nothing in his sermons that cannot be endorsed
by every well-thinking man or woman. If you expect to get to heaven, live up
to the commandments of the Lord; if you do not, you cannot expect to reach
that goal." In Baltimore, a city with a large community of German and Rus-
sian Jews, Jones urged Christians to overcome religious bigotry. "God bless
the Jews, the most neglected race upon the earth. Eighteen hundred years
ago an old Jew couldn't see how God would save a Gentile, and now some
Christians can't see how a Jew can be saved. It is a scandal." A week later
he held a special service "for Hebrews" during which he reduced the dif-

ferences between Jews and Christians to a quibble over "creeds or tenets." He ended the service by asking for contributions to the Hebrew Hospital: "Let us send a collection to the institution of humanity for the glory of our common father." [81]

Like the Pharisee of old Jones delighted in the law and found solace in its boundaries, its call to radical restraints. "Set all the commandments to music in your soul. Even the angels will be charmed." Other Christians might swoon over the love of Christ, but Jones would preach the God of the burning bush and the smoking tablets. "Mr. Moody lingers about Calvary more than I do," Jones admitted. "I linger more about Sinai." [82]

While liberals found Jones's emphasis on law distasteful, they admired his iconoclasm. After hearing Jones preach "What Must I Do to Be Saved?" a liberal noted with approval that there was "not a drop of the sacrificial blood of Christ in the whole sermon." What commended Jones to the liberals, however, condemned him with the orthodox, one of whom accused Jones of aiming at "mere surface reformation," preaching "Unitarianism in uncouth dress." Jones's explanation of repentance "would make an ass laugh," a correspondent from Scotland predicted, concluding that like John Wesley, Jones was "essentially a papist teaching salvation by works, a damnable doctrine." [83]

Others were more grieved than angered by Jones's failure to "preach Christ, and him crucified." Writing after the evangelist's death, the Reverend Flournoy Rivers of Tennessee concluded with regret that the evangelist had preached repentance but not faith.

> He would show men their sinfulness and lead them to repent of their sins, and when they cried out, "What Must I do to be Saved?" instead of answering them as Paul did the jailer, "Believe on the Lord Jesus Christ and thou shalt be saved," he told them "Quit your meanness and join the church." There he failed—failed, sad to say, at a vital point. He could preach Christ. We have heard him preach Christ beautifully and powerfully. But he did not always do it. In fact, he seldom did it. His whole effort seemed to be directed to getting men to repent. And there he would leave them. . . . Many were saved under his preaching and led to better lives, [but] in truth, he was more of a reformer than a preacher of the Gospel." [84]

"I know it has been said that I'm going around preaching only reformation," Jones would say, "but what is better to preach? What does the world need more than reformation from head to foot?" Many agreed with Theodore Culyer, a minister who became a great supporter of Sam Jones, that what America needed was a revival—a revival "which keeps God's commandments. . . . A revival which will sweeten our homes and chasten our press and purify our politics and cleanse our business and commerce from roguery and rottenness would be a boon from Heaven. A revival which will bring not only a Bible-knowledge, but a *Bible-conscience* to all is what the land is dying for."[85]

To many Sam Jones was a necessary antidote to a religion that "emphasized the dogmas, and said but little of the duties that lay behind them." Jones was not the creator of a new type of Christianity—he had neither the mental nor the organizational abilities for that—but many saw him as the "harbinger" of a new day when Christians would be judged more by their works than their testimonials. Theodore Flood, editor of the *Chautauquan*, was right when he predicted in 1886 that Jones's "movement will touch millions. It will modify methods. It will refresh Christian hope in all lands. It will build nothing, but it will cut stones for other men to build with."[86]

Break off your sins by righteousness and your

iniquities by showing mercy to the poor.

—Daniel 4:27

I didn't mind the war so much; it's this

everlasting peace I can't abide.—Bill Arp

5

❧ Priest of the New South

One day in July 1868, two young men sat spellbound, oblivious to the passage of time, unconscious of the heat that enveloped them like a hot fog, alive only to the oratory and the wild thrill of righteous anger. Georgia was again being reconstructed. A military commander was headquartered in Atlanta, and his troops had made their hated presence felt at the polls the day before, keeping disfranchised Confederates away and protecting freedmen. As a result, Republican Rufus Bullock was now governor, and twenty-two blacks sat in the state legislature.

But Georgia Democrats felt hopeful that wealth, education, and white skin would soon hold sway again. President Andrew Johnson had proclaimed amnesty for former Confederates, and the Democratic party had denounced the Congressional Reconstruction Acts as "unconstitutional, revolutionary and void." Georgia's "natural leaders" had returned: the angrily unreconstructed Robert Toombs had ended his exile in Europe, Howell Cobb had been roused to oratory, and Benjamin Harvey Hill, master of logical invective, was issuing anathemas. On July 28 these men and twenty thousand Georgians met under an immense arbor in Atlanta.[1]

Sam Jones was there, a young man just short of twenty-one, so caught up by the crisis he was having trouble concentrating on either his courtship or his readings in the law. Henry Grady was there, an eighteen-year-old senior at the University of Georgia, already known for his astonishing oratorical imagery. That day Ben Hill became their idol. All his life, Sam Jones would remember how the eloquence of "the grandest man Georgia ever produced" washed over him that hot day, how he thrilled as Hill thundered against "the miserable spawns of political accidency" that had enabled blacks to "spring with one bound from the cornfields of Georgia into the legislative halls of the State to make laws for decent people." Young Grady, too, was stirred by Hill's soaring oratory. "I don't think I was ever so much impressed by any human being as by Mr. Hill that day," Grady remembered. "Such a speech, of such a compass, pitched upon such a key, was never made in this State before or since."[2]

Eighteen years later, these two men were in the North. Priest and prophet of the New South, they wooed Yankees with a mixture of repentance and self-respect, dry wit and dewy nostalgia, announcing that the Old South had died an honorable death and its offspring had come of age, longing for fellowship and itching for money. They still drew their inspiration from Benjamin Hill, but now from the Hill who, first as a congressman and then as a senator, informed the South that Reconstruction and the political suffrage of the black man must be accepted. Yankee ways and Yankee money must be cultivated; industry, not aristocracy, was the way of the New South.[3]

Like most New South spokesmen, Jones and Grady were not tied by birth to the plantation South. The offspring of entrepreneurial fathers, they had come of age during Reconstruction, and their experience made them critical of the leaders of the Old South who had brought ruin upon their people. Both men saw the cost of war to north Georgia in the early seventies, when Grady was editor of a Rome newspaper and Jones served a series of pastorates nearby. It is likely they met at this time through their mutual friend Charles Smith, better known as Bill Arp. The friendship that began then lasted until Grady died in 1889 at the age of thirty-eight.[4]

Henry Grady was olive-skinned and round of face, and his clerical counterpart was sallow and cadaverous; Grady was elegantly casual, and Jones was unkempt. But in personality and beliefs, the two disciples of Benjamin Harvey Hill were strikingly similar. Both had a commanding presence that overshadowed their small physical frames. "I remember one day in Chicago, we ran into a group of Chautauqua lecturers, such as Governor Hanley, Senator LaFollette, the Hon. W. J. Bryan and others," Walt Holcomb reminisced. "They all stood around and let Sam do the talking. He became the center of attraction in every group." Grady was equally magnetic. "When he had the incentive of sympathetic friends and surroundings, he was the most fascinating talker I ever heard," Joel Chandler Harris remembered. When their powers of persuasion failed, both men were master manipulators, working behind the scenes with ruthless charm to achieve their object.[5]

Their speaking styles were similar—even their posture was alike as they lazily leaned up against the podium. Blessed with astonishing memories, both men refused to speak from a manuscript, their mental agility and knowledge of local conditions allowing them to adapt a set speech to specific circumstances. Both had a high-pitched, penetrating voice that made it possible for them to speak with ease at outdoor gatherings; both avoided the affected oratorical elegance of the day. Both men had an uncanny ability to communicate wordlessly, their eyes expressing "fear, enthusiasm, conviction, tenderness, pathos, persuasion, humor, [and] seriousness when no spoken word was heard."[6]

Grady and Jones were ardent exponents of crop diversification and contended that the indebtedness of southern farmers and the increase in the tenant system was a result of the South's debilitating dependence on cotton. But though they paid obligatory homage to the farmer, both believed that industry, not agriculture, would save the Southland. Like others in the band of boosters who traveled north in the eighties and nineties, Jones and Grady grew eloquent as they extolled the bountiful resources of the South to industrial investors, presenting its possibilities as proudly as a mother showing off a marriageable daughter.[7]

One of the attractions southern promoters trumpeted was the availability of a cheap and docile labor supply in the large black population. "No section shows a more prosperous laboring population than the negroes of the South, none in fuller sympathy with the employing and land-owning class," Henry Grady assured the moneyed members of the New England Club in his famous speech. Economic interests dovetailed nicely with the belief that blacks could not benefit from anything more than rudimentary education;

higher learning led to "frustration and criminality in the negro." Sam Jones voiced a southern truism when he said there was no place for an educated black person to go but to "preaching, teaching, or the chaingang." It was senseless for a black man to get a degree in business, Jones contended; no one would hire him because the other employees would quit. Besides, education clouded their sunny natures and made them less "quiet" and "orderly": "The best negroes I know of in Georgia today were never in a schoolhouse."[8]

The revulsion such remarks now inspire make it difficult to understand the mind of the South in the years after Appomattox, years when the battle to maintain white supremacy took on the holy glow of a righteous crusade. "Standing in the presence of this multitude," Grady said at the Texas State Fair in 1887, "I declare that the truth above all others to be conserved un-sullied and sacred in your hearts, to be surrendered to no man, sold for no prize, compromised in no necessity . . . is that the white race must domi-nate forever in the South." Jones was equally emphatic. "Law and order, protection of life and property, can only be maintained in the South by the supremacy of the white man and [his] domination over the inferior race," he told a San Francisco reporter in 1889. Hoping to strike a sympathetic chord in a state inflamed over Chinese immigration, Jones suggested that if California had 150,000 more Chinese than white people, and "they all had the privileges of the ballot, you could then realize the fearful menace to civilization which the domination of an inferior race presents to the South."[9]

Winning the war of the blood lines depended on maintaining the "purity" of the racial stock. Like most southerners, Grady and Jones equated mis-cegenation with mongrelization. "Assimilation means debasement," Grady said; Jones quipped that if God had wanted the black to mate with the white, "He never would have colored him at the start." The tranquillity of the social order—indeed, the well-being of the blacks—demanded seg-regation, paternalists insisted. Applauding the advent of Jim Crow laws, Grady asserted that separate accommodations restored racial harmony, for "each has his place and fills it, and is satisfied." Jones echoed, "The best negroes and the best white people don't want social equality," a phrase that would ricochet into the next century.[10]

To white conservatives like Sam Jones and Henry Grady, the separa-tion of the races was part of a divine order. "The fiat of the Almighty has gone forth," Grady announced, "and in eighteen centuries of history it is written." Neither had any difficulty reconciling his views on race with his religion. "No, I do not think Christianity requires that the white race should meet the negro on terms of social equality," Jones told a California reporter.

"That will never happen in this world. It will only come about when they meet before the throne of God." Such sentiments raised not an eyebrow in southern churches that railed against "the wickedness of attempting to break down that social distinction between the black and white races which Nature, God, and the best interests of mankind have so far preserved." [11]

Good paternalists, Sam Jones and Henry Grady were personally kind to blacks and famous for their generosity. As an employer Jones took the remarkable position of paying women and blacks the same wages as white men, and repeatedly reminded his audiences that they were accountable to God for their record with their servants. "It is said that negroes will steal," he told southerners. "If we were working for them at the same wages we pay them we would steal them out of house and home." [12]

The blacks-only meetings were often initiated by blacks who wanted to participate in the Jones meetings more freely than they could from the corners to which they were usually confined. Jones reveled in these rollicking events and frequently told the story of "old black Sally" who had waddled up the aisle after such a meeting and crushed the undersized evangelist to her ample bosom, exclaiming, "Mr. Jones, you'se got a white skin, but praise de Lawd, you'se got a black heart!" These meetings revealed the message of the New South to blacks: work hard, be honest, know your place, acknowledge your betters. "Quit your stealing, whiskey drinking, gambling and lying and do right," Jones would urge, "and after awhile you will get home to heaven and your old black skins will peel off." Though his scoldings make the modern reader flinch, blacks of that time were accustomed to being talked to as children. Painful evidence of this is the phrasing a minister used to invite Jones to a black Chautauqua: "We need you here to skin us niggers." [13]

The limitations of the conservative credo were illuminated by Grady and Jones, and they betrayed themselves with their protestations of friendship. While Jones spoke fondly of "his colored man," Charlie, Grady bragged to Bostonians: "I want no better friend than the black boy who was raised at my side, and who is now trudging patiently with downcast eyes and shabby figure through his lowly way in life." Both found "darkeys" humorous and sprinkled their speeches with tales of outlandish situations in which these "childlike people" found themselves. Supposed racial characteristics were always good for a laugh: when Jones wanted to illustrate the hardheadedness of church members he often told the story of the mule who "kicked a nigger on the head" and couldn't "put his foot to the ground." Poverty and misfortune had little effect on these carefree folk. Docile and lighthearted, blacks were deficient, Jones believed, "in acquisitiveness, ambition and self-respect." While acknowledging that blacks were religious, Jones contended they were not pious. "It does not hurt [a black man] so much when he does a wrong, but it lashes and pains him when he gets caught in a wrong."[14]

While Jones and Grady insisted that the black man be allowed to exercise his citizenship rights—Jones often warned southerners they would go to hell if they defrauded him of his vote—this would occur under the control of his "best friend," the conservative. The untutored black was, Grady said, "credulous, impulsive—easily led and frequently easily bought." The safety of the republic depended upon the black person's being "left to those among whom his lot is cast," the southerner who understood his needs and limitations. "Bred and buttered among the colored brethren, I know them as they are," Jones would say, voicing the usual litany. "No man can know the negro unless he has been acquainted with him from his infancy up."[15]

That these views faced little resistance in the North is evidence that racism was not confined to the South but was "a general tenet of American thought." By the time Sam Jones and Henry Grady went north, the erosion of racial liberalism was advanced, and they found many eager to believe that the conservative southerner was solving "the negro problem" with justice and charity. The people of the North were worn out with the exertion of idealism. As Turmon Post recognized soon after the war, "it is a sad truth that men, for the most part, are not heroes or martyrs. From the extraordinary tension requisite to act the part of such, they must in time relax from sheer exhaustion." Even northerners who retained their idealism were discouraged by the limits of legislation. "If the colored people of the South are doomed to an inferior position," a northern clergyman traveling through the old Confederacy concluded in 1869, "they and their votes will be controlled by the more cultivated and competent whites; and no plans of Reconstruction, no legislation at Washington, can permanently prevent this." To the nods of northern conservatives, Grady announced that "to liberty and enfranchisement is as far as law can carry the negro. The rest must be left to conscience and common sense."[16]

Sam Jones and Henry Grady were only two of the league of southern conservatives evangelizing the North in the winter of 1885–86, a critical time when Republicans, smarting from their loss of the presidency, were lobbying for federal troops to oversee elections in the South. However, Jones and Grady were the most charismatic of the southern battalion, and there is no doubt that they made racism more respectable. Through their efforts, northern support for Reconstruction was eroded, leaving blacks defenseless when radicalism engulfed the South in the nineties. Racial conservatives like Sam Jones and Henry Grady "opened the beachheads that allowed the

Radicals to land." The woefully inadequate protection paternalism provided from radical delirium was made vividly explicit during the Atlanta race riot of 1906. Dragging two Negro corpses to the statue of Henry Grady on Peachtree, the mob spotted a black man crouched behind the monument. Shots rang out, but then the voice of reason: "Don't shoot—you'll kill good white men!" Obediently, the frenzied mob clubbed the man to death and left him to mutilators and souvenir hunters, a gory offering to the father of the New South.[17]

With the same gospel, Grady and Jones preached from a different text. While Grady's efforts to eulogize racial harmony in the South were dewy and mellifluous, Jones's attempts were cruder. He got off to a bad start in St. Joseph, Missouri, when a caustic remark about hypocrites in the church caused hilarity in the black section, provoking the evangelist to say with a smile: "That's enough to make a fool nigger laugh, isn't it?" This remark was not remedied by his description of the church and the world as being "thick as niggers." Though St. Joseph was largely populated by former Confederates, Jones felt compelled to explain a few days later that "when I say 'nigger' I mean a colored man who has ostracized himself by his meanness, or a white man with a soul black on the inside. . . . I respect the colored race. I was raised among it. I wouldn't for the world say anything to offend a respectable colored person."[18]

By the time he reached Cincinnati a few months later, Sam Jones was more circumspect. Noting "with pleasure" the presence of "colored people" sprinkled throughout the audience, Jones endeavored to explain the practice of segregated seating in the South. "I preach to the colored people in the South as much as any white man there, and some of my best friends are among that race," Jones protested defensively. "We have our own social usages down South, of course, but I have no choice about where the people sit. It is my business to preach; and it's the usher's business to seat the people."[19]

Though Jones's revivals in the North and Midwest attracted some, northern blacks did not respond to him with the fervor of those who had remained in the South. It may be that they saw in his paternalism a part of what they had endeavored to escape. Commenting on the Jones meetings in Minneapolis, a black newspaper editor remarked that the evangelist has "the reputation of being willing to help [his] colored brothers and sisters into heaven by a sort of side entrance." However, the Bible teaches "there is only one way; and whoever tries to enter in any other way, is as a thief and a robber, and we have not, as a rule, taken much stock in their Christianity."[20]

In order to make themselves and their message acceptable to Yankees,

Jones and Grady took pains to dissociate themselves from the slave South. Grady opened his historic speech to the New England Society with the magnificat of that born-again Unionist, Benjamin Hill. "There was a South of secession and slavery—that South is dead; there is a South of union and freedom—that South, thank God, is living, growing every hour." To a cheering Chicago audience, Jones, son of a slave owner, confessed, "I am sorry that America has it in her history—they used to put a colored man up down South and sell him to the highest bidder. I am glad that is done away with forever." In Boston, a hotbed of abolitionism, Jones said, "We had brave soldiers on both sides. I believe as I love and honor the noble Grant and Logan on your side, so you honor Lee and Jackson down there." But, praise the Lord, "it's over now. We love one another, and I can find as true brethren in the North as in the South. We can be friends though our fathers have been enemies."[21]

This combination of loyalty to the Union and fidelity to the Confederacy was irresistible in the mid-eighties, when Old South literature was at its most compelling. Amid the spoils of war and the noise of industry, Yankees longed for the balm of mythology, for tales of chivalrous knights in gray and belles who moved gently through a magnolia-scented world. While novelists created a common myth, northern industrialists participated in the expositions held in Atlanta, Louisville, and New Orleans in the early 1880s. At these events, as at hundreds of fairs and festivals across America, ritualistic reconciliations were staged. Soldiers from both sides dressed up in the old uniforms and celebrated courage, acknowledging the verdict of war and the blessings of peace on "Blue and Gray Day."[22]

Religion was doing its part for sectional reconciliation as well. Catholics, Lutherans, and Episcopalians had not formally separated, and the breach between their northern and southern factions was quickly repaired. Though in the heat of war, northern Presbyterians had called their southern brethren sinners and schismatics, passions had cooled sufficiently by 1868 for the Presbyterian Assembly to officially acknowledge its southern counterpart, the Presbyterian Church of the United States. Baptists refused to fraternize until the mid-nineties, but 1876 Methodists staged an emotional reunion during which they sang "Blest Be the Tie That Binds" and proclaimed that "henceforth they may hail each other as from the auxiliary ranks of one great army."[23]

Such public celebrations of brotherhood did not erase the deep sectional suspicions that kept the two branches of Methodism separate until 1939. Four years after Appomattox, southern Methodist bishops protested that the northern church was sending missionaries to "disintegrate and absorb our societies." Many northern Methodists were Radical Republicans and supported protecting blacks' right to vote. Southerners viewed this as an attempt to subjugate the South under "negro domination." Northern charges of southern bigotry were countered with accusations of Yankee hypocrisy. The very northerners who characterized southerners as "brutes and cutthroats" after a lynching "commended and applauded the course of a few thousand white men in taking violent possession of Hawaii, without even showing the semblance of respect for the wishes of the natives," the Reverend E. E. Hoss pointed out in 1899. The fact that the provisional governor, Sanford Dole, and his accomplices in the sugar and pineapple trusts were mostly descendants of New England missionaries, the future bishop added wickedly, may "have given some consecrating touch to this action." This it-takes-one-to-know-one attitude reached its childish crescendo when a contributor to the *Advocate* claimed that southern mobs were more orderly about their lynchings than their northern counterparts, for the Yankees "want to kill all the Negroes that can be found instead of merely punishing some guilty criminal. As we have said before," the writer noted with a sniff, "racial antipathy is one thing, and bitter race hatred is another."[24]

But though divisions continued, the erosion of liberalism in the North, the emergence of the New South conservative, mutual trade interests, and the unifying effect of literature and religion bound the country together again. When Sam Jones came north in 1886, Lost Cause literature was at its height, and things southern seemed quaint and engaging. Northern businessmen were eager to accept and underwrite a southern conservative, and a growing ecumenical accord created conditions in which a successful union revival was possible. The stage was set. One more thing was needed: a sophisticated approach to revivalism that would make "the Georgia Cracker" acceptable to his northern audiences. The addition of two men to his small entourage achieved this object. These men were an evangelist named Sam Small and a singer, E. O. Excell.

An elegant, cultivated man, Samuel White Small had been brought up on a plantation near Knoxville. His father was editor of the first Democratic newspaper in Tennessee and president of an express company. Young Small was sent to Emory and Henry College, then to Nashville to study law. By the time of his death in 1931, Sam Small could boast of having "clasped hands with every president from James Buchanan to Herbert Hoover"; his involvement with politics began in 1875 when his father's influence secured him the position of personal secretary to Andrew Johnson. A brief stint covering the southern tour of President Rutherford B. Hayes for the *Atlanta Constitution* led to an appointment as secretary to the United States commissioner general of the Paris Exposition. After working briefly with Jones's hero, Benjamin Hill, and marrying a congressman's daughter, Small returned to journalism, working in Virginia and Oklahoma before returning to the *Constitution*.[25]

At that paper Small was known for his wickedly accurate mimicry of black speech, a talent he parlayed into national popularity with his "old Si" column. Though his stories appeared in the *Century Magazine* and other leading periodicals, Small "declined all invitations to join the literary world" and studied briefly for the Episcopal ministry. Long a "close student" of the Bible, obsession with politics and addiction to alcohol made priesthood impossible, so Small took a job as a court reporter, free-lancing as a journalist. "Picturesquely drunk," Sam Small took the train to Cartersville in September 1885 to report on the Sam Jones revival.[26]

The transcription of "Conscience—Record—God" was lost to the *Constitution*, for in the midst of the sermon, Small dropped his pen, overwhelmed by a conviction of sin. Dazed, he returned to Atlanta and for forty-eight hours he "wrestled with the angels" until he obtained "assurance of salvation." His wife, Annie, doubting that his ecstasy had its origin in religion, worried that her husband was slipping into madness. Atlantans wondered the same thing when Small climbed atop four whiskey barrels at the corner of Peachtree and Marietta and began to hand out circulars entitled "Beware, Beware That Fatal Cup." News of the spectacular conversion reached Cartersville, Jones came to hear Small preach, and he asked him to be an apprentice evangelist.[27]

Jones considered the conversion of this extraordinary man providential. Delicate health would not allow the evangelist to continue at his frantic pace, and friends fretted that his ceaseless labors would burn him out or burn him up. "If the Rev. Sam Jones undertakes to do all that is asked of him this heated season, he will not see another," Dr. Fitzgerald warned in the summer of 1885. "He is tough and elastic, but there is a limit to human endurance." Jones himself predicted that the work would soon kill him: "I have lived long enough to know that I won't live much longer." Gratefully, Jones acknowledged that "the Lord put [Small] into the work just about the time I was obliged to have him. I have nearly worn myself out in middle life, and God put him in just at the right time, and just where I have no strength." Small's fame and newspaper connections ensured that his conversion would garner publicity: "God wouldn't have kicked up a bigger fuss in all Georgia if he had gone down and restored sight to a man born blind than He did when, two weeks ago, He touched Sam Small," Jones told a St. Louis audience. "I tell you this conversion is the talk of all Georgia."[28]

Joined just two weeks before the beginning of Jones's northern and midwestern tour, "the two Psalms" delighted northerners as the embodiment of the two traditions of the South. Small represented the refined plantation South, while Jones was the typical southerner to the Yankee mind: "rough, uncouth, impulsive, inclined to exaggerate, slangy, but withal bright, witty, keenly sensitive to the humorous and sarcastic side of things." Newspapermen enjoyed comparing the two, amused that Jones was small and Small was large. Otherwise, the two Sams "dress alike, walk alike, talk alike and look alike." Both were lean, favored the old-fashioned Prince Albert coat over a more clerical costume, and wore their hair slicked flat "in true Southern style." A Chicago reporter found the difference in the two men epitomized in their mustaches. Small's mustache was "luxuriant and soft," reflective of a "fanciful" and artistic nature; Jones's bristled like a "fire fighter or a politician from the Irish wards."[29]

Six months after Small joined the evangelical entourage, Jones added Excell, a singing evangelist so "full of music" he seemed to have "swallowed a brass band." With the revivals of Dwight Moody and his singer, Ira Sankey, audiences had come to expect gospel singing with gospel preaching, and Professor Marcellus J. Maxwell, a small round-faced musician from Oxford, Georgia, had been traveling with Jones intermittently. But Maxwell was overshadowed by Excell, a "big, robust six-footer, with a six-inch caliber voice," whom Jones imported from Chicago for the Baltimore revival of May 1886. Like Jones, Excell used jokes and threats, molding hundreds of singers from a multitude of churches into a single choir, culling out the sisters "who mistake a talent for calling chickens for ability to sing," and the brothers who "would make a discord in a chorus of bullfrogs." "He is the biggest choir singer that ever struck Dallas," one reporter wrote of the physically ponderous Excell, "and he knows how to pull a melody out of a choir just like a dentist knows how to pull a tooth."[30]

Like Jones, Excell could shift moods quickly, adapting to the requirements of the moment. Beginning with foot-tapping music like "Bringing in the Sheaves," "When the Roll is Called Up Yonder," or "Marching On to Zion," after the pastoral prayer he would move into songs that focused on Christ, such as "Lily of the Valley," or "There Is a Fountain Filled with Blood." At the end of the service, Excell's deep, liquid voice would wash into the corners of the building, pulling the people like an undertow toward the altar, singing dirgelike songs that spoke of death and rebirth: "Just As I Am, Without One Plea" or "Who'll Be Next to Follow Jesus?" If Jones's sermon was heavy with warnings, Excell's solo would be leaden and ominous, such as "Are You Ready for the Judgment Day?"

Should the death angel knock at thy chamber
In the still watch of to-night,
Say will your spirit pass into torment
Or to the land of delight?[31]

Excell's music reflected the change in revivalism; it was becoming "more frankly entertaining, even folksy," a camp meeting come to town. Jones's musicians, "Ex and Max," complemented the evangelist's casual, irreverent style. While Ira Sankey was solemn and starchy, Excell had an "Everyb-o-d-y sing!" exuberance, erasing ideas that the audience needed any Sunday stiffness about them. But music did more than set a mood; it was a great healer of war wounds, and melodies crossed sectional lines where speeches and sermons stopped. The songs of Sankey and Excell were restorative, allowing Christians to remember a common heritage and form a new national culture. The way in which music eased sectional tensions was illustrated by two songs written especially for Sam Jones in his first two years of national prominence, 1885 and 1886.[32]

The first "welcome song" was written for the St. Louis revival by Gilby Campbell Kelly to generate enthusiasm for Jones's visit. It was written in "darky dialect" at a time "negro romance" was convincing northerners that southern blacks were as carefree as children. Unlike many southerners—even his colleagues Sam Small and George Stuart—Sam Jones never romanticized the life of the slave; instead he pictured it as drudgery sharpened by a longing for freedom. However, he frequently used black dialect for humor, so the song was a fitting tribute to him. Through fourteen verses of tortured prose, Jones is extolled as a champion for "de Lawd," as "true to natur'" as "John the Baptis' wuz."

> Sam Jones he love de white;
> Sam Jones he love de black:
> Yass, suh, he's de man of might;
> He'll never tu'n he back.

This was followed with a rousing chorus of:

> Sam Jones is comin',
> Sam Jones is comin',
> Yass, Sam Jones is comin',
> In de name of de Lawd.[33]

The more popular welcome song was written by R. Kelso Carter of Baltimore, composer of the famous "Standing on the Promises." Kelso took the phrase associated with the evangelist—"Quit your meanness"—and encased it in words that reflect the individuality, irreverence, and urgency in the gospel according to Sam Jones. Like Jones's sermons, the verses were full of injunctions not to overlook omens that the end was near and inescapable:

> Now my friends, salvation must begin with number one,
> Sleeping in a sinking ship is very little fun,
> And God has many whales on hand for those who try to run,
> So you better quit your meanness!

This verse was followed by a menacing chorus of:

> Take care, take care, the doom of sin is nigh!
> Beware, beware, or you will surely die!
> The Judgement Day is coming fast; O sinner hear the cry—
> Now you better quit your meanness!

What is amazing is that Kelso put these words to the tune that celebrated the incendiary success of General Sherman, "Marching Through Georgia." That such a song could become popular with a southern evangelist and his northern audiences illustrates the willingness of Americans to incorporate the gains and losses of the Civil War into a new and common culture.[34]

Again and again during his northern and midwestern tour, Jones urged Christians to stop the sectional skirmishes that were sapping the strength of the American church. "We'll never conquer America for Christ, till the Methodist Churches, North and South, unite, but general conference resolutions won't do it, nothing but love." In the spring of 1886, Jones's enthusiasm for reunion prompted him to suggest that during his visit that summer the director of the Round Lake Chautauqua in New York stage a Blue and Gray Day, a symbolic union of the northern and southern churches. The director considered it "a grand scheme" and borrowed some of the evangelist's soaring prestige to prevail upon his board to sponsor "a good hearty meeting of both parties where they can pray and sing and shout together."[35]

In St. Louis, Jones encountered a different kind of denominationalism in the acidic editor of the Catholic periodical the *Western Watchman*. Father Phelan warned the "unparsable evangelist" that "St. Louis has been the mausoleum of all those evangelical mountebanks who have ventured within her gates. . . . Protestantism is dead in this town, and Catholics have no use for religious burlesque." Delighted by the attack, Jones publicly turned the other cheek, an action that endeared him to the Catholic editor of the *St. Louis Globe-Democrat* and ensured the evangelist the newspaper coverage that made him a national figure. "I saw in the paper the other day that St. Louis was a Catholic city," Jones announced. "Take this city with all its saloons, lewd houses and say it is a Catholic city. I will say it is a lie. The proud Catholic church will never father the vices of this city." [36]

Jones's stance was startling in a day when anti-Catholic sentiment had been stirred up by an enormous influx of immigrants—more than two million during the 1870s and five million during the following decade, most from Catholic countries. Many Protestants feared that American democracy would be corrupted by a people they believed were more accustomed to taking orders than to exercising independent judgment, that the public school system would be endangered by parochial schools, and that the prohibitions of the Puritan Sabbath would be ignored by immigrants accustomed to the revelries of the continental Sabbath.

Anti-Catholic sentiment was less pronounced in the South because the majority of Catholic immigrants settled in the urban areas of the Northeast and Midwest. However, in port cities with a significant Catholic minority, there was considerable hostility to the "Romanists." Explaining why Methodism failed to flourish in Shreveport, Louisiana, a minister blamed the Roman Catholic church, which "ruins the city and gives color to the general condition of things. One does not wonder at the debased condition of the people in the lands under the influence of this gigantic ecclesiastical fraud." Jones refused to take part in the Protestant pillory. When a Baptist evangelist named Len Broughton execrated the Catholics in Atlanta, Jones was asked why he did not join the fray: "When I get through with the Methodists, it's bedtime," was his laconic reply. [37]

In St. Louis, Jones was at first unperturbed by Father Phelan's prediction that he would founder. "I can afford to fail in some places," he answered. In some towns, even Christ "did not do many wonderful works." The predominantly Catholic, foreign-born population did fail to respond to him, and Jones was forced to admit that St. Louis was "the hardest rock I ever attempted to drill." Told at the end of the revival that a committee was forming to collect a compensation for him, Jones confessed tearfully: "I don't think I've done any work here to warrant anything like that." A month later his swagger had returned, and he labeled the rumor that he had failed in St. Louis a "fabrication of the father of lies." [38]

Though their accents and idioms had excited comment in St. Louis, it was not until they went to Chicago in the winter of 1886 that the two Sams encountered overt hostility. "Sam Jones and Sam Small were rampant rebels down in Georgia during the War, but that was when both of them were very wicked," one Chicago paper informed its readers. "We don't wish to ask any impertinent questions; but out of curiosity we should like to know if, when they repented of their sins, they also repented of the rebel business." Reading the editorial aloud, Sam Small announced that "at that period, if I was a rebel at all, I was one of the dastardly class that was ten years old at the time, and if I did the Government any damage I am sorry for it." As for Sam Jones, "he was thirteen and if he hurt them I have never heard of it." A contrite sinner, "I stand here tonight singing amen to that good old Methodist hymn, 'Let a repentant rebel live.'" Sam Jones was equally adept at penitence without servility. There "is not a Union soldier that marched to the front to defend that grand old flag" that he would not hope to see in heaven, despite his private conviction that he had never "seen a man born north of the Mason and Dixon's line fully recover from the fact."[39]

Protestantism was hardier in Chicago than in St. Louis; the churches were not divided into sectional factions, and the Moody Bible Institute provided regular infusions of evangelical energy. Doubtless Jones felt a rapport with the citizens of the Windy City; he was an offspring of the aggressively materialist New South talking to aggressively materialistic Chicagoans. In a short time the newspapers were tripping over themselves in praise. The evangelist's "easy, unpretentious self-possession soon won him the entire confidence of his audience," a *Tribune* reporter wrote, noting that unlike some southern revivalists, Jones never gave way to "ranting or shouting." Though the Georgian initially tried to overcome "the pronounced nasal Southern accent and idioms," the effort was unsuccessful and "the flavor of his section seeped through." Soon he was leaving off final *g*'s and punctuating points with a "heah" or a "naow."[40]

Southerners were thrilled by the success of their spokesmen in the North, feeling that this acceptance represented their own readmission to American life. Grady was mobbed getting off the train in Atlanta, and Jones and Small became cultural heroes. They became a living bridge between the sections, healing spirits. "God sent you to Chicago" to break down the "prejudice against southern men," Atticus Haygood wrote Jones. The editor of the *Chicago Daily Inter-Ocean* concurred, pointing out that while Jones and Small were in the North, Moody and Sankey were in the South. "These men, with the enthusiastic multitudes that have thronged to hear them, may be taken as personal proofs of the fact that the once lurid gulf between the two great sections of our country is fast disappearing."[41]

Sam Jones and Dwight Moody continued this cross-pollination through the eighties and nineties, with Jones conducting occasional campaigns in the North and Moody sometimes coming south. The two evangelists admired each other. After hearing Jones preach, Moody had telegraphed the young evangelist: "God has given you a sledge-hammer with which to shatter the formalism of the church, and to batter down the strongholds of Satan. The good Spirit is helping you mightily to use it." Once Jones and Moody conducted simultaneous revivals in Boston, and on several occasions, America's premier evangelists held meetings in the same city in the same year. Both preachers of great power, their styles were very different. "Moody came here and sprinkled cologne over the people," one man explained when Jones followed Moody to San Francisco in 1889. "Sam Jones came along and gives them a dose of carbolic acid and rubs it in." On the whole, women preferred Moody and men preferred Jones—"I expect I have preached to more men than any other man in this or any other time," Jones would boast. Both attracted the godly middle class; it was not unusual for them to ask all Christians to stand and have nine-tenths of the audience rise. Though most often Moody followed Jones, as conversion follows conviction, in 1895 Moody preceded the southern evangelist to Atlanta, phoenix city of the New South.[42]

Made great and brought low by the war, Atlanta manifested an eagerness to get on with business. Though a plea for victims of the Chicago fire in 1871 elicited a smouldering reply, ten years later the city was so willing to overlook the past that it gave General William Tecumseh Sherman a hero's welcome. Atlanta was, it boasted, "a new place—modern—democratic— a fresh production, wholly practical, without antiquities or prejudices." The city's unconcealed arrogance did not endear it to neighboring towns. "The Chinese at one time believed that China was the center of the world [but] it has lately been discovered that Atlanta is. Their rocks are the hardest, their mud is the softest; their thunder is the loudest and their rain is the wettest that was ever known," Milledgeville sniped, still smarting over the loss of the state capitol to Atlanta. "If Atlanta could suck as hard as it blows," Savannah snorted, "it would be a seaport."[43]

It was at the Cotton States and International Exposition that Booker T. Washington pronounced the "Atlanta Compromise," publicly conceding what seemed unobtainable—social and political equality—to claim for his people what seemed possible—economic opportunity. To southerners, it seemed their solution to the "Negro problem" had been offered by a black man: recognition that reform must occur gradually and under the control of the white southerner, that social and political equality was a dangerous fancy, that it was up to the black people to elevate themselves through loyalty, industry, and thrift. Moved to make a donation to Tuskegee Institute,

Sam Jones described Washington as "the greatest negro on earth, and a negro who leads his race and leads them right."[44]

To Atlantans it seemed fitting that Washington made his historic act of appeasement in Atlanta, that people were flocking to see the "brave and beautiful city" that had risen from the ashes. Atlantans congratulated themselves on their chosen status, and propagandists never failed to include a glowing tribute to Atlanta's churches amid descriptions of fabulous mineral wealth and a salubrious climate. As the Exposition Ode proclaimed, where once "the clods were trampled red by the avenging gods," now stood "skyward pointing steeples."[45]

Thus it was natural that when plans were made for the exposition, attention was given to the "great multitudes of the unconverted" who would be drawn to Atlanta. Four days after bonds began to be sold, the Evangelical Ministers' Association invited to Atlanta Dwight Moody, the man who had drawn attention to the godly side of Chicago during the 1893 World's Fair. While Chicago's businessmen had worked to establish the city's reputation as a center for transportation, distribution, and manufacturing, Moody's gospel campaign had focused attention on Chicago's churches and God-fearing citizens. It was just this balance of piety and profit that was hoped for from the man Sam Jones described as having "go and vim and push."[46]

Moody accepted, and a tabernacle was constructed able to accommodate seven thousand people, accessible by streetcar, and strategically located between downtown and Piedmont Park, where the exposition was being held. In spite of these advantages, attendance was disappointing. Though Moody had stressed the importance of newspaper coverage, the *Atlanta Journal* reported only the evangelist's arrival, departure, and three sermons. The *Atlanta Constitution* did little better, burying "Moody's Farewell Sermon" on page 8 among other "Church News." In execution as in preparation, the Moody revival was eclipsed by the exposition.[47]

There are several explanations for the revival's failure to flourish: lack of coverage, poor timing, the fact that Methodist ministers were away at their conference for much of the meeting. Nor was the Atlanta campaign as well organized as the one in Chicago, with its 257 ministers and 25 evangelists conducting simultaneous revivals in eighty churches around the city. But most basic to the failure of the Moody meeting was the fact that important Atlantans were more concerned with having a successful fair than with saving souls. There was evidence of this months before opening day, when the *Constitution* called on Atlanta ministers "not to interfere with the success" of the exposition by insisting upon Sunday closing, strict enforcement of liquor laws, and the prohibition of bullfighting. "The *Constitution* must have a small eye and a narrow range to think for a moment that a little Exposition is comparable to these great interests which the preachers represent," the outraged editor of the *Wesleyan Christian Advocate* answered, urging Methodist ministers not to hesitate in the choice "between mere money and manhood."[48]

If they were not overly particular about civic morality, city boosters were interested in establishing the city as a religious capital. Giddy with compliments, they prophesied that a resurrected Atlanta would regenerate the nation. With the exposition Atlanta "has gained the applause and admiration of the world," the *Constitution* bragged, "a reputation as the pluckiest and most enterprising city on the American continent. But she is destined to figure in a new role and one which is no less bold and original," that is, "the purification of the nation's life."[49]

The National Christian Conference, which met in the Moody tabernacle in December, did not achieve this lofty aim, and two days before Christmas, a discouraged committee of ministers bought the tabernacle for $250, less than a tenth of what it had cost to build only months before. There was one last chance to spark the revival that would fire the nation, and the Evangelical Ministers' Association took that chance: they invited to Atlanta the irreverent Reverend Sam P. Jones, a man who stood for "God, home, manhood [and] municipal welfare."[50]

Jones believed in Atlanta's special destiny and could be counted on to endorse any project designed to aggrandize the city. He helped raise money for the Cyclorama to commemorate the Battle of Atlanta, a new railroad depot, and a couple of hospitals. He had been thrilled by the exposition's public reaffirmation of faith in the New South creed in the face of economic depression and the challenge of political radicalism. "I felt proud of the south when I witnessed the display of pluck and vim and generosity and enterprise" demonstrated during the exposition, Jones wrote in his newspaper column. "We shall all know each other better and love each other more as a nation" because Atlanta gathered the states together in recognition that "whatever may have been the conditions of the past, we're now all one people."[51]

Sam Jones had never lost faith in the creed of the New South. While the region's iron, steel, railways, and mineral wealth fell into northern hands, Jones recited the old message: "We would soon be the richest section of the United States if we had the thrift and industry of Yankee Doodle, and play keeps with what we got." Three years into a depression that was ruining thousands of farmers, Jones blithely assured southerners that low prices were a blessing because they would force the farmer to diversify and spur production to the point that soon there will be "a place for every human brain and hand." The real problem was that too many folks were looking to get on the dole. "I believe the curse of the South, to say nothing of the other sections of the country," Jones drawled, "is the long list of idle men, and an idle man is like a dead man, it don't take him long to become offensive." [52]

When approached by the Evangelical Ministers' Association about conducting a revival in Atlanta, Jones was initially cool. He agreed to come, but not before March. Jones was in demand; his career as an evangelist was experiencing an upswing after a slump in the early 1890s, and he was never able to fill all the dates offered him on the lecture platform. That he did not postpone other commitments, his usual practice when an urgent invitation was extended, indicates that he was not eager to arrive in the city in December, when people would be occupied with the holidays. If he came to Atlanta in the spring, he would arrive when classes for new members were conducted and Sunday school students prepared to make their profession of faith; this movement into the churches would add momentum to his campaign. The exposition ended on December 31; with that out of the way and the Easter holiday at hand, attention would focus on religion and his revival. He could thus become heir to the excitement created by the Exposition rather than its rival. Also, he could establish his revival as a separate entity instead of an appendage to the Moody meeting, an important consideration for a man who gloried in individuality. "Mr. Moody is like St. Peter," he liked to say, "and I am like—Sam Jones." Whether Jones delayed his arrival in Atlanta out of necessity or native shrewdness, his decision to conduct a spring campaign was an important factor in its success. [53]

Jones had a perverse formula for victory: persecution equals publicity and publicity produces success. Since he had been unanimously invited by the EMA, was respected in the business community, and had friends in the Atlanta press corps, persecution might have been hard to provoke. Sam Jones was equal to the task. He gave two lectures in December aimed at giving the greatest offense to the greatest number. He hinted he might provoke another divisive prohibition election, denounced the "jackasses" who sat in the Georgia legislature, the "red-nosed whiskey devils" at that exclusive "hog wallow," the Capital City Club, and the hide-bound, hell-bound church members and their ineffective, effeminate "pitty-patty" preachers. The Atlanta press looked upon the whole thing as great fun and good copy, as the headline of the *Constitution* indicates:

Sam Jones Hits the Georgia Legislature a Hard Lick.

Said Members of the Legislature Were Not Able to Pass Anything

---

NOT EVEN A CHEAP BAR ROOM

Having alienated many of his backers, Jones could now enter Atlanta with the air of a fearless crusader. "I may be alone," Jones said with satisfaction, "but I'm still in good company."[54]

The revival opened to enormous crowds, and thousands flocked to "listen to the magic words of the gifted speaker." Days of rain did not discourage those who came three times a day to hear Sam Jones and his assistant, horse-faced, jug-eared George Stuart, the man Jones called "the ugliest man and the best preacher alive." Never more powerful than that month in Atlanta, the evangelist pulled people from laughter to tears and back again, and the people listened "as if they were listening to some miraculous prophet sent from God. Their fixed attention was almost painful in its tension."[55]

Even Orth Stein, editor of the iconoclastic paper the *Looking Glass*, acknowledged that Jones was "the most notable figure in the local horizon." Every day the papers devoted four or five columns to the revival, detailing the meetings for special groups. Seven thousand men were present at one of these, causing an old Confederate to declare, "I saw Sherman's battalions descend on Atlanta and never since then have I seen so many men on one spot." Three days later, eight thousand gathered to hear the evangelist denounce décolleté, dancing, and "dudines" (female dudes). On two successive Saturday nights, Jones conducted meetings for black people only, at which he announced that "a colored man can have religion just like a white man," even though "many a nigger in Georgia never raises any chickens until they are half grown."[56]

Jones resisted having his revivals used to serve secular purposes. In 1885, when he discovered that the merchants had invited him to St. Joseph to attract crowds to their businesses, Jones sputtered: "God forgive them, for I cannot." However, though Jones saw his revival as a moral mission, city boosters used it to glorify Atlanta. "Atlanta is grand," Jones was quoted as saying. "She is grand, and capable of doing anything." While the meetings at the railroad shops emphasized Atlanta as a center of distribution and transportation, the meeting at police headquarters pointed out the city's devout police force. The service at Boy's High School publicized the new facility built under the direction of the evangelist's old teacher, Professor William Slaton. The blacks-only meetings illustrated one of the themes of the exposition: social equality was unthinkable. Jones also voiced another theme of the exposition: there is no North or South, just one glorious nation, forged "in a struggle that did much to civilize and bless the world." The Blue and Gray Day at the tabernacle was a "striking spectacle" with "the old, battle-scarred veterans rallying round the standard of a common leader, listening in common brotherhood to a common gospel."[57]

If Jones's special meetings underscored Atlanta's successes, they also revealed some of the tensions in the city in 1896. When the evangelist arrived, the black community was in a state of millennial excitement, and on March 5 a group gathered in Grant Park to await the whirlwind that would sweep the saints into God's presence. The rapture was delayed, though one of the believers attempted to fling himself into the millennium by jumping from a tree. The Atlanta papers treated the whole affair as hilarious and featured cartoons of apelike creatures with enormous lips frantically flapping their arms in a futile attempt at flight. Soon a rumor circulated that an Atlanta judge of the "hanging variety" had declared that "if the coons fail to go to heaven on the fateful morning" he will "have them all arrested on writs of lunacy." The story was unfounded, but it threw "the Negroes into a state of fright bordering on terror." Perhaps the Jones meetings, prominently attended by mainstream black clergy, were efforts to channel the religious energies of Atlanta blacks toward outlets more acceptable to white society and provide social control on two potentially explosive Saturday nights.[58]

Tensions were also high in the police department, which had been "almost overwhelmed by dissension" during a fight for control of the police commissioner's board; at one point Mayor Porter King and Police Chief Connally almost came to blows. Fifty policemen were members of the anti-Catholic American Protective Association, while Chief Connally was an Irish Catholic. Jones's visit to the police station and his public endorsement of Police Chief Connally was an effort to end animosity. "I would see

Atlanta in moral life what she is in commercial life," Jones would say the next year in Atlanta. This meant "every Protestant living up to his vows, every Catholic as devout as grace could make him, every Jew come back to the God of his fathers and the ten commandments."[59]

The question of woman's rights had been the subject of heated debate in Atlanta since 1892, when two Baptist pastors, J. B. Hawthorne and Henry McDonald, and Bishop Warren Akin Candler of the Methodist church accused Frances Willard, leader of the Womens' Christian Temperance Union, of subverting marriage and "pressing women into the gospel ministry as preachers and leaders, contrary to Scriptures." The battle was still being fought three years later. On December 16, 1895, the day after Jones's lecture, the church page of the *Constitution* was divided between the revivalist's inflammatory remarks and Hawthorne's charge that the suffragist Elizabeth Cady Stanton was a "blasphemer" because her *Women's Bible* deleted passages she deemed demeaning to women. The National Women's Suffrage Convention, which met in the Moody Tabernacle in January 1896, did nothing to diminish public passion over "the woman question."[60]

Early in his ministry, Jones had forbidden his female members to give their testimonies, much less "pitchin' and rarin' and prancin' in the pulpit." "I was narrow in my views, conceited of my sex," he confessed; since then "I have heard some women talk in public that made me feel I was not even capable of saying grace at the table." Frances Willard—"the most charming talker I have ever heard"—changed his mind, and he became convinced that God called women to the ministry. "Women were not only the last at the Cross, and first at the Resurrection, but they have been in the forefront of every hard fought battle for Christ."[61]

As for Paul's insistence that "it is a shame for a woman to speak in public," Jones said Paul was "simply reporting the custom of that day. He said women oughtn't to cut off their hair, but about two-thirds whack off bunches in the front, anyhow. When they quote St. Paul, they are simply hunting excuses." While Jones did not like "she-males"—"I ain't got no use for a cackling rooster or a crowing hen"—he advocated giving women the right to vote. Sure that the blight of alcohol would be obliterated by women wielding the ballot, Jones announced that he preferred "women's suffrage to women's suffering." Jones's position was shocking for a southern preacher, and his endorsement of the WCTU and decision to turn his pulpit over to Emma Tucker, director of a rescue mission for prostitutes, caused controversy during the Atlanta revival.[62]

The conflict between labor and capital, a critical issue in this decade of depression, was also a source of tension. The labor leader Samuel Gompers had visited the city in 1895, and a month before the Jones revival, Eugene V. Debs, just released from prison for his participation in the Pullman strike of 1894, arrived in town. The visit was part of a national tour designed to rebuild Debs's American Railway Union, which had been dismembered by the Pullman debacle. The ARU, founded by Debs to unite railroad men without regard to craft, class, or caste, had encountered resistance from elite unions like the Order of Railway Conductors. During the Pullman strike, some unions had combined with management to destroy the ARU, and this marriage based on mutual malice was reestablished in response to Debs's attempts to resurrect the union.[63]

Whether labor and management were drawing together as a response to the ARU or because depression made union agitation unwise, their unity explains why Jones was welcomed by both the elite workers, such as conductors, engineers, and machinists, and also by management. It may be that Jones's appearance in the railroad shops was a tacit endorsement of the brotherhoods and encouraged by management, either because elite unions were the lesser evil or in order to keep the unions from combining. What is certain is that when Jones announced that he wanted to hold a special meeting for railroad men, his usual practice in a transportation center, the superintendent of the Western and Atlantic made the unusual suggestion that the meeting be held in the shops. This arrangement was endorsed by Jones's good friend John W. Thomas, Jr., owner of the railroad.[64]

The service was a great success, and the *Constitution* reporter found it marvelous "to see the sturdy fellows, some of them in their shirt sleeves, greased and smoked, sitting spellbound under the pathos and eloquence of the famous preacher." At the end of the sermon, "they came up in their everyday working clothes, leaping over benches as they came, and with tears streaming down their faces. . . . The scene," the reporter wrote with sudden restraint, "was one seldom witnessed in this city."[65]

The service may not have been a management plot to subvert the labor movement, but Colonel Thomas knew he had nothing to fear from Jones. Though he gave away most of his earnings, Jones was a wealthy man; on his death he left an estate valued at $250,000. An instinctive entrepreneur, Jones had plowed money into the Cartersville economy, and as owner of a sawmill, bottling factory, icehouse, several buildings downtown, and part of a nearby mine, Jones was one of the largest employers in his hometown. His sympathies were with management. Throughout the long depression of the nineties, Jones urged workers not to strike. "When you strike you can look around and see ten fellows sitting up waiting for your job," Jones warned. "When you strike you generally send your wife to the wash-tub."

He urged the "sweet working girls" struggling to live on half of what they made ten years before to "live within your income, if it means bread and water, pay as you can on the debts already contracted; sooner or later the clouds will break away and the sunshine of prosperity will come to you." Every word in the railroad service endorsed Christian capitalism; Jones even recommended religion to the railroad workers because "godliness is profitable." [66]

Twelve days later the revival ended. At the last meeting, twenty thousand people crowded onto the corner of Cain and Williams streets: eight thousand inside the tabernacle and twelve thousand outside. "The day will be recorded as one of the most remarkable in the religious record of the south," the *Constitution* predicted, for "never has Atlanta been shaken by such a tremendous force." The paper estimated that five hundred decks of cards had been burned, two saloons closed, arrests for drunkenness curtailed, attendance at theaters reduced, and a thousand people added to the church rolls. Two weeks later, the *Constitution* reported revivals in all the major churches "as a result of the religious wave that swept over Atlanta during the Sam Jones meetings." [67]

The revival did not bring a thousand people into the churches. If Jones is credited with all the accessions in March, April, and May for the five churches that participated most prominently, his converts would total 135; 70 if those who joined on profession of faith are credited to his eternal account. Only Grace and Trinity Methodist churches showed a significant increase in the number of professions of faith in 1896. However, these churches may have been demoralized by the revival, because the average number of accessions by profession dropped in the five years following the revival to a lower number than during the five years before. Central Congregational, the church of R. V. Atkisson, president of the EMA and the man who had gone to Cartersville to plead with Jones to come to Atlanta, showed a decrease in accessions by profession during the revival year. Central Congregational was suffering from adverse publicity because it had admitted a black man to membership four years earlier, and it may be that the church's appeal to the working class made it appear radical compared to the middle-class churches. It was just this middle and upper-middle class to whom Jones appealed: of the fifty-one men coming into the churches in April, May, and June, three-quarters were proprietors, managers, or white-collar workers like clerks and bookkeepers. [68]

In less than a year, Jones was back in Atlanta. Four hundred railroad men had petitioned him to conduct another revival. Again the crowds were enormous—"he draws like mustard plaster"—with the *Journal* estimating that in the first ten days alone, the evangelist preached to 150,000 people, 5,000 of whom professed conversion. "No man can in two successive years hold a series of meetings, take the same texts, preach the same sermons, tell over and over again the same stories, and hold the crowd as he can," a Methodist minister remarked. But two weeks after the revival, the Methodist churches had not received a single accession from the hundreds of people who had signed cards signifying their decision to accept Christ.[69]

It may be that the revival faltered because Jones was in poor health, or because the reporters had lost their crusading zeal. In the first few days of the revival the *Constitution* devoted a page of coverage a day, but it soon cut back to a single column. The *Looking Glass* mentioned the campaign only in two unflattering cartoons, one of which depicted the devil dancing a jig and shouting at the retreating figure of the evangelist: "Ha! Ha! Never touched me!"[70]

The most important ingredient in the formula for failure in 1897 was the defection of the clergy. While Jones's charm and success had wooed the disaffected into the fold in 1896, the following year many ministers could not be seduced or shamed into supporting the meeting. It may be they remembered the disappointments of the year before, or they may have considered Jones too closely identified with the Atlanta power structure to lead a crusade against it on any issue other than prohibition. Although Jones had the backing of prominent businessmen, he did not have the support of most clergy, and the reason will explain not only why the meeting in 1897 was a failure, but also why the evangelists J. Wilbur Chapman in 1899 and R. A. Torrey in 1906 faced disunity and defeat.

In the months before Jones returned to Atlanta, the tenuous alliance between businessmen and religious leaders broke apart. Angered that a city which advertised its sanctity tolerated Sabbath desecration and a divorce rate of one out of every hundred marriages, the EMA took up arms. On March 1, 1897, three days before the Jones revival began, the headline of the *Constitution* read:

ATLANTA MINISTERS DECLARE WAR
No Mail on Sunday / Divorces Must Stop.[71]

To the editors of the *Constitution*, this announcement seemed an attack on the city itself. The preachers had forgotten, W. A. Hemphill, business manager of the *Constitution*, wrote, that "people congregated here for business. They did not come here primarily to attend the Young Men's Christian Association Movement and revivals. These things are incidental and are not the main factor of a city's growth." What the city needed, Hemphill declared, was fewer evangelists and more entrepreneurs. Naturally, this injunction did not apply to Jones, for "Sam Jones would never interfere with the proper and beautiful growth of any truly good city like Atlanta, but would aid in building it up." [72]

Orth Stein was also alarmed by the resurgence of a Puritanism unimpressed with pragmatism and profit, exactly the brand of fanaticism that had fastened prohibition on Atlanta a decade earlier. It was true that there was "a growing indifference to religious duties" in Atlanta. " 'Pon my word," the editor of the *Looking Glass* exclaimed, "as long as the pastors dawdle with such fatuities as card-playing and dancing, to the exclusion of living issues, I am not surprised." Stein was aghast that Atlanta preachers had endorsed the Baptist evangelist Len Broughton while he slandered the city three times a day from the pulpit of the Second Baptist Church. Such "reckless sensationalism" was destroying an image Atlanta had spent millions to acquire. "A decent man will think twice before bringing his family to a place that is publicly denounced as the wickedest spot in half a continent." [73]

With ministers accusing Atlanta of immorality and boosters charging ministers with treason, the exposition alliance had clearly ended. The estrangement between the Evangelical Ministers' Association and the business and newspaper community was not complete. They continued to agree on certain issues—that God had incited the Spanish-American War to present America "with an exceptional opportunity for the expansion not only of political but also religious liberty," that "summary justice" might be called for in cases of rape, that disfranchisement was a reasonable solution to the "Negro question." There was little agreement about what Atlanta needed, however, and while the EMA pursued blue laws and prohibition, businessmen relied on an occasional revival to reaffirm Atlanta's allegiance to the Almighty. [74]

Ministers for the most part did not participate wholeheartedly in these municipal rites. Though they were pressured into public support by their prominent members, privately they were wary, even deprecating. When the Business Men's Gospel Union brought R. A. Torrey to Atlanta in the spring of 1906 amid talk of another exposition to counter another depression, ministers were openly critical. Disgusted by the infighting that hobbled the revival—a meeting during which Jones's old sidekick Sam Small renewed his conversion—Sam Jones scoffed at the churches bickering over how to get rid of Satan. Baptists wanted to drown him; Presbyterians hoped to freeze him out; Episcopalians were afraid that without him "their members would die of loneliness." [75]

It was not until the Billy Sunday revival of 1917 that the coalition between business and religious leaders was re-formed in the spirit of wartime unity. With his words being transcribed by Sam's son Paul for the *Constitution*, Sunday again invoked the vision of Atlanta as the key to the Kingdom. With sweat pouring in rivers off his face, Sunday begged God to deliver Atlanta into his hands. "O God! If this city of Atlanta, pearl of the south, will fall on her knees before You and come over to Christ, then I say that this whole southland, drenched in tears of repentance, will do as Atlanta does." Thrusting a hand heavenward, Sunday pleaded: "Men and women of Atlanta, I hold before you the bleeding form of Jesus Christ. Take him if you will." As the audience watched in intense silence, his hand dropped and his face collapsed in exhaustion. "Good night, my friends, good night." [76]

The Rev. Samuel Gamble Jones and
Elizabeth Edwards Jones, Sam Jones's
grandparents. As a young boy Jones
lived for two years with the couple,
and later credited his grandfather
with his salvation. Elizabeth Jones
was also known for her piety: she
was said to have read the Bible
thirty-seven times "on her knees."

John Jones, Sam Jones's father, as
a captain in the Confederate army.
(Hargrett Rare Book and Manuscript
Library, University of Georgia
Libraries)

Jones as a young man. (Special Collections Department,
Robert W. Woodruff Library, Emory University)

Laura McElwain Jones soon after her marriage to Sam Jones in 1868.
(Courtesy of Howell Jones)

Laura and Sam Jones (top) with their children and grandchildren on the steps of Roselawn, their home in Cartersville, Georgia, circa 1896. Robert, Laura, and Julia Jones are seated at bottom; Robert's wife, Lillie, Mary Jones Mays, Paul Jones, and Annie Jones are seated in the second row. The grandchildren are Mary's daughters Eva (top) and Laura (middle), who became a well-known lingerie designer, and Robert's son Sam Paul Jones. (Courtesy of Howell Jones)

Laura M. Jones with her daughter Mary. (Special Collections Department, Robert W. Woodruff Library, Emory University)

Jones's daughter Laura, who fashioned herself into everything her father hated, in a characteristic pose. (Courtesy of Howell Jones)

Jones circa 1885, the year of the three-week Nashville revival that made him
a national figure. (Special Collections Department, Robert W. Woodruff Library,
Emory University)

Samuel White Small, a journalist and the author of popular black-dialect stories who was converted in 1885 while reporting on a Jones revival. He subsequently became Jones's chief apprentice. (Hargrett Rare Book and Manuscript Library, University of Georgia Libraries)

E. O. Excell, Jones's choirmaster. According to a contemporary news account, Excell was so "full of music" that he seemed to have "swallowed a brass band."

Walt Holcomb (left) and Thomas Dunham, Jones's closest and most-faithful associates during the final years of his life. In 1895 Dunham was placed in charge of the rehabilitation of Jones's twenty-year-old son Paul, who was experiencing a period of depression and substance abuse. Holcomb married Jones's daughter Julia soon after her father's death and assisted Laura M. Jones in writing her husband's official biography.

Jones and George R. Stuart, an itinerant Methodist minister who frequently traveled with Jones on the revival circuit. (Courtesy of Howell Jones)

Editorial cartoon published in the March 14, 1896 *Looking Glass*.
(Atlanta History Center)

Editorial cartoon published in April 1896 in the *Looking Glass,* an iconoclastic
Atlanta newspaper. (Atlanta History Center)

Yet the Lord pleads with you still: Ask where the good road is,

the godly paths you used to walk in, in the days of long ago.

Travel there, and you will find rest for your souls.

—Jeremiah 6:166

The Bible is good enough for me: just the old book under which I

was brought up. I do not want notes or criticism, or explanations

about the authorship or origin, or even cross-references. I do not

need or understand them, and they confuse me.

—Grover Cleveland

6

❧ That Old-Time Religion

Today the late nineteenth century is portrayed as a simpler, less imperiled era, a time free of acid rain, holes in the ozone shield, and the awful umbrella of The Bomb. When Madison Avenue wants to evoke home or health or nature, it assembles the icons of the "good old days": straw hats, bandstands, spacious front porches, white lace. In modern mythology, America of a hundred years ago was a graceful place where life was sure and faith was fixed.

The reality was far different. While the South struggled to overcome the devastation of a war that had destroyed its wealth and disrupted its carefully layered society, the raw West worked to establish the necessities of civilization. The North wrestled with the burden of victory: a reputation for prosperity that pulled people like a magnet. Millions streamed into the cities, not only those "yearning to breathe free" but American farmers, who were plagued by natural disasters, rising railroad and interest rates, and the tedium of isolated life, and gave up on farming with a curse or a sigh. Blocks away from fetid slums, Italian villas, French chateaus, and Rhineland castles were constructed by those lucky or skilled or unscrupulous enough to benefit from the enormous expansion of the economy. The city, the Reverend Josiah Strong wrote in *Our Country*, became the place where "Dives and Lazarus met face to face," the arena where "surfeit" met "starvation." [1]

By the last decade of the century, a great weight had shifted: America was no longer primarily an agricultural society. In a country where virtue was thought to be taught at the end of a plow, the growth of the city was disturbing. Antiurban sentiment, always a part of the American mentality, became more insistent, and evangelicals talked anxiously about the need to sanctify the "vicious and degraded populations which form the slums of our cities." Poverty produced heresy, it was said, awful errors not just in theology but in economic thought as well. Either the city will be evangelized, Dwight Moody warned after the Haymarket Riot of 1886, or "the leaven of communism and infidelity will assume such enormous proportions that it will break out in a reign of terror such as this country has never known." [2]

The creation of two new economic entities, the corporation and the holding company, was also viewed uneasily. As corporate empires feasted upon small businesses and family companies, monopolies grew to enormous proportions. The corrupting power of these vast corporations was evident as money flowed freely into the coffers of politicians: these were the years that "Standard [Oil] did everything to the Pennsylvania Legislature, except refine it." Those behind this enormous consolidation of wealth and power were admired for their initiative, appreciated for their benevolence, and despised for their greed. Made envious by accounts of lavish parties and sumptuous "cottages," many read with satisfaction that for all his wealth, Jay Gould was unable to digest a simple meal; that Cornelius Vanderbilt could not walk in the park without being "accosted by tramps or insulted by socialistic philosophers"; that the bereaved family of George Pullman had to sink his coffin in cement in order to prevent an untimely resurrection at the hands of disgruntled employees. [3]

When the labor question forced itself into the popular consciousness with the strikes of 1877, 1886, and the prolonged agony of 1892–94, anxiety expanded exponentially. Even the South, free for the most part from strikes and "foreign agitators," was afflicted by this pervasive paranoia. When the editor of the *Southern Evangelist* analyzed a series of train accidents, he acknowledged that they might have been caused by the "criminal negligence" of the railroad, but he thought it far more likely that they were evidence of "a deep-laid scheme of destruction and ruin that could only be born of communism." Some expected a capitalist dictatorship, predicting that people would surrender freedom for security. "It would not take too many panics for Property to cry aloud for some strong man to come forth as the savior of society," an alarmist warned in 1886.[4]

If life was not sure, was faith at least fixed? When people turned to the church in this anxious age, did they find assurance in ancient answers, the fellowship of believers, "the shadow of a great rock in a thirsty land"? Certainly, in many ways, the late nineteenth century was a thrilling time for Christian Americans. It was a time of almost insufferable optimism, a time when America's Manifest Destiny seemed to intersect with Christ's Great Commission in benevolent colonialism. Revivalism, that "uniquely American ritual," was so widely accepted that even Catholics embraced it. Fed by "seasons of refreshing," churches grew at an astonishing rate: in 1870 only 17 percent of the population belonged to a church, but by 1910 more than a third were inside the fold.[5]

Interdenominational congresses were touted as proof that Christians had outgrown the infighting of their ancestors, and union revivals, where mainstream churches combined to evangelize an entire city, were cited as evidence of a newfound spirit of unity. Evangelicals aligned as well to overcome the outcroppings of sin: prostitution, alcohol, tobacco, gambling, and the abuse of children, prisoners, and the poor. While the first fifteen years after the Civil War had been a time of "almost frantic solicitude for the spiritual welfare of the rich," complacency cracked during the turbulent eighties. An awakened social conscience spawned a multitude of institutions: the Young Men's and Young Women's Christian Associations were established to protect rural offspring from urban evil, and the Salvation Army marched with militant empathy. Lay witnesses were sent into slums, city missions were founded, and institutional churches fed the mind and body as well as the spirit. Jones's neighbor Lottie Moon, a missionary to China, was only one of thousands who responded to the call to carry Christ to heathens abroad. The devout began to look with confidence to the day when the Gospel would be preached in every tongue. "No intelligent person can doubt whether Protestant Christianity is a setting or a rising sun," Daniel Dorchester proclaimed in 1895. "Every year it is robing itself in fuller effulgence, and pouring its blessed illumination upon new millions of earth's benighted children."[6]

However, the Gilded Age was no Golden Age. To many, it seemed that the church was substituting social welfare for spiritual growth, the loaves and the fishes for the bread of life. Numerical growth did not cheer those who feared that church rolls were padded by people seeking respectability instead of Christ, and towering spires failed to encourage those convinced that costly churches glorified man, not God. Christians who cited statistics on new churches neglected to notice that many were the result of the abandonment of the city's core by the middle and upper classes; for every Protestant church that elected to stay in the inner city, many more followed their members uptown. From 1868 to 1888, when two hundred thousand people moved into the area below New York's Fourteenth Street, seventeen Protestant churches moved out. All too often, when ministers did address the problem of poverty, their remarks were marred by ignorance and condescension. The aptly named Alexander Proudfit boasted that the doors to his church were always open to economic outcasts: "I have every Sunday of my life, in the city of Baltimore, tramps sitting in the best pews of my church—men without a linen collar and without a whole coat—although my ushers bring them in and seat them very comfortably, yet I get very few of them."[7]

Such shallow sympathy for the dispossessed was easily overcome when fear or outrage arose. "Bring on the troops—the armed police—in overwhelming numbers," the *Congregationalist* shrilled during the railroad strike of 1877. "Bring out the Gatling guns. Let there be no fooling with blank cartridges." Workers must recognize that labor is a "commodity, and like all other commodities, its condition is governed by the imperishable laws of supply and demand." Besides, with their addiction to vice and alcohol, the poor manufactured their own misery. From his Brooklyn pulpit only a few miles from the slums of New York City, Henry Ward Beecher proclaimed as a "general truth" that "no man in this land suffers from poverty unless it be more than his fault—unless it be his *sin.* . . . There is enough to spare thrice over; and if men have not enough, it is owing to the want of provident care, and foresight and industry, and frugality, and wise saving."[8]

While some blamed the moral bankruptcy of the poor for the spreading stain of slums, others accused immigration. To nativists, a common enemy invited an end to sectionalism, as the Reverend Bristol, a northern Methodist, suggested at the general conference of the southern church in 1890. While the South now enjoyed the "purest Americanism," Bristol said, distance from the teeming cities of the East provided no security against those foreign elements who threaten the "integrity of labor" and the "security of capital," the evil agitators who were working to substitute the "Sabbath of Paris or Berlin" for the "quiet, peaceful and holy American Sabbath." The once warring sections must now unite, Bristol urged, unite in opposition to that "Italian citizen" who would "make the Mississippi a tributary of the Tiber."[9]

Not only were Protestants faced with an invasion of immigrants whose very numbers endangered their culture, they were threatened as well by erosion from the inside, the eradication of chunks of belief by biblical critics who used the techniques of modern scholarship to analyze the Scriptures. On the basis of findings in anthropology, archeology, and geology, biblical critics concluded that water never covered the entire earth, that the Pentateuch was not written by Moses, that many of the sayings of Jesus were common to a small cult called the Essenes. Ministers trained in universities brought these ideas to the people in the pew, as did newspaper and magazine articles and a host of lyceum lecturers. A crack opened that would widen for the next hundred years, the division between those who insisted the Bible was the inerrant Word of God and those who viewed it as a book that revealed the efforts of imperfect people to understand the Incomprehensible Almighty—inspired as art, inspired as ethics, but not infallible.[10]

Some in evangelical denominations viewed biblical criticism as a way of "taking in the old from higher heights and with broader range." Others were incensed by clergymen who seemed willing to relinquish the Bible to keep Christianity. "The heinousness of finding fault with the Bible at this time by a Christian minister is most evident," DeWitt Talmage wrote indignantly; such a minister is like a crew member on a sinking ship who tries to "saw off some of the planks" because "the timber did not come from the right forest." The bitterness of the beleaguered crept into the remarks of evangelicals, and revivalists became more defensive, more exasperated. "What is the use of talking about two Isaiahs when most people don't know there's one?" Dwight Moody moaned.[11]

Equally upsetting to evangelicals was the controversy over evolution, and many connected a decline in morality with Charles Darwin's *The Descent of Man*. The idea of sharing ancestry with an ape was so outrageous and interesting that it captured the imagination of the age. Chautauqua lecturers and lyceum speakers alternately defended and derided the theory, and monkey jokes were the order of the day. To the Methodist Episcopal Church, South, however, heresy was no laughing matter, and in 1878 Alexander Winchell, a part-time lecturer in geology at Vanderbilt University, was relieved of his position. Though university officials denied that Winchell's dismissal was connected with his contention that people—black people—had existed before Adam's creation, conservatives claimed victory in angry exultant letters, while liberals labeled Vanderbilt a priest-ridden, medieval institution. Conservatism triumphed again six years later when James Woodrow, uncle of Woodrow Wilson, was removed as a professor of natural science at the Presbyterian Theological Seminary in Columbia, South Carolina, for maintaining that since "the Bible does not teach science" Christians need not choose between God and Darwin.[12]

While real infidelity may have been "much too weak in America to be of any grave importance," biblical criticism and theories of evolution made inroads into the aggressive certainty of Protestant belief. More important than the actual number of defectors from the faith was the perception of defeat. In the heart of the Bible Belt, with church membership rising around him, Henry Grady fretted about the "atheistic tide that is sweeping the country." Convinced the contamination came from the North, southern clergymen constructed an intellectual blockade against infidelity just as their predecessors had excluded abolitionist ideas, trying to protect their people from "the godlessness of the truly damned Yankess."[13]

Thus insulated, southerners congratulated themselves on their freedom from insidious "isms"—Darwinism, spiritualism, Christian Scientism, biblical criticism—and boasted that there was "no part of the world in which ministers of the Gospel are more respected than in the Southern States." However, there as elsewhere, churchmen worried that an increasing number of men were delegating piety to their wives, sending the women and children to pay homage to God while they worshiped mammon in the marketplace. Women so outnumbered men in Protestant denominations in the nineteenth century that one clergyman confessed that he was tempted to change the emphasis of the psalmist to "O that *men* would praise the Lord!" and quoted a parody of Longfellow:

> In the world's great field of battle,
> In the bivouac of life,
> You will find the Christian soldier
> Represented by his wife.[14]

Related to this feminization of the church was a decline in the status of the minister, especially outside the South. "Real" men, aggressive, energetic men, went into commercial life, it was thought; soft, idealistic, indolent men entered the ministry. Throughout the nineteenth century, ministers of all Protestant denominations increasingly came from the lower echelons of society, and while the status of professionals like doctors and lawyers was rising, that of the minister was slipping. Separated from those above him by social and economic boundaries and removed from those below by his education and profession, the minister was vulnerable to being viewed as an effete failure by both segments of society. Their very manhood was under attack: in October of 1882 one writer in the *Homiletic Review* felt called upon to refute the popular notion that religion robbed men of virility and urged brother pastors to remember Paul's injunction: "Quit you like men." A month later, another writer bemoaned the fact that men of the cloth were widely seen as dreamy, unrealistic, "even physical cowards."[15]

Contributing to the decline in moral authority was the popular perception that ministers pandered to the rich, assuring their moneyed members that they could attend the Great Barbecue *and* the banquet of the Lord. Mark Twain joked about the "Church of the Holy Speculators," and most of the "robber barons" were ecclesiastically connected. John D. Rockefeller taught a Baptist Sunday school class, and the railroad and stock market magnate Daniel Drew founded a Methodist seminary and attended prayer meetings "when he was not printing bogus shares or devising the technique of watering stock." Though some clergymen shrank from accepting plundered money, many echoed the sentiments of the denominational college treasurer: "The only tainted money I know is tain't enough."[16]

That Sam Jones bubbled to the top during this time of religious effervescence and cultural dislocation was no accident: he provided comic relief to an anxious age, nostalgia in an era of unsettling change, and the irresistible appeal of emphatic answers to gnawing uncertainties. As forthright and independent as the circuit riders of old, to westerners Jones was a reminder of those wonderful camp-meeting days when folks would gather from miles around, having fire and brimstone for the first course and grace for dessert. To the northern sons and daughters of Calvin, Jones was a funny man who reassured them that God loved laughter and scorned the choking compression of creeds. To the southerner, caught "in the two currents of Puritanism and hedonism," Jones offered both at the same time.[17]

In a prudish age where table legs were called "limbs" and chicken breasts were never mentioned, Jones spoke with rare anatomical exactitude. Though he usually euphemized brothels as "houses of shame," when told where the fire engines were headed during a Cartersville meeting, he exclaimed, "Praise the Lord! Hattie's whorehouse has burned to the ground!" His diatribes against fashion both aroused prurient interest and endorsed puritanical disapproval, as when he said: "The girls have cut off the tops of their dresses for the ballroom and the bottoms of 'em for the bicycle until, I'll tell you, I'm getting uneasy." No wonder that reporters covering Jones's lectures and revivals noted the startling shifts in the audience's mood. Where else could a person be titillated, tickled, and edified all at the same time? [18]

Against the enemies of evangelical Christianity Jones used his sharpest weapon: wit. And there were plenty of enemies to aim at, for alien creeds were cropping up everywhere: Christian Science, Mormonism, theosophy, and spiritualism, along with a host of sects spawned by a fascination with the occult and astrology. Jones fought heresy through hilarity, delighting his audiences by shrinking it with ridicule, then knocking it out with a punch-line. Brought to Tennessee to counteract the Mormons, Jones undermined the influence of Joseph Smith's disciples with good-natured contempt. "I could eat a big mess of pork before bed-time and have more visions than all the Mormon nation." And though spiritualism is "catching them by the thousand," the ones they hooked were not worth reeling in. "You can run after new tricks and new isms if you care to, but here is one fellow that's going to stay by the God of his fathers, and the church of his mother." [19]

Jones enjoyed advising the Christian Scientists the many ways in which the vacuum above their eyes might come in handy. There was no way to drown with a head as light as balsa wood: "Just lift your handkerchief for a sail and you will come in with the first favorable breeze." "You know that the Christian Scientist believes that everything is true they think is true," Jones would say.

> An old negro came up to see a friend of mine, and my friend, who was the negro's employer and a Christian Scientist, said: "Ben, you're late again. What's the matter?" "My brother's got the rheumatism," said the nigger, "and I stayed up all night and nursed him; that's why I am late." "He hasn't rheumatism, Ben," said the boss, "he just thinks he has." The next day the nigger didn't show up at all, but came the following day. "Hello, Ben," said his boss; "guess your brother thinks he's got the rheumatism again, doesn't he?" "No, boss, he thinks he's dead—we buried him yesterday." [20]

Concerned that evolution was eroding the foundations of Christianity? No need to be, when the doctrine could so easily be laughed out of court:

> They say we came up through evolution. I wonder if that is so, and whenever nature will evolute again. I have been watching that thing. [Laughter and applause.] My old grandfather was 91 when he died, and he told

me, not twelve months ago, that he never had seen nature evolute, and he said his father told him he never saw it, and I have traced it back through my kinfolks, and they, not one of them, ever saw nature evolute. It's a fact! It wouldn't evolute when they were around. Now, how many of you believe that you came from an animalcule? From an animalcule to a tadpole, from a tadpole to a lizard, from a lizard to a squirrel, and from a squirrel to a monkey, and from a monkey to a man? We don't! I don't believe man came from monkeys, but when I look at some fellows I think they are heading that way, and will likely reach there. (Applause and laughter.)[21]

No wonder the simple stumbled when even ministers had fallen into heresy, and it seemed to Sam Jones the more educated a man was, the more likely he was to join the "unorthodoxy brethren." "Half of the literary preachers in this town are A.B's, Ph.D's, D.D.'s, LL.D.'s and A.S.S.'s," Jones would say. "And when you find a fellow with a whole alphabet on him you can turn him out." At a "big Chautauqua" Jones had occasion to listen to one such D.D. ("dudle digger") lecture on the "ologies": geology, biology, and zoology. Jones was immediately offended ("I don't like a joke on God") and listened with angry incredulity as the minister ridiculed the biblical account of creation. As "the people whooped and hollered" Jones accosted the man, and what followed was a confrontation he recounted ever after. "Hello, Bud, you dug up more snakes to-day than you can kill the balance of your life," a seething Jones said. "It is a sin and a shame for a minister of God to dig up snakes and throw them on the crowd, for you can easily unsettle the beliefs of the weak these days, but it is mighty hard to settle them back again." As for the stupidity of believing that God "picked up a piece of mud and blew upon it and a living, perfect man walked away," he did not know about that, not being present at creation. He was, however, "right on the spot" when God came to Cartersville "and picked up the dirtiest piece of mud in the town, called Sam Jones, and blew upon it, and a living man for God and right has been walking forth from that day to this. . . . And I believe the breath of the Almighty is omnipotent," Jones would end triumphantly.[22]

Few people were eager for a confrontation with Sam Jones, for his righteous humor made him a perverse opponent, something William Jennings Bryan understood. While Jones liked Bryan and worked with him on prohibition and religious issues, he was baffled by the infatuation of Democrats with the flatulent free-silver ideas of "the Great Commoner." The man "should have been born a woman," Jones concluded: he "could have talked himself to death as the president of a woman's club." Traveling on the Chautauqua circuit, Jones and Bryan were thrown together frequently, and on such occasions the acidic evangelist took pleasure in tormenting the man whose recurrent quest for the presidency made him a tempting target. "Why don't you answer back?" Jones once asked Bryan, after prodding him with remorseless wit in front of a circle of mutual friends. "Ah, Jones," Bryan said with a hangdog look, "nobody can answer a joke."[23]

It may be that Robert Ingersoll understood this, for despite Jones's repeated efforts, the most notorious infidel of the century refused to match wits with the Georgia evangelist. "The Apostle of Agnosticism" on occasion did debate evangelicals, and he was peculiarly fitted to enumerate the shortcomings of the brethren, for he was the son of a Congregational preacher noted for an ability to make sinners smell sulphur. Brought up in rigid orthodoxy, with vivid memories of the confinement of Calvinism and the grim sacrifice of the Puritan Sabbath, Ingersoll turned his knowledge of the faith against the church, aiming with angry accuracy.[24]

It is a shame that agnostic and evangelist never met, for they had much in common. Both lost a mother at an early age and enshrouded the dead parent in "sacred memory"; both passed the bar at the age of twenty-one. Both were devoted family men frequently away from home; both opposed alcohol as the enemy of women and children. Both were at ease in front of immense audiences, with expansive voices that allowed them to talk to the thousands as if they were speaking to each alone. Both won audiences with humor, then ended with a "burst of fiery earnestness." One Boston reporter wrote in words that were often applied to Jones: "The great secret of Ingersoll's success is that he does not aim too high. He is eminently simple and direct and straight forward with the dash of humor and flavor of quaint idiom which are always popular with American audiences." While both were popular lecturers, Ingersoll commanded twice the compensation Jones received, for when the eloquent infidel spoke, even churchgoers came to hear him "give hell hell."[25]

Jones and Ingersoll had similar quarrels with hypocrites, scoffing at the piety that sought sanctuary from the gritty realities of life and the "heartlessness" of a church that had turned away from the poor. Both were contemptuous of men who took the cloth to hide behind the skirts of the church, and in 1895 the people of St. Louis enjoyed the spectacle of evangelist and agnostic railing at effeminate defenders of the faith on successive nights. While Jones ridiculed the silk-hatted preacher who "gets up in his velvet cushioned pulpit and preaches about angels and stars and moon," Ingersoll scorned men who "never had the constitution to be wicked" and took refuge in the ministry. "They mistake weakness for piety," Ingersoll would say, "and remind me of the remark by John Randolph, concerning some land on the upper Potomac, that it was nearly worthless by nature and had been rendered entirely so by cultivation."[26]

It is difficult for people today, exposed to Ingersoll only through the rather appealing agnosticism of his oration at his brother's grave, to understand how bitter Ingersoll was against believers. "The only difference between Catholicism and Protestantism," Ingersoll concluded, "is that the Catholic does not care to think; the Protestant said you must think, but if you did not think right you would be eternally damned." To Ingersoll, the "religion of Jesus Christ" was a "religion of blood," a fearful creed that started with the sacrifice of one man and continued with the bloodshed of thousands, a faith that inspired men to bigotry and butchery. As for the Bible, that pope of the Protestants, it was a savage book that "decrees the destruction of innocent children and unborn babies." Ignorance was its ally: "The reason so many people believe the Bible is that so few read it."[27]

Such pronouncements left Sam Jones sputtering about that "blatant, blab-tongued fool." Ingersoll became the embodiment of evil to Jones: a man of enormous personal charm who used eloquence to undermine moral authority. "His words, put into sentences, look like streams of pearls; but they are merely bracelets and necklaces for swine." While Ingersoll "clamors for free thought and moral liberty," he was in reality agitating for anarchy. "Establish the fact that men can think as they please," Jones growled, and "you establish the fact that they can act as they please."[28]

Jones ached to debate him: "I've tried to get old Bob to meet me on the platform," he said in 1897. "There'd be a box full of monkeys at feed time, sure." In 1895 when Ingersoll was in Louisville, Jones sent his lyceum agent to challenge the agnostic to a debate on "the pros and cons of Christianity" in the six largest auditoriums in America. Ingersoll refused "point blank." "Maybe he thought I was some poor clod-hopping preacher," Jones speculated. Two years later when both men were in Boston, Jones reissued the challenge, and Ingersoll again refused, claiming that since Jones had left the Methodist ministry, he no longer represented a "great religious body." "Colonel Ingersoll admits that Sam Jones is a good man, but says that he addresses himself to the emotions, not the intellect," the *Atlanta Constitution* explained. "He thinks Sam Jones is afflicted with religious hysterics— a state of mind in which facts are worthless and reason dangerous." The "blating blasphemy" was afraid, Jones chortled. "I tell you Bob doesn't want to back up against a buzz-saw going 300,000 rotations a minute, or he might find himself out in the woods at fly time."[29]

Frustrated because he could not get at Ingersoll directly, Jones contented himself with artillery from afar, using the agnostic as an enemy whenever local opposition was low. "Thank God," Jones would say, "I never had a man closer than forty-fifth cousin" that would pay "to see Bob Ingersoll chip the words off his mother's tombstone, 'I am the Resurrection and the Life.'" Far from being a defender of intellectual freedom, "Old Bob" was just "after the dollar." Sacrilege was shocking, and "men love to be shocked." Ingersoll was "the devil's dynamo, and when a man stands upon the damp soil of a sinful life, old Bob can turn a current on him that will make him almost leap out of his hide."[30]

If Ingersoll would not meet him officially, Jones would not meet him informally. Once, both men were on a train from Boston; Ingersoll only glanced at the caustic cleric, while Jones studied his adversary with silent intensity. Neither moved to meet. Invited to Atlanta to hear Ingersoll lecture on "The Mistakes of Moses," Jones answered: "No, I can't give a dollar to hear Bob on 'The Mistakes of Moses,' but if I could get a chance to hear Moses on 'The Mistakes of Bob,' I would pay any reasonable sum." Jones's one-way war ended only with Ingersoll's death in 1899. "Peace to his ashes," Jones wrote, adding wickedly that it was a shame the man who mocked judgment could not deliver a lecture "based on the experience of the past few days."[31]

Jones's hatred of heresy, evolution, and infidelity appears to link him to those trying to "arrest the drift from the old moorings," the forebears of the fundamentalists. Certainly most southerners at the end of the nineteenth century endorsed revivalism, were interested in personal piety, and were suspicious of modernism, sentiments that would ultimately make the South the repository of orthodoxy. However, the forerunners of fundamentalism, or prefundamentalists, were largely Presbyterians and Baptists from the North, a section where social change and theological upheaval made a defense of old-time religion imperative earlier. The evangelical conservatism of the South and the doctrinal orthodoxy of the North did not merge until the great battles against evolution and liberalism during the 1920s, two decades after Jones's death. However, Jones was aware of the Bible institutes and conferences where the essential tenets of Christianity were being defined; he even attended one in Atlanta in 1906. In revivals he worked with several of the fathers of fundamentalism: the Baptist ministers A. M. Gordon and George C. Lorimar of Boston, and A. C. Dixon of Baltimore, Thomas Dixon's brother and one of the men who wrote the book *The Fundamentals*, giving the movement its name. Through his reaction to these events and these people, it is possible to decide whether Sam Jones was, as many fundamentalists today believe, a pioneer of the movement, a warrior who fearlessly raised "the standard against liberalism and radicalism."[32]

Like the forerunners of fundamentalism, Jones believed that a commitment to Christ would propel the believer into sacrificial service and evangelical activism. Like them, he insisted that Christianity was "the great conserving and preserving force of the age," without which the United States would collapse like the temple under Samson's wrath. Certainly Jones shared the fundamentalist insistence that lines must be drawn, stands taken, that the church's accommodation with the world must cease. Like the fundamentalists, Jones reserved his harshest criticism for the enemy within, the liberals who craved peace at any price, who preached the remission of sin without sacrifice, resurrection without death. He shared, too, the anti-intellectualism that marks fundamentalism, an indignation at the idea that the God who made Balaam's donkey proclaim his truth needed four years of college and three years of seminary in which to teach his Word. "If some college should give me a D.D. I'd sue 'em for damages," Jones would say with an anger echoed by fundamentalists. "My divinity don't need doctorin!"[33]

Like the fundamentalists Jones gloried in the narrow gate, and like them he erected pharasaic fences, going beyond the commands of Scripture to impose new standards of behavior. The twentieth-century fundamentalist warns of the insidious influence of television and movies; Jones denounced the theater. Even things not inherently evil were to be avoided because they might lead to evil things: card playing to gambling, sports to Sabbath desecration, dancing to fornication, drinking to drunkenness.[34]

Like the God of the fundamentalists, Jones's God was one whose anger, once kindled, consumed. "Here is a man who is afraid not to do right," Jones would say. Many times he had gone home to rest when a telegram came that seemed "to be charged with electricity from the sky." "Pack my grip," he would say to Laura. "I'm afraid not to go, for I'd rather be in Boston, Texas, Colorado or New York, away from my home and my children, than be at home with them and have either of them die." "It is only in the path of duty I can walk safely."[35]

Such a God should be feared, and those heedless of eternal judgment were as foolish as the Cartersville dipsomaniac who decided one night to wrestle with a locomotive. When he grabbed the fender, "the wheels turned and rolled his flesh under them and ground him to powder." But that drunk was "a philosopher and a wise man compared to the one who rushes up into the presence of the great eternal God, who has in the beginning made known his laws and his eternal purpose and thrown around it his own power-ful arm—the mighty spirit that made the world." Jones warned in a sermon that "blanched faces" in Toledo, Ohio, "Some of you say, 'I'm not one to be frightened into Christianity.' Let me tell you if the fact that all you lack of being in hell is being dead doesn't frighten you then you are a braver man than I ever was or want to be this side of the judgement seat of God." [36]

Like the fundamentalists Jones preached a "bottomless hell" and a "top-less heaven," and contrasted the ghastly, unending death of the unrepentant with the "bright world" that God has prepared for the faithful, a world full of "crowns, and psalms, and harps, and towering spires, and jasper walls, and pearly gates." As fundamentalists do today, Jones used literalism as a rallying point against those who would explain everything away through allegory. "I have been twitted many a time, and it makes me feel good from head to foot, with—'Oh, he is one of the old-line fellows, running on brim-stone like John Wesley.' Law, it is the greatest compliment you can pass on a nineteenth century preacher." [37]

Sam Jones proclaimed Scripture as "the voice of God which never mis-guided a footstep." On many of the touchstone texts of fundamentalism he was a literalist: he believed Moses wrote the first five books of the Bible, and he accepted the account of creation "as written." He even defended the chronology of Archbishop James Ussher, the seventeenth-century Irish prelate who determined God created the heavens and the earth on Octo-ber 26, 4004 B.C., at nine o'clock in the morning. "Jones, are you willing to take the Bible as it is?" he was asked after a Bible conference in 1906. "Well," he drawled, "I just reckon I am, for I certainly don't think I am going to take it as it ain't." [38]

Fundamentalists today speak of the Bible as a "rule book": unchanging, certain, pointing the true way. Jones thought of it that way as well, and liked to illustrate his point by telling of the time a box of unmarked parts arrived at his house. Jones was befuddled for a week, until a book arrived describ-ing what the machine was and how it was to be assembled. "The book and the machine go together," Jones discovered. "Then I got to thinking, and I said to myself, 'Look here, Sam Jones, twenty-three years ago you were not put together as you should have been. You'd run backwards and sideways, and you'd run anyway but straight ahead. Twenty-three years ago I took down that old book, the Bible, and I was put together again." No doubt about it, that book "has done a great deal for my wife's husband." [39]

Behind this public position of unblinking literalism, however, the evan-gelist interpreted some Scripture symbolically. Parts of the Bible are "alle-gorical," he admitted to a San Francisco reporter, "and the holy book contains a great deal of beautiful imagery. Christ taught in parables." Insisting that God created the universe in seven days, he acknowledged that "this term 'day' is used indiscriminately in Scripture," meaning anything from twenty-four hours, to the span of a man's life, to an eternity. Like the liberals Jones surrendered the authority of the Bible on issues of science, while claiming its infallibility on moral questions. "The Bible was not given to teach men the way the heavens go, but the way to go to heaven," he was fond of saying. Late in life Jones confessed, "I used to think that a man could not get religion unless he believed everything in the Bible. I made a mistake there." Only one belief was essential: belief in Christ Jesus. "If a man will admit that Jesus died to save sinners," Jones said, "I will chain him there and let him graze all around that peg."[40]

This statement reveals the deepest difference between Sam Jones and his prefundamentalist friends: theology. A. C. Dixon relished doctrinal disputes: "Next to peace I love a fight, and I believe the next best thing to peace is a theological fight." Jones hated infighting among believers, and he despised theology, dismissing it as "a good thing to stuff with sawdust, like the skin of a fish, and put in a museum as a relic of antiquity." He scoffed, "A creed never saved anybody, and it splits the Church and kindles the fires around the martyrs and brought to bear the Inquisition." All were purely human inventions, for "there never was a creed till Jesus Christ had been in heaven 300 years."[41]

Jones believed in "progressive theology," the idea that man's understanding of unchanging Truth was itself changeable. In Chicago in 1886, Jones went to hear Dr. David Swing, a Presbyterian minister tried for heresy for proclaiming that "a creed is only the highest wisdom of a particular time and place." Afterwards, he told other ministers that "Swing put more Christianity into one of his sermons in five minutes than they did in an hour," noting happily, "That raised a storm." Jones urged the denominations to build one another up, rather than tearing one another down. "You Methodists, stop biting that Baptist, and you Presbyterians, stop fighting among yourselves." Emphasis on doctrine merely alienated believers and nurtured spiritual pride. "Now the general pulpit style of America is about like this," Jones said with disgust: "Here I am, Rev. Jeremiah Jones, D.D., saved by the grace of God with a message to deliver. If you repent and believe what I believe, you will be saved, but if you do not you will be damned, and I don't much care if you are." Thus, while the orthodox devised a creedal defense of the faith, Jones tossed away everything he considered nonessential in the interests of unity; while the orthodox worked to shore up belief, Jones labored to change behavior.[42]

Jones's boast that he "never made theology a study" did not keep him from having a theology, and one that differed significantly from the orthodox views. Most prefundamentalists were Baptists and Presbyterians who believed in the substitutionary atonement of Christ's death. While Jones accepted that Christ's death made reconciliation possible between God and man, he rejected the idea that Jesus died to appease God's anger at sinful, fallen man. "My intellect, my manhood, could never love a God who made Christ die to satisfy his wrath," Jones protested. He also disliked the doctrine that man is utterly depraved. While his orthodox friends "say they get it from the Bible that he is," Jones remained unconvinced: "They never showed me the special place yet." Nor did he have much use for the orthodox emphasis on "imputed righteousness," the notion that Christ's virtues are attributed to each believer regardless of individual inadequacy. "I am sorter like the fellow who, when the choir sang, 'Jesus Paid It All' rose up and said, 'Well, if Jesus paid it all, what do you keep dunning us for?' "[43]

In some ways, Jones's view of women and their role in life merges with fundamentalist thought today. Like them, he believed that except in extraordinary instances, God meant women to marry: whenever he saw a "spinster," he knew "some old bachelor wasn't doing his duty." Jones, too, emphasized the nurturing side of women, and believed that the greatest contribution a woman could make to her country was to give it a "half dozen good men." However, unlike the fundamentalists who stress man's role as the spiritual leader of the family, Jones believed "that the women ought to be in the lead religiously, and in business let the men ride the horse in front." Nor would Jones have much use for the fundamentalist insistence upon Ephesians 5:21: "Wives, submit yourselves unto your own husbands, as unto the Lord." Jones had this advice to the women who told him the Bible commanded them to follow their husbands: "You better go slow. Let your husband go on first and send word to you whether to come or not."[44]

While the prefundamentalists and their theological offspring were pessimistic about human nature and the future of human history, Sam Jones was an optimist who saw life as constantly improving, an upward climb to the Kingdom fulfilled. "Surely humanity is getting better," Jones wrote in 1903. "No man who mixed with men twenty years ago and mixes with them now can fail to see the fact that men are behaving better," citing as evidence that Texans no longer toted pistols on trains. Jones had little patience with those who had given up on the world, resigned that evil would reign until Christ ruled. He was angered by those obsessed with the end days, who mooned about the millennium while the world was going to hell around them. "This old world needs heaven," he would say. Like the liberals, Jones insisted it was time to stop dreaming of the "Sweet Bye and Bye" and do something about the "Nasty Now and Now." Jones's book was Acts, not Revelation: "It is not a prophetic religion with me." Jones urged those pining for the Second Coming to bring it about by fulfilling the Great Commission, for the Shepherd would not return until the last sheep was in the fold: "Let us rush in the millennium and get to work," Jones urged. "That is the only way I know to bring it about."[45]

However, despite disagreements on theology, Jones and the orthodox worked together because of their common goals: converting as many people as possible and making everyone else behave. If he were alive today, he would be condemning liberals for emptying the mainline churches, ridiculing the infighting of the Baptists, dismissing modern millennialists as people with "more religion than sense," and urging moderates and conservatives to work together for the redemption of the world. Jones opposed even the ineffective methods of birth control available in his day; he would be appalled by abortion. A man who discerned God's wrath in natural catastrophes (they were just "God getting after somebody about something") would surely describe AIDS as the harvest of immorality. Instead of ordering Christians to the polls to vote for prohibitionists, Jones would be commanding them to vote for candidates who support school prayer and the teaching of creationism, who favor tax credits for private schooling, who oppose abortion, who would crack down on pornography and drug use, and who would refuse to recognize homosexuality as a legitimate life-style.[46]

This "master of audiences" would surely have his own television program today, and it would be a powerful voice for those who want to put "God's people" in power. So many of the slogans of this "most quoted man of his generation" could be rallying cries for the religious right. On the need for Christians to involve themselves in the political process: "Some fellows say, don't mix politics and religion. When you hear a fellow talk that way, you know he hasn't got any religion to mix." On pornographers taking refuge behind the First Amendment: "The less character a man has, the more he talks about his constitutional rights." On the Bible as the true source of law: "The only way to tell whether anything is right, is just to lay the straight edge of the Bible to it."[47]

Jones's evangelical activism might appear to link him with another group emerging out of the cultural convulsions of the late nineteenth century: the Social Gospelers. They were an amorphous group of intellectuals who wanted the church to look beyond individual conversion to the salvation of society and advocated far-reaching economic changes to make America conform more closely to the Kingdom of God. Dr. Elmer T. Clark, an authority on American religion, saw Jones as an advocate of social Christianity, a man with a vision that was "world-wide and socially redemptive." Bishop Edwin Hughes of the Methodist church similarly described Jones as a minister who "walked in the ways of the social gospel, yet never became a mere tinker on the surface of damaged life."[48]

Like the Social Gospelers, Jones deplored the way Christians clustered together in economic classes, making the church seem like a club. Like them, Jones was fiercely critical of churches that rented pews to underwrite the budget: "God Almighty has a quarrel with every crowd that perch themselves on hired pews and shut the doors on the poor and perishing in the town," Jones scolded. Convinced that middle-class churches were failing the poor, Jones threw his support to the Salvation Army, an organization newly arrived in America. The very things many found repugnant endeared the Army to Sam Jones: their militant Christianity, their concern for society's castoffs, their indifference to theology, their sensational antics, their unabashed enthusiasm for the cause of Christ. "You Methodists ought to keep your mouths shut, and not turn up your noses. One-hundred years ago you were just like the Salvation Army, except you didn't have money enough to buy a drum and a red shirt," Jones would say when he took up collections to aid the Army. "Don't you criticize the Salvation Army. They've got religion, and that's all that ails them."[49]

Jones often took time during a revival to commend specific local charities, especially "rescue missions" for prostitutes and the Florence Crittenden homes, where "fallen women" could have their illegitimate babies. "I used to say to the police, 'Run out these women.' God forgive me for saying that. Poor women! Poor women!" "If any creature on earth needs your sympathy, the woman who has lost her character needs it," Jones would say. "Jesus was tenderer with the Magdalene than anyone else."[50]

Although Dwight Moody is the evangelist most frequently linked to the Young Men's Christian Association, in 1885 and 1886 Jones singlehandedly raised over one hundred thousand dollars for buildings in Nashville, Cincinnati, St. Joseph, and Omaha. At a critical stage of development in the 1870s and 1880s, the YMCA needed to establish permanency in cities by moving out of rental rooms and into buildings that could house dormitories, reading rooms, "swimming baths," and Bible study groups. Jones persuaded businessmen that an organization that strengthened character, promoted temperance, and guarded virtue was a good investment for employers. Jones had an "effective species of begging," a Nashville reporter wrote after observing the evangelist sending ushers out into the audience and directing their efforts with nudges of "Fish awhile over this hole, Brother Gibbs," or "Are there any more minnows in your pool, Brother Thruston?" So productive were Jones's appeals that he raised fifty thousand dollars in less than half an hour at a St. Joseph rally—men stood on chairs and shouted out their pledges faster than the secretary could record them. Jones finally had to send them away so the ladies could be admitted for their meeting, during which an additional fifteen thousand dollars was subscribed.[51]

Jones frequently began fund-raising rallies with an impressive personal donation. "He never asked for a dollar where he was not willing to give two or more," one neighbor remembered. Once a week he fed forty poor children at his own table, and the letters he received testify to his reputation as a generous man. He contributed liberally to Methodist colleges and was credited with educating more young men than anyone in Georgia. In spite of his obstreperous opposition to theological education, Warren Akin Candler at Emory and W. F. Tillett at Vanderbilt knew they had only to mention a struggling seminarian to receive funds. In Cartersville he founded the Sam Jones Female College, later the public high school, and subsidized many young girls interested in teaching or industrial education. "I always help girls who have ambition and want to be something," Jones would say. "I will help them till my heels fly up and then I'll help them skating along the ground." Usually evasive about the extent of his private charity, when accused of saving souls for the money that was in it, Jones angrily retorted that he had given away $275,000 of the more than $300,000 he had earned, an estimate confirmed by friends after his death.[52]

The evangelist was suspicious of those less generous, and characterized the rich as greedy and shallow, criminal in their business transactions, and hypocritical in their professions of faith. "I say it and I believe it and I want you reporters to get it down; I believe that the devil will get ninety-nine out of every one-hundred men in the United States that die worth $50,000," Jones announced to a Texas audience. "Guess that will make many an old fellow buzz around." The rich may try to take it with them, but their arms will be "too stiff to get into the pocket of their shroud."[53]

Jones was appalled at the spectacle of surfeit in a starving world. "A man who piles up a million in this day, when the poor are suffering and the laboring men are idle, and the cry of the destitute is heard on every corner—a man that can pile up a million is a hog," Jones said during the depression of the nineties. Such selfishness stoked the fires of socialism, driving the poor to believe relief would come through the destruction of capitalism. "The anarchy that will some day burn up this country will come from overworked underpaid women," the evangelist predicted in 1899. "The merchant that pays $30 for the same work that he pays a man $100 for will go to hell when he dies sure as it ain't burnt out." Wild with indignation when he read of a "hungry freezing woman" huddled with her children on a cot "sewing men's garments at fifteen cents a dozen," Jones lashed out at the sweatshop owner: "I tell you 15 cents a dozen from making garments by the poor women of this country, paying that, you are putting the torch to your own mansion, sir—you are putting the torch to your own storehouse, and God himself will laugh at the conflagration."[54]

Jones shared the repugnance of the Social Gospelers for the "gamblers" in the stock and commodities exchanges who take the risks for which others pay. "Every little while you read of a Wall St. plunger killing himself. I think it would be a good job if they could all be cleared up in one night," Jones told a Boston audience in 1897. He was convinced that most stock-market machinations were criminal, and the perpetrators escaped justice because of white skin and green money. "A nigger can steal a chicken and they'll put him in the workhouse or the chaingang, but a white man can steal a hundred thousand dollars, and they'll call him 'Colonel.' You see," Jones explained, "the nigger stole the chicken, but the white man just misappropriated the funds."[55]

For all his indignation over ill-gotten gain and his lamentations over the victims of industrialism, Sam Jones was not a Social Gospeler with a Dixie dialect. Though the language is the same, when Sam Jones and the Social Gospelers spoke of Christian ethics, they meant very different things. Social Gospelers spoke of ethics in societal terms: the need to restrict unbridled competition, protect the weak, endorse the rights of workers to organize, establish free schools, lobby for government ownership of transportation, reform prisons, impose progressive taxation to equalize wealth. Sam Jones, on the other hand, spoke of ethics in personal terms: people were to be kinder to their families, fairer to their employees, more considerate of their servants. "We have sentiment enough today; so brethren, let us run on the ethical awhile, let us run on the moral awhile, let us tell the truth, pay our debts, be good husbands and good wives."[56]

While northern Social Gospelers inveighed against industrialism, Sam Jones and other southerners pined for investment and industry, and dismissed the idea of dismantling capitalism to save its casualties as being as foolish as abandoning the railroad to save a few cows. The rise of monopolies that liberals found so alarming represented progress to Jones, who pointed out that before Standard Oil fuel cost four times as much. Monopolies "hurt a few," Jones concluded, "but they benefit the masses." Suspicious of the expansion of government, Jones opposed antitrust acts, sure that companies that fail to serve the public "will fall with their own greed."[57]

His fear of government growth led Jones to oppose another idea advocated by many Social Gospelers: federal control of the railroads. The railroads were "magnificently merged," Jones gushed; trusts led to better prices and better service. Who would not rather go "a mile a minute" than ride on the independent railroad that traveled so slowly farmers were likely "to sue for shading their crops"? So effusive and constant was Jones's praise of the railroads that he was frequently forced to deny that he was influenced by the free passes railroads provided him as a minister and a columnist.[58]

Jones also opposed another reform favored by progressives: free public education. "When a father can't feed and clothe and educate his own kids, the best thing he can do for his country is to get out of the 'kid' business." It was as absurd to have free schools as it would be to have "free restaurants or free clothes." In its efforts to provide for people what they should get for themselves, the government was extorting money, taking so much—nearly 2 percent of property value in Georgia—that it seemed "the state has gone into the robbery business." Soon the country will be a "nation of paupers and pap-suckers," Jones predicted, with the lazy living off the efforts of the industrious. Nor did Jones support the idea that wealth be equalized by the progressive income tax, a measure not passed until 1913. Such notions were pure socialism, Jones scoffed, dreamed up by those who "spend their money on whiskey" and "are now calling upon you to divide." The bottom line was this: "People who work should not be left to the mercies of those who don't."[59]

Sam Jones did not like taxation even with representation, and his tight-fistedness led him to support something progressives condemned in a chorus: convict labor. The Tennessee Coal, Iron, and Railroad Company leased thirteen hundred convicts from the state, and when Sam Jones hit Nashville in 1885 the controversy had reached a boiling point. Though the legislature had found the labor camps "hell holes of rage, cruelty, despair and vice," Sam Jones's investigation revealed that "the most happy laborers in Tennessee were those who had on striped clothes." Managers were equally satisfied; as one explained, "free labor is always complaining about the work they have to do, but convicts do not care but for one thing—

that they get plenty to eat, plenty to wear, and the quarter for every extra ton of coal they dig out and they are the happiest lot out." Convict labor, Jones concluded, served the taxpayer by saving money, served the employer by providing dependable labor, and served the prisoner by giving him useful employment. Laborers, who rightly suspected that the convict lease system was being used to forestall unionization, were appalled by the evangelist's glib assessment, one writing that Jones had become "a toady of the rich and aristocratic element."[60]

Obviously, Sam Jones was not a Social Gospeler. He was that far more common creature of his day: a Social Darwinist. It is one of the ironies of the age that evangelicals who denounced Darwin embraced Social Darwinism as fashioned by Herbert Spencer and popularized by the former Episcopalian minister William Graham Sumner. A harsh moralism that derided government assistance and institutional charity as an "artificial" device to preserve the unfit, Social Darwinism extolled the benefits of laissez-faire. Sam Jones helped popularize this brutal doctrine, translating a famous Sumner expression into country southern. "If a hog don't root, let him die. Them's my sentiments."[61]

Like those today who claim that poverty is a result more of moral failure than of unjust conditions, that public assistance merely finances drunkenness and drug use and underwrites illegitimacy, Jones warned against subsidizing the "unworthy poor." Charity was for assistance, not maintenance, Jones instructed his audiences; if unwisely applied it sapped the moral and physical fiber of the poor and weakened the economic strength of the middle class. "I have long since contended that promiscuous charity means professional tramps," Jones said, voicing the popular view. "Where our charity is promiscuous, the undeserving live fat, and the deserving starve." Such sentiments made him wary of institutional churches that offered training and recreation to the urban poor. "I have heard reform until I am tired of it," Jones said near the end of his life. "Man's remedy for sin is Jesus Christ in the heart."[62]

Sam Jones looked for reform one conversion at a time. "There is but one way I know of to light up this city by night and that is for each lighter to go along the streets and turn on the gas of one lamp at a time and light it; and bye and bye light jumps to light and ray meets ray until the whole city is flooded with light." Just so, "if we get the regeneration of the individual then we get the necessary reformation of the masses." Revival was the answer, not revolt. Through this view Sam Jones linked himself with his evangelical ancestors, those who expected temperance and abolition and education to follow in the wake of spiritual upheavals, and whose expectations were frequently rewarded. He also linked himself to his evangelical offspring, those who would support Jimmy Carter and Ronald Reagan and Pat Robertson, weaving their way through political parties to catch the thread of righteousness, to add to the tapestry of American life.[63]

Be Ye Therefore Holy

And they were all filled with the

Holy Spirit and spoke the word of God boldly.

—Acts 4:31

May God defend me from my friends.

From my enemies I can defend myself.

—Motto of the House of Visconti

7

❧ Be Ye Therefore Holy

One of the reasons that Methodists did not get entangled in the doctrinal battles that beset the Presbyterians and the Baptists at the end of the nineteenth century was that Methodism was proudly indifferent to creed. "The distinguishing marks of a Methodist are not his opinions of any sort," its founder, John Wesley, had declared. For Sam Jones, this freedom from orthodoxy had allowed individuality to flourish. "If I had to quit the Methodist Church to talk like I'm talking now I would be ready to walk out," he told Nashvillians after a particularly eccentric invective. "But the

Methodist Church has enough India-rubber about it to let me say what I want and still stay in it."[1]

Sam Jones was wrong. Seven years after that exclamation of independence, the Methodist church had splintered into angry factions, and Jones had been forced out of the regular ministry. Although the Methodists did not fight over the five fundamentals or squabble about scriptural inerrancy, their battle against modernism was just as fratricidal. Theirs was the fight over holiness.

Holiness was the watchword of early Methodism. "All our preachers should make a point of preaching perfection to believers constantly, strongly, and explicitly," Wesley had commanded, "and all believers should mind this one thing, and continuously anguish after it." Wesley stressed that no mortal could be free from mistakes, sickness, temptation, or "involuntary transgression"; yet it was possible for believers to be so completely "renewed in the image of God" that their hearts would reflect "the full likeness of Him that created it." Wesley explained: "The perfection I teach is perfect love," love for God and love for man.[2]

Wesley's command to "spread scriptural holiness throughout the land" propelled the Methodists across the ocean and inspired circuit riders to push the frontier, but the doctrine was not a monopoly of the Methodist church. In 1839 two Congregationalists, Charles Grandison Finney and Asa Mahan, began promoting perfectionism at Oberlin College in Ohio, and in 1858 a Presbyterian named William E. Boardman published one of the movement's best-sellers, *The Higher Christian Life*. In the New York City parlor of a Methodist named Phoebe Palmer, Episcopalians, Quakers, messianic Jews, and Methodist bishops struggled together to obtain "the blessing of holiness." In an era when northerners were in aggressive pursuit of the millennium, perfectionism answered both the optimism of the age and its insistence upon a practical piety that reformed the drunkard, educated the ignorant, and freed the slave.[3]

Though the holiness movement helped ignite the famous layman's revival of 1858–59, it was soon submerged in the need to wage total war. Indeed, in the first few years after Appomattox, it seemed the movement had foundered, overcome by the moral exhaustion that followed the war and a "sophistication" that holiness advocates found lamentable. Determined not to let the movement die, a group of ministers met in Philadelphia and organized themselves into the National Camp-Meeting Association for the Promotion of Holiness. Though there was a strong interdenominational impetus, the thirteen original organizers were Methodist ministers from New

York, and one of the organization's stated purposes was to "initiate a new era in Methodism."[4]

Many factors contributed to the revival of interest in holiness in the last quarter of the nineteenth century. Perfectionist movements occur in times of social and economic dislocation. Plagues, wars, waves of immigration, and periods of moral decline make holiness seem a necessary corrective. For Methodists, unsettling changes in society were mirrored by distressing changes in the church. Even before the Civil War, the plain speech and plain dress of Wesleyan Methodism were being replaced by elaborate sermons by "please-the-people preachers" who, like their choirs, were robed in "heathen" splendor. The church became even more sophisticated after the war, fed by fabulous wealth in the North and spectacular church growth in the South. Those loyal to primitive Methodism were convinced that the church had been devastated by success.[5]

There were those who rejoiced in Methodism's rising social stature. The Reverend Follansbee of the Baltimore Conference remembered revivals in which he had "toiled all day and caught nothing" because the converts went to the Presbyterians, who could promise them salvation *and* social standing. When the Baltimore Methodists got rid of their drafty "old barns" and built new churches with "stately towers and spires," business boomed. However, it was expensive to replace wooden churches with Greek temples and costly to "praise God by proxy" with "quartets, choirs, and musical machines." There was widespread concern that churches were accepting "indulgence money" to wink at the transgressions of the mighty. In 1893 the Reverend E. E. Hoss, editor of the *Nashville Christian Advocate*, made the sensational accusation that Methodism had sold itself to the highest bidder. "Good men are rejoiced that a sinner has repented, the angels are thrilled to rapture that a soul is newborn to heaven, [and] a first-class Methodist Church joins in the harmony moved by the fact that its bank account will be increased," Hoss charged angrily.[6]

As the gap widened between "high-steeple" city churches and the "hard-scrabble" rural circuits and urban missions, many old-fashioned Methodists felt estranged. The Reverend Joseph A. Reynolds blamed refinement for the scene he observed with disgust at the North Georgia Conference in 1886: "The subduement during the devotional exercises could not have shocked the most orderly Episcopalian. It is a great pity that our increase of culture, laxity, or both . . . trenches upon our hearts and subdues our old honest amens." Reynolds added with a wicked flourish, "Maybe the elaborate finish of the Church buildings dazed them."[7]

Others blamed the decline in enthusiasm on education. When the clamor for formal theological training had started in the southern church in the early 1870s, Bishop Lovick Pierce had stood against it, convinced it would end the itinerancy and enfeeble evangelicalism. Now the bishop looked around the southern connection and saw "nothing is left in many places but a petrified respectability." A man who would soon be bishop himself, O. P. Fitzgerald, unhappily concurred with this assessment. "Many of our preachers need the class meeting to thaw them out," he wrote in 1884, "to bring them down from metaphysical abstractions in their preaching to the actual wants of living souls—in a word, to make them spiritual leaders instead of moral essayists and theorizers."[8]

The loss of the old institutions—the camp meeting, the mourner's bench, the class meeting, the probationary period for prospective members—left traditionalists feeling that the church of their fathers had changed beyond recognition. The substitutes seemed tepid by comparison: the after-meeting to which "seekers" were discreetly conducted; the Sunday school, with its emphasis on education instead of conversion; and the Chautauquas, which tended to "mix Christianity and sea-bathing a little too confusedly." The conviction that thousands of the unconverted were crowding into a church that was abolishing the means of conversion was expressed repeatedly in denominational papers. When the southern church announced its aim of a million members by the hundredth anniversary of Methodism in America, many agreed with the Reverend T. W. Lewis of Lexington, Mississippi, who suggested that the occasion be commemorated by casting out the one-third of its members who neither enjoyed the benefits nor displayed the fruits of religion. If pared down to the fighting few, Lewis wrote, the church "might start out upon another march of a hundred years better equipped for active service."[9]

Another source of anguish for conservatives was the church's unwillingness to enforce sanctions against the buying and selling of liquor, card playing, Sabbath desecration, gambling, dancing, and attendance at circuses and the theater. While the liberal faction contended that such statutes were unenforceable, conservatives argued that just as the state does not rescind the law against murder because it is ignored by killers, the church should not abolish its laws because sinners break them. The solutions, conservatives insisted, was not repeal but aggressive enforcement through preaching, counseling, church trials, and expulsion of "unworthy members."[10]

Invections against worldliness were delivered more shrilly but were less heeded. In 1887 Warren Akin Candler, then minister of McKendree Methodist Church in Nashville, was hailed as a hero when he denounced the theater. Six years later, Candler's successor, S. A. Steel, rebuked a steward for dancing. His salary was cut by 25 percent and he was told "to preach nothing but 'the love of God.'" A typical jeremiad ran: "In the nineteenth century we have laid down in the lap of worldliness and had our locks trimmed, and now . . . we raise our sightless eyes to Heaven, amid the hisses and jeers, and pray for the strength to raise the foundation pillars of darkness and throw down the tower of sin."[11]

A significant minority of Methodists believed discipline could be restored and the spiritual decline could be reversed by a renewed commitment to holiness—"the Holy Ghost can burn out what the Discipline can't turn out." Though the connection between holiness and the antislavery movement made southerners hostile to the movement before the war, conditions in the South were ripe for a holiness revival. It began in 1872 when John Inskip, president of the National Camp-Meeting Association for the Promotion of Holiness, conducted the region's first holiness camp meeting. Six years later, A. J. Jarrell, pastor of the St. James Methodist Church in Augusta, Georgia, "accepted sanctification" during one of Inskip's meetings in Ocean Grove, New Jersey, and invited Inskip to conduct a revival in his church in Augusta the following year. During that meeting Inskip spoke to crowds so thick that people stood in the aisles. Nine months later, Inskip returned to St. James for a longer campaign and went on to Trinity Methodist Church in Savannah for a ten-day revival. By the beginning of 1881, a cell of sanctificationists was meeting in Savannah, and three hundred were gathering every Monday night in Augusta. The holiness movement had begun in Georgia and the South.[12]

The movement quickly spread to Macon and Milledgeville, where Georgia's first holiness newspaper, the *Way of Life*, began publication in 1882. In an effort to "localize the contagion," most holiness preachers were assigned to the Gainesville District. Jarrell seized the opportunity to introduce holiness to north Georgia and invited the evangelist George Watson of Boston to assist him in a three-day revival. During this campaign two events electrified public opinion. The presiding elder, W. A. Parks, a man in the fiftieth year of his itinerancy, claimed the second blessing, and Mrs. John D. Wimpy, an invalid for twenty-two years, felt herself healed while alone in bed. She got up, walked to church, and testified to her sanctification. "An apparition from the dead would not have produced a more profound impression," the holiness brethren declared. Soon sanctification was "sweeping through the District like an evangel of love."[13]

In August 1882 the Georgia Holiness Association was founded in Gainesville. Insisting that "the Methodist Church is all the organization they want," the group resolved to promote holiness "as taught in the Bible, the Discipline, Hymn book, and standard authorities of the Methodist Episcopal Church, South." They claimed that sanctification had given them "a fountain of happiness, strength to live right, and of power to win souls to Christ which we did not have in our former, simply justified or converted state." They begged Methodists to "cooperate with us in our effort to bring the Church up to this high ground of Christian experience and life." The document was signed by sixty lay people and fourteen ministers, among them one "S. P. Jones."[14]

It is not surprising that Sam Jones felt a kinship with holiness brethren. He, too, fretted that the church was taking off "after strange gods" and forsaking "the New Testament Savior." Rising church membership failed to cheer him, for he believed that there was never "a time when the Ten Commandments and the Sermon on the Mount were so little thought of" or had so little to do "with the ruling of the nation." He agreed that the decay of public morality was mirrored by a decline in church standards. "If the Methodists of Nashville were to violate the laws of Tennessee as they violate their discipline, they would be in the penitentiary in a month," he declared. Also, he was attracted to the unabashed enthusiasm of the sanctificationists. "The holiness people will holler 'Hallelujah' if you drop a ten pound weight on their toes," Jones declared. "I like the holiness people because they are alive."[15]

By signing the organizational statement of the Georgia Holiness Association, Jones did not only express sympathy for the movement. He claimed to have experienced sanctification. It is difficult to discover when he obtained the "second blessing." He does say that John 3:9—"Whosoever is born of God doth not commit sin"—gave him "pain and trouble" for the first seven or eight years after his conversion before it became "the sweetest Bread heaven ever gave to me." In 1886 he told a Baltimore audience: "I overhauled my religious life four years ago and found that I had quit every sin I wanted to quit, and those I didn't want to quit I was still a-running." Inspired by the preaching of Bishop Joseph Key at the Georgia Holiness Association meeting in 1887, Jones stood up and testified. "Brethren, I know what you are thinking about—there was a time in my life, when I laid all on God's altar and reached a point where for months my soul bathed in a sea of glory."[16]

It was not until 1897, as the holiness revival was receding in schism, that Jones gave a "clear testimony" of his experience to a Nashville audience. If "Brother P——" is his friend W. A. Parks, this testimonial suggests Jones's experience occurred in 1882, when the holiness revival swept the district of Gainesville. "Never shall I forget an association with a holiness preacher down in a Georgia town a few years ago," Jones reminisced.

That brother had preached this great blessing with all the earnestness and power of his soul. The tidal wave of salvation was sweeping over the people. He was urging a full and uncompromising consecration of all to God, and that accompanying supreme act of faith which procures the downpour of the Spirit in all His fullness.

We were walking alone after one of the services had closed, and turning to me, he said, "Sam, why in the world, brother, don't you turn loose of everything that lies between you and God's fullness and lay hold on this great blessing?" I said, "Brother P——, everything that stands between me and my God and the uttermost which he can do for me is not worth a nickel. . . ." Brother P—— said, "Then, you are just within one nickel of the blessing." I replied, "Well, a nickel shan't split such an important matter."

When I got back to the church at the next service the meeting had commenced, and this brother was praying as I entered the church and sat down; and he truly had hold of the horns of the altar. Such praying I never heard since I was born in this world. The very windows of heaven seemed open. I felt the very presence of my God. Heaven and earth came together. It was a time of soul-searching, heart-emptying, heart-surrendering, and heart-filling. At that meeting, in that solemn and never-to-be forgotten hour, I turned loose the willows that overhang the banks and swept out onto the very midst of the ocean of God's infinite love, and the joy of that moment lingers sweetly and ineffaceably today. Its memory and power have swept over the lapse of years, and it has been my solace in a thousand sorrows, my strength in a thousand struggles, my star of hope through a thousand nights, and like a sheen of glory will canopy with its light and peace and triumph in my dying hour. Thank God, there is water enough in the River of Life to cleanse every heart from all sin.[17]

For the rest of his life, Sam Jones contended that "the doctrine of sanctification is as clearly taught in the Word of God as the doctrine of justification." However, few obtain this sacred grace because few expect it. "Some of you worldly gang in the Church are whining, 'I just can't live without sin; I am just a poor worm of the dust, and poor human nature is so frail that I just can't live without sin,'" Jones scoffed. "Well, now, just tell me, what sin is it that you are compelled to commit every day? Just sit down and write it out on a piece of paper and look at it, and see which of the commandments you have to break every day of your life. What a libel on the Savior!"[18]

Jones recognized that many Christians scoffed at the idea of perfection. "You cannot raise a bigger, higher, deeper howl in the churches of God in this country, than to preach about sanctification, than to say that a man can be a sanctified man throughout soul and body and spirit, and made to walk arm-in-arm with God everyday," Jones said in 1886. "People will say: 'That man is running off like wild-fire, now he has got off on a tangent, and the first thing you know he will be in an asylum.'" But why was the idea so surprising? "If I should say an honest man can't steal, if I should say a truthful man can't lie, or that a chaste man cannot indulge in filthy conversation, you would all say, 'That is so.' Why should you think it strange, then, when John says, 'A son of God cannot sin?'"[19]

"Did you ever watch a woman paring apples for preserving?" Jones would ask. "She cuts out the little spots and blemishes." This is what sanctification does for the believer. "The difference between regeneration and sanctification is that the first is being saved from big sins, and the other is being saved from the little ones, too," Jones explained. "Regeneration cleans out the heart, but it leaves little sins like prejudice and pride still there, and it's sanctification that cleans out even these little enemies inside the citadel of the human frame." Sanctification "puts the last enemy of man on the outside."[20]

This is not to say that the sanctified never sin. "It's a mighty poor Christian that can't say on one day, 'Thank God, I haven't sinned today, or if I have I don't know it.' But when a man stands up and says he hasn't sinned for five years, I know he either has a very low conception of God's law or a very high conception of himself. Who can measure up to God's standard?" The state of the sanctified reminded him of "the fellow that had one eye knocked out. His father kilt a cat and put the cat's eye in the place of the one knocked out. It fit in the place all right but when he went to sleep at night the cat eye kept open to look for rats. You'd better keep one eye on the devil," the evangelist advised, "for you seldom get such a twist on him that he won't come back."[21]

But though they slip, the sanctified do not fall far.

A man says to a merchant when he buys some goods: "I'll pay you that dollar at nine o'clock tomorrow." The merchant says, "I won't put it down in my book, because he'll pay and I'll just have to scratch it out again." So when a man whose intentions and desires are right begins to wobble,

God says to the recording angel, "Don't put that down. I'll show him his error. He'll repent and come out all right." I'll tell you, a man can get where God can bank on him, because his "seed remaineth in him." Like the sterile soil under those big trees in Georgia, which is shut out from the sun by the overlapping boughs, if you get the fruits of the spirit planted in your soil, the devil may sow the seeds, but the ground is preoccupied, and they will not sprout.[22]

Though today a Methodist can go from the cradle to the grave without hearing a sermon on sanctification, holiness was the enthusiasm of the eighties. By 1883 it was estimated that more than a thousand Georgians had professed sanctification. A branch of the Georgia Holiness Association was organized in Griffin, and the evangelist J. B. Culpepper wrote from south Georgia that "most of the Methodists in this circuit think it is possible to live without sin, and that they are not saved till they do. . . . Many of these people are after more of Christ in their soul, social life, business intercourse, and they are not disappointed in the search." With the support of Bishops George Pierce and Joseph Key and the allegiance of many of the clergy—240 ministers of the North Georgia Conference ultimately claimed a sanctification experience—it seemed that "the year of the Jubilee" had come. "We are on the old Wesleyan platform," W. A. Dodge, editor of the *Way of Life*, announced. "We hold the fort, and have got all the guns."[23]

However, the backlash against "the second blessing brethren" had begun. Over the next fifteen years official opposition would become so powerful that Jones and Culpepper would be forced out of the regular ministry, A. J. Jarrell would flee to St. Louis to escape "persecution," and many other holiness brethren would be punished for their announced lack of sins by appointments to "hard-scrabble" circuits. The turning of the tide began in the summer and fall of 1885, and it began with two situations that convinced many that the holiness movement was dangerous to Georgia Methodism.[24]

The first incident occurred during a holiness revival conducted by Dodge and Parks in Lawrenceville. After a particularly emotional service, the pastor of the local Methodist church, M. D. Turner, professed sanctification. Within a few days he sinned, then murdered himself by drinking strychnine. He left behind a note that read: "I have lost faith and hope for the world, and that which is to come."[25]

The *Atlanta Constitution* seized upon the Turner incident and began an investigation of the holiness movement. The paper found many Lawrenceville folk blamed the "wild ravings" of Dodge and Parks for Turner's suicide.

"The conduct of these people will bring about a schism in the Church," reported one Methodist. "They are bent upon rule or ruin, and if they cannot have their own way they will drive off large numbers of members." Another article described Dodge's techniques: fervent exhortation, harrowing warnings, emotional testimonials, and songs of sanctification sung "with a rotary motion" until the congregation was "drunk with joy." To its glee, the *Constitution* also uncovered the "faith cures" that accompanied holiness. Eight people in Lawrenceville had testified that a healing was the "witness" to their sanctification. Soon the paper was crowded with claims of miracles and the rebuttals of physicians. The controversy was further inflamed by the death of a missionary to Africa, Charles L. Miller, who had claimed holiness as his protection from disease.[26]

The other controversy that alienated moderate Methodists from the holiness brethren occurred in Augusta. Warren Akin Candler, pastor of St. John's Methodist, was concerned about the spiritual declension in his church and invited Sam Jones to conduct an eight-day campaign in April 1884. "If this old church is not revived this year I despair," he confided to the evangelist. It may be that during the campaign Jones persuaded Candler to reconsider his aversion to the holiness movement, for in October 1884 Candler invited Jarrell to conduct a revival at St. John's.[27]

Candler was thrilled with the results: 150 church members were converted and many others claimed sanctification. In the summer of 1885, Jones's old pastor, Clement Evans, established a holiness camp meeting near Augusta; it attracted four thousand seekers the first year. A year after the revival at St. John's, Augusta was again in the grip of holiness excitement, as twenty-five hundred people a day attended a tent revival conducted by George Watson.[28]

For someone who claimed perfection, George Watson was a very prickly person, and he and Warren Candler were soon at odds. Candler came to agree with Methodist officials that the holiness movement was unnecessarily clannish and would lead to "divisions and strife." Suspicion of the northern Methodists who headed the national organizations also was a factor. Candler speculated that northern Methodists might be encouraging dissidents to defect.[29]

Candler had theological differences with the movement as well. A man of searching faith and stringent integrity, Candler had concluded that because true conversion is an "entire surrender" to God that "cleanses entirely," the sanctificationists' belief that an "evil infection" remained in believers until they obtained a "second blessing" was in error. This declaration was treated as apostasy by George Watson, who sentenced Candler "to hell by obstinancy or to heaven by ignorance." Watson was further enraged by the transfer of holiness ministers to poor city missions and rural circuits. "In the days of the Spanish Inquisition, wandering priests sat up at night inventing ways to torture the saintly heretics," Watson wrote venomously. Now, "tobacco-chewing, if not wine-drinking ecclesiastics sit up in the bishop's cabinet, devising how most to afflict and fetter the most pious preachers in the conference."[30]

For many Methodists, the events of 1885 solidified opinion against the holiness movement. A rupture did not occur at this time only because of the mediating influence of Bishops George Pierce, Charles Galloway, and Joseph Key, and because moderates in the Georgia Holiness Association, led by Charles and A. J. Jarrell, acknowledged "the grievous blunder of touching in any way the Faith Healing question, and, of allowing ourselves to be drawn into [the] secular press." However, the controversy did not quiet. Opponents became more outspoken, branding holiness an extremist movement that flirted with scandal and produced schism.[31]

While Georgia Methodists were treated to the unedifying spectacle of their ministers hurling scriptures and quotations from John Wesley at each other, Sam Jones was becoming famous. The Nashville revival that made him the best-known southern evangelist of his day occurred in April 1885. As Jones's closest friends in the conference were defending the doctrine of holiness, Sam Jones was suddenly lifted out of his parochial boundaries and placed on a national platform. Why did Jones not use his new prominence to promote the holiness revival? Though he would continue to hold "consecration services" for those seeking sanctification, his name does not appear on the roster of any holiness association after 1882. Why?

One answer is temperament. Sam Jones was a "one in a hill" kind of fellow, and as the holiness revival became institutionalized, it became less appealing to him. Another reason was that Jones was "fishin'" for sinners, not for saints. "Tain't no use bringing some old backslider up to the altar and putting holiness in him," he explained. "He's got no foundation for it. No use giving him a second story if he ain't got a first story." Also, Jones realized that an association with the holiness movement would hamper his effectiveness as a revivalist. Though the movement in Georgia was led by respected ministers and educated laypeople, in the West it was run by radicals characterized as "cranks and fanatics."[32]

Another factor was Jones's aversion to extremism. He was especially opposed to the "holiness or hell" faction who contended that there was no salvation without sanctification. "Sanctification is to regeneration just as dessert is to a big old-fashioned country dinner," Jones said: a nice treat, a glorious finish, but not necessary. Besides, if heaven were populated only with the sanctified, it would be settled pretty sparsely. In 1892 Jones estimated that he had shaken hands with ten thousand preachers in the United States and Canada. Though he had met "many good people," only about a hundred were "thoroughly consecrated men." Out of the million church members he had met, only about five hundred were thoroughly consecrated.[33]

Many Methodists worried that the holiness brethren were "rather advanced on the women's rights question," and they were scandalized by the spectacle of women praying—even preaching—at holiness meetings. The sight did not disturb Sam Jones. Nor was he overly disturbed by the claims of faith healings. Unlike the Christians who believed that healings had stopped with the death of the apostles, Jones openly attributed the recovery of his wife in 1887 to divine intervention. His daughter Mary was so ill with blood poisoning in 1900 that newspapers reported her dead. Jones was convinced that her recovery was the result of prayer. However, he objected to the "holiness is health" equation held by a minority in the movement. "Some of the greatest Christians I have seen were terribly sick or afflicted," he insisted. "It is the mangled, bruised violet that gives out the sweetest odor."[34]

Many Methodists were offended by zealots who seemed to "arrogate to themselves more grace than is graceful," or who manifested a pharasaical spirit that made them "as touchy as a half-skinned eel." Jones, too, was dismayed by the irritability of the saints. "There are a lot of these holiness folks who must have been preserved in vinegar, they are so sour," he concluded. Jones suspected that many holiness folks had at least one sin: pride. "I knew a man in my congregation who wouldn't sing the last verse of 'Jesus Lover of My Soul' because it said 'Vile and full of sin I am,' and he said he had no sin in him," Jones confided. "That man deserted his wife and ran off with his cook, but he's learned to sing, 'Vile and full of sin I am.'"[35]

As the holiness movement solidified, it relied more on a formula experience called the "second blessing." The process involved a crisis experience, followed by a "second birth" or sanctification. To those who pointed out that neither Jesus nor John Wesley had used that term, it seemed that the holiness brethren "would reduce qualification for entrance into the Kingdom of Christ to being able to remember and pronounce a password." The most aggressive intellects in the southern connection, E. E. Hoss and

Atticus Haygood, combined to denounce a dogmatism they believed over-ruled Scripture for what Hoss characterized as an "ill-assorted compound of impossible psychology, absurd exegesis, and misread experience."[36]

While others wrangled over whether holiness was an "interminable pro-cess" of "growth in grace" or an "instantaneous cleansing," Sam Jones tried to strike a middle ground. Sanctification was both gradual, preceded by a long period of growth and struggle, and instantaneous, culminating in a moment. "I never saw an old backslidden Methodist secure sanctification at the altar in five minutes," he contended. Sanctification cannot occur until a man "has reached the springboard where he leaps out onto God's grace." And yet, "you don't want to 'develop' into sanctification; you want to be cleansed. I don't want my washerwoman to develop my dirty clothes; I want her to cleanse them. There's a good many of you that's developed too much already now: you want to be cleansed." Above all, Jones urged Methodists to avoid being entangled in semantics. "Never mind so much about the 'first blessing' or the 'second blessing,' " Jones advised. "If it takes a hundred 'blessings' before you're saved, get 'em all."[37]

For a while in the mid-eighties, it appeared that the appeals of moder-ates like Sam Jones and A. J. Jarrell would keep holiness enthusiasts in the fold. Most were devoted to Methodism—many of them had been reared in its parsonages. Again and again, they tried to convince fellow Methodists that they were simply preaching the doctrine of John Wesley. "The only second blessing we preach is that taught in the 'Discipline,' " Jarrell wrote in one of his many efforts at mediation. "When we go out of the grand old Methodist Church it will be feet-foremost."[38]

Jarrell did go out of the church feet foremost. He died in Cartersville in September 1896. Alienated from the church that had first moved him to the South Georgia Conference and then sent him to minister to a St. Louis con-gregation that was "poverty-ridden" and actively hostile to the doctrine of holiness, Jarrell had requested retirement and returned to Georgia. He told his wife the move had "broken his heart." He died shortly after of "softening of the brain and paralysis" at the age of fifty-six. Embittered and grieving, his widow wrote to George Jarrell that local Methodists had given only ten dollars to help with funeral expenses. There was nothing else from "the people he had served so faithfully and long."[39]

By the time Jarrell died, Methodism was dividing in the North and in the South. The holiness revival birthed dozens of new denominations and was midwife to the pentecostal movement of the twentieth century. In the eleven years between Jarrell's plea for unity and his death in disillusionment, it became clear that the enthusiasm that fueled the holiness movement would not result in a Wesleyan revival but would create more new denominations than had ever been founded in so short a time.[40]

There are a number of reasons why revival resulted in schism. One is the revulsion of moderate Methodists at what they saw as the excesses of the movement: faith healing, women evangelists, an emphasis on the role of the Holy Spirit at the expense of the other members of the Trinity, an emotionalism many found unsavory and suspect, and a piety that regarded all who were unsanctified as "beyond question lost." The noise of controversy silenced some who might have added reason to the debate. William Green, pastor of McKendree Church in Nashville, wrote to the *Advocate:* "As the discussion presents itself at this time, I am reminded of an old deadbeat who was lifted on a goods-box to make a speech during the Know-Nothing excitement. He looked around at the crowd in a dazed sort of way and drawled: 'Gentlemen of the jury, I would be happy and willing to make a speech, but in the general confusion and concatenation of things, I cannot discover which side I am on.' "[41]

For their part, the holiness brethren felt alienated from a church that appeared to be forsaking its own tenets and traditions. Though Jarrell had promised that "the church will never 'split off and leave us,' " by the end of the century it seemed that this calamity had occurred. Sanctificationists felt that they were faced with the choice of staying to defend Methodism against Methodists, or using their periodicals, associations, and colleges to form their own denomination. "The serious question arises: Shall we go further?" H. C. Morrison, a holiness editor and evangelist, asked. "Shall we build up the spiritual life of this and that congregation and community, to have it torn down by some higher critic, who has no well defined faith or deep conviction about anything, only that he has a contempt for the doctrine and experience of sanctification? Shall we pour our money into the hands of ecclesiastics who will use it to defeat the great revival for which we work and pray?"[42]

Morrison's questions hint at the final issue that splintered the church: ecclesiastical control. By 1890 the conditions for schism existed. There was a growing chasm between Methodists rising in social stature and those who were poor and uneducated. There was disaffection between those who were complacent about society and those who railed against moral decay. And there was alienation between those who loved liturgy and ritual and those who longed for informality and the "amen corner" of old. Into this gap was wedged the question of the power of bishops, an issue that had spawned the Republican Methodists in 1792, the Reformed Methodists in 1814, and the Methodist Protestant church in 1830, and had contributed to the creation of the Wesleyan Methodist church in 1843. Though the South was traditionally deferential, even there dissidents looked upon the Methodist form of government as "autocratic, almost monarchical." In 1890 murmurings about ecclesiastical "tyranny" became a clamor when Bishop Robert Hargrove forced David C. Kelley out of the pastorate over the protest of the Tennessee Conference.[43]

David Campbell Kelley was one of the most fascinating men in a conference rich in fascinating men. Though he entered the ministry at nineteen, he was awarded a medical degree one year later. He combined his thirst for souls and concern for bodies as a missionary to China. He was an abolitionist but joined the Confederate army after secession and rose to become second in command to the flamboyant cavalry commander Nathan Bedford Forrest. Colonel Kelley, a British observer wrote, was "as brave a man as ever smelled gunpowder." After the war, he returned to the ministry and married his cousin Mary Campbell, daughter of Governor William B. Campbell of Tennessee. This connection sparked Kelley's interest in politics as a way to promote prohibition. In June of 1890, while a minister in Gallatin, Tennessee, Kelley accepted the nomination as the Prohibition party's candidate for governor. His presiding elder, B. F. Haynes, and his bishop, John C. Keener, opposed his decision, believing that Kelley could not serve both God and Caesar. Though Kelley surrendered his salary to pay a substitute while he stumped the state, he was firm in his insistence that political activism was an extension of his ministry.[44]

Because Methodist bishops, like preachers, were itinerant, it was not Keener but Robert Hargrove who presided over the Tennessee Conference held in October 1890. "A compact man bodily and mentally," Hargrove "moved upon straight lines," a cautiously worded obituary noted upon his death in 1905. "He was not a reed shaken by the wind, nor a man clothed in soft raiment." By the fall of 1890, Bishop Hargrove was convinced that Kelley was a partisan "seeking to stab the Church and bring ruin upon it." He confided to his old friend B. F. Haynes that he intended to force Kelley to "locate or leave," that is, to sever his bonds with the pastorate in part or entirely. As Kelley's supervisor, Haynes was shocked and insisted that if the bishop believed Kelley had "deserted his post," the man must be tried for immorality. That is how the character of the upright D. C. Kelley came to be impeached on the floor of the Tennessee Conference.[45]

The proceedings that followed were illegal according to Methodist polity. Kelley had not been given formal notice that his character would be impeached and was not allowed to speak in his own defense, both violations of the *Discipline*. Though 116 ministers voted for "non-concurrence" with the motion to impeach Kelley's character, Bishop Hargrove appointed a committee of investigation drawn almost exclusively from the 25 men who had voted against Kelley. Not surprisingly, this committee recommended a trial. Over the written protest of 87 members of the conference, Kelley was tried before the 25 who had voted against him and was suspended from the conference for a period of six months. An infuriated B. F. Haynes charged Hargrove with falsehood, "improper motives in making appointments," and a host of illegalities, but the college of bishops upheld Hargrove's decision. Haynes appealed this decision to general conference, and Kelley added a doctorate of law to his doctorate of ministry and medicine in order to conduct his own defense. In 1904 Hargrove's ruling was reversed, and the seventy-one-year-old Kelley was vindicated.[46]

Though Hargrove's arrogation of power was ultimately overruled, it was part of an extension of the episcopacy that had begun even before the secession of the southern church in 1844. Reacting to the holiness movement, political prohibition, and professional evangelists, in the last decade of the century some of the best minds in the Methodist Episcopal Church, South, argued for expanded ecclesiastical control. E. E. Hoss, editor of the *Nashville Christian Advocate*, and J. M. Tigert, editor of the *Methodist Review*, used their papers to fight those they believed would cripple the bishopric, reduce the church to a holiness association, and "leave the fountains of living water to dabble in the foul pools of party politics."[47]

In opposition to this "high prerogative" party was the "low church" group, whose opinions were advanced in smaller conference journals like the *St. Louis Christian Advocate*, the *Texas Christian Advocate*, and the *Tennessee Methodist*, the new manifesto edited by B. F. Haynes. "Low churchers" tended to be sympathetic to the holiness movement and advocate legal prohibition over moral suasion. They were apt to favor strict enforcement of the *Discipline* and a return to the "old-fashioned" Methodism of the class meeting, the camp meeting, and the revival. Because they were a minority and vulnerable to persecution, "low churchers" advocated making bishops more accountable to the clergy. One suggestion made by a faction styling themselves the "termites" was that bishops be elected for a specified term, after which they would be reelected if their performance was satisfactory to the preachers. "Democracy" was the rallying cry of these reformers; down with "secret trials" and the "divine right" of bishops! As one Kentucky preacher put it, "Methodism needs to be Americanized."[48]

It is not surprising that the obstreperously independent Sam Jones would be drawn into this battle against authority. "My mother and father and all my relatives were Methodists," he told an Indiana audience in 1886. "I was born one, just like I was born Jones," but "when the Methodist Church or polity says I can't go where I please, and with whom I please, to save souls to Christ, I'll say, 'Down with your issue, I don't want nothing to do with you.' If I belonged to any church, and it would try to keep me from doing good, I'd cut loose from it in a minute." And cut loose he did in 1893, when he was forced by Bishop Atticus Haygood to choose between taking a church and continuing as a roving revivalist.[49]

Jones's treatment at the hands of a church he had served for twenty-one years was partly the consequence of his own abrasiveness. But it was also the result of conflicts between the episcopacy and the "second blessing" brethren. By the end of the eighties, the holiness revival had spawned more than two hundred evangelists, many of them radical in their interpretation of sanctification, healing, and the role of women. The *New Orleans Christian Advocate* was not alone in associating the "new evangelists" with heretical teaching and in speaking out against the "wild, irresponsible, self-made system of evangelism now operating within the Church." Thus holiness and evangelism became, Jones's coworker George Stuart explained, "companion irritants classed together by the opponents and defenders of either."[50]

Though the possibility of regulating evangelism by creating an office of evangelist had been repeatedly raised and rejected, the church considered the issue again at the general conference in Richmond in 1886. The name of the newly famous Sam Jones was invoked by supporters and opponents. "If you pass this law, you will clip Jones' wings," J. B. McFerrin of the Tennessee Conference warned, "and he goes no more out of Georgia." Dr. A. R. Wingfield of Kansas conceded, "There is only one Sam Jones in the world, and there is not going to be another. You ought not to try to duplicate him. Boarding at a hotel for $5 per day and getting $100 a week is a grand institution." Another critic created a sensation by announcing that "as much as I honor Sam Jones, and would throw up my cap for him, yet I don't hesitate to say that Sam Jones is sailing under false colors. He was, by appointment of the Georgia Conference, an agent for an orphan's home."[51]

Sam Jones was conducting a revival in nearby Baltimore, preaching some of the strongest holiness sermons of his life. Aware of the rumblings about his unbounded itinerancy, he cannily refused to define himself: "If I am a revivalist, I've grown to be one just as the fingernails have grown on my fingers." He was careful to emphasize that he saw no conflict between "fishers" and "feeders" and careful to give credit to settled pastors. "What is an evangelist?" he asked his audience in Baltimore. "He's the extra hand you hire at harvest to work the cradle. It's very good to swing your cradle into another man's wheat, but to these brethren here" (turning to the ministers behind him on the platform) "credit is to be given. I reckon Jones and Small and Moody would have a time over in China, where no sowing has been going on." [52]

To make his case in person, he took the midnight train to Richmond to speak before the conference. He began by announcing his "spirit of submission." "I am willing to go back to Georgia and take any circuit the bishop may appoint me to, but while I am out I am going to give it to the old cities about right." He was relieved that the conference had "set down upon" the idea of employing evangelists. "The first thing you would be doing would be to hunt around for evangelists, and the second thing would be to try to get rid of those you thought were evangelists." He preferred the loose system of nominal appointments that allowed him to serve as agent of the Orphan Home and roam the country at will.[53]

Many Methodists were dismayed by the conference's failure to regularize revivalism and fretted that "lawless" evangelists were "running over the country" and "vilifying the churches and pastorate." The problem was particularly acute in California and the Southwest, where holiness evangelists were most schismatic. "Many lack discretion," the *Pacific Methodist* warned, "some lack experience, and others, apparently, lack religion." Loyal Methodists worried that through the "heterodoxy" of roving revivalists, "seeds of disaffection and discontent" are spread and "strange fires are kindled upon Methodist altars."[54]

Many Methodists fretted about the church's becoming enthralled by "peripatetic" evangelists. "A revival is within the reach of every congregation," the *Texas Advocate* insisted. "No Church need despair because it cannot secure the services of Sam Jones or other evangelists; you can get the Holy Ghost by asking." What churches usually asked for, however, was a clerical celebrity, and frequently communities went from one revivalist to another. The day after Jones closed a successful union revival in Knoxville in 1905, Protestant ministers voted to invite J. Wilbur Chapman, head of a Presbyterian network of revivalists, to continue the campaign. The apparent inability of Knoxville ministers to harvest the fruits of the Jones revival was common, and critics charged that such dependence on the "wandering stars" of evangelism enfeebled the regular ministry.[55]

Sensational preaching was another criticism of revivalists. Far too many evangelists bring to their sacred calling "the arts of the patent medicine vendor of the street-corner," a contributor to the *Homiletic Review* charged, and "grin and grimace to tickle the risibles of the gaping crowd." Simon Peter Richardson, a strong supporter of evangelists, also found the "clap-trap" preached to produce a collection repugnant. "What a burlesque to beat a tamborine, or blow a horn, or sing a sentimental ditty in the presence of a condemned man seeking at the throne of grace mercy and pardon." Others found offensive the gimmickry of revivalists like "Weeping Joe" Harding, who piled stones in front of his pulpit and invited those without sin to throw one. Such theatricality produced an "abnormal appetite for the sensational" and turned church members into "whining dyspeptics" unable to stomach "unadulterated gospel bread." [56]

Roving revivalists were also vulnerable to the charge that they went where the money was best instead of where the need was greatest. Theodore Flood, editor of the *Chautauquan*, noted that unlike the circuit riders of old, the modern itinerant evangelist "does not precede civilization, but follows it on the railway train—not to the frontier, but to the godly town or city." The income of some evangelists, garnered from "love-offerings" collected at the end of revivals, seemed inappropriate as well. "Covetousness is the most subtle of all temptations," E. E. Hoss warned. "The disciples of John Wesley should be careful to emulate his example. Imagine that great and holy man making a public boast that he was the best-paid preacher of his generation, or haggling and wrangling over the terms of a ten-day meeting in Bristol or London?" [57]

Staging evangelical extravaganzas drained resources. There is only "a given amount of money in any community for ministerial support," the Reverend J. V. Enochs warned in the *New Orleans Christian Advocate*. If "these popular evangelists" take it, "the tendencies are to weaken or, rather, cripple the pastorate." W. C. Dunlap, a holiness man himself, fretted that if ten thousand dollars was spent to build a tabernacle and bring Moody to Atlanta during the Cotton States and International Exposition, "we will be in no condition financially or otherwise, to do the work God has sent us to Atlanta to do." [58]

The paucity of conversions from the Moody meeting—"fewer than reported"—confirmed fears that the return did not equal the investment, even from Moody, "the best of the professional evangelists, full of faith and the Holy Ghost." The pattern of enormous expenditures, reports of an "entire city turning to God," and the reality of few accessions occurred again and again with professional evangelists. Reporting on the B. Fay Mills meeting in Kansas City, a "W.M.L." wrote that most of the 150 profession cards turned over to Methodist pastors came from "unfaithful members" who had felt a momentary tug toward reform. "It was the uniform testimony of those who attended the preacher's meeting, after the meeting had been in progress two weeks, and after the papers had reported hundreds of conversions at a single meeting, that if there had been any cases of spiritual regeneration they had not found it out."[59]

Too often revivalists conducted "an inquiry-card, raise-the-hand, church-made-easy" revival and reaped "shake-hand professors," those swept in by a moment of religious excitement and swept out again as soon as it ended. Others who crowded the altars were "grasshopper Christians" who were "on the jury during revival times, but hid away the rest of the year." Even when revivalists made conversion more than a show of hands or a stroll down the sawdust trail, they left follow-up to local ministers and lay leaders. "Most evangelistic efforts could be likened to the action of forest rangers who, finding a man lost in the woods, would turn him around in the direction of civilization, and then would go off looking for lost souls, trusting that the bewildered fellow could find his own way back home."[60]

While Sam Jones was often exempted from criticisms of itinerant evangelists, his imitators were not. Striving for "oddity" if not originality, the sermon of the imitator was "an off-hand, disconnected, shot-gun deliverance in which grimaces, bad grammar, and mixed metaphors constituted no inconsiderable part," complained "A Hearer" in the *Christian Advocate* in 1890. Nor were these mimics confined to the South. "If the rising generation of so-called evangelists do not stop aping Jones," a critic wrote in the *Michigan Christian Advocate*, "the Church may die off with nausea and disgust. . . . No one else can successfully fight the devil and win trophies with this man's war-clubs."[61]

However, it was impossible to restrict Jones's imitators and allow Jones to run loose without creating a special office for the man, something far too novel for the church to consider. By the late eighties Jones recognized that southern bishops were going to call independent evangelists in from the field. Thus he was not surprised in 1890 when George Stuart got a telegraph from Bishop John Keener ordering him to appear at the Holston Conference to receive an appointment as a minister to a church in Chattanooga. "George, are you going to take your hand off the throttle of the locomotive engine to roll a wheelbarrow?" Jones asked when Stuart read him the telegram. Stuart answered that he "must obey." He told Jones he would preach his last sermon as an independent evangelist that day.

However, after a meeting of such "great power" that two ministers on the platform embraced each other and shouted "Hallelujah!" Stuart was "struck dumb by the Holy Ghost." Interpreting this as a sign from God, Stuart told Jones back at the hotel: "Well, my brother, my life's work is settled. God has spoken; let man be silent. I shall tell the bishop my experience. I shall continue my work as an evangelist, but I must obey orders, be loyal to my

Church, and report to the Conference, as directed by the bishop." Moved by Stuart's testimony, John Keener did not pressure him further.[62]

The moves by Bishop Keener to restrict Stuart and by Bishop Hargrove to control Kelley made Jones uneasy about being under the control of the church. He began to consider becoming a "local preacher," a minister who is authorized to preach but who has no church or authority to administer the sacraments of communion or marriage. A week after Hargrove had Kelley's character impeached on the floor of the Tennessee Conference, Jones asked his old mentor, Simon Peter Richardson, to succeed him as agent of the Orphan Home so he could locate. Richardson dismissed Jones's fears that he was about to be "set down upon" by the bishops. "You are now beyond the reach of all your critics," Richardson insisted. "Continue, the Conference will make you an exception."[63]

Jones made no further attempts to locate. Nor did he try to appease the critics of itinerant evangelism. Instead, with characteristic recklessness, he attacked the "stale old" doctors of divinity who were "putting all the pressure they can on the Bishops" to stop revivalists. "Some talk of stopping the whole evangelist business," he scoffed, "but they must get in the forefront of the procession before they can stop it. I'm sure that the old pokey crowd I hear talking against evangelists can never catch up with us, much less get ahead." His tactlessness extended to the bishops. "Take the power of making appointments out of the Bishop's hands," Jones told an Indiana audience a few weeks after the Kelley-Hargrove incident, "and he could no more throttle a conference than he could successfully combat the business end of a mule."[64]

Theoretically, Methodist bishops had the authority to send any minister anywhere. In practice, their autocracy was informally hampered by the ability of individual churches to refuse support to preachers forced upon them. It was also restricted because bishops were required to consult with presiding elders, who formed the advisory council for "stationing the preachers." However, since bishops controlled the selection and appointment of the presiding elders, there was danger that through the skillful use of patronage and intimidation a bishop could develop a "truckling ministry" of "sycophants." Inclinations toward tyranny were held in check by making bishops itinerant, thus disrupting bossism before it became deeply rooted, and by making the bishops accountable every four years to the general conference, which reviewed the decisions of the bishops and reversed those in conflict with church law. Though bishops were elected for life, they could be impeached for "inefficiency" and "immorality." It was a formidable system of almost militaristic elegance. In the hands of a personality like Atticus Haygood, its power was irresistible.[65]

Jones recognized Atticus Haygood as a man "with heart and brains, and *will*" who "would, if he believed he were right, wreck a world to carry his point." Blessed with a vigorous body and an energetic mind, Haygood had served both as president of Emory University and as editor of the *Wesleyan Christian Advocate*. In 1880 he preached his famous sermon "The New South," in which he urged his section to overcome provincialism and feel "the heart beat of the world outside of us." One year later he ignited southern opinion with *Our Brother in Black: His Freedom and His Future*. While he found it regrettable that the freedman had been given the right to vote, Haygood insisted that black people were capable of being educated into worthy citizens—by northerners. After "The New South" Haygood had been hailed as a Moses. Now he was a "Yankee fanatic," the "Nigger College President."[66]

Though southern presses railed against him, one northerner, John F. Slater, was so struck by Haygood's courage that he asked him to administer the Slater Fund for the education of the freedman. In 1882 Haygood was elected bishop of the Methodist Episcopal Church, South—evidence that many preachers regarded him as a hero. He declined in order to continue his work in education. Two years later, he resigned from Emory to devote himself entirely to the Slater Fund, though he continued to influence appointments and worked to contain the "heretical" doctrines of the "holiness cranks." In 1890 Haygood became the only man to be elected bishop twice, this time by the largest margin ever.[67]

Haygood accepted. At the time of his elevation to the bishopric, Atticus Haygood was fifty-one, the "picture of health" with a body "unimpaired by dissipations." When the college of bishops appointed Haygood to the Pacific Conference, the *Rocky Mountain Methodist* predicted that the "severe wit" of this "pointed and brusque divine" would suit the western style. "He stands flat-footed and is always ready for a tilt," the editor noted approvingly. "He is in the thickest of the fight, and seldom hit." However, by the time Haygood came back to Georgia in 1893, he had lost thirty pounds and "tons of strength" after catching a "bone-break fever" in Mexico. In this debilitated and "abnormal condition" he presided over the North Georgia Conference.[68]

Haygood's opinion of Sam Jones had deteriorated since he had endorsed Jones to the ministers of Memphis in 1884. When William Leftwich asked the bishop to provide an introduction to Jones's book *Sermons and Sayings*,

Haygood demurred. "I do not feel prepared to do what you ask," Haygood replied. "I don't understand his genius." By 1893 Haygood's determination to rein in evangelists overrode whatever personal affection might have remained. He resolved to make Sam Jones a public example that no man was above Methodist law.[69]

Sam Jones arrived in Gainesville during the last day of the conference expecting a confrontation. He had been warned that Bishop Eugene Hendrix said that if he had presided over the North Georgia Conference of 1892 as he expected, "he would have forced Sam Jones to take a Pastorate, or locate." Jones's apprehensions were aggravated when he bumped into Dr. Wilbur F. Tillett of Vanderbilt University at the Union Depot in Atlanta ten days before the North Georgia Conference began. Tillett told Jones that "the bishops had decided in Nashville last May" how his "case should be disposed of." Jones heard also that Bishop Haygood would no longer appoint Sam Jones as fund-raiser and Howard Crumley as administrator of the Orphan Home. Jones instructed John B. Robbins, chairman of the board of the home, to request Crumley.[70]

When the conference recessed for lunch, Jones sought a private interview with Bishop Haygood. "Bishop, I think I know your heart; it is all right, and I want to know your mind touching me and my case," Jones said. In a "kindly way" Haygood replied: "I will appoint but one Agent to the Orphans' Home, and that Agent must confine himself within the boundary lines of the North Georgia Conference."

"Is there no appointment available to me by which I can hold my conference relations, and go on with my work?"

"None," Haygood answered.

"Bishop, under all the circumstances, if you were me which would you take, a pastorate or locate?" Jones asked.

"I would locate, Sam."

"Bishop, I locate," Jones answered.[71]

At the last session of the conference, Bishop Haygood asked, "Who are located this year?" Sam Jones stood. With a voice choked with emotion, Jones said his "feeling for the Conference and his love for his brothers made him ask for location." Haygood explained to the stricken assembly that "the law of the Church precludes nominal appointments." A resolution of "confidence and regret" passed unanimously. The issue appeared closed when Haygood wrote on the back of the location certificate: "The location of Sam P. Jones, at his own request after the passage of his character, had nothing to do with his personal or ministerial character, but with the law of the Church, which does not authorize the appointment of preachers to the work of general evangelism without reference to regular pastoral charge." [72]

Jones wrote a saddened but conciliatory article about his location for the *Atlanta Journal* on December 11. The event had sidetracked him momentarily, he admitted, "but I am out on the main line again," zipping along. "You have no idea how free a fellow feels when he feels like he owes allegiance to no power greater than himself under the shining stars, God as his king, Christ as his elder brother, the Holy Spirit as his comforter and friend, the Word of God the manifestation of his counsel, the praising millions around him helping him on in his work. With wings like these, a man can fly around the world." [73]

A month later, after conducting a revival in Nashville, Jones's tone turned angry. It may be that his friends there, B. F. Haynes, J. O. McClurkan, and William Leftwich, had convinced the evangelist he had been ill used by Haygood, who himself had served out of the pastorate for twenty years. It is possible that his loss had just penetrated, or that he had gotten a glimpse of how discredited he appeared to the outside world. He was especially angered by Robbins's charge that he could have been the sole agent of the home but chose voluntary location instead. "I did so as voluntarily as a man ever went to jail after the sheriff laid his hands upon him, no handcuffs were necessary," Jones scoffed. [74]

"Looking back over the field," Jones wrote bitterly,

if I was back again where I was at the moment I stood up and asked for my location at the hands of my Conference, I would say "Brethren! Under the decision on law by our presiding Bishop, I find in order to do my work I must locate and withdraw from your ranks. I am perfectly willing to do so if the Bishop presiding will make every man in the Conference who ought to do so, put on his hat and walk out with me. . . . such as Real Estate dealers, Carriage Manufacturers, Business Managers of church papers, Professors and Presidents of Colleges, not Methodist. . . . If our presiding Bishop will make all these fall in line, and follow me out, I will go willingly." [75]

Even then Jones seemed willing to retire quietly. When the *Texas Baptist Standard* praised Jones for opposing "this tyrannical and unscrupulous system," Jones refused to return the salute. "Be it understood once for all that I am a Methodist, [and] I take no part in furnishing clubs to others not Methodists to cudgel my Church." After exchanging public letters for two months, Jones announced he had laid down his pen. "I'm too busy in my work to be discussing this matter in the papers with every old mother in Israel who would provoke discussion." [76]

However, the General Conference of the Methodist Episcopal Church, South, held in Memphis in May 1894 shattered any hope of a peaceful settlement. To evangelists and to the holiness faction, the collective address of the bishops seemed to declare a "war of extermination." The bishops affirmed that sanctification was a doctrine that should "still be proclaimed," an experience that should "still be testified." But there had "sprung up among us a party with holiness as a watchword; they have holiness associations, holiness meetings, holiness preachers, holiness evangelists, and holiness property." Those merely possessing "the new birth" are disparaged, and terms like *sanctified* and *holy* are "improperly denied to the body of believers." While not questioning "the sincerity and zeal of these brethren," the bishops said, "we deplore their teaching and methods in so far as they claim a monopoly of the experience, practice, and advocacy of holiness, and separate themselves from the body of ministers and disciples." [77]

Every reproach against evangelists—that they visited "the centers of population where Christ is regularly preached," that they fostered discontent, friction, and superficiality, and that they tended to "disparage and weaken the regular ministry"—was presented by the bishops as fact. "We do not want an order of pastors to keep up a routine, and a higher, freer, and bolder order of prophets to bring down fire from heaven." The answer to the evils of worldliness and apathy, they insisted, was not "to transfer the work of soul-saving to a distinct office" but to encourage ministers to "stir up the gift that is within them, and make full proof of their ministry. The efficiency of the regular army is more important than any guerilla warfare, however militant." [78]

Responding to petitions asking for legislation controlling evangelists, the bishops concluded that the responsibility for religious services belonged entirely to the appointed preacher and suggested that the conference pass legislation putting all local preachers under the control of the minister in charge of the "circuit, station or mission to which they belong." The conference complied, and local preachers became local indeed: unable to leave the parish without the permission of the minister, unable to go into a district—even to preach in a private home or a public park—without the permission of the presiding elder. [79]

The bishops' address convinced a lot of people that there was no place for them in Methodism. Between 1893 and 1900 twenty-three holiness denominations were established, the largest of which, the Church of the Nazarene, would eventually be the denominational home for Jones's Nashville friends

B. F. Haynes and J. O. McClurkan. But while one-third to one-half of the four million American Methodists claimed sanctification, only one hundred thousand left the church. Moderates like J. B. Culpepper, forced to locate from the South Georgia Conference to continue as an itinerant evangelist, deplored "come-outism" as "religious anarchy." Others, like Sam Jones, thought Christianity was fractured into too many churches already. "I've got no patience with these people who are going out and organizing new churches; the 'go outers,' the 'come outers' and the 'kicked outers,'" he said in Kentucky, heart of the southern holiness movement, in 1899. The Methodist church was "sacred to him," Jones insisted. "I propose to set up with the sick man until he is either well or dead."[80]

After the general conference of 1894, Jones agreed to invest in and help edit the *Tennessee Methodist*. This was Haynes's vituperative journal, and it had faced bankruptcy since it declared against the "usurpation" of preachers' "rights" by "tyrannical bishops." Jones created a sensation with his article "A Wrong Interpretation of a Bad Law," in which he attacked the decision by John Sawyer, the presiding elder of the New Orleans District, to refuse Dr. Beverly Carradine permission to conduct a holiness revival in his district. "This new law, as interpreted by Presiding Elder Sawyer, virtually puts ten bishops in charge of the fifteen thousand church organizations within the bounds of the M. E. Church, South. A pastor in charge is no longer a pastor in church, but simply a yearling calf staked out in the back yard or tied to a peg, to be removed or put back at the will of the presiding elder."[81]

Now identified with the most radical of the dissidents, Jones became a clearinghouse for discontent. "Such unrest I have never known among the preachers, nor such an undercurrent of dissatisfaction," a minister from Newnan, Georgia, wrote after reading Jones's attack on "ecclesiasticism" in the *Tennessee Methodist*. "We are tired of the shameless prostitution of authority, of being 'bossed' by flunkies and imbeciles, and the thing must end." The church must "rectify or revolutionize," a minister from Tuscumbia, Alabama, wrote. "Has it actually come to pass that in order to be an itinerant Methodist preacher one has [to] sacrifice his manhood and independence, and surrender his freedom?" J. A. Thompson wrote from Thomasville, Georgia.[82]

The controversy took an ugly turn in August 1895. A Dr. William Stradley had received a letter from Bishop Haygood charging Jones with pretending "to kill a louse on his fingernail to show how easily he could crush the 'Hicky Bishop' if he wanted to." Stradley led the ministers of Augusta to withdraw their invitation to Jones to conduct a revival. Jones retaliated by denouncing Stradley as a drunkard. Though details are shrouded in innuendo, apparently it was this allegation that prompted Haygood to write his inflammatory article "Syndicate of Liars." A part of the syndicate "saw Z, a man of good character, stagger on the sidewalk, and support himself by catching at a garden fence," Haygood wrote angrily. "A told B that Z was drunk. Z, overcome by heat, had an attack of vertigo. But B told C—the town talker. Wounds were made, deep and incurable, and it was all a lie." These men, Haygood charged, constituted "a syndicate of liars equal to almost any demand that Satan may make upon his children."[83]

It was rumored that the members of Haygood's "syndicate" were Sam Jones, George Stuart, and J. B. Culpepper. Enraged, Jones asked Warren Candler to deliver a letter to Haygood. Candler refused, saying the letter was improper. Jones also wrote Stradley. "I have never lied on any man," the evangelist insisted. "If it is a sin to repeat a statement of facts as given by a brother Preacher without equivocation or qualification then I am a sinner and beg God and man to forgive me." While claiming to bear no malice toward Stradley or Haygood, Jones warned that if he were named publicly as a member of the syndicate he would vindicate himself in the newspapers. Tensions rose throughout the connection, and some feared that "Jones and Haygood will split the Church wide open with their hostility towards each other."[84]

Haygood's health continued to decline, and his slurred speech and unsteadiness on his feet caused speculation about his sobriety, as well. He was able to preside over the Kentucky Conference in September 1895, but the next month he suffered a stroke on the way to the Holston Conference that left him with a slight paralysis. Jones had said that he would not put his "proof" in print if the bishop did not "get perfectly well." Haygood died on January 19, 1896, at the age of fifty-seven. Abruptly, Sam Jones withdrew from the fray. He had already restricted his participation in the *Tennessee Methodist* to one column an issue. After Haygood's death he severed this connection, forcing Haynes to sell the paper when the Tennessee Conference disowned it in October 1896. A penitent Jones not only attended Haygood's memorial service but raised money for a memorial fund honoring the late bishop.[85]

"I want to say, Bishops and Brethren of the Church, there was a war up a year or two ago," Jones said on the floor of the general conference in 1898, where he represented the Rome District as a lay delegate. "There was a war up, indeed, and I was in it, too, but I laid down my sword and put my hands in my pockets two years ago, and I ain't 'fit' a thing since. I 'fit' until I backslid, and I have tried to get the whole business to quit 'fitting' since."

Sam Jones would not fight a dead man, and Haygood's death stunned him into realizing how destructive the "war" had been to his church. However, he continued to oppose restrictions on local preachers, and it was the proposal to strengthen penalties against local preachers who defied the church that brought him to his feet in St. Louis at the General Conference of the Methodist Episcopal Church, South.

Jones realized that if a local preacher could be accused of immorality and expelled from the church for holding an unauthorized revival, he was a prime candidate for expulsion. Any member of any conference can "arraign and clean me right up on the very law you are passing today," Jones warned. For example, he had been invited by a layman to Selma, Alabama, and had accepted, only to receive a note signed by all the ministers of evangelical churches asking him not to come. After he canceled the campaign, he received a petition with two thousand names of "businessmen, lawyers, doctors, farmers, merchants, Jews, Gentiles, Catholics, gamblers, horse racers, the whole business from snout to tail." "Dear Brother Jones: Our pastors never agreed on anything. Our boys are going to destruction; our town is heaped in sin; Oh, come help us." Deciding that "the voice of the people is the voice of God," Jones wrote the people of Selma he would come to "help you save your boys and help run the devil out of town."[86]

Now he could be censured or expelled for this action, and even his friends thought he was being "disloyal" to the church. "In the name of heaven, I don't mean to be," Jones protested. "There is no more loyal Methodist on this platform, because I don't know anything else but Methodism. I can't enjoy any other Church. You needn't think you are going to run me out of the Methodist Church into any other, because if you turn me out tomorrow, I am going to 'jine' again. I expect to live in the Church and die in the Church; and I say, brethren, the best thing we can do is to stop this whole war. The best thing we can do is, in love and harmony, help each other, stand by each other in friendship and help and counsel. . . . I am fifty years old, and I have been a Methodist fifty years; and if I live fifty more years, until this head is white, Sam Jones is going to be a Southern Methodist preacher, unless we all get religion enough, brethren, to unite, and then I am going to be just a plain Methodist Episcopal."[87]

The general conference passed the legislation. With the laws in place and the extremists leaving, it seemed that the "war" would end at last. However, in the aftermath of the campaign against the "second-blessing" folks and the evangelists, anger was replaced by inertia, and the rate of church growth dropped precipitously. Articles about the "decrease of the increase" replaced the columns on holiness and revivalism. Some agreed with E. E. Hoss that the reaction was merely an indication that the "intoxication had passed." "Let us all of us return unto God," Hoss urged, "and God will return to us." Others were not so sanguine. "On every devout lip is the earnest question, 'What is the matter?'" Dr. J. J. Tigert of Vanderbilt wrote. "Has the Church so dishonored herself as the Bride of Christ that she has lost power to bear and train prophets for the Lord?"[88]

There is no doubt that Jones's identification with the dissidents hurt his career. He was barely mentioned in the *Nashville Christian Advocate* after his location, and calls for campaigns, even in the South, came less frequently. Location was "a kind of religious ostracism," and a "ban was placed on all such." However, his popularity as a lecturer continued unabated, and he was able to use his leisure time to compile editions of his sermons with B. F. Haynes and to write his autobiography, *Thunderbolts*. Though handicapped by uncertain health and declining prestige, increasingly he turned his attention to the issue that would reunite Methodists, conservative and liberal alike: prohibition.[89]

Do not gaze at the wine when it is red,

when it sparkles in the cup

when it goes down smoothly!

In the end it bites like a snake

and poisons like a viper.

—Proverbs 23:31–32

Lean-look'd prophets whisper fearful change.

—William Shakespeare

8

❧ Apostle of Prohibition

During the first two decades after the Civil War the South was busy reinventing itself. That which was dead—the aristocracy slavery built—was embalmed in mythology. The characteristics thought to be the offspring of the Old South—honor, courtesy, hospitality, reverence for the past, piety, social deference, and racial control—were carefully preserved. Within this continuity of culture, however, there was change, and voices calling for more change, for a New South with a broader democracy, a place where efficiency would enliven courtesy and industry would be softened by charm.

Nor were these voices speaking of economics and politics alone, for there were those who called for a New South religion, one that would appropriate the social evangelicalism of the North without losing the spirituality and emotion of the South. Sam Jones was a spokesman for this New South religion, and to understand the opposition he encountered, particularly within his own Methodist denomination, it is necessary to understand how that church's idea of its role in society had evolved.

In the years before Methodism divided, two distinct theories had developed on how the church should act upon the world. Prompted by the need to defend slavery, southern Methodists contended that the sacred and the profane should be separated, and that preachers should condemn only those sins specifically forbidden in Scripture. However, this refusal to "meddle" in politics did not prevent Methodist ministers from preaching numberless sermons on slavery as God's way of bringing pagans across the sea to salvation and extolling Abraham as a model slaveholder.[1]

These eloquent defenses of the southern system reduced northern Methodists to sputtering contempt. The fact that Abraham owned slaves did not mean God approved of slavery, they fumed. Abraham also had a concubine and an illegitimate son: did that mean God endorsed fornication and bastardy? Theirs was the broad view of the role of church and society, and northern Methodist preachers did not hesitate to condemn practices as contrary to the spirit of Christ even if they were not censured in Scripture. Emboldened by this approach, they embarked with solemn abandon upon the task of perfecting the world by reforming prisons, improving asylums, restricting alcohol, eradicating prostitution, and overthrowing slavery. Their noisy activism further alienated southerners, who hardened their hearts against what they perceived to be a radical spirit of politicized reform in the northern church.[2]

The Civil War intensified distrust between the two halves of the Methodist church. The North, proud in victory, perceived its evangelical activism to be vindicated. The South, proud in defeat, renewed its determination to keep church and state separate. The Palmyra Manifesto of 1866, the southern church's announcement that it would not die with the South that spawned it, reiterated the resolve not to mix God and politics. Reunion with their northern brethren was impossible, the manifesto proclaimed, because southern Methodists abhor "political churchmen" and "oppose the prostitution of the pulpit to political purposes." Fifteen years later, southern Methodist papers were still editorializing against political meddling. "There is a secularity about them, a style that brings them into near fellowship with worldly enterprises and organizations," the editor of the *New*

Orleans Christian Advocate wrote in its critique of northern evangelists. "They *run* things up there—churches as well as factories and railroads. Their style of preaching is in contrast with ours, and is largely of the politico-sensational order."[3]

When a wave of prohibition sentiment swept the South in the early eighties, arguments that the sacred should not mix with the civil were heard less frequently. D. C. Kelley spoke for a large number of southerners who wanted a "practical Christianity" that would convert the world rather than flee from it. The church must not abstain from moral issues to maintain political purity, Kelley contended. While "good men under great trial" had surrendered their prophetic role, there was no reason "we at this late date shall be bound to regard their declaration as the lamp of truth." Such a narrow interpretation of responsibility would eliminate the church from all areas where civil and moral jurisdiction overlapped, such as Sabbath desecration, the liquor question, prostitution, and gambling.[4]

This evangelical activism got mixed reviews. While O. P. Fitzgerald praised the proliferation of "religious and benevolent enterprises" that aligned the church with "the great moral movements of the day," E. E. Hoss, a professor at Vanderbilt, denounced those who would "go down to a secular Egypt for the help that can only come from the living God." However, in 1894 Hoss—by then editor of the *Christian Advocate*—conceded defeat. "Practical Christianity" had won the day to the point that "in many places the old theme of personal religion has been virtually banished," Hoss lamented. In place of the gospel are "mere discussions of current issues," a policy Hoss predicted would be "disastrous beyond measure."[5]

Sam Jones, embodiment of the New South theology of political activism and the first American evangelist to "turn revival campaigns into civic-reform crusades," became the litmus test for those for and against "practical Christianity." Fitzgerald favored him with flattering editorials and D. C. Kelley hailed him as a "harbinger" of a "new type of Christianity." Hoss fashioned oblique criticisms of Jones and made frontal assaults on activists who yoked the church to political parties to achieve prohibition. The Methodist church should never underwrite a candidate or endorse a political party, Hoss fulminated, "even were that party to formally incorporate into its platform the principles of the Ten Commandments, the Apostles Creed, and the Lord's Prayer." The battle against holiness factions had enfeebled opposition to prohibition, however, and many Methodists were relieved to turn from internecine skirmishes to a war on an external enemy: alcohol.[6]

Sam Jones was easily the most famous prohibitionist in the South. His own alcoholism made prohibition a personal battle, and his intolerance of ambiguities caused him to dismiss temperance as a truce with the Devil. The humorist Robert Benchley once divided the world into two types of men: those who divided the world into two types of men and those who did not. Sam Jones was a divider. He viewed the world as composed of unflinching opposites: God versus Satan, good versus evil, abstinence versus alcohol. "I am a concentrated-consolidated-eternal-uncompromising-every-day-of-the-year-stand-up-to-be-knocked-down-and-dragged-out prohibitionist," Jones would boast. "I'm not only *not* going to drink it but I'll fight it to perdition, and when perdition freezes, then I'll fight it on the ice. If you can make it stronger than that, I'll put my name to it."[7]

Because of different drinking patterns and cultural attitudes toward alcohol, during the nineteenth century three out of every ten drinkers became abusers. Thus Jones was contemptuous of people who claimed "one little drink" never hurt anyone. Folks have been using that line for fifty years, he would say. "You are not only wicked men, but you have got no originality about you." Jones was particularly alarmed by the rise in beer consumption, from 36 million gallons in 1850 to 855 million in 1890. The efforts to promote beer as a temperance drink caused him to snort: "Don't talk to me about it. Why, I got stinking drunk years ago on beer. And of all the nastiest, suck-eggiest, doggiest drunks a man ever got on, a beer drunk is the worst."[8]

Jones dismissed those who argued for constitutional rights and individual liberty as scoundrels hiding a sordid motive and a depraved appetite behind lofty ideals. "The less sense a fellow has the more he talks about the constitutionality of a thing; the less character he has the more he talks about individual rights; and when he has neither sense nor character then he begins to talk about his blood and training." Any judge who ruled prohibition laws unconstitutional should be booted out of office: that would take care of a lot of the "old mash-tubs sitting on the bench." If he were in charge of America, he would reintroduce "whipping posts for drunkards," he boasted, and if grand juries were too cowardly to return judgments against law-breaking liquor dealers, he would declare martial law.[9]

Along with their personal-liberty arguments, opponents of prohibition stressed the economic consequences of banning alcohol. They insisted that without liquor, farmers would have grain rotting in their barns, cities would languish for lack of industry, and taxes would soar. Prohibitionists countered that it was precisely because America was becoming an urban, industrial country that prohibition was imperative. A drunken farmer could do little but bankrupt himself; a drunken worker on an assembly line could wreck expensive machinery, and a drunken train conductor could kill hundreds and incur enormous liabilities for his employer. Abstinence became even more urgent with the advent of the automobile at the turn of the century. In the words of Henry Ford, "Booze had to go when modern industry and the automobile came in."[10]

Jones did not advocate prohibition to make America safe for industrialism. Prohibition was at bottom a moral issue for Jones. "It is not a question of statistics," Jones said in St. Louis. "It is a question of blood and death and hell." In Augusta, Georgia, where an earlier revival had sparked a local option election, Jones reassured an anxious audience: "I am not here for a prohibition campaign. If I said so you old fellows would say that it would kill the town and that long grass would grow up right in the streets. Well, let it grow. We'll raise more hay and less hell, and the crows and old women will be happy." For those who think that abolishing alcohol would devastate the local economy, Jones had this suggestion: "If you think saloons increase the value of your property, have one put up next to your residence."[11]

Nor was the evangelist indulgent of those who pleaded that without alcohol their appetite would wither and their nerves would fray. A "pill-pusher" had prescribed liquor for him, and the result was seven years of intermittent drunkenness. "I detest these dirty little devils of doctors who prescribe whiskey for every ill and inject morphine until we have a tramload of morphine wrecks here," Jones snarled. "When he dies he'll go to hell like he was shot out of a gun." So insistent was Jones that the medicinal use of alcohol was unwarranted that when a doctor wanted to administer alcohol as a "stimulant" to his typhoid-stricken son Robert, Jones contended that it was better for the boy to die sober and go to heaven than to live to be a drunkard and wind up in hell. As for himself, "when the doctor tells me I must drink whiskey or die, you may order my shroud and I will get into it."[12]

Sam Jones was so intolerant of alcohol he did not believe wine should be served at communion. Prominent Methodists like Bishop Lovick Pierce and E. E. Hoss saw the substitution of grape juice as immoderate, since they interpreted Scripture as favoring temperance rather than abstinence. Antiprohibitionists listened closely to their theological arguments and then hurled verses at the prohibitionists: "Give strong drink to him that is ready to perish," or, "Not that which goeth into the mouth defileth a man, but that which proceedeth out of the mouth." The marriage at Cana was cited as evidence that Jesus enjoyed an occasional taste of the grape, and in Savannah "Uncle Mingo" speculated that if Sam Jones had been present when water was turned into wine, the evangelist would have denounced Christ as a "humbug preacher" who worked magic with the help of "de debbil."[13]

"How did I get to be a drunkard?" Jones would ask. "Why by drinking wine, like you do; and I stood up for it too, and argued that the Savior made it." But Jesus made wine out of water, not California grapes, Jones told a San Francisco audience. "Show me some such a wine an' I'll take a drink with you three times a day." God expressly ordered people to "taste not, touch not the accursed thing" and warned that "no drunkard shall enter the kingdom of heaven." "Take a little wine for thy stomach's sake," a scripturally literate heckler shouted out in a tent meeting. "The fool's god is his belly," Jones countered.[14]

Jones was not surprised that Christians were confused about liquor since their shepherds were so often silent or in error. Told that only ten preachers in Boston were "straight out prohibitionists," Jones curtly informed the clergy: "Well, I've been a prohibitionist ever since I got religion, and if you're not, you need another dip." He was equally unrelenting with the person in the pew. "A man can't drink whiskey and be a Christian, and don't you forget it," Jones insisted. "Red liquor and Christianity . . . won't stay in the same hide at the same time. As one goes down, the other's coming out sure!"[15]

Jones admitted that his most intemperate remarks were on temperance. "I never mention this whiskey question that it doesn't start all the blood in my nature," he confessed. "Some may think this is rather a prohibition meeting instead of a revival," Jones said during a Baltimore campaign. "For every barroom that I could close, I would be doing a better thing than bringing in fifty converts to the church. First let God help me destroy the machinery that is wrecking men's souls." Near the end of his life, Jones estimated that "in my time, I have got 100,000 men to quit drinking, and if I have done nothing else, I think that's a pretty good job, don't you?"[16]

The fact that this boast was invariably greeted with foot-stomping applause indicated how drastically public opinion had changed from the colonial era, when alcohol was viewed as "God's good creature," or the fifty years following the Revolution, when Americans drank more heavily than at any other time in their history. However, alarm over the erosion of values, concern about drunken workers and voters in an expanding industrial democracy, and evidence that alcohol was a "poison" rather than a food made temperance an important reform movement. By 1835, 1.5 million people belonged to temperance organizations, 500,000 had renounced the use of distilled liquor, 4,000 distilleries had closed, and the annual consumption of alcohol had been cut in half.[17]

When fourteen states passed laws prohibiting the manufacture and sale of distilled liquor, there were widespread expectations of a dry millennium. It was not to be. The slavery issue diverted the resources of reformers, and medical evidence that moderate consumption of alcohol was not dangerous led some to question the need for absolute abstinence. The demise of the friendly Whig party, difficulties of enforcement, reversals in the courts, the unwearied opposition of the liquor industry, and the attitude of immigrants who regarded drinking as a part of their culture led to the "dry debacle" of the late 1850s.[18]

Many local temperance societies survived, however, and in 1869, re-formers founded the Prohibition party. Resolving to take the "broad-gauge" approach, party leaders advocated an income tax; direct election of the president, vice-president, and senators; and public regulation of railroads. Though the party was never strong in the South, between 1880 and 1884 the number of men voting the Prohibition ticket grew from 10,000 to 150,000. However, rather than widening their appeal, the party's endorsement of a hodgepodge of reforms alienated moderates and made prohibitionists ap-pear ridiculous, an "army of crack-brained, visionary cranks." By 1890 the "golden age of the reform" was over.[19]

Paralleling the rise and decline of the Prohibition party was that of the Woman's Christian Temperance Union, an organization born out of a women's crusade in a small town in Ohio in 1872. Following the "Do everything" motto of its charismatic leader, Frances Willard, members pressured legislatures into mandating temperance education in schools, organized local-option campaigns, combatted tobacco addiction, lobbied against child labor and for raising the age of sexual consent, "rescued" pros-titutes, worked with immigrants and blacks, and agitated for pure food and drugs. "One of the most powerful instruments of women's consciousness-raising of all times," the WCTU grew by almost 70 percent between 1885 and 1890.[20]

However, the WCTU was tarred with the brush of political heresy when Willard endorsed populism, Christian socialism, and woman suffrage. With the WCTU branded a "menace to true womanhood," the southern societies went into steep decline. WCTU chapters in the North languished as well, with Willard's absence in England. When the WCTU began to focus on prohibition alone, its membership sank in status. By Willard's death in 1898, the perception of the organization was changing. In the popular view, the WCTU once attracted "the best, most respected, most forward-looking women in town." Its members were now thought to be "narrow-minded antilibertarians riding a hobby horse."[21]

In 1896 with the prohibition movement foundering and the nation sunk in depression, the Anti-Saloon League was founded in Oberlin, Ohio, a town famed for its role in the antislavery crusade. By courting clerics and other "public opinion makers," marshaling women and children, and concentrating the evangelical vote into an instrument of "pressure politics," the ASL became a fearsome "politico-ecclesiastical machine." Rather than dispersing its energies trying to achieve statewide prohibition, the ASL worked to abolish saloons through local-option elections in which an individual community could vote itself dry. Appealing to middle-class folks who disliked having a saloon in their neighborhood and to loyalists who would never vote for a third party, the ASL took a pragmatic approach: "Better to have a scoundrel who will vote right than to have a saint who will vote wrong." To the dismay of purists, the ASL accepted what was possible instead of holding out for what was ideal, taking "a half loaf where it could not get a whole one—a crumb, even, if there was no more to be had."[22]

Though Sam Jones was dead before the ASL perfected its speakers' bureau, both George Stuart and Sam Small were popular and highly paid speakers. In every lecture, circular, and newspaper article, the saloon was made to seem the "source of all misery and vice." "Liquor is responsible for 19% of the divorces, 25% of the poverty, 25% of the insanity, 37% of the pauperism, 45% of child desertion, and 50% of the crime in this country," a typical poster proclaimed. When the saloon was gone, the ASL contended, taxes would be lower because there would be fewer inmates of hospitals, asylums, orphanages, and prisons; children would thrive because paychecks would be spent on food and education instead of alcohol; and profits and productivity would soar with a sober work force. Nor would the scope of reform stop at the borders of the United States. Pass prohibition, Sam Small prophesied at the ASL convention in 1917, and America would become "not only the savior but the model and monitor of the reconstructed civilization of the world in the future."[23]

The ASL billed itself as the "Church in Action Against the Saloon," and by 1908, 40,000 churches supported it. The ASL's effort to isolate the saloon as an urban vice was so successful that by the outbreak of World War I, only 26 percent of the total territory of the United States was wet, though more than half the population lived in these areas. There were only three dry states at the beginning of the last prohibition wave in 1904; by 1914 fourteen states had outlawed the sale and manufacture of alcohol. A revolution had occurred in public sentiment, and the stage was set for the moral fervor of war to achieve national prohibition.[24]

It is no coincidence that Sam Jones's career and prohibition sentiment rose and fell and rose again together, for Jones's brand of civic righteousness matched the needs of the dry crusade. He gave quotability to the prohibition movement, and some extravagant admirers believed that the Georgian brought down John Barleycorn. "The prohibition movement which resulted in the 18th Amendment to the United States Constitution in 1919, was without a doubt the result of Sam Jones' powerful appeals for temperance and his merciless exposure of the liquor traffic and its hellish methods," the Reverend John G. Garth of Virginia wrote in 1948. John Temple Graves, editor of the *Atlanta Georgian*, took to the platform after statewide prohibition passed in Georgia in 1907. In lectures around the country, Graves attributed the "prohibition wave" that dried up Georgia and other southern states to the attempt of "liquor men" in Bartow County "to take an ungenerous advantage of Sam Jones' death" in October 1906. Enraged by the assumption of "liquor leaders" that without Sam Jones the county would go wet, Bartow County residents overwhelmingly voted for "Sam Jones and prohibition." "The news flashed an inspiration to the temperance ranks throughout the state," Graves claimed, and a stunning victory in Lowndes County prompted prohibitionists, now "wild with enthusiasm," to successfully push for statewide prohibition.[25]

It is excessive to attribute national prohibition to an evangelist who had been dead for more than a decade when it was enacted. What can be claimed for Jones is that he helped change public sentiment. Before the Civil War and to a lesser extent afterward, the southern host's "first expression of hospitality to a guest was to summon the negro with the ice, the sugar, and the mint, and to draw the cork himself." Even ministers on their pastoral rounds rarely refused a "toddy." But Jones and the legion of preachers he inspired insisted that drinking, not just drunkenness, was a sin. Their persistence changed southern sentiment so dramatically that, "in many counties, even in rather sophisticated family groups, claret or sherry displayed in a decanter or served at dinner parties aroused a feeling akin to 'horror.'" This alteration in attitude was accompanied by an emphasis on political evangelicalism—taking the Bible into the voting booth—also promoted by Sam Jones. It was in this way that Sam Jones prepared the way for prohibition.[26]

Though preachers and politicians jumped on the prohibition platform after the shift of public opinion, Sam Jones began preaching prohibition when he began preaching. In 1883, after convincing four bar owners in Putnam County, Georgia, to shut their saloons, Jones wrote an exuberant letter to the *Wesleyan Christian Advocate*. His upcoming revival in Jones County would be followed by "a *voluntary* abandonment of the traffic," he predicted, "and that is prohibition with a vengeance. Get any county to Christ and prohibition is inevitable." Jones's reverence for private property led him to believe the right way to close a saloon was to "pay the owners and burn the whiskey." Publicly unsympathetic to saloon keepers who whined they could not live without their livelihood—"Better men than you have died"—Jones was privately more compassionate. When a convert confided that he could not afford to get out of the whiskey-dealing business, Jones gave the man five hundred dollars of his own money to take the axe to his inventory.[27]

However, Jones was not opposed to slinging some sulphur at those unwilling to stop selling the Devil's brew. Preaching in Robertson County, home of Tennessee "sippin' whiskey," Jones warned bourbon barons that there was "no more loathsome thing crawling through the dark corridors of hell than an old distiller, hiding and shrinking from the groans and cries of the poor devils who gather around them and accuse them of their ruin." He was equally outspoken in another whiskey capital, Owensboro, Kentucky. "I see you, Dick Monarch," the evangelist said, pointing a bony finger at a local "distiller of death." "You are making this damnable whiskey sour mash that is sending our boys to hell." Monarch held his tongue until Jones made his habitual plea for money to cover the expenses of the revival. "Mr. Jones," Monarch drawled, "if it is only seven hundred dollars you need, here is my check for that amount. I figure your advertising my brand is worth at least that much."[28]

Jones's willingness to accept "the devil's dues" made for a humorous encounter in his hometown of Cartersville. Seeing the evangelist walking down the street, a local bootlegger nudged a crony and said, "I am going to show you what a hypocrite old Sam Jones is. Sam," the whiskey runner said, "here's a hundred dollars to help you in your work of saving souls."

"Thanks," said Sam, walking on.

"I think I ought to tell you, Sam, that I made this money bootlegging."

"Well," drawled Sam, "the Devil has had it long enough; we will let the Lord use it awhile."[29]

There was a limit to Jones's willingness to deal with the Devil, however, and that limit was high license—regulating alcohol through heavy charges and taxes. To Jones, suggesting that liquor be controlled but not abolished was like offering a person a rotten egg, saying, "That's rotten: you can compromise and just eat half." He was especially alarmed that high license made liquor more lucrative to the government: by 1903 the liquor traffic was paying more than $100 million in state, county, and municipal taxes, and almost $231 million in federal taxes. "I expect many professing Christians in this town will be astonished when they get to heaven and find how God Almighty can run the Celestial City without a few saloons to help keep up the taxes," Jones speculated in St. Louis.[30]

Jones briefly advocated the dispensary system, giving the state or local government a monopoly on the sale of alcohol. He believed this system, tried first in Georgia, "would at least keep the dog chained." However, he became convinced that it hindered the passage of local-option bills, deflected the drive for statewide prohibition, and created the same unholy alliance between liquor dealers and taxpayers as high license. "I had rather have the smallpox and get over it than have the measles forever, and, gentlemen, when the dispensary is inaugurated it has come to stay, because it pays the taxes for the people, and the majority of humanity can't see any harm in a thing that pays their taxes."[31]

Jones's reversal raised cries of treachery among some temperance reformers, however. "Politics make strange bedfellows, but when Sam Jones and Red Nosed Devil and Barroom Bill all bunch up under the same quilt it seems to us it's about time the cover and the mattress were fumigated," the pastor of the Second Baptist Church in Rome, Georgia, wrote angrily. Since the dispensary was opened, this cleric claimed, there was less crime, thirteen saloons were out of business, and "our streets are clean of the dirty negro element." Jones's invitation to conduct a revival in Rome during 1904 was abruptly withdrawn and the dispensary was voted in for another year.[32]

Sam Jones favored the local-option approach, a technique which dried up small areas until public opinion favored statewide prohibition. Naturally, he worked hard to exterminate alcohol in his hometown of Cartersville, even though during the first local-option election, antiprohibitionists blew up his buggy house and threatened to dynamite his home if he did not "hush up." He decided he would "rather be a dead lion than a live dog," but he did suggest to Laura she take the children away until after the election. "Do your duty, and stand up for the poor women and children of this country," Laura told him. "I would as soon go to heaven by the dynamite route as any other that God or men can get up." With his house guarded by a group of black volunteers, Jones led the successful campaign, then offered five hundred dollars to anyone who could get drunk in Cartersville. One fellow managed it and was paid; the man running the "blind tiger" was sent to jail for ten years.[33]

Although local option prohibited the sale and manufacture of alcohol, it did not forbid consumption. Those determined to drink could import alcohol or make their own home brew, a practice that led the humorist Mr. Dooley (Peter Findlay Dunne) to remark that though there was less drunkenness after prohibition, "what there is is a much more finished product." When folks in Cartersville had liquor shipped from Atlanta or from distillers in Kentucky and Tennessee, Sam Jones discovered what other prohibitionists had found: "local option was too local and too optional." Jones fumed, "What advantage to me to keep my premises clean, when the filth of my neighbor's premises gives me the typhoid fever?"[34]

The United States Supreme Court ruling that alcohol could be shipped from wet to dry territory in the "original package" posed a special challenge. Coming home from a revival, Jones was met at the train by neighbors who told him that two fellows had rented a house in town and proposed to set up an original package store. "Shucks! No, they ain't," Jones answered. He immediately had handbills printed for an "anti–original package meeting." That night "the woods was full of folks," all of whom endorsed the evangelist's resolution: "We will make an original package out of any damnable scoundrel" who tries to sell whiskey in Bartow County. The two men left "for parts unknown."[35]

Despite his unwavering opposition to alcohol, Sam Jones was a pragmatist. He realized that prohibition could not be accomplished by a single blow: "If I can't chop off a snake's head, I'll chop off his tail—and then I'll keep on chopping off his tail until I get right up to his head." He appreciated the practical approach of the Anti-Saloon League and in 1900 was principal speaker at a mammoth rally in Atlanta to launch the organization in Georgia. The following year the Methodist minister James Cannon established an ASL branch in Virginia, and Jones agreed to serve as treasurer without pay, a position he held until his death.[36]

Jones claimed he faithfully voted the Prohibition party ticket: "I may be throwing away my vote," he acknowledged, "but I had rather shoot it in the air than in the mud." However, his pragmatism made him incompatible with many in the Prohibition party, and it is surprising that he was considered as a presidential candidate in 1904. After a disastrous flirtation with populism, the Prohibition party was trying to take a leaf from the ASL and woo the church, the South, and the conservative middle class. It may be that this unsuccessful courtship provoked the flurry of interest in Sam Jones. One enthusiastic promoter of "the Sage of Cartersville" was James W. Bodley of Memphis. Predicting that "the southern delegation for Jones will go to the convention in power," Bodley was confident that female delegates would support "their champion, Sam Jones."[37]

"I think that we are getting the levers well under the ball and that it will roll," Bodley confided to Jones in early June. A few weeks later, however, talk turned to having General Nelson A. Miles, hero of the Spanish-American War, as standard-bearer, with Jones filling the vice-presidential spot. Dismissing the ticket as "an old woman's dream," Jones wrote in his column that though Miles was an honorable man, he doubted that he was a prohibitionist. Miles agreed and refused to run. The Prohibition party returned to the ticket of four years before, Silas Swallow and G. W. Carroll.[38]

Although Jones endorsed both the Prohibition party and the Anti-Saloon League, most of his energy focused on local elections unconnected to specific political parties. In 1887 Jones made a whistle-stop tour of Tennessee, and in 1894 he stumped that state on behalf of candidates pledged to vote for the "Mississippi Plan," a system that required applicants for a liquor license to present a petition signed by a majority of the registered voters. In 1893 Jones went to Virginia to campaign against "Parson" John E. Massey, a Baptist minister running for the school board as an antiprohibitionist. Five years later Jones turned a revival in Marietta, Georgia, into a crusade against Georgia Supreme Court Judge John Gober, who was suspected of selling his homemade wine in dry territory. Jones's forays into politics failed, however. The Tennessee antiliquor candidates were defeated, and "Parson" Massey and Judge Gober were elected. Everywhere he went "the people would slap their hands and holler and take on terribly" over prohibition, Jones lamented. "But there's a heap of difference between slapping hands and voting."[39]

Jones was somewhat more successful in his campaigns to make the public "remember the Sabbath day and keep it holy." This was a battle related to the war on alcohol, for saloon owners were the most blatant "Sabbath desecrators," but it also appealed to evangelicals ambivalent about prohibition. The silent Sabbath had ended with the beginning of the Civil War, when demand for news had eased restrictions on Sunday mail and newspapers, and the upheaval of war had made even devout Christians question the necessity of blue laws. By the 1880s public sentiment was often indifferent to legal enforcement of the Sabbath, and in some states blue laws were repealed.[40]

In response, the American Sabbath Union and the Sunday League of America were organized to lobby for the reinstitution of old laws and the enforcement of existing legislation. Jones supported such efforts; it was his hope that the full force of the American legal system would one day descend on the Sabbath breaker, "because the desecration of the Sabbath works ruin to humanity." "You can go in your Missouri Penitentiary; you will pull them in one at a time," Jones told a St. Louis audience. " 'What was the first step that brought you here?' and ninety-nine men in a hundred will say my first downward step was Sabbath desecration." Whole nations fell under the weight of this iniquity. "France has demonstrated what Sabbath-breaking will do," Jones contended. "When you allow Sabbath-breaking you let in a wedge that will open the way for communism and anarchy."[41]

Just as Jones was sometimes brought in to provoke a local-option election, he was occasionally engaged to arouse public opinion about Sabbath desecration, as with the Louisville, Kentucky, campaign in 1899. Lamenting that the "revival fire" was "burning low" in Louisville, M. P. Chapman, a Methodist minister, admitted that a visit by the manager of the Sunday League of America had failed to inflame the city. His hopes were now pinned on the irascible evangelist from Georgia, for with nine hundred saloons open every Sunday in flagrant violation of the law, "there are few cities in this country where the Sabbath is so desecrated, and where the whiskey element is so dominant." [42]

"What I want is a revival in this city which shall not only help individuals but shall reform the city," Jones announced at the outset of the campaign. Told that some feared he would make things worse, Jones scoffed: "You can't knock a man down who is on the flat of his back to save your life. . . . If the devil himself were mayor of the city he couldn't do worse." Saloon keepers sat on the city council, and there was a distiller on the school board. Not only were the saloons open on Sunday; they never closed at all. "I have no respect for any dirty scoundrel who won't go home at night." [43]

Jones usually received flattering attention from major newspapers during revivals, for even irreligious editors recognized the chance to win the goodwill of church folk. Such was not the case in Louisville, however. The alcoholic son of Henry Watterson, editor of the *Courier-Journal*, had been converted during Jones's revival sixteen years earlier; yet the evangelist charged that the paper was straining out the "clear gospel truths" and printing only his "rough" remarks. The *Louisville Times* was undisguisedly hostile, suggesting that "it is not everlastingly too late for the irrepressible Sam Jones" to correct the mistake he had made "in responding to some other man's call to preach the Gospel." [44]

After Jones labeled Louisville a "damnable, devil-ridden and rum-soaked city," the *Times* parodied the evangelist's hyperbolic style in a column printed next to the form sheet for the race track. "The Onlooker" explained to Louisvillians:

> Mr. Jones is after the devil. If collections remain good he will dig the devil up if he is in the ground, shoot him on the fly if he is in the air, hit him with a brick if he is swimming in the river—and when Mr. Jones gets the devil, he will chop off his tail, knock out his teeth, trim down his hoof, take out his heart, liver and lights and otherwise make him wish that when he was first thrown out of heaven he had gone into a legitimate natural gas business in the center of the earth instead of rigging up a

red-hot hell there and manufacturing damnable damnation with which to overthrow the righteous.[45]

Jones could rarely resist responding to critics, and he hurried to denounce the "little jackass editors" of Louisville. Though at the end of the revival thousands of signatures were on a petition asking public officials to enforce Sunday closing, Jones felt rebuffed. "In the fifty-second year of my life and the twenty-seventh year of my ministry," he announced at his departure, "I have received less sympathy in Louisville than in any town, city or country place in which I ever worked."[46]

Though Jones's stance on the Sabbath is severe by modern standards, he was not rigid enough to suit some. In 1893 the Methodist ministers in Wheeling, West Virginia, boycotted the local campground for leaving their gates open on Sunday, thus enticing the godly to ride excursion trains from nearby towns. Jones was the only preacher who came to the camp meeting. "But the crowds are here," Jones wrote in his weekly column. "God is blessing the people, and so it goes." Though Jones publicly prayed "that this country may soon have a Congress that will make it unlawful for trains to run on Sunday," when he preached in Atlanta, he frequently made the short trip from Cartersville just after dawn on the Sabbath. One Sunday morning, two Atlanta men spotted a small, wiry man slouched down in a seat with his hat pulled down over his face. They demanded to know "if you are that Sam Jones fellow who preached all week that people who ride trains on Sunday are going to hell."

"Yep," Jones replied in a laconic drawl, "but I ain't going that far."[47]

It would be wrong to suggest that drinking and Sabbath desecration were compartmentalized in Jones's mind. Saloon owners—especially those in immigrant communities—fused the issues by keeping their bars open in defiance of local laws and middle-class mores. The most dramatic example of the melding of the issues occurred in April 1899, when Sam Jones of Georgia met Sam Jones of Ohio. By the time this confrontation occurred, Jones's career as an evangelist was in eclipse, and he was estranged from the Methodist hierarchy, afflicted with poor health, and tormented by troubles with his children. His humor had grown sharper and more sour. It was this Sam Jones who arrived in Toledo, Ohio, in April 1899 to meet his nemesis.

Samuel Milton Jones was a sucker-rod magnate who converted to Christian socialism and transformed his factory into a company run strictly "upon the basis of the Golden Rule." He shortened the workday to eight hours, shared profits with his workers, provided paid vacations, and gave other benefits that seemed to go beyond generosity and end in folly. A Methodist and president of the local YMCA, Jones had been known as a staunch teetotaler and was almost defeated for mayor when his opponents suggested that if elected, Jones would shut down the saloons.[48]

This was the expectation of evangelicals as well, and they were enraged when the mayor concluded that attempts to enforce saloon laws had been an expensive failure that tied up courtrooms and deflected the police from controlling more serious criminal activity. He made little effort to close brothels, refused to enforce the state law forbidding bars to open on the Sabbath, and pressured the city council into repealing the ordinances closing saloons at eleven during the week and those prohibiting plays and concerts on Sunday, the only day off for laborers. At the next election all but one candidate pledged to shut saloons, gambling parlors, and "disreputable resorts." Mayor Jones maintained that "it would not be consistent for me to sign a paper pledging myself to make Toledo anything more than what its citizens desire it to be."[49]

The *Toledo Bee* angrily charged that although the mayor claimed that arrests had declined in the previous two years, "no attempt has been made to restrict crime. Wine rooms, bawdy houses, assignation houses, low concert halls, pool rooms, crap joints, gambling hells of every possible shape and form have been as free from police interference as the churches have been." The mayor's advocacy of organized labor and public ownership of streetcar and gas companies was interpreted by the *Bee* as an attack on capitalism: it "arouses the poor against the rich and appeals to the basest passions of men." Outraged, evangelicals and alarmed businessmen determined to put out "the fanatical torch of atheism, socialism, anarchy and Jonesism" and called upon the man they believed could define the coming election as a choice between "righteousness and iniquity, law and lawlessness, the church and the saloon." They summoned the man they believed could defeat Mayor Sam Jones: evangelist Sam Jones.[50]

Jones was in poor health; at one meeting he asked all present to pray that he would have the strength to finish the service, saying "I have never felt more physically unwell than I have today, but I am trusting in God and leaning on the Almighty arm." He appeared exhausted. "The arduous work he has been engaged in has begun to tell on him," one reporter wrote, "for his hair shows silver streaks and the lines of care in his face are plainly drawn." He has "a perceptible stoop" and a "habit of running his fingers through his hair which leaves it in a condition bordering on the disheveled." However, his "indomitable will and tenacity of purpose" are immediately apparent, and compassion shows through his "splendid eyes."[51]

Just days before Sam P. Jones arrived in Toledo in the midst of a snowstorm, Sam M. Jones had been denied the nomination as the Republican candidate for mayor. Charges of "boodling" or payoffs abounded, and even Democrats "were carried off their feet by sympathy" for an honest man denied office through corruption. Thus, when Mayor Jones came forward to introduce the evangelist Jones, he was warmly applauded. "My faith for the final saving of the world rests upon nothing else but the love of Christ at the heart of society," the mayor said. He had devoted his life "to realizing the kingdom of Christ" by being "tongue to those who cannot speak, eyes to those who grope, and help to those who are crippled."[52]

Sam P. Jones, who had "hinted pretty broadly that he would raise the devil" with Sam M. Jones, surprised the audience by praising his nemesis as "the champion of a holy cause." Lest folks fear the revival would be dull, Jones of Georgia announced: "I'm here for a fight and I'm going to say things to start it." He explained: "I just leave myself as God made me, a sort of mixture between a mule and a billy goat" that can "kick with one end and butt with the other."[53]

When "Golden Rule" Jones announced that he would run for mayor as an independent, the evangelist's remarks became more pointed. "I don't know any town that the devil has done more for than Toledo," he said. "Toledo is the widest open town, not except Chicago, that I have ever been in. No door is shut at all. They have done taken them down." With one quarter of the population foreign born, Toledo celebrated the "continental Sabbath" with "theaters running every Sunday and everything else that wants to. For every decent German or reputable Irishman I have the hand," Jones snarled, "but for a white-washed Dutchman or an anarchist Irishman I fix my foot. If you don't like this country go back."[54]

The Georgian's attacks filled the armory every night past capacity, and his afternoon meetings at the auditorium attracted exactly the "busy businessmen" that he was after. During the men's meeting, which attracted seven thousand, Jones made an obvious allusion to the other Sam. "Somebody told me there was an apostle in this town who believed you could run everything in this town by love. If love turned the devil loose on this town let's hate one another. The saloonkeeper don't care how much you love him if you just let him keep open. I believe if the devil himself was mayor here he wouldn't change anything. He wouldn't want more than 800 saloons and 400 bawdy houses. . . . You say I'm fooling with politics. I'm not. I'm naming no names, but I am running my engine on the track, and if anything gets in the way it's going to be run over. I'll fight the saloons till I die. Give it up tonight boys; give it up."[55]

Evangelist Jones soon broadened his attack to the other mayoral candidates, one of whom "played a good poker game" and was known as "a liberal patron of the saloons." Though he "used to get drunk on democratic whiskey and was as good a democrat as ever flopped a wing," Jones admitted, "thank God, I never ran with you republicans." As far as he could tell, "the only difference between the two candidates is that one is high cockalorum and the other is low cockahighrum." [56]

None of the Georgian's scouring remarks provoked a reply from a mayor determined to turn the other cheek, despite press predictions that "Evangelist Jones has cost Mayor Jones 1,000 votes since he struck Toledo." Under "tremendous pressure," Jones extended the campaign three days, in order to continue "to preach as full gospel as ever was preached—reconstruction for society and regeneration for the individual." At the final meeting, the southern Sam aimed a parting blow at a man he regarded as a weak-minded visionary. "I have nothing to do with politics, but I have to do with a theory that will land your town in ruin. . . . I see a mad dog coming over my fence and my wife and children are there. Do I say 'I believe in the Golden Rule for that dog?' The mad dog in this town is the saloon and the shameless houses. . . . I say the way to meet a mad dog is with a shotgun." [57]

When asked by the *Bee* about the results of the revival, ministers agreed that "under Jones' preaching businessmen and public officials have certainly been made to see their obligation to the citizenship of Toledo, and their duty toward purifying the morals of society." Jones himself felt he had "never touched so many hearts in such a short a time as I have here." And though "lots of these doctors of divinity are as cold as a dog's nose," he had never "worked with a heartier, more tender, more unanimous pastorate than I have met here." In her biography of her husband, Laura Jones claimed that he "won a great victory for municipal reform in Toledo, and changed the moral atmosphere of that city." If he did, his "victory" was not reflected in the mayoral election. Though he had been elected by a small margin in 1897, "Golden Rule" Jones was reelected by a landslide and continued in office until he died in 1904. As Samuel Milton Jones liked to say, "everyone was against him but the people." [58]

Both Sam Joneses identified themselves as progressives. Clearly, if progressivism contained two such antithetical people, it was a broad and contradictory movement. Mayor Sam Jones advocated a minimum wage, public ownership of utilities, and a system of collective production and distribution. He supported drastic political changes as well, trusting in the ability of ordinary men to make sensible decisions for the state. On the other end of the progressive spectrum was evangelist Sam Jones, an enthusiastic capitalist who advocated moderate reforms such as the direct election of senators, the merit system, professional city managers, and the establishment of a federal agency to ensure pure food and drugs. He believed in democracy: "There is one thing stronger than political bosses and political machines, and that is the people." However, Jones's faith in the common sense of the common man was not as strong as his elitism. He was convinced that the "cesspool" of politics would not be drained until the electorate was limited to property owners with mental and moral fitness.[59]

The two Sam Joneses also illustrate progressives' conflicting attitudes toward alcohol. The saloon was the "poor man's club," Welsh-born Sam M. Jones said, often the only place a working man could enjoy fellowship, get an uncontaminated drink, or use the toilet. Bars and brothels were only "evidence of wrong social conditions." Relieve poverty and broaden democracy, Mayor Jones insisted, and they would wither on their own. "You have grown white men in your town who say that saloons don't make poverty, but poverty creates saloons," the evangelist said in disbelief. "Don't you believe it; that's the biggest lie was ever told." Nor did Sam P. Jones believe that the "Whiskey Trust" would voluntarily relinquish its hold on the body politic if persuaded liquor was harmful to the republic. "It makes me tired to hear people talk of moral suasion," he snorted. "Put a lot of hogs into a cornfield, and you can sit on the fence and lecture them all day about the evils of overeating and they will keep on cracking corn. The only way to make them quiet is to set the dogs on them."[60]

In the opinion of Jones of Georgia, progressivism must move beyond overthrowing trusts and undermining political bosses to concentrate on the single most important reform: prohibition. It was alcohol, he charged, that promoted poverty and disease and illiteracy; if alcohol were abolished, there would be enough for all. "What would the discussion between labor and capital amount to if the $1,200,000 wasted on drink could be emptied into the pantries and upon the tables of all our homes? If whiskey was banished from our land no more children would cry for bread." Taking a swipe at the socialists, anarchists, and union "agitators" who congregated in saloons, Jones speculated that if you were to stick a knife into the bloated bellies of these foreign labor agitators, "four gallons of beer would run out."[61]

Alcohol not only devoured paychecks, Jones insisted, it ate away at individual morality. At first, there would be only petty evasions and little lies. "I drank whiskey, and if you don't lie to your wife, it's because you haven't got as much respect for your wife as I have for mine," Jones would say. Soon greater sins would be committed, until finally nothing seemed too heinous. It is whiskey that "makes men murder their wives," Jones insisted, "it makes them kill their children, it peoples hell with immortal souls." The worst crime any man can commit is to get drunk, Jones would thunder. "When a man gets drunk he is heated up for anything the devil wants done."[62]

Nor was the teetotaler free from the ravages of alcohol, Jones warned, for its corrupting influence had permeated every level of American political life. "We have lain low and said nothing until tonight the strongest power in America is the whiskey power," Sam Jones charged. "The Congress of the United States just stands and trembles in its presence. The legislatures of three-fourths of these states stand and tremble in its presence, and the pulpits of this country say 'I don't want to preach politics.' "[63]

It is tempting to dismiss Jones's claims as hysterical overstatement. In fact, objective sources have found evidence indicating that Jones's charges that alcohol contributed to poverty, crime, insanity, and political corruption have merit. Urban reformers, city officials, and social workers of the time blamed alcohol for creating at least 20 percent of the city's poor. The poor did benefit economically from prohibition. While antiliquor laws had little effect on either the pocketbooks or the drinking habits of the wealthy, it was estimated that during the dry years of the 1920s, wage-earning families had approximately one billion more dollars than they would have had without prohibition.[64]

There was a connection between liquor consumption and insanity and crime as well. The Massachusetts Bureau of Labor Statistics concluded that one-fifth of mental illness was abetted or induced by alcohol, and a survey of court records of inmates in twelve states found that alcohol was listed as the sole cause of crime in 16 percent of cases, the primary cause in 31 percent, and a contributing cause in 50 percent of the cases. Even given criminals' natural predisposition to blame outside agents, such figures are reminiscent of recent statistics indicating that the majority of prisoners in American penitentiaries consumed either alcohol or drugs in the hours before they committed a crime.[65]

Jones constantly insisted that he was working for "women and children" who were terrorized and pauperized by drunken, brutish men. It is easy to dismiss his melodramatic tales. However, in a society in which women had few opportunities to earn a living and no legal recourse if sexually attacked by a diseased husband, in which birth control was ineffective or unavailable, in which children had no "safety net" to ensure them access to medicine, food, clothing, and an education if their father drank his wages, the "terror of the old-time drunkard" was quite real. Sam Jones personally experienced the economic consequences of addiction for a family; it was whiskey that took a promising young lawyer and turned him into a wagon driver, that took an affluent girl and sent her to live in a shanty. "My objection to the saloon-keeper is the same I have to the louse," Jones would say. "He lives off the head of the family." [66]

It is also easy to dismiss Jones's shrill charges of political corruption as hysterical overstatement. However, a large number of political machines were lubricated with liquor: one-third of the aldermen of Detroit and Milwaukee in the 1890s were saloon keepers, as were half of the Democratic precinct workers in Chicago. It was a standard joke that the quickest way to clear a city-council room was to shout, "Your saloon's on fire!" The liquor industry raised millions of dollars to defeat high license and local option, and some of the money went toward purchasing votes. The alcohol industry subsidized candidates, paid for press opinions, organized political lobbies, manipulated the courts, and bought public officials outright. Though Jones's picture of a conspiracy of corruption was overdrawn, there was enough truth in his accusation to make it credible to millions of Americans. [67]

It is impossible to comprehend the progressive impulse of prohibition without understanding that these reformers were convinced that through prohibition they would free America from a tyrannical power that was corrupting and subverting democracy. Nor was there any doubt in their minds that the "Whiskey Trust" was strongest in cities like Chicago, Boston, Cincinnati, and New York, where a majority of citizens were foreign-born, places that seemed to Protestant Americans to be "practically parts of foreign countries set down in our midst." This enmity toward the immigrant gave prohibition a strong nativist strain, and the pronouncements of prohibitionists were often an amalgamation of antiurban, antiimmigrant sentiments. "In our large cities the controlling vote is that of the dangerous classes, who are readily dominated by the saloon," the Presbyterian Committee on Temperance explained. "City government is 'boss government,' and the boss rules by the grace of the grog shop." [68]

Sam Jones was frank about his belief that prohibition was desirable because it would slow the tide of immigration and control aliens already within the gates. In an impromptu interview on a ferryboat, Jones told a reporter from the *San Francisco Examiner:* "I am a Know-Nothing in politics" (referring to the defunct political party whose cornerstone had been nativism). "The country is being weakened by the influx of a lower and alien element. I greatly desire to see this country become and remain thoroughly American." Perhaps, Jones ventured, a party could be formed uniting the "better class of Southern people with the better class of the Northern people" against "negro rule" and foreign domination. [69]

The connection between prohibition and race was openly discussed in the southern press, and appeals to "racial pride" were made without fear of reproach. In an editorial that appeared a few days before the Atlanta prohibition election of 1885, the *Journal* suggested that "respectable anti-Prohibitionist citizens" should "take a walk past the cluster of whiskey dens on Decatur Street; or other localities similarly cursed, and see the crowd of loafing, bloated, hang-dog looking Negroes who stand around these places with red badges on their rags, advertising the bar-rooms and their own degradation. If the sickening sight is not enough to turn their stomachs and cause the blush of shame to rise in their cheeks at being found in such company, we will acknowledge that we are not able to understand the meaning of self-respect." [70]

Religious periodicals were equally unabashed in their insistence on white superiority and racial unity. "The first fact to be grappled with," the Reverend J. M. Hawley wrote in the *Christian Advocate* in 1904, "is that the Anglo-Saxon and the negro are at the poles of humanity. The one has largely made the civilization of modern times; the other, left to itself, has risen very little above the beasts of the African wilds." Hawley's solution to dealing with this "shiftless" race with its "low moral sensibilities" was the same solution reformers in the Northeast and Midwest clung to as the answer to immigrant inundation: prohibition. "Only those who are thrown into close contact with [black people] know of their passion for strong drink," Hawley wrote. "Where they are allowed to vote prohibition is well-nigh impossible. But the greatest blessing the whites can confer upon them is to put liquor beyond their reach, even if it is necessary to disfranchise the whole race." [71]

Hawley's position was far from unique. Southerners' support of prohibition was motivated not only by humanitarian concerns but by deep racial fear and loathing. Many southerners were convinced that the uncontrolled sale of alcohol was unsafe in a multiracial society: with "one gallon of whiskey," Sam Small warned, "flint meets steel over an open keg of powder." The belief that drinking "inflamed the passions" and augmented the "criminal propensities" of blacks explains why in Alabama "the strongest voices for temperance came from the counties where Negroes formed a large part of the population" and why, as Will Rogers quipped, "Mississippi would vote dry as long as the voters could stagger to the polls." [72]

Southerners were often quite frank about this source of prohibition sentiment. In 1881, fearing that the tax on alcoholic beverages was about to be removed, prohibitionists petitioned the North Carolina legislature to pass "an absolute and unqualified prohibition law." If liquor were available for twenty-five cents a gallon, "with our mixed population, and the passions and prejudices of races, and our small and unprotected families, who can contemplate the possibilities without horror?" The Louisville editor Henry Watterson confessed, "The pretense is temperance, [but] the real underlying, compelling cause is the negro."[73]

Southerners were candid about their expectation that prohibition would be most prohibitive to blacks. Noting that 100 of the 136 counties in Georgia had gone dry, the *Atlanta Constitution* acknowledged that there was no "expectation that it will impede the drinking proclivities of the whites, but that it will prevent the sale of intoxicating liquors to the negroes." In fact, prohibition in Atlanta from 1885 to 1887 mainly prohibited alcohol to blacks by raising the cost and by granting "wine-room" licenses to operations restricted to white trade. This fact convinced many blacks to vote against prohibition in future referendums.[74]

Like the overwhelming majority of southern prohibitionists, Sam Jones believed that social conditions made prohibition imperative. As long as liquor was available, Jones argued, "negroes will drink it and steal to get money to buy it." In the spirit of southern paternalism, he tried for years to persuade blacks to vote for prohibition. "Don't go and sell yourselves like sheep, my colored friends," he implored on the eve of a prohibition election in Milledgeville. "Here are these barkeepers living in purple and fine linens and faring sumptuously every day, and you poor negroes go from the saloon by way of the courthouse to the chaingang." Denied liquor in slavery, blacks regarded alcohol as a symbol of freedom, and some believed liquor agents who told them prohibitionists were trying to reenslave them. It was their resistance to prohibition that would convince Jones that the black man must be barred from the polls, and he would work to marry the "progressive" reforms of disfranchisement and prohibition.[75]

Though Jones supported prohibition for moral, social, and political reasons, much of his animosity toward alcohol came from his own experience with addiction. Unlike most prohibitionists, Jones had personally battled John Barleycorn, and his war against liquor had all the markings of a personal vendetta. "If I did not fight the saloon," Jones admitted candidly, "I might go into them." Tormented by temptation in a western town in the summer of 1906, Jones told Walt Holcomb that the craving which had been quiet for years had come upon him again. "I ran to my room, locked the door and fell upon my knees telling God that I could not withstand a stronger temptation than the one that seized me on the street and I would go down before it," Jones confided a few days later. But then God had called to mind the words to "our grand old hymn":

When through the deep waters I call thee to go,
The rivers of woe shall not thee overflow,
For I will be with thee, thy troubles to bless,
And sanctify to thee thy deep distress.

"God seemed to say to me, you have passed through the darkest valley,
pulled the steepest hill, the worst is over, the best is ahead." Sam Jones
died that fall.[76]

All the ways of a man are clean in his own eyes; but the
Lord weighs the spirit.
—*Proverbs 16:2*

But th' throuble with this here plan is th' higher ye boost
th' naygar be askin' him up to th' White House, th' farther
he has to fall when he gets about two blocks South 'iv th'
White House.

   Me frinds down South don't believe in this way of ilivatin'
th' coon. They have ways 'iv their own.
—*Mr. Dooley*

9

❧ Poli-ticks

Sam Jones relished the clash of politics: "I love to see the fur fly, especially when I don't have to furnish any fur to do the flying." His revival meetings mimicked political rallies, with public officials extolled or excoriated, prohibition lobbies organized, and crusades for "law and order" launched. Jones's respect for the system made his denunciations of purchasable politicians stinging: "There is no dirtier cesspool this side of perdition than American politics," he concluded. "I think we better leave off the poli and just call it pure 'ticks.'"[1]

Beginning in 1892, Sam Jones had a new platform for his political opinions: a weekly column for the *Atlanta Journal*. The commencement of Jones's column coincided with the rise in the South and West of populism, an angry expression of agrarian revolt against the Democratic party and its affiliation with the oppressive eastern banking system and railroads. Control of the national government had passed from the agricultural to the industrial interests, and farmers were dismayed by their loss of status and economic clout. This erosion was particularly acute in the South, where planters had dominated economic and political life before the Civil War, and where credit was now unavailable except on unfavorable terms. The panic of 1893 and the deflation that followed made debts loom larger and business failures multiply. By the end of the "heart-breaking nineties," farmers sold a bushel of wheat or a bale of cotton for less than it cost to grow. "We make the clothes for all the world," one Populist song lamented, "But few we have to wear."[2]

Casting about for a way out of economic ruin, Populists seized upon several solutions. One was a subtreasury plan, by which farmers could store nonperishable products until a fair price could be obtained. To counter deflation, Populists proposed that the money supply be enlarged by restoring silver to its old ratio of sixteen ounces of silver to one ounce of gold. Believing that the demonetization of silver in 1877 had been engineered by the banks, Populists wanted the government alone to have the right to issue currency. Other proposals included government ownership of railroads, a graduated income tax, the secret ballot, improvement of public schools, abolition of the convict lease system, restrictions on immigration, and the reclamation of surplus land held by railroads.[3]

Initially, Jones was sympathetic. His hometown of Cartersville was a center of Populist stirrings, and in his travels he came face to face with hard-pressed folks. His own acreage made him realize the truth of his neighbor Bill Arp's lament that "farming is a slow way to make money." He agreed that there was a currency famine, estimating that "our money property is too small by one half." However, Grover Cleveland's unflinching advocacy of the gold standard convinced Jones that inflation would be unfair to creditors. When the silver forces in the House and Senate worked to marshal a majority for unlimited coinage of silver, Jones announced, "I am for Cleveland first, last, and always, and would like for him to come out in a message dissolving parliament and give the country a rest."[4]

Jones was convinced that the Populist belief in a conspiracy of "plutocrats" was an overblown phantom, and their anger at "class legislation" was a cover for personal failure. "God Almighty gives us all an even start in this world, and if you don't make a man of yourself it's your own fault," Jones declared. "I'll give you my head in a hat, and you may use it for a foot-ball—and you couldn't use it for a much worse purpose—if you'll show me a law that discriminates against any man." Told that Populists contended that legislation favoring railroads and corporate monopolies had concen-trated wealth in the industrial East and robbed the farmers of the South and West, Jones scoffed: "The babies! It's no loafers and kickers country!" Such weaklings only "want to get hold of the government's nipple." [5]

To Jones, many of the People's party proposals sounded like the ravings of men who had never made a payroll. "As for myself," he wrote in his col-umn, "I have very little confidence in the ability of the third party orators to revolutionize and regulate the finances of this great government, when at each political meeting they pass around the hat to send the orator to the next speaking place." He was especially critical of Populists who rejected overtures by Democrats, behaving like a "mule" who would "turn its heels and kick the fillings out of everything that approaches." [6]

During the gubernatorial race of 1896, however, it seemed that Jones might be forced into supporting the People's party. Bidding for the middle-class church vote, Tom Watson persuaded Populists to support a state dis-pensary which would give the government a monopoly on the sale of alcohol and abolish saloons. "We 'fool Populists' have adopted a platform with an ante-bar-room plank in it," James K. Hines, former Populist candidate for governor, wrote Jones triumphantly. Hines challenged Jones to fulfill his promise to "stump the state" for any party with a prohibition platform and support Seaborn Wright, a fervent prohibitionist. The evangelist saw little advantage to a dispensary over Governor W. Y. Atkinson's plan, which allowed each community to vote itself wet or dry. The "Pops," Jones warned, were merely trying to "snare Methodists." [7]

Though Jones refused direct support, he inadvertently helped the People's party in 1896 by exposing the Democrats' fraudulent activities in the congressional elections of 1892 and 1894. The Democrats had trucked in so many votes to defeat Tom Watson in the Tenth District that in 1892 there were twice as many votes as registered voters. "You needn't be afraid of negro domination in Augusta," Jones scoffed. "When you want to you Democrats can pile up a majority bigger than all the white men, black men, mules and dogs that there are in the county." The Democrats' defense that the Populists' appeal to black voters compelled corruption caused Jones to snort that these "loose-jointed and rattle-brained visionaries" had never threatened the Solid South. "They may get to heaven, but they'll never get to Washington." While he admitted that "both parties bear watching," Jones insisted that his visit to the state archives to study the election returns—

returns which had taken seven days to "fix"—revealed that the Populists had been more sinned against than sinning.[8]

Jones was especially incensed by the machinations against his old teacher, Dr. William Felton, who had tried to regain the seat he had held as an independent from the Seventh District. Making use of corrupt commissioners, Democrats had disfranchised three hundred Cartersville residents suspected of Populist sympathies. Black voters were rewarded with barbeque and free liquor for voting Democratic. When Felton and other Populist candidates challenged the election results, they found the grand juries packed with Democrats. "I had as soon try to arraign a litter of kittens before the old mother cat as to try to get a grand jury to find a true bill against a set of ring tricksters and ballot box stuffers," Jones scoffed. The Populists had been defrauded in 1894. Any editor who disagreed was "too ignorant to edit a journal in the jungles of Africa."[9]

Jones's solution to fraud was blackmail. "My dear Steve," Jones wrote in an open letter to Steve Clay, chairman of Georgia's Democratic committee, "we must have an honest election in Georgia this time." Jones warned that if he heard that Democrats were planning fraud or enticing blacks to vote for them by promises of jobs, cash, or political preferment, he would bring on another divisive prohibition campaign in Atlanta. Worse, he would "take to the stump" and reproduce correspondence that would "bring the charges on you boys from the wire grass regions of the South to the mountains of Northeast Georgia where the whangdoodle mourneth."[10]

The Democrats did not take long to furnish the fuel for Jones's match. Outraged by the rising tide of lynching, Governor Atkinson goaded the Georgia General Assembly into stronger legislation against mob law. On the strength of that legislation, Atkinson took the extraordinary step of punishing five police officers who had allowed a suspect to be taken by a mob. As election time neared, black constituents were reminded of Atkinson's record in a leaflet containing this sentence: "Atkinson pardoned Adolphus Duncan, a negro who was twice convicted of rape against a white woman and was sentenced to be hanged." No mention was made of Duncan's innocence, an oversight whites feared would encourage black men to rape in the expectation that a sympathetic governor would overlook their crime. "See for yourselves what impression it will make on the ignorant and besotted fiend that roams at will in our exposed districts," Tom Watson's *People's Party Paper* shrilled.[11]

When Steve Clay denied knowledge of the "rape circular," Jones applied his match, publishing a memo from Clay to Atkinson that mentioned the offending leaflet: "What Governor Atkinson Has Done for the Colored

People." "No more incendiary literature was ever circulated from the hot-beds of abolitionism or the fury of Reconstruction politics than the rape circular," Jones fumed. "The fearful outrages upon Georgia women in the past three or four days must make the hearts of the Campaign Executive Committee tremble with horror."[12]

Though the uproar cost Atkinson white votes, it convinced blacks that their interests were not with the the Populists, who six years earlier had passed a record number of antiblack bills. Atkinson defeated Wright, and the disillusioned Populist party began to work angrily for disfranchisement. White people would never be free to divide as long as the unscrupulous could frighten voters with the "africanization" of the state. "For more than a generation 'the nigger' has been the stock-in-trade of the Democratic Party in the South," Watson fumed. "Nothing can be done as long as the South is forever frightened into political paralysis by the cry of 'negro domina-tion.'" As for Sam Jones, he dropped the topic abruptly, writing with impish evasion that "Georgia has had as fair an election as she has had for years."[13]

Jones's interest in Georgia politics continued, and on February 19, 1898, the headlines of the *Atlanta Journal* revealed that the evangelist intended to be more than a political commentator in the next governor's race:

REV. SAM P. JONES ANNOUNCES FOR
GOVERNOR; DECIDED THIS MORNING
TO ENTER THE RACE.
He Says it is Nobody's Business
Whether He is in Earnest.[14]

Suggesting that Georgia might need a Christian governor more than an evangelist, Jones insisted he was interested only in "the greatest good for the greatest number." He announced his platform as "unadulterated, un-purchasable, unbulldozable manhood" and promised to cut the state budget in half or resign. "Down with extortion—even the extortion of a sovereign State," Jones proclaimed. "Let's pen up the jackasses for a while in the back lot and trot out some throroughbreds."[15]

For days little was discussed on courthouse steps and in the homes of the devout than the candidacy of Sam P. Jones. While predicting that the evangelist was playing one of his famous practical jokes, the *Atlanta Con-stitution* acknowledged that Jones could control an enormous number of votes. "His wit, wisdom, and eloquence have made him famous and it goes without saying that on the stump in a political campaign he would be one of the most unique, picturesque and powerful figures ever seen in the arena of politics."[16]

Much of the speculation centered on what party the eccentric evangelist would represent. He had gone to the torchlight processions and drunk the campaign whiskey of the Democrats while a sinner, and after he "got religion" he had seen no pressing need to alter his political affiliation. Being a Democrat "is a mighty hard thing to get over," he admitted, and "if there is anymore pressure on any one thing than there is on another it's on a citizen of Georgia voting the Democratic ticket." However, when the Democrats came out in favor of "the liberty of individual conduct unvexed by sumptuary laws," Jones felt he could not support a political party so expressly against prohibition. However, his memories of Reconstruction were too fresh to allow him to join the Republican party. As far as he could tell, there was only one difference between the two parties: "the Republicans have shouldered the nigger and the Democrats have straddled a barrel of whiskey," proving that "the rascal predominates in one party; the fool, in the other." When the *Constitution* inquired about his party affiliation, Jones answered: "I am a horse in the field, loose, without any saddle or bridle and I am dead sure I have no rider on board."[17]

The Populists, orphaned by Tom Watson's decision not to run for governor, rushed to endorse Sam Jones. Seaborn Wright telegraphed Jones not to develop a political doctrine: "You are platform enough." John Fullerwood, editor of a Populist paper in Jones's congressional district, wrote that if Watson remained firm in his decision not to run "I believe our people would rally to your support almost to a man." Privately, Fullerwood predicted that Jones "would probably get enough democratic, populist and republican votes to make him governor of Georgia."[18]

It seems puzzling that Populists would support the man who advised them "not to sleep lying on their sides" as "their brains would all run out their ears." However, the People's party was in disarray after state and national defeats, and the charismatic evangelist offered Populists that combination of down-home demagoguery and eccentric individualism they favored in political leaders. An outspoken opponent of political chicanery, Jones could be counted on to ensure there were no "irregularities" at the polls if Populists garnered strength for another run. And though Populists sometimes sounded like "modern-day levellers," many of them were middle-class folks who shared Jones's concern about the high cost of government.[19]

While some Populists supported prohibition out of political expediency, many honestly shared Jones's view that the "Whiskey Trust" was an insidious conspiracy that endangered public and private morality. Finally, Sam Jones and the Populists feared foreigners and favored restriction on immigration. Though Jones did not feel strongly on the issue of "alien" ownership of land, he exceeded many Populists in his zeal to disfranchise the "foreign hoards" who frustrated his prohibition campaigns. He suggested that all immigrants be tested on their ability to read and write in English, and none be enfranchised before they had lived in the country twenty-one years. "We who are born here cannot vote until we have been here twenty-one years," Jones reasoned. "Why should any foreigner have the advantage?"[20]

However, on the issue of education Jones was at odds with both the Populists, who favored free textbooks, and the newly rising Progressives, who favored free, compulsory public education. While Jones agreed that education should be universal and compulsory, it should not be free: "first free schools, then free stores." Jones's individualism was offended by the idea of a uniform education that would turn out a standard product "like round sausage, just the same in diameter and length and about the same substance." His elitism was affronted as well, for he was convinced that in public schools the "best" children would be mixed with the "worst." To avoid this calamity with his own children, he built a charming little school-house behind his large Victorian house and engaged a Christian lady to teach his six offspring along with neighbors' children, carefully screened.[21]

Jones not only advocated pinching off the incipient educational bureau-cracy, he lobbied for weeding out the parasitic "pap-suckers" and "time-servers" who lived off the public. Overtaxation—the government got two of every hundred dollars—had made so many "perjurers" that "no one man in a hundred would sell his property for double what he swears it is worth on the tax books of our county." To keep costs down Jones proposed elimi-nating homestead exemption and pensions for veterans and their widows. The situation was bad in the South, where the states paid the pensions; it was ludicrous in the North, where the federal government footed the bill. If Confederates had known "we had maimed 1,400,000 [Yankees] as bad as they say we did when they go after those pensions we would have made another rally and whipped 'em."[22]

Jones's views were consistent with the antiintellectualism, individualism, and suspicion of central government embedded in southern society. Jones's contention that the government should serve those who pay the bills, that the South could not afford to educate its offspring, and that government costs were out of control were all echoes of the Reconstruction South. In 1898 Sam Jones was running for governor as a Redeemer. Even his platform was drawn from the issues of 1870: "I believe in penitence for the past and glorious hopefulness for the future."[23]

The time had passed when a Redeemer could be elected governor of Georgia. Hoke Smith, an owner of the *Atlanta Journal* and a leader of the education movement, ridiculed Jones's platform as regressive. If the education crusade were abandoned, Smith scoffed, Georgia would be known as "the most backward and miserly state in the Union" and would be unable to attract desirable immigrants or retain "intelligent parents." More effective than this straightforward editorial was the parody of Jones's platform presented by candidate "Sam Peajay Buncombe." "I am against the free lunch but I am hell on free speech," Buncombe announced. As for public education, "if any old flop-eared hound is unable to educate his children, let them remain ignorant and we will take care of them in the jails and prisons and penitentiaries and on the gallows." Buncombe ended: "I shall resent any assertion to the effect that I am a candidate for advertising purposes only, that I may attract large crowds when I extort, that the collections may also be large, and that my vanity may be well fed." [24]

Though Georgians enjoyed the stir, Jones's closest friends were appalled by his candidacy. "In my judgement your running for Governor would be the mistake of your life, Hit or Miss," coworker George Stuart telegraphed from Tennessee. Jones's old convert Thomas Ryman begged Jones to withdraw before more damage was done to his reputation as an evangelist. John W. Thomas, Jr., owner of the L and N Railroad, worried that his friend was making a "terrible mistake." Though Thomas had no doubt Jones would make a good governor, no job, not even president of the United States, was "equal to bringing men to God. . . . You do not belong to the State of Georgia but to the Christian people of the country at large," Thomas insisted. [25]

After five days of running for office, Jones announced that he did not "want to be interviewed any more as a candidate—never!" "I see a fellow has to be sorter cautious when he is a candidate not only of what he says but what he has been saying for years," Jones explained; "it don't suit me to be cautious." He advised supporters to vote for the poor man's friend, "the one-eyed ploughboy of Pigeon Roost," Allen D. Candler. [26]

Even at the beginning of his "campaign" Jones had said, "I am a Candler man, next to myself." It seems likely that Jones's candidacy was simply a demonstration of the evangelist's political muscle designed to pressure Candler into supporting temperance education and statewide prohibition. Candler had declared statewide prohibition unworkable because of the hostility of urban dwellers, but cynics wondered if his ownership of a hotel in Gainesville where the bar had brought in nine hundred dollars a year before local option dried up Hall County might have been more of a factor. Even though Candler's platform was silent on the issue, Jones predicted that "Allen D." would come out on the right side of the prohibition question, or "arrange to vacate the gubernatorial mansion at the expiration of this present term." He was right. In 1902 Candler signed a Scientific Temperance Law to provide for education in the schools and vetoed a bill that would have established a dispensary in Georgia.[27]

One of the planks in Candler's campaign was an endorsement of the Spanish-American War. Sam Jones was not swept away by the prospect of American empire; his prejudices prevented him from being an enthusiastic expansionist in those heady days when there was talk of planting the flag from Manilla to Mexico City. He opposed the annexation of Hawaii and was not impressed by the attempt of newspapers like the *Atlanta Journal* and those in the Hearst chain to drum up a war with Spain. "It would be like a strong, vigorous man hitting a frail, puny, sickly, weak little woman," he chided.[28]

When the war began, however, Jones was thrilled by accounts of American heroism, touched by the spectacle of the sons of Confederates and the sons of Federals donning the same uniform, and converted by declarations that the war was God's means of "bringing light" to those in darkness. "If this Spanish-American war shall wipe out forever the sectional differences in America and broaden the circle of Christian civilization, then we will not have spilled our blood or spent our money in vain," Jones concluded. "Spain has shown herself utterly incapable of Christian civilization, and God himself may be behind the guns of America."[29]

The rhetoric of imperialism was the rhetoric of racism, as Jones's remarks reveal. America has been getting the "offscouring of creation" for twenty-five years, Jones growled, and "we may need some of these islands to dump that foreign element back on." First on his list for deportation would be the Germans, who, though racially acceptable, had been so contaminated with socialism and "irreligion" that "they have no Sabbath and they resent any encroachments of their personal rights." His belief that "the difference in man is organic" made him equally unenthusiastic about assimilating the inhabitants of Spain's conquered empire. After all, Jones pointed out with characteristic delicacy, "the fellow don't always keep down everything he swallows."[30]

The imperialist creed, based as it was on the pseudoscientific theories of Social Darwinism, supplied southerners with the ideological underpinnings for their own resurgent racism. If the Filipinos, Cubans, and Hawaiians were intended by the Creator to be ruled by a superior Caucasian civilization, surely blacks were, as well. If participation by those of Latin blood would contaminate the political process, surely the participation of blacks invited disorder and regression. These statements by Congressman John Sharp Williams of Mississippi illustrate the implications of such thinking. "You could wreck ten-thousand illiterate white Americans on a desert island," the congressman speculated in 1898, "and in three weeks they would have a fairly good government, conceived and administered upon fairly democratic lines. You could shipwreck ten-thousand negroes, every one of whom was a graduate of Harvard University, and in less than three years, they would have retrograded governmentally; half of the men would have been killed, and the other half would have two wives apiece."[31]

Other factors besides imperialism contributed to the movement toward disfranchisement and segregation. The fact that Social Darwinism could be so readily embraced illustrates that the "overwhelming majority" of Americans believed that blacks were "innately inferior." As southerners never tired of pointing out, the very communities that reared with indignation at "southern outrages" habitually practiced racism at home. Northerners were content for 90 percent of the black race to reside in the South. Informed in 1905 that a group of blacks were immigrating to Indiana to find work, armed white men met them at the state lines and refused them entry. In 1908 the Committee for Improving the Industrial Conditions of the Negro in New York asked black leaders to use their influence to keep their people in the South; discrimination, an unkind climate, and atrocious living conditions had made the condition of southern refugees desperate.[32]

Northerners were weary of racial issues; even reformers were more interested in railroad tariffs, tenement houses, and child laborers. The old champions who might have called the country back to earlier ideals were feeble or dead. The development of the West had displaced the South in congressional issues, and northern capitalists were more interested in stability than in social justice. Further, many northerners were convinced that black enfranchisement was a failed reform, and their every defection was gleefully reprinted in the southern press. One dramatic example was that of William H. Thorne, editor of the *New York Globe Quarterly* and an old abolitionist. On a trip south in the late nineties, Thorne denounced the "insufferable self-assertion of our negroes" and their "shiftless, unteachable, immoral" ways, which rendered them "unworthy of American citizenship." He predicted that within thirty years the South would be forced to "re-enslave, kill or export the bulk of its negro population."[33]

Though Thorne's apostasy was extreme, there were only muffled outcries in the North when Supreme Court decisions gutted the Civil Rights Acts and endorsed the South's solution of "separate but equal." Unopposed from the outside, radicalism swept through the South, accompanied by laws providing for disfranchisement through poll taxes and property and literacy requirements, and for segregation on trains, streetcars, theaters, and hotels.

Lynchings peaked—235 in 1892. By 1895, when Governor Atkinson announced that "the dark cloud of prejudice had passed over" the South, the existence of blacks was one of insult, intimidation, and oppression.[34]

Former moderates, who had viewed blacks as unequal but teachable, slipped into racial radicalism. This descent was dramatically demonstrated by Sam Small, Jones's assistant in the great northern and midwestern revivals of the eighties. Brought up a southern aristocrat, Small was unable to scale back his style of living to fit a minister's salary. Despite frequent loans from Jones, problems with creditors constantly threatened scandal, and in 1887 the "two Psalms" went their separate ways. Though he served briefly as agent for the Paine Institute in Augusta, a college for blacks, by 1892 Small had joined the Populists and sunk to a racism even the *Atlanta Constitution* found "terrifying." In a rabid speech before the Populist convention, Small lambasted Grover Cleveland for inviting Frederick Douglass—"the leader of niggerdom"—and his "low" white wife to the White House for dinner. Small was still a prohibitionist, and his brawl with a saloon keeper contributed to the defeat of the Populists in 1892.[35]

Historians have found the ferocity of racism difficult to explain. Some blame politics, pointing out the South's anxiety in 1888 when Republican Benjamin Harrison appointed black Republicans to public office in the South. One year later, Republicans controlled all departments in the national government. Southern fears of a new Reconstruction were exacerbated when Henry Cabot Lodge proposed a bill that would provide for federal oversight of national elections and prevent disfranchisement through fraud and intimidation.[36]

Southern politics played a part as well. The inflammatory tactics of the politicians are infamous, tactics arising not only from the desire to tar an opponent as soft on white superiority but also from a real fear of black political power. At the very time southern whites were insisting upon the blacks' inability to participate in self-government, black people were getting cannier about using bloc voting to win concessions from political factions. The fact that Populists and Democrats vied with each other to win the black vote is tacit acknowledgement of the ability of black leaders to obtain results for their race at a time when disfranchisement was shrinking their power. The "accommodationist" maneuverings of Booker T. Washington, the writings of W. E. B. Du Bois, and the founding of the National Association for the Advancement of Colored People reveal the existence of a highly developed sense of political survival and a determination to remain part of American political life.[37]

Some historians have found an economic explanation for racial radicalism. As the standard of living for whites declined, many families were forced into a sharecropping system designed to control black labor. Yet in Georgia blacks had been able to increase their landholdings by more than a million acres in a single generation. Though confined by discrimination to largely unskilled jobs, blacks were finding a place in southern industry as well. By 1900 half of the trackmen and nearly one-third of the firemen and brakemen working for railroads in the South were black. Two-thirds of the dockworkers in New Orleans, the shipbuilders in Virginia, and the tobacco workers in North Carolina were black, as were a fourth of the cowboys in Texas.[38]

Blacks were also making educational progress, cutting their illiteracy rate in half by the turn of the century. Visitors to the South, like Ray Stannard Baker, a reporter who came in the aftermath of the Atlanta race riot, spoke of the "astonishing and pathetic" eagerness of black people for education. Whites recognized and feared it. "The future is fraught with danger," F. P. Venable, governor of North Carolina, warned. "The negroes are being rapidly educated, and the whites not in proportion. If Anglo-Saxon superiority is to be maintained," this was "a very suicidal course." Such comments led W. E. B. Du Bois to suggest that the rise of racism was due not to black retrogression but to black progress. "There is one thing that the white south feared more than negro dishonesty, ignorance, and incompetency," Du Bois wrote, "and that was negro honesty, knowledge, and efficiency."[39]

A "new Negro" was emerging, a black person the *Fisk Herald* described as unbroken by slavery, "ignorant of the so-called instinctive fear of their fathers . . . more sensitive to injustice and quick to resent." To whites, however, "new Negro" meant insolent rather than self-respecting, sullen rather than sensitive. Whites contended that this "new Negro," unschooled in the "civilizing effects of slavery," away from the benevolent effects of white oversight, was retrogressing. Their most convincing evidence was the exponential growth of the "new Negro crime": rape.[40]

Returning to Georgia from California in 1893, Bishop Atticus Haygood commented on the increased incidence of rape. He could recall only one instance in which a white woman was raped by a black man before the Civil War; now he thought that the estimate of three hundred rapes in three months was "too low." If Haygood—a man whose liberal stance on race relations had caused him to be ostracized ten years earlier—believed this, it is not surprising that those less friendly to "the brother in black" would give credence to the most hysterical accounts of a rape epidemic. It became an article of faith that when black men had been invested with civic equality through "mistaken philanthropy and deluded fanaticism," the way seemed open for them to realize their fond, secret wish: racial amalgamation.[41]

Historians have cast about for explanation for this sexual hysteria. Some contend the increased crime was an inevitable part of urban life. Some blame the press for creating an atmosphere of paranoia, noting they were abetted by an 1896 law which defined "rape" as any physical assault upon a woman—even a hostile gesture. The overwrought nature of the claims have indicated to some historians that the explanation lies in pychotherapy. Sexually repressed Victorians, captive to a culture that worshipped the white female as an unapproachable Madonna, projected their fantasies on the black male. Killing, disenfranchising, and excluding the "sexual beasts" released and empowered white men and "fit the psychic needs of a generation who had been fatherless and powerless during the war [and] destitute and vanquished during Reconstruction."[42]

However, to those caught in a "crisis of sex and race," the solution was not a searching of the psyche, it was the "rope and the faggot." Though laws passed under Governors Northen and Atkinson made penalties for lynching more severe, from 1888 to 1903, 241 blacks were lynched in Georgia, making the state second only to Mississippi in dispensing "summary justice." Lynching became more ghoulish as the "juries in the woods" decided that hanging was "a mercy." Rebecca Latimer Felton proclaimed: "It is not possible to inflict upon the black rapist any punishment comparable to the suffering already endured by innocence and virtue. If he was torn to pieces limb by limb and burnt with slow fire, or hung by the thumbs until the buzzards swarm around him, he would still be saved some of the revolting torture already inflicted upon a harmless victim." Another Cartersvillian, Bill Arp, was equally vehement. "As for lynching, let the good work go on. Lynch 'em! Hang 'em! Shoot 'em! Burn 'em!"[43]

In the midst of this carnage, a few clergymen spoke out. In 1902 Andrew Sledd was forced to resign as a Latin professor at Emory College for publishing an article in the *Atlantic Monthly* that denounced lynching as a "wild and diabolical carnival of blood." Sledd's father-in-law, Bishop Warren Akin Candler, was angered that Sledd's family had been forced to flee the South under death threats, and he took up the fight for social justice. Candler stripped the hood off the "morality" of the mob. "He who incites a mob to lynch a human being is in the sight of God an accessory to murder, if not an outright and downright murderer," Candler insisted. "It is a contradiction in terms to say that Christian men have been members of murderous mobs."[44]

However, most clergymen equivocated about lynching. In 1895 the *Advocate* contained an article typical of the time. Citing a lynching in Cole City, Tennessee, which had followed the "outrage" of a "highly connected young lady," the *Advocate* concluded that "in the case before us the negro deserved what he got." The black man had been taken out of jail, his body riddled with bullets, mutilated, then burned. After the Atlanta race riot, it was the consensus of the ministers of the city that "when raping stops riots will cease." Dr. A. R. Holderby, pastor of Moore Memorial Presbyterian Church, summed up popular opinion. Though he regretted the riot, Holderby said, it did demonstrate "that the people of the South will protect their wives and daughters and sisters, regardless of the consequences and at all hazards."[45]

Sam Jones also equivocated about lynching. "I've got no respect for a mob," he often said. "A mob is the most infernal, cowardly thing in this world. Ten thousand men screw up their courage to the sticking point and rush up to a handcuffed, defenseless negro and mob him on the spot. That's courage, ain't it?" However, Jones continued to mouth the southern maxim that lynching was provoked by rape, and "rape means rope in every state in the Union." To thunderous applause in Evansville, Indiana, in 1903, Jones announced that "Anglo-Saxon blood is the same everywhere. The only way to stop lynchings and riots between the races is for the colored race to stay from over the dead-line, for when the brother in black crosses the dead-line they will get him every pop. They are slow to learn that fact, but they will learn it, and the sooner the better."[46]

There is no doubt that Sam Jones was influenced by the rising tide of racism. How thin the veneer of paternalism had worn on him was demonstrated by his reaction to the lynching of Sam Hose, to which Andrew Sledd had been an unwilling witness. Hose, a "ginger negro," allegedly killed a white farmer and raped the man's wife on the bloody floor next to the body. According to the Cartersville paper, Hose was lynched in Palmetto, Georgia, "in the presence of nearly 2,000 people, who sent aloft yells and defiance and shouts of joy" while "depriving" Hose of "his ears, fingers, and other portions of his anatomy." After mutilating, hanging, and burning Hose, "the crowd fought for place about the smouldering tree, and with knives secured such pieces of his carcass as did not fall to pieces." Souvenir hunters who rode special excursion trains from Atlanta were offered ghoulish relics: "small pieces of bone went for 25 cents, and a bit of the liver, crisply cooked, sold for 10 cents."[47]

Initially, Jones insisted the lynching had been unnecessary since Georgia has the "best judiciary and best law enforcement in the nation"; most criminals are "hung within five days of sentencing." He especially objected to Hose being "cooked," since he felt "a lynching ought to be a decent affair, if it is obliged to be done." Within a few months, however, Jones concluded that in the case of such a moral monster, "then anybody, anything, anyway to get rid of such a brute." [48]

The Atlanta Evangelical Ministers' Association held an emergency session the day after the Hose incident. Len Broughton, pastor of the Baptist Tabernacle and outspoken opponent of lynching, expressed his conviction that the white and black race could not live together in peace in the South. He called for a "gradual, voluntary removal of the colored to the tropics." Broughton's church was vandalized and he received a charred fingerbone in the mail. [49]

Broughton was not alone in his belief that exodus was the answer. Blacks weary of prejudice and made desperate by the increasing savagery of racism responded to the "Back to Africa" movement led by Bishop Henry McNeal Turner of the African Methodist Episcopal Church. The expenses of transportion, tales of awful living conditions in Liberia, and the deaths from fever of many who actually emigrated caused the effort to collapse. Another Georgia clergyman, Lucius H. Holsey of the Colored Methodist Episcopal Church, led a more moderate separatist movement. Holsey was convinced that flight to the North was futile and emigration to Africa was impractical. Nor could the Negro remain in the South unless "he lives in the submerged realm of serfdom and slavery." Given this impasse, Holsey proposed that the United States government establish a Negro state, possibly in Oklahoma or New Mexico. In this state, blacks could enjoy full manhood suffrage, and whites would be refused residency except through marriage. [50]

Sam Jones recognized that much of the meagre prosperity enjoyed by the New South was founded—as the vast wealth of the Old South had been—on the labor of blacks. "We need the negro South," Jones admitted in 1894. "We want him, not at the polls specially, not in politics, but a negro and a mule is the best cotton combination in America." In 1896 he wrote, "I have always been an abiding friend to the colored race. They are the best servants we have ever had." However, within a few years the ferocity of racial radicalism made him wonder if separation of the races might be best. "Our Brother in Black holds a rather anomalous relation to the state of things, being a weaker race, seemingly settled down amidst a stronger one," Jones wrote in 1897. Perhaps the government should gradually "settle them in one

of the balmy climates along the Southern shores of our great Southwest."
But even if man failed to act, Jones was confident time would take care
of the problem: "the survival of the fittest will settle that question sooner
or later."[51]

Jones continued to insist that whites were the moral and economic over-
seers of the negro. "God will have to do with us by and by when the question
of our relationship and duty towards the colored men will come up for settlement," Jones warned in 1894. However, Jones's language began to reflect
the rising racism. He had always deplored miscegenation; now his remarks
became angrier, cruder. "I never knew a society man who didn't drink and
dance and sleep with nigger women," he said in 1892. On his visit to Boston in 1887 he had stressed racial harmony. Ten years later, he seemed
unafraid of northern disapproval—aware, no doubt, of the erosion of concern in the North. Asked by a Boston reporter if it was true the southerner
was not in sympathy with the instincts of the black, Jones quipped: "It's
generally his outstincts that we are not in sympathy with."[52]

The Negro is "improving all the time, and in many respects doing well,"
the evangelist reassured a St. Louis audience in 1895. "I suppose there is
no race in the world getting along so well on the work they do. They don't
have to work much. [Laughter.] They can work three months in the year
and that puts them to blackberries, and the blackberries puts 'em to persimmons, and persimmons brings 'em to possums, and possums lasts 'em
all winter." The *New York Times* quoted Jones a few months later advising
Yankees not to "waste your sympathy on the niggers of the South. They are
contented and are better off than the poor working girls in the city."[53]

Southerners' suspicions that their "social usages" were under assault by
Republicans determined to appoint blacks to public office were inflamed in
1901 when Theodore Roosevelt became president upon McKinley's assassination. Despite his assurance that "half my blood is Southern," after less
than a month in office, Roosevelt invited Booker T. Washington and his wife
to dinner at the White House, an act of hospitality that caused him to be
vilified in southern presses as "the Black President." Three months later,
Roosevelt hosted a reception at which five blacks were present. Southern
congressmen immediately withdrew their wives, outraged that these "fair
ladies of the South whose instincts and breeding have held them above
social intercourse with the Negro" should be thus affronted. As his final
insult to southern sensibilities, Roosevelt appointed a black woman to be
postmistress at Indianola, Mississippi.[54]

Sam Jones was not disturbed by Roosevelt's dinner with Washington.

Although he felt that Roosevelt's invitation demonstrated that "he himself is an ass," he allowed that it is "a matter of taste, as the old woman said when she kissed the cow." When Roosevelt appointed the black postmistress at Indianola, however, the evangelist joined the chorus of southerners accusing the president of pandering to blacks. "Most of you people don't know what Roosevelt means by this," Jones told a Houston audience in 1903. "He is simply a politician. You are not aware of the fact that in a number of States the negro holds the balance of power." Jones concluded with a crowd-pleasing piece of demagoguery. "The South has said, and the South will stick to it, that this is a white man's country. [Applause.] I like the colored brother. I have stood by him when it cost me something to do it. I would not harm a hair on the head of a colored man in the South, but this is a white man's country. God gave it to the Indians, and we took it away from them. [Laughter and applause.]"[55]

Jones counseled forgiveness for the president, sure that the roar coming out of the South would prevent Roosevelt from repeating his breach of racial etiquette. "White will remain white and black will remain black long after the president has been gathered to his fathers," Jones wrote. His prediction proved correct. To the disillusionment of blacks, the chastened politician reversed his southern policy. On a tour of the South in 1905, the old Rough Rider praised the heroes of the Confederacy and advised students of the Tuskegee Institute to give up the idea of training for the professions and be loyal to "their best friends," the southern white conservatives.[56]

Jones praised Roosevelt, writing that his talk at Tuskegee Institute had done "much toward solving the race problem," as had his admission that "the white man who was closest to the black man was in the best position to help him, not someone 2,000 miles away." Jones was among the luminaries who attended Atlanta's luncheon for the president, and at the public rally afterwards, Roosevelt staged a reconciliation. Calling Jones up to the platform, Roosevelt said: "Mr. Jones, you, in your way, are doing for this country and the people what I am trying to accomplish in mine. I heartily endorse your good work, and hope that success will continue to crown your efforts. The next time you visit Washington, I want you to telegraph me in advance, and I want you to be my guest during your stay in the capitol city."[57]

One year later, a report of Roosevelt's patronizing address to the black students at Hampton Institute was sandwiched between articles about the most savage political campaign yet waged in Georgia. The contest received inordinate press coverage because its two principals were Clark Howell, editor of the *Atlanta Constitution* and candidate of the Democratic "machine," and Hoke Smith, a former owner of the *Atlanta Journal*, and secretary of the interior under President Cleveland. The central issue was reform: first, reform of the railroads; later, reform of the ballot box.[58]

It was Clark Howell's contention that poll taxes, residency requirements, and the white primary had already disfranchised the black man. There was no need to amend the constitution of Georgia, Howell insisted; "the negro has no more to do with the politics of the state than the Chinaman." Constitutional disfranchisement would merely provoke the Republican Congress to reduce Georgia's representation. Literacy requirements would "keep out the votes of many an old democratic hero who was too busy shedding his blood in defense of Georgia to learn 'readin', 'ritin' and 'rithmetic.'" Worse yet, it would give the vote to ninety-three thousand educated blacks and drive other "ballot chasing" blacks "from the cotton fields where they are so badly needed, into the schools to equip themselves with an education that was not enjoyed by thousands of the sturdy young white men of the state." Already, Howell quipped, "throughout the state countless thousands of negro children are getting bowlegged with the burden of carrying their books to school."[59]

Hoke Smith assured Georgians that he did not favor education for blacks: "It is folly to spend the money of white men to give negroes a book education." Nor would disfranchisement be used to eliminate uneducated whites, for "heredity brings qualification for suffrage even when unequipped with education." However, Smith insisted that the white primary was insufficient protection from "negro domination." Many elections were not preceded by a primary, Smith pointed out, and "in case of division" the black vote could "give trouble at any time." Nor was the poll tax sufficient; if poll taxes were paid by unscrupulous politicians, black voters would outnumber whites in sixty-five counties in Georgia. However, Hoke Smith acknowledged that his "broader reason" for disfranchisement was racial rather than political. "If we study the true character of the negro," Smith said, we find that "a white man's control is more or less necessary for a large majority of the negroes. Any thing that fills the average negro with the idea of any kind of equality with the white man injures him, and lessens his usefullness, and gives him ENCOURAGEMENT IN HIS FOUL DREAMS OF A MIXTURE OF THE RACES."[60]

Never one to miss out on a fight, Sam Jones used his column in the *Atlanta Journal* to discuss disfranchisement. Jones had long adhered to the New South doctrine of black enfranchisement under white control. At first he was not even enthusiastic about the white primary, a turn-of-the-century effort to "purify" the ballot box by restricting the nominating process to the Caucasian constituency. Far from attracting better candidates—ones who would not "sully" themselves by courting black voters—Jones contended that white primaries often nominated "the lousiest devil in the entire county." It was too bad the white primary was thought necessary, Jones lamented. "If the negro had realized that the best white people of the South were his best friends and he had quit ganging with the liquor crowd and let Yankee Doodle alone, he would have been much better off today."[61]

Though Jones was on a lecture tour in the Midwest, "the land of hog and hominy," he kept in touch with the political situation. In March 1906 he announced he would vote against his "personal friend" and boyhood companion, Clark Howell, because "I am with Mr. Smith, teeth and toenail, on the disfranchisement of the ignorant, viscious voter and the purchaseable voter." Jones did not fear backlash from the North. "I believe that Yankee Doodle has long since admitted to itself that it was a mistake to have given the negro the right to vote."[62]

Nor did he fear the black man would be hurt. Politics has "done more to dissatisfy and debauch the negro" and "cause racial strife than anything else." The southern states that have amended their constitutions to "eliminate the negro from the ballot box" have found their negroes "most contented and happy." Besides, "how much good does the negro get out of the privilege of voting? He knows his vote is not counted, if it is in the way of Democratic domination. When he goes to the polls he makes a fool of himself and afterwards admits it." Jones ended: "If Hoke Smith will carry through this plank of his platform, we will then put the saloon out of business in Georgia. That is the biggest move and the biggest reform that can come to this grand old state."[63]

Sam Jones's comments reveal the intimate association of disfranchisement and prohibition, "reforms" that came to be wedded in the minds of many "progressive" southerners. While prohibitionists earlier had dissociated themselves from disfranchisement, fearing to divide their energies, in 1906, Georgia prohibitionists reversed this stance. They came to believe that Sam Jones was right when he said that if blacks were barred from the polls, Georgia would go dry at the next election.[64]

Disfranchising prohibitionists repeatedly insisted that their reforms were fashioned with the "true welfare" of the blacks in mind. These "child people" need to be "protected from the perils of liberty," John E. White, pastor of the Second Baptist Church in Atlanta, insisted. Just as Indians were denied access to "firewater" for their own protection, blacks should be required to have a physician's prescription before purchasing whiskey.

Above all, they must not be allowed to mix with lower-class whites in the saloon. "It is realized that in any southern community with a barroom a race war is a perilously possible occurrence," White wrote. "There are thousands—should we say millions?—of our own Anglo-Saxon stock, not yet raised to a safe level of civilization, not yet, by education and opportunity, strong enough to reckon this social responsibility and to resist the elemental impulse of lawlessness, when racial antipathies are aroused."[65]

In Atlanta on Saturday night, September 22, 1906, "racial antipathies" became genocide. After days of special editions screaming headlines about a "rape epidemic," a mob of 10,000 whites attacked Negro restaurants, pool halls, and barbershops. Streetcars—the last place blacks were allowed to ride as "free citizens"—were stopped, their ropes cut to plunge the cars into darkness, and the passengers clubbed. On Monday the riot moved to Brownsville, an affluent black suburb and home to Atlanta University and Clark College. By the time the terror subsided on Tuesday, at least 25 blacks and 1 white policeman were dead, 150 blacks were critically wounded, 1,000 black people had fled the city, and countless others were hiding from the "nigger hunters" in the homes of their white employers.[66]

Atlanta's leaders were appalled that the image that they had worked years to acquire had been damaged in a weekend. "Mob rule" was loudly condemned, streetcar companies ordered their employees to treat blacks more courteously, and one-fourth of the police department was fired. Many of those guilty of inflaming public opinion expressed pious horror of the deeds of a mob they (wrongly) insisted was made up of lower-class ruffians. Hoke Smith, who had ended many speeches with the incendiary question "Shall it be ballots now or bullets later?" boasted that he had hidden blacks in his own house. John Temple Graves, a prohibitionist whose paper, the *Atlanta Georgian*, had spent the weeks before the riot debating whether rapists should be "denatured" and branded with an *R* or whether it might be best to eliminate the source by "unsexing" black women, bragged that he had kept rioting out of East Point at the request of blacks who came "humbly" to his back door.[67]

Why had this explosion occurred? Modern historians have blamed the inflammatory political campaign waged by Smith and Howell, a contest that Hoke Smith won largely because he "out-niggered" his opponent in order to win the support of Tom Watson and his Populist followers. Blame is also attached to the sensationalist press, which had whipped up public sentiment with their relentless rape count and reports of raids on "negro dives." Sam Jones and his prohibitionist friends have also been assigned blame for inflaming opinion on the issues of alcohol and disfranchisement.[68]

Sam Jones was in Cartersville when the riot broke out, conducting his annual revival in the tabernacle a block away from his house. He had long spoken out against the bars that laced whiskey with cocaine, making a concoction so potent that Jones claimed it would "make a jack-rabbit spit in a bulldog's face." He had long denounced the "disgraceful Decatur Street dives of debauchery and sin" that exhibited lewd pictures of white women that inspired blacks to commit the "nameless crime." His comments after the race riot epitomize the position of many southern white conservatives. Several themes were sounded: blacks were not the victims but the perpetrators of crime that awful weekend; the whites that were involved were "lower elements" provoked by the "rape epidemic" and by the spectacle of black vagabonds loitering outside saloons; prohibition was needed to bring the "riotous and disorderly elements in both races" under the control of conservatives.[69]

"Of course, back of the present riot was the frequent assaults of brutish negroes upon the white women of Atlanta," Jones told his audience of fifteen thousand in Cartersville. "But this gives no reason for race riots or race extermination or for the killing of innocent persons." The real spark, Jones announced, was the "whiskey devil." The rioting began in front of the "dives of Decatur and Peters streets," and when Mayor James Woodward closed the saloons, the rioting stopped. "Liquor was behind all those atrocious deeds committed by blacks in a crowd," Jones ended, and if "you fellows will go to work and eliminate political chicanery and work in the interest of prohibition and accomplish the destruction of the liquor traffic I will personally account for every rape committed thereafter."[70]

One month later, Sam Jones died. Within two years blacks had been disfranchised, and Georgia had gone dry.

The crucible for silver and the furnace for gold,
but the Lord tests the heart.—Proverbs 17:3

Nothing is intolerable that is necessary. Now
God hath bound thy trouble upon thee, with a
design to try thee, and with purposes to reward
and crown thee. These cords thou canst not
break; and therefore lie thou down gently, and
suffer the hand of God to do what he please.
—Jeremy Taylor

10
❧ Heart Trouble

Sam Jones liked to joke that when bringing up a boy, "you have to raze him often to raise him right." In reality, Jones indulged his own to the point that "each one of his children believed himself or herself to be his particular favorite," his daughter Mary remembered. Laura was the disciplinarian of the family. "I think the children look on me more as their own brother than they do as a father," Jones confessed. "Wife is the mother of us all."[1]

However, tender playfulness did not obscure enormous expectations. "I can't be satisfied with my children," he admitted in 1885. "I want them to be everything that God would honor, and that will be useful in the world." When his children were young and his hopes high, Jones was contemptuous of preachers with uncontrollable offspring. "I don't go much on a preacher that hasn't a religious family," Jones would say. "He hasn't generally got it himself. If I turn loose a godless set of children on the world, someone can chip upon my tombstone the words, 'Here lies the most errant hypocrite that God ever let live.'" Though he knew of "no-count, trifling" girls who go from the parsonage to the ballroom, "I hope to God I'll never see the day when one of my children want to go to those places, much less scandalize the professions of their father."[2]

That prayer was not answered. Annie, a headstrong girl whose curly hair refused to be tamed into a bun, was the first to experience the publicity that attended the indiscretions of the children of one of the most public Protestants in the land. In 1888 the *New York Times* reported her wayward-ness with barely concealed satisfaction. It seems that when Sam and his brother Joe conducted a revival in the Tennessee town where Annie attended school, a young theology student had prayed loud and long for the girl's soul, saying that while her father was saving the souls of strangers, Annie was headed for hell. An indignant Annie withdrew from school, declaring she would not stay where ladies were insulted in church.[3]

On Christmas Day a year later, sixteen-year-old Annie eloped with her father's personal secretary, William Graham. An Episcopal minister in Chattanooga with the unfortunate name Dr. Dumbell had performed the "runaway match" when Annie lied about her age. Initially angry with Graham for "stealing his daughter," Jones soon welcomed the young couple back. The marriage lasted only three months, however, and Annie, pregnant, came home again.[4]

The scandal was particularly embarrassing to Jones because he had taken an unyielding stand against divorce. "Woman, if you have married a dog, live with him," Jones commanded. "Don't turn him loose to ruin the life of some other woman." He blamed the exponential rise in divorce on the "yellow-backed" novels spawned by cheap printing. These "weird, wild, flashing novels" of romance had become an addiction, the evangelist growled, turning girls into vapid creatures who mistook sentimentality for compassion and infatuation for love. "I wish parents could see that the literature of the nation is debauching the nation," Jones growled. "You will never get over a bad book in your family."[5]

Soon after Annie returned home, the oldest daughter, Mary, married Dr. Evans Mays. Living first in Atlanta, the couple moved to Cartersville when Jones offered one of his properties on Main Street for a drugstore.

Mary was a dark, quiet girl, emotionally unstable and physically fragile. In March 1891 she was so ill after the birth of her daughter Mary Laura that the *Wesleyan Christian Advocate* reported her dead. When Mary contracted blood poisoning a year later, the family was told that she was beyond medical help. Jones telegraphed a friend in Meridian, Mississippi, to pray for her. Though Mary's obituary again appeared in the papers, his friend telegraphed: "God told me at 5 o'clock yesterday afternoon that your daughter would recover." Mary passed a critical stage at that very hour, and when Jones asked why he had sent the telegram after Mary was reported dead, his friend replied: "If every paper in the United States had told me she was dead, I would not have believed it, for God told me she should recover." Though she bore another daughter, Eva, Mary's health remained uncertain. In the summer of 1895 she was sent to Johns Hopkins for treatment, and in 1900 Jones was forced to break off a meeting in Baltimore because Mary was again dangerously ill.[6]

Mary was widowed young; her second marriage was to William L. Turner, a prosperous carriage manufacturer, in 1904. She moved to Marietta, a town between Atlanta and Cartersville, living in a house her parents bought her, a place known locally as "the Villa." Like her brother Paul, Mary became addicted to drugs, and her new home was close to her supply, Brawner's Sanitarium. Dr. Brawner, a friend of the family, invited the Jones children to come to the sanitarium every two weeks for their "medications" so that they would not have to travel to Atlanta. Thus, a steady source of unadulterated drugs was made available.[7]

Mary spent her second widowhood with her daughter Laura, who had become famous from New York to Hollywood for her exquisite lingerie designs. B. C. Sloan, Laura's second and third husband, lived in the house as well and was referred to as Mary's "boarder." One of Joe Jones's grandchildren remembers visiting "Cud'n Mary" and "Laura Mays" in that Marietta house and seeing both women under the influence of "dope." Laura Mays died in a New York City hospital in 1943. Four years later, Mary was declared incompetent and her sister Julia appointed as guardian. Mary died in a nursing home, scalded to death in the bathtub.[8]

Jones had a heartbreaking time with his brother Charles also. On November 20, 1890, the front page of the *Courant-American* announced that Charlie Jones had shot a black man named Jim Young three times in front of "the Jew store" (Frankel's) in downtown Cartersville. With Young dying on the street, the sheriff told Jones to turn over his pistol and come to jail. "All right, Bob," Jones answered. "I have done what I aimed to do and I will go with you."[9]

Charles Jones had been working as the foreman at the Etowah Iron Company, overseeing blacks who dug out the ore with picks. Jones blamed Young for having lost that job in July; his suspicion that Young had "lied on" him to get him fired seemed confirmed when the black man was made foreman. The two men thundered at each other for months; Jones told Young "to prepare his box"—his coffin—and warned that if Young "fooled with him he would shoot Young's liver out." For his part, Young "started at Jones with his knife" and "cursed him for five minutes" so loudly the shouting was heard for "near a quarter or a half mile." This was a fatal violation of racial etiquette. Young's "great fault was his disposition at times to place himself on an equality with white men," the Cartersville reporter wrote. "I have heard him curse white men, not to their face, of course, and I have often remonstrated with him about it, telling him it would surely get him into trouble sooner or later. He did not seem to fear anything, however." In Charles Jones he cursed a man as volatile as himself. Even the Cartersville paper, while praising Jones as a "gentleman of undoubted courage" who is "as true as steel," acknowledged "his haste to resent an insult." [10]

The incident nearly caused a race riot: "strong men were about wild with excitement; mutterings, curses and threats came from the negroes." When Young died after suffering for four hours, the blacks talked of breaking Charlie Jones out of jail and lynching him. "The hardward stores were raided for implements of warfare," the paper reported; the whites intended "to protect the prisoner at all hazards." Indeed, in the white community sympathy for Jones was overwhelming; hundreds visited the jail. Jones maintained that he had merely upheld the racial code. He had been insulted and threatened by a black man. "If any of you gentlemen were placed in the same position I was, and did not do as I did, I would not want to know you." [11]

Ten weeks later the trial began. The first two witnesses were "of ebony hue," the paper reported; with a "surly" and "sullen" attitude. Both testified that Charlie Jones had threatened Young, and that Young carried a knife in order to protect himself. A number of white witnesses followed for the defense, testifying that Jim Young was a dangerous, "high-tempered, overbearing man" who had cursed and threatened Jones. A physician testified that while Jones was "disabled" in his legs and "clumsy," Young was an "active, vigorous man." [12]

Sam Jones did not take part in Charles's case, though it is likely he paid for the team of defense lawyers. Friends who fretted that Jones was "under affliction," both from Charles's arrest and the recent death of his first grandchild, were relieved to see that the evangelist was still "cheerful and witty," able to josh with Simon Peter Richardson, his old friend who had become pastor at the Cartersville Methodist Church. One day the two preachers stood on the street corner swapping altar-call stories. Jones's tale was of a sinner he spotted sobbing at the railing. Jones eased over to him and asked if he felt "all his sins were forgiven." The old man mopped his eyes with a red bandana and sighed, "Not all, Brother Jones, not all; but I think a majority of 'em." [13]

However, the toll of personal tragedy was reflected in an incident that took place in Palestine, Texas, just as Charles's trial was getting under way. In a revival Jones had conducted there in November, he made his usual charge that local officials were conniving with saloon owners to frustrate liquor laws. Mayor Word was out of town at the time, but he heard that Jones had suggested that he was "in collusion with violators of the law." He resolved to avenge himself. [14]

Three months later Jones came to Palestine to deliver his lecture "Git Thar." The next morning, Mayor Word tracked him to the depot and asked, "Is this Sam Jones?" Jones answered, "That is my forgiven name." Word then hit the evangelist across the face with his cane, causing a deep slash. Jones, having promised his wife he would "take care of her husband," wrenched the cane away from the mayor, and, in his own words, "wore him out" before leaving him "in the hands of doctors for repairs." Both Jones and Word were bleeding profusely, though the evangelist clearly won the scuffle. In fact, the *Atlanta Constitution* wrote, the mayor's face looked "like a piece of raw beef." [15]

Triumphant, Jones cabled newspapers all over the country about the "one-gallus mayor" and his dastardly attack. Popular sentiment was overwhelmingly in favor of the evangelist. The *Atlanta Journal* reported that Jones's actions were "universally endorsed" and that "Mr. Jones has been praised on all sides." The *Constitution* was equally effusive, writing that "the Bible admonished [Jones] to turn the other cheek, but Georgia grit inspired him to 'close in' on his antagonist." [16]

The newspapers do not mention whether Sam Jones was in the courtroom a few days later when his brother was pronounced not guilty. As the *Journal* acknowledged, "the opinion all along" was that Charles Jones "would be acquitted." In the South of the late nineteenth century, a black man who killed a white man would be lynched; a white man who killed a black man would be acquitted. "A loud long shout of joy pronounced the commendation of the public upon the righteous act of the jury"; presumably the friends and relatives of Jim Young knew better than to come to the courtroom. [17]

Charles Jones continued to have emotional and financial troubles. In

1903 Sam became legal guardian of three of Charles's nine children: Queenie Jones, sixteen; Henry Grady Jones, thirteen; and Annie Laurie Jones, six. Two years later, Charles was fined for "bastardy"—fathering an illegitimate child. Despite his turbulent life, Charles outlived Sam Jones by twenty-five years.[18]

Jones's relationship with his sister, Annie Stocks, was also troubled. Annie was a morphine addict whose dependency drove her in and out of Brawner's Sanitarium. In 1892 that family's tragedy worsened when her son, Porter Stocks, shot a man named Holland Cassin in an Atlanta saloon. Jones blamed alcohol for his nephew's downfall and begged to be allowed to talk to the jury, predicting that after two hours of listening to him the jurors would free Stocks and hang instead "every bottle-bellied bull-necked barkeeper in Atlanta." Jones's appeal was denied, and Stocks was found guilty of voluntary manslaughter, a verdict that outraged Atlantans who believed that Stocks had deliberately murdered Cassin. A year later, Jones visited Porter Stocks in prison with the unhappy news that his mother had been "given up as an invalid for life by her physicians." Sure he had broken his mother's health, Porter swore off alcohol. Six weeks later, he got drunk and hanged himself in his cell.[19]

In the summer of 1895, the emotional imbalance of the family emerged in Jones's twenty-year-old son, Paul, who came home from a two-month vacation in Europe to find his sweetheart had died. In despair Paul gave up the study of law and turned to opium and alcohol to assuage his grief. "Colonel" Thomas Dunham, a simple man who lived to serve the man who converted him, was moved into the family home and put in charge of Paul's rehabilitation. "Don't think of me as your poor lost wicked and ruined boy that can no longer be trusted," Paul pleaded with his parents, "but as a young man who is trying to take a new lease on life and to live down the errors he has committed."[20]

Jones's relationship with his daughter Laura was made more difficult by his emphatic ideas about women. Jones admired good looks—when he heard a man with a homely wife remark that ugliness was "just skin deep," Jones said he "believed if she was his he'd skin her." However, the evangelist insisted that his wife and daughters be unembellished by paint and unrevealed by décolleté. "If any of my daughters cut anything from their dresses I want them to cut it from the bottom," Jones would say. He would not have them behave like the society girl who lured "a virtuous country boy" onto the dance floor by "showing him a couple of things he hadn't seen since he's been weaned." Nor would he allow a "French dancing master" to instruct his girls in elegance. "I would rather a daughter of mine go trotting through life like a jersey cow than to learn grace from a devil with a fiddle."[21]

Laura listened and fashioned herself into "everything her father hated," a saucy seductive woman, fond of dancing, fashion, the theater, gambling, cigarettes, champagne, and morphine. Because he "could never throw a child out, no matter what they had done," Jones allowed this prodigal daughter to live under his roof. A neighbor remembered fearsome fights between stubborn father and stubborn daughter, and was shocked to overhear this interchange: "Good morning, daughter of the devil." "Good morning, father." More often, Jones relied on guilt to control his daughter's behavior. Reminding Laura that happiness is a "reward for *right doing*," Jones wrote "you must love me . . . so that you will be a joy to me always." Laura remained defiant and ended their relationship with a final affront. She showed up drunk at her father's funeral.[22]

Julia was the last of the children, born just as her father was becoming a clerical celebrity. "Pet," Jones called her, and of all the children, she was the most company to him. She frequently traveled with him; once they were trapped for hours in the wreckage of a train outside of Toronto. "I love my girls very devotedly and I want my girls with a loyal love to stay by Mama and Papa," Jones wrote possessively in 1903. "I don't care how much you love Mr. K [Dickie Knight], for you owe your Mama and Papa a debt that ain't settled yet. Now remember that my dear Julia girl." Two years later, Jones was stressing the same theme to the twenty-year-old girl. "Your peace of mind can only come to you in the down right loyalty of your whole life to your father and mother and the most constant integrity of purpose. Don't forget that."[23]

Julia was devastated by her father's death and committed herself to seeing his work continued by marrying his coworker Walt Holcomb, who had lost his first wife in 1904 when the turpentine she used as a linament ignited. Julia had fallen in love with the twenty-nine-year-old Holcomb as he worked feverishly with Mrs. Jones to produce *The Life and Sayings of Sam P. Jones*, published just weeks after the evangelist's death. The "only normal child" of Sam and Laura Jones, Julia had a strong marriage. The Holcombs' first child, Julia, lived only a day, but they later had a son, John, and daughter, Laura Louise. They became one of the most admired couples in the North Georgia Conference; both outlived everyone else in the family. Walt Holcomb's remarkable energy stayed with him all his life, and at the age of eighty-four he threw himself into the 1960 presidential election, "attacking those who objected to Senator John F. Kennedy's Catholicism." Holcomb died in 1965 and Julia two years later, a week after celebrating her eighty-second birthday. Unfortunately, they lived to see their son die of alcoholism and their daughter marry a man named Louis Cade, himself afflicted with manic-depression.[24]

A public man, Sam Jones lived out his family tragedies in public. At a meeting "for men only" in Louisville, Kentucky, in 1899, Jones told of his nephew's drunkenness, imprisonment, and suicide. "Mr. Jones wept," a reporter noted, "and took his seat completely exhausted." The evangelist often confided to audiences of the suffering his children had brought him. He had hoped his oldest son, Robert, would "make a preacher." Now, he told a Nashville audience in 1898, Robert was "running away from God" and "wanting in health." Paul had a "kind, loving heart" but doctors had pronounced him "well-nigh incurable." His children were "the best children I can persuade them to be," he wrote in his column that year. "Sometimes my persuasion don't make them very good." At the first service of the Cartersville revival of 1901, Jones confessed tearfully: "While I'm preaching the gospel all over these United States I find that my own children are going to hell and damnation. If they should die now, they would be lost forever." He asked for prayers that one daughter would be saved and another begin to enjoy the "fullness of grace." Both girls were on the mourners' bench at the end of the revival, weeping penitents.[25]

"Life is a circle," Jones concluded sadly. Just as his wild and liquorous youth had wounded those who loved him, his children's behavior now hurt him. Psychology and biochemistry suggest that the answer to his children's addictions and instability may be found in parental patterns and in family genes. All of the memories of his mother Jones mentioned in his sermons—accompanying her to church, learning his alphabet at her knee, even reciting his prayers on the final night of her life—have to do with instruction, not nurture. "Queenie" Porter Jones, of the distinguished family and regal manner, emerges from her son's worshipful memories as a cold and proper woman. It is suggestive that, although the family had a tradition of naming children after relatives, not one of Jones's five daughters or nine granddaughters was named Nancy or Queenie.[26]

The memory of John Jones was sacred to Sam as well, and in sermons he is depicted as a war hero respected in his community, a pious parent whose last act was to beg his son into heaven. "The death of the father was the life of the son," the story went. In reality John Jones was a glib scoundrel until days before his death, a man who scorned the ministry because of poor pay, and whose actions in the service of the Confederacy earned him a courts-martial. Even given the grief of a man who lost a daughter and a wife within a year and a half, leaving his four surviving children in the care of his parents for two years verges on abandonment. It is significant that Sam's "dissipation" began when his father left to join the Confederate army only three years after the family had been reunited. For a boy who had lost a sister and a mother and been deprived of a parent's comfort during those losses, this last departure was more than he could withstand.[27]

Unconsciously, Jones re-created the pattern of an aloof, judgmental mother and absent father in his own family. Though Jones misted when he talked of home and hearth, he was away from his family for much of his marriage. He first abandoned them because of alcoholism, then because of his itinerancy, then as agent of the Orphan Home (a job his wife recognized as ironic), then as an evangelist. When he was home, he was restless and bored. Though he explained to his family he must "be about the Master's work," he may have sensed that the terrible undertow of depression became more powerful when he did not have a battle to become caught up in, and an enemy to drain off anger and anxiety.[28]

For a wife, he chose a woman as coolly correct as his mother. In family pictures Laura sits stiff and unsmiling, a thick-waisted woman "of queenly bearing" who judged the world and found it wanting. It comes as no surprise to read in one of Jones's endorsements for "King's Royal Germateur," a patent medicine he invested in, that for twenty years before Laura ingested that elixir, she had been "an invalid from [a] nervous sick headache." The ingredients of this potent brew are lost to history, and it is unlikely that it contained any alcohol, as Jones railed against imbibers who rationalized their tippling as "medicinal." However, one wonders whether Laura's tightness might have been loosed by opium, morphine, or cocaine, all common ingredients in tonics before the Pure Food and Drug Act of 1906.[29]

Laura's need for order was as great as her husband's need for activity. A grandchild remembers that "Mangie" allowed her to play in a scrap box only if she replaced each piece of fabric before taking out another. Her naturally stern instincts with children were reinforced from afar by her husband. "Just use some good straight bossing," he wrote from Iowa in 1899, when their youngest child was fourteen years old. "Don't feed their vanity, it's fat enough now. Hold a tight rane over all of them. I am not afraid if my wife is in full command of the fort." Though prevented from rejecting the prodigals when her husband was alive, after his death the children who disappointed her were cut off from funds and banished from her presence. Laura lived for twenty years as a widow. She enjoyed good health until her final year, and died at the age of seventy-six in 1926. The Kentucky girl who feared losing her identity in marriage now lies under a stone reading "Mrs. Sam Jones."[30]

Only illness and trouble could bring Sam Jones home for any length of time, and his children were manipulative enough to realize they could get his attention through tribulation. "Jones, which one do you love the best?" he would say. "I'll tell you: its the one that is sick and in trouble. That's the one that gets me every time. . . . When one of my little fellows gets sick and begins to suffer, I don't know I've got but one of them, the other five don't count at all." One wonders whether Annie's early marriage, Mary's and Paul's addictions, and Laura's long history of disorderly conduct might have been motivated by a need to be noticed by a faraway father.[31]

If poor psychology and a dysfunctional dynamic were at the root of some of the emotional instability, genetics may have contributed as well. Addiction and mental illness, very likely bipolar (manic-depressive) disorder, afflicted Sam, his brothers, his sister, and five of his children.

Those afflicted with this biochemical imbalance can become promiscuous and commit criminal acts in the grip of an acute episode, since their judgment and control are impaired and their sexuality heightened. The court records show that Charles Jones had assaulted several people before his arrest for murder; this behavior and his siring of an illegitimate child may well have been a manifestation of manic depression. The alcoholism of Joe and Sam Jones and the drug addiction of Annie Jones Stocks also suggest an affective disorder, since manic depression and substance abuse "go hand in hand and may be related genetically in the same family tree." The only child of Queenie and John Jones who escaped was Mary Elizabeth, dead at the age of seven. Given the family's calamitous history, perhaps Queenie Jones's unexpected death at the age of twenty-nine was a suicide. Profound mood swings can provoke exhaustion and cardiac insufficiency in an acute manic phase, and suicide during a depression. It is suggestive that though Sam spoke often about the effect his mother's sudden death had upon him, he did not speak of what killed her.[32]

Mary was addicted to drugs; in hindsight it seems her first marriage to a pharmacist might have been one of convenience. Her younger brother, Robert, was delicate and sensitive. "If religion consists in crying," Jones would say with fond disgust, "I have the most religious boy in the land." Bob and his wife, Lillie, had a son, Sam Paul Jones II, the first year after their marriage; seven years later, Lillie had twin girls. Mary Elizabeth lived only a day; her sister, Julia, died twenty-four days later. Given his father's belief that God allowed children to die in order to provoke spiritual life in the parents, it is not surprising that Bob swore off alcohol and reclaimed salvation during the Cartersville revival of 1906. After his father's death Robert felt "impressed to preach" and had been giving trial sermons at local churches when he contracted pneumonia and died. It is impossible to say whether his gloominess was a manifestation of manic depression, but it is suggestive that his only child, Sam Paul Jones, was eventually deported for what may have been treasonable activities.[33]

While Mary and Bob struggled with addiction, emotional illness clearly emerged in three of the children. Laura, "a noted beauty of unusual intellect," had the unnatural gaiety and sexual magnetism often associated with bipolar disorder. Unlike her siblings, mania rather than depression controlled Laura, though the results of her reckless behavior were just as destructive. Her agitation and pathology would lead her to marry and divorce four times. "Men were always falling in love with Laura," her nephew Paul Jr. remembered, but after they married her, "they just didn't know what to do with her." (One did: David Flournoy sent Laura packing after two weeks with a note telling her parents she was "entirely unsuitable as a wife.") The children of the family were warned not to kiss Laura on the mouth, since "there's no telling where she's been." Laura's promiscuity and emotional turbulence caused her to lose custody of her only child, Sam Jones Sloan, to her mother in 1908. That child, nevertheless, inherited his mother's love of risk: he grew up to become a stuntman in movies directed by Howard Hughes.[34]

Laura's mental health continued to deteriorate. In 1919, after treatment at Brawner's Sanitarium and the Louisiana State Asylum in Alexandria, Laura was arrested for disorderly conduct in New Orleans. Her bizarre behavior may have been a manifestation of the assaultive overactivity associated with severe episodes of manic excitement. Released from custody on the condition that she never return to New Orleans, Laura restlessly traveled the country, supporting herself by writing bad checks and conning money out of her late father's admirers. Her mother put a stop to her activities by putting a warning in several Methodist *Advocate*s. Illegally, she returned to New Orleans and found a job but, broke, had to ask her "dear old mother" for sixty dollars "for dental work and a new bridge." Ultimately, Laura landed at Mary's house. Laura Mays wrote Julia in disgust that Laura Jones looked "as though she had her a big spree and was in serious condition upon her arrival home. She is penniless and homeless—I took her to St. Joseph's [Hospital]." Many in the Jones family had their nervous depression lifted and were able to stop drinking late in life. Laura, too, eventually recovered her sanity and her religion, serving at the end of her life in a Christian mission in Miami, Florida.[35]

The portrait that emerged of Paul Jones from his son, Paul Jr., was one of a chronically depressed man whose addictions made it impossible for him to hold a job for more than intermittent periods. He made several stabs at business in Cartersville; in 1896 his father set him up in a store. "Everything in fine groceries in my stock, and I will sell cheap," his advertisement promised. "Give me your trade and you will profit by it." That business quickly collapsed, and Paul moved to Atlanta at the age of twenty-one to become a reporter. For the rest of his life, he bumped among the city's three main newspapers: the *Atlanta Journal*, the *Atlanta Constitution*, and the *Atlanta Georgian*. Paul's career choice excited some disapproval; Sam Jones estimated that "the average newspaper correspondent tells one lie a day." However, if Sam had been alive, he would have been pleased by his son's coverage of the Billy Sunday revival in 1917, reporting that gained Paul national recognition.[36]

Paul had always chafed at the restraints his family attempted to impose. His first marriage in 1904, to Alya O'Neill, caused a stir because of Alya's Catholicism. Relations between Alya and the family were strained; in fact, Alya once exclaimed, "Hell won't be full till all the Joneses are dead." Alya died young, leaving Paul with a son, Porter. Paul's second wife was Leila Booker, his nurse at Brawner's Sanitarium. The couple had four children: Catherine, Paul, Howell, and Anne. Leila's animosity to the Jones family was only fully revealed after her husband died. She not only refused to have him laid to rest in the family plot in Cartersville, but as soon as she could afford to, she had his body exhumed from the Atlanta cemetery plot that Julia had provided and moved him to a resting place of her own choosing.[37]

The family treated "Poor Paul" as an outcast after Sam's death, though he protested in a letter to his mother that he was the victim of circumstances beyond his control. "My life is drawing much more rapidly to a close than yours and my perplexities are great. Life is full of irony and sadness." Friends had deserted him during his breakdown; "all my desires and hopes fall about me like a house of cards," Paul wrote. "I rebel against a God who could allow a man to make the efforts I have made and would deny me any chance to have a reward for doing the honest thing."[38]

Paul outlived his mother by only eleven months. When he died at the age of fifty-one, his friend Frank L. Stanton, poet laureate of Georgia, wrote a eulogy in which he expressed his bitterness toward the Joneses. While naming no names, the venomous poem is clearly aimed at a stingy, sanctimonious family Stanton believed had aggravated Paul's suffering. It ended:

> A curse on their gold and their grain
> And God strike the sun from the sky

Who prate of the cross where the Christ was slain
　　Yet let his children die.
Dear friend, asleep 'neath the voiceless sod,
　　They wait the storm and the wrath of God.[39]

　　If mania seemed to predominate in Laura and depression in Paul, Annie's diary reveals both. A lively girl with her father's charm, eighteen-year-old Annie was plunged into depression when her baby, Laura, died at the age of two months. "The angels came and bore our darling to a more congenial clime," Annie wrote in the obituary for the Cartersville paper. "Too pure and beautiful for earth, God called her home ere she was tainted by sin or saddened by sorrow." Overwhelmed with grief, she was sent to Rome, Georgia, for a stay in an "Infirmary for the Treatment of Nervous Disorders," operated by a doctor with the improbable name of Henry Battey.[40]

　　The elevated mood of manic states often increases sexuality, and patients frequently speak of being "in love." In her five-month stay at Dr. Battey's, Annie "fell in love" with three men. While such emotionalism may only indicate an overly romantic nature, her diary reveals a startling juxtaposition of feelings. "I am afraid, I am miserable, I can't trust anyone," she confided to her diary on July 5, 1891; the next day, after a beau sent a band of Italians to the infirmary to serenade her, she wrote: "My, my, what happy days." Three days later she confessed, "I stuck a pen in Dr. Henry this afternoon and I am awfully sorry." Estranged from her mother, Annie's days were cheered by visits from her father, who brought her pretty dresses and pleaded with her to stop reading romantic novels.[41]

　　Annie was discharged after three months, but her depression returned on the anniversary of Laura's death. "Fall is here and the melancholy days have truly come." Spring brought more treatments. When her father fell ill, Annie prayed to God to "spare my dear father as long as I have to live," and she remembered with remorse how her father pointed to his graying hair and said "that's where Annie hit me." Feeling "no good" to anyone, Annie wondered if death was not preferable to such a life. A month later, Annie felt "reckless"; a month after that she was depressed, writing, "I don't believe there is any such thing in the world as true happiness." The second anniversary of her child's death brought the preoccupation with sin and guilt characteristic of depressive episodes. "I am sure I was not worthy of being her mother and so God took her away." Remarriage to Will Graham did not raise her self-esteem: "He surely loves me far more than I deserve."[42]

　　Annie did not write in her diary during the second marriage: "I got tired of it like I do everything else." Her emotional inconstancy quickly undermined the marriage. Graham's angry prudishness contributed as well. Graham, who coveted the goodwill of his former employer, explained to Jones that he was divorcing Annie because of her "jokes about the intimate marital relations" in front of other men, because her card playing made her a slothful housewife (his breakfast was once three hours late), and because she adopted "another man's child" (an orphan named Ollie her father brought her) "after saying publicly she would never have his." Annie was relieved: "I would have left him but for my dear father."[43]

Her father bought her a 185-acre farm near the family home—the old Bill Arp residence, which was haunted, according to local lore. Annie continued to be puzzled by her own emotions and actions. "This day I promised Mr. Glyck I would be his wife. . . . I wonder if I will be fool enough to do such a thing." Eleven days later she decided, "I wouldn't marry that man if he were the only man living." In 1896 she was sent to Baltimore, ostensibly for the treatment of "impoverished blood" but more likely to wean her from the morphine to which she had become addicted after surgery for an ovarian tumor. "Everything is sadness it seems to me," she confided to her diary. Though she longed for "the rest of the soul and mind" heaven promised, she was angry with God: "You make us breathe corruption and wonder that we lose our health." Annie's diary ended in 1900 with a resolution to develop her musical talents.[44]

In the next years Annie found self-confidence by playing piano for her father's revivals and personal happiness in marriage to Rouhs Pyron, a wealthy farmer and cotton broker. Annie never bore a second child. However, one day a black servant went to the outhouse and came back saying that she had just given birth (she was overweight and had not noticed an additional bulge). Convinced the woman was unfit for motherhood, Annie fished the newborn out of the slop jar and announced she would bring up the girl herself. Annie spent her last years mothering that black child, playing with the monkeys that filled her house, organizing mission churches, and inveigling the sheriff of Bartow County to let her take home prisoners she thought showed promise of reformation. She died suddenly at the age of fifty-one of "acute dilation of the heart."[45]

Besides explaining his emotionally unruly brood, a diagnosis of manic depression would explain many of the contradictory facets of Sam Jones's personality: the braying arrogance and soft humility, the feeling of forgiveness and nagging guilt, the curious blend of grandiosity and inferiority, buoyant cheerfulness and leaden pessimism. Manic depression would also explain the cycles of frantic overwork and disabling depressions, the restless chattering and the deep lethargy when it seemed an effort to form a

single word. It would explain the undercurrent of melancholy people perceived in Jones even at his most exhilarated, his morbid guilt over Beulah's
death, and his fears that God might take another child from him if he
ignored his obligations to eternity. "I am afraid not to do my duty, because I
don't know what will happen," Jones once said. "You go putting up at home
and the first thing you know your wife will die and one of your children will
die." Even Jones's somatic complaints—constipation, ulcers, weight loss,
insomnia—are symptoms associated with bipolarity.[46]

Many people with this illness have long periods of normality or hypomania (mild mania) between bouts of manic excitement and depression, and
most of the time Jones's behavior was normal or only mildly disturbed by
hypomania. Indeed, mild mania fueled him, giving him energy, flash, and
enough lack of inhibition to allow his humor free expression. Contemptuous
of caution and intolerant of criticism, hypomanics can slide into psychosis
under stress, however, and this may be what happened to Jones in March
1885, when he was close to a breakdown. There were periods throughout
the nineties when Jones retreated to Cartersville unable to work, sometimes
because of stomach ailments, influenza, or neuralgia, other times for reasons that remain obscure. After the stress of Annie's elopement, Jones was
forced to cancel a series of revivals in 1890. The following year the newspapers reported that the evangelist was "suffering from nervous prostration
due to overworking," and Jones wrote a "despondent letter" to a friend in
Texas expressing the belief that his days as an evangelist were over, "as the
excessive labors of several years have impaired his health." Mrs. Jones's
diary records a cryptic entry at that time, writing on Friday the thirteenth
that her husband had suffered another week-long "attack."[47]

The worst collapse occurred in October 1900. Canceling all appointments, Jones came home in a state of frenzied exhaustion. "He is oh so
nervous and I am so worried about him," Annie fretted in her diary. Though
Jones recovered sufficiently to resume his speaking tour in November, he
collapsed again in December and for two months was under the "close
care" of an Atlanta osteopath, undergoing chiropractic treatments to restore
his nerves and digestion. In April 1902 Jones again broke off his work,
and that autumn he felt "too weak and nervous" to take an active part in
the Georgia gubernatorial race. A break occurred in September 1903 and
another in June 1904, at which time he canceled all engagements to go to
Catoosa Springs for his health. Lithium, a chemical now used to control
mood swings in manic depressives, was present in the mineral waters at
places like Catoosa and Lithia Springs; its properties even then were advertised as an aid to mental health. The Jones family often scheduled vacations

around springs where Jones could "take the waters," an effort, perhaps, to even out his emotions.[48]

Though his marriage was strong, problems with his children distracted and debilitated Jones during the nineties. "They say I've been three weeks in Boston," he said at the height of Paul's addiction and Laura's school problems, "but, I tell you, about three-quarters of the time I've been about a hearthstone in Cartersville, Georgia." Jones became moodier, more subject to prolonged depression. "If your children turn out badly," he warned, "it is good-by to happiness." The man who threw stones was suddenly living in a glass house. But though his children disappointed him and damaged his reputation, Jones would not turn them out. "God has endowed me with a father's heart. I never will, I never can, turn my back on my child."[49]

Jones's impulsiveness had always been a trial to him; one of the things he remembered about his years on his grandfather's farm was that the strict rules helped him control his temper. "The hardest fellow I have to deal with is my wife's husband," he admitted. "I found out," Jones confided to an audience at a prohibition camp meeting, "that I was half dog and half human. You needn't laugh at that, Bud. You're in the same fix. By the time I was twenty-four I had starved the human and fed the dog, until I was half ready to go running rabbits." After his conversion, he thought his dog days were over, until "some fellow would throw him a chunk and he would get to growling again."[50]

In 1899 the dog growled again. Jones had forced through a "anti-jug" law which required package stores to pay a thousand-dollar license fee to receive liquor in Cartersville and ordered buyers to pay a tax of five dollars per gallon. This was declared unconstitutional by his neighbor, Judge J. W. Harris. A bitter controversy ensued during which townspeople divided into hostile factions. Jones charged in his newspaper column that Harris's ruling was influenced by his "appetite," pointing out that Judge Harris had privately partaken of the "jug" of Canadian Club whiskey before rendering his decision. Allies of Harris countered by warning Jones that he was no longer "czar of Cartersville." Harris himself wrote two bitter letters to the *Atlanta Journal* accusing Jones of "profanity" that "no newspaper would print" (Jones had called him an ass, a term the evangelist insisted was biblical), and suggesting they submit to a morals trial at either the First Methodist Church or the Masonic Lodge, organizations to which they both belonged.[51]

The situation worsened when James B. Heyward, the man who had challenged the constitutionality of the package laws, joined the fray. Heyward lived in the house between Jones and the judge, and he offered to "wager my salvation that there is less whiskey, opium or other intoxicants used by self and family of Judge Harris in a year than is used by Sam Jones and his family in a month." Jones is "either crazy or in some reprehensible daze," Heyward concluded; "his extravagances are simply incompatible with sanity."[52]

The controversy wounded Jones, and after B. P. Allen, pastor to both parties, pleaded with him to relent, he went to the judge and apologized. Judge Harris, who had spoken of Jones as a man with "Jekyll and Hyde" shifts in character, accepted the evangelist's apology. "I think I know something of his temptations—something of the undertow [that] is drifting him out to sea, and whether he wants it or not, he has my pity," Harris said sanctimoniously. "Let them talk and we will try to serve God and do right," Jones wrote Laura. "Hope God's grace will keep me from ever getting mad again."[53]

It did not. Four years later, Sam Jones again was the center of controversy in Cartersville and the Atlanta press was buzzing about the pugilistic preacher. "Georgia has among her varied and valuable resources, one of those good old-fashioned factors of civilization, a fighting preacher," Hoke Smith of the *Atlanta Journal* wrote with careful contempt. "We often hear of ministers of the gospel winning souls to the straight and narrow through talents of eloquence and oratory. Georgia, though, is one of the few commonwealths that has one that wins through the strength of his good right arm. 'Quit your meanness' emphasized with a crack on the eye if the mandate is not heeded, is a much more forcible text than 'virtue is its own reward' in these strenuous times."[54]

Outraged when two drunks were found on tabernacle grounds during the Cartersville revival, Jones had denounced the "dirty dogs" who were rolling "their barrels, demijohns and jugs over our boys and our homes." Because one of the drunks was black, the issue was inflamed by charges that alcohol was being peddled "promiscuously" to "improper persons." Jones threatened to write President Roosevelt about Walter Ackerman, the local postmaster who supplemented his income by selling homemade wine, and announced that "he had rather have a decent negro to hand out his mail than to have a white man for postmaster who was engaged in dealing out damnation to the boys and the poor negroes in this community."[55]

Ackerman took offense and punched the preacher. Jones hit back. "I am not physically hurt or morally abashed," the evangelist announced in the *Atlanta Journal.* "I will take care of my integrity, my manhood, and my cause, against all comers. . . . To me the grave is preferable to the gag." As with Judge Harris, Jones's conscience soon pricked him into a reconciliation. At the evangelist's death three years later, Ackerman said of Jones that "no one could stay angry with him for any length of time." [56]

Some of Jones's difficulties in Cartersville sprang from naked jealousy of the evangelist's opulent life-style. In 1895 the Joneses renovated their house, jacking up the original two-story "cottage" and building a story underneath. The house, known as Roselawn for the two hundred roses that filled the front yard, was "one of the most magnificent homes in North Georgia." Its twenty-one rooms were decorated with "subtle elegance," an Atlanta reporter wrote, and "Mrs. Jones' collection of silver, china and glass is probably the largest and wealthiest in Georgia." Each room had brass chandeliers, the downstairs was paneled with ornately carved wainscoting and lit by spectacular stained glass. Most sumptuous was the living room with its domed ceiling gilded with golden garlands and angels. A lifesized portrait of the evangelist and another of his wife faced each other in the foyer. [57]

"Petty animosities" in the town almost caused the family to move in 1893 and again in 1900. Both times, when word got out that the Joneses were leaving, the yard filled up with locals, whites in the front and blacks in the back, who begged them to stay. "Sam Jones's removal from Cartersville would be a calamity," the local editor wrote after hearing that the Jones family had bought a house down the road in Marietta. "As a citizen he is a progressive liberal and broad. There is no other that could take his place." Jones decided not to leave his "peaceful town" in the gentle "blue mountains" where the ten o'clock whistle of the Western and Atlantic was his "signal to go to bed." Besides, he joked, in Cartersville he lived on "the banks of the Jordan," right across from the First Baptist Church. Placed on the National Register of Historic Sites in 1972, Roselawn has been restored to its earlier elegance and now serves as the Sam Jones Museum. [58]

Even his enemies could not deny that Sam Jones labored for his wealth, and much of his exhaustion and irritability stemmed from overwork. Even after Sam Small joined him in 1886, Jones kept up his frantic schedule, using his assistant for "overflow meetings" instead of allowing him to carry a significant part of the load. Though he admitted, "I am often so tired I can't rest," Jones was scornful of preachers who worked less: "I tell you it's a calamity when a minister can only preach about half an hour a week, and then get so tired that he must have a vacation in the summer." As for himself, Jones bragged, "The only rest I get is when I have preached two or three times a day all the year, I go home and preach once or twice a day for a week or two." [59]

Stomach problems were complicated by the constant change in drinking water while traveling, and Jones wrote with exasperated euphemism to Laura of his unsuccessful attempts to "move Bili." "My bowells have pained me much since I got here," Jones wrote from Clinton, Georgia, in 1880. "If you will come over Thursday you will find comfortable quarters here if you are well enough to come—I get along so much better when you are with me." His indigestion was so well known that the inventor of the "Jo-He" patent medicine sent a bottle to the evangelist with the promise that not only would it cure dyspepsia, but "if one is suddenly stricken down with paralysis, it never fails to cure in a few hours if used freely." [60]

One "nerve cure" Jones used was common in the nineteenth-century South: tobacco. Smoking, chewing, and snuff dipping was not confined to the laity. When a North Carolina Baptist suggested that preachers who refused to give up the "enslaving weed" be defrocked, he was told that such a policy would "unchurch, and depose two-thirds of the most pious, learned, and efficient and consecrated ministers." Such a policy would be catastrophic for church offerings as well. Tobacco "is our Southern style," one prominent Methodist explained, "and our churches are largely supported by it." Some thoughtful clerics even provided parishioners with spittoons. "Somehow or other," one distressed visitor remarked, "I cannot keep from thinking that if Jesus had been there" he would have "driven them out for making His home a tobacco chewer's spitbox." [61]

Such practices appalled northern Christians, many of whom regarded tobacco as physically harmful and morally unsound. To ensure that northern congregations would never sit under the pulpit of a nicotine addict, the Presbyterian General Association refused scholarships to smoking seminarians, and the General Conference of the Methodist Episcopal Church required those presenting themselves for ordination be "free from the habit" which was "hurtful to their acceptability and usefulness among our people." [62]

The condemnation of tobacco by Christians outside the South proved troublesome to Jones. In 1886 criticism of the evangelist became acute in Chicago, center of the antitobacco movement. Sam Small was jeered at when it became known that he smoked cigarettes, and the *Chicago Herald* printed a letter from a woman who predicted that no one "with clothing scented like a stableman, and fingers and teeth stained with the offensive nicotine, can hope to do much good in Chicago." When his ability to spit tobacco "with amazing effects upon the coals" was reported, Jones also became an anti-tobacco target. The Women's Christian Temperance Union held a prayer meeting asking God to deliver the southerners from their "fearful habit." [63]

Sam Small succumbed quickly, throwing his entire stock of tobacco into the fire. He announced that he would "give up tobacco in all forms, now and forever, so help me God." Five days later Sam Jones announced that "down in my country I have never been in a soul's way that I know of." But since coming north, "in a hundred different instances I have been notified that 'a habit that you are given to is a stumbling-block to souls in this city,' and I want to say to the congregation to-night from this day until we meet up in heaven you can tell this world that Sam Jones has got no habit that is a stumbling-block to anybody." This announcement was greeted with "great applause" and "amens." Jones ended by asking for the prayers of all assembled. "I have had a fight that none but God knows anything about. I have struggled. Thank God! I have the victory."[64]

Newspapers across the country were entranced by the reformation of the southern Sams. The *Indianapolis Times* was glad to hear the evangelists had taken "the motes out of their own eyes," while the cynical *Cincinnati Enquirer* remarked that "if Sam keeps on he may reform himself yet." "Admiring citizens of Atlanta, Georgia . . . lately sent to the Rev. Sam Jones fifty pounds of A.A.A. plug tobacco," a Chicago reporter wrote wickedly. "It appears now that this was a.a.a. mistake." The Chicago papers cautioned against premature celebration: the "general rule is once a slave to nicotine always a slave."[65]

Such prophecies proved correct. Tobacco proved indispensable to Jones because of its calming effects. Within six months Jones was "entrapped" by a company that used Jones's letter of appreciation for a box of cigars as an advertisement. During the Boston revival of 1887 Jones was silent on the subject of tobacco, and a few years later a Texas newspaperman discovered Jones backstage "trying to stink out a lot of brethren with a miserable cob pipe, upon which the ages have thrown the dust of rank decay." The reporter explained, "Brother Jones used to chew tobacco and smoke cigars." When he gave it up "it broke out on him again in the shape of a pipe." Reproached by a Pennsylvania minister who found the evangelist's hotel room "blue with tobacco smoke," Jones said that "while he regarded the use of tobacco a senseless and harmful habit the temptation was too much for him."[66]

Some believed it was hypocritical for Jones to condemn alcohol and use tobacco. After spotting the evangelist taking bites out of a tobacco plug after a meeting, a reporter for the *Los Angeles Times* wrote disdainfully, "Either Sam approves tobacco chewing, or he is too weak to give it up. In the former case, he is no fit instructor on manners and morals; in the latter, decency should induce him to refrain from taunting others with their shortcomings, until he has overcome his own." Two young men in Minneapolis were equally contemptuous. "You ask how Christ would look on a theatre or ballroom," they wrote in an open letter, "and we ask how Christ would look upon smoking a pipe or cigar or chewing the filthy weed."[67]

Jones was unrepentant. "Why do you chew tobacco?" an old deacon asked. "To get the juice out," Jones shot back. Growing up "in the shadow of a tobacco leaf," Jones began smoking and chewing when he was a schoolboy, and though he quit many times, he always took it up again. "The odor of tobacco had saturated him and stood out around him like the perfume of a wooden Indian before it is aired out in the morning," a Minneapolis reporter sniffed. "It should be a consolation to those anxious souls to know that we don't take our breath to heaven with us," was Jones's response.[68]

The evangelist admitted that a man could not be a gentleman and use tobacco, but he could be a Christian. "Do you ask how I know? I have tried it." Jones insisted, "There's nothing in tobacco to damn a man and nothing to save him. It's a question of good manners, while whiskey drinking is a question of morals." He offered to give up tobacco as soon as someone could point out a scripture that said "Look not upon the tobacco when it is yellow in the leaf, when it showeth its color in the plug." When an old brother jumped up and shouted out "Let him that is filthy be filthy still," the unflappable evangelist simply smiled: "That's as good a verse of Scripture as I ever heard quoted. We'll have the benediction now."[69]

Given the Jones family's tendency toward sudden death, tobacco was an unfortunate addiction. Sam's brother Joe died in his arms of "paralysis of the heart" after declining Sam's offer of a cigar. Though the connection between smoking and heart disease and stroke was less well documented than it has become, there was anecdotal evidence even then. Until his unexpected death, however, Jones suffered more from digestive and nervous disorders, with an occasional recurrence of malaria.

After a mysterious collapse during the Cartersville revival in the fall of 1889 and continued health problems during 1890 and 1891, Jones's health improved for a time, and he preached some of his most powerful revivals. He resolved to give what evangelical energies he had to the South, as southerners were "more easily moved" and unhampered by "the intellectual difficulties that curse the other portions of the country." In truth, his soul-saving services were not much in demand elsewhere. Sales of his books had fallen off dramatically; in 1893 royalties for *Living Words* amounted to only $14.75. In 1895 Sam Jones and Robert Ingersoll lectured in St. Louis on the same night; Jones drew forty people while Ingersoll packed the house. Two years later, Jones's column was discontinued by the Kellogg Newspaper Syndicate and ran only in the *Atlanta Journal*.[70]

Jones collapsed again in 1899, and continued to decline to the point that by 1903 his health was so "broken down" that he was "unable to digest a cracker." Beginning in 1900 and continuing for the next four years, Jones turned from strenuous two- to six-week revivals to the less stressful requirements of the camp meeting, lecture, and Chautauqua circuit.[71]

Jones had preached at camp meetings from the beginning of his ministry, and he loved the unvarnished evangelicalism of the services and the atmosphere in which "every cottage is yours, and every table ministers to your wants." But by Jones's day the camp meeting had become a rural southern phenomenon. The urban middle class required a different diversion: the Chautauqua.[72]

Founded in New York in 1874 by John H. Vincent, a future bishop of the Methodist church, the Chautauqua became a popular retreat for the devout to refresh their souls in worship, their bodies in recreation, and their minds in classes on such subjects as archeology, literature, painting, or elocution. "The moment one treads that sacred enclosure," William James rhapsodized, "one feels one's self in an atmosphere of success. Sobriety, industry, intelligence and goodness, orderliness and ideality, prosperity and cheerfulness, pervade the air. It is a serious and studious picnic on a gigantic scale. . . . the middle class paradise, without a victim, without a blot, without a tear."[73]

Though it was a perfect setting for Jones's unique talents—"a cross between a camp meeting and a country fair"—Jones initially refused the lure of the lecture circuit. "The idea of peddling around the Word of God on the lecture platform," he said in Baltimore to thunderous applause. "I shan't do it." But in the summer of 1886, Vincent personally asked him to speak at the Chautauqua in Round Lake, New York, and Jones found the atmosphere of relaxed respectability his "greatest delight."[74]

Jones attributed his success in evangelism to "the plain truth, plainly spoken." At a dinner at Dr. Vincent's home, Jones revealed that his approach would be the same on the platform as well. Dr. Vincent asked another dinner guest, a "distinguished Fifth Avenue pastor," what methods he used "in dealing with young and immature minds." The divine unctuously confided that "in the effort to establish relations of sympathetic receptivity . . . I try to employ language that is essentially simple." Always eager to puncture pomposity, Jones chortled: "I just put the fodder on the ground, where anything from a jackass to a giraffe can get at it."[75]

So great was Jones's delight at finding this "easy way to make money" that he urged eloquent friends—General John B. Gordon, for one—to follow him on the lecture circuit. While walking down the sidewalk one day in

Chattanooga, Jones encountered Bob Taylor, the former Populist governor of Tennessee who had transformed political campaigns into revival meetings with his fiddle and his hymns. Jones asked Taylor how he was "getting on." Despondent, Taylor confessed that his law practice had been such a bust that he was waiting on the sheriff to seize his assets. "Bob," Jones said, "if you'll do what I tell you to do, I'll get you out of that hole and put you to walking on velvet." Jones ordered Taylor to go home to East Tennessee and write a lecture on "human nature, how it acts and what fine and funny stunts you have known it to be guilty of. Call it 'The Fiddle and the Bow' and that will make everybody want to hear it." Jones paid off Taylor's debts and arranged for the Southern Lyceum to book him for one hundred dates for a hundred dollars each. Taylor became a premier attraction on the lecture circuit and used his newfound popularity to win a seat in the United States Senate.[76]

Jones viewed lecturing as "a great opportunity for doing good" while being "relieved of the close tension of revival work." He signed with several lyceum bureaus, and when his evangelical career waned and his health could not withstand the stress of a meeting, he spent winter months lecturing and summers at Chautauquas. Especially popular in small western and midwestern towns, Jones became one of the most sought-after speakers on the circuit, earning between twenty-five and thirty thousand dollars a year. The summer before his death, he spoke at seventy Chautauquas in seventy-six days, and proudly declared his seniority on the circuit: he was, he bragged, "the oldest rat in the barn."[77]

During the fourteen years he was losing ministerial support, popularity, and health, Jones blamed lukewarm Christians and cold clerics for his disappointments and decline. Angered by the unresponsiveness of the Knoxville churches in 1892, Jones blamed the "tide of worldliness" that was submerging piety and extinguishing revivals everywhere. "You can't reach the young people," Jones said bitterly. "Most converts are made from people over forty years of age." There were still times he felt the "spark of the Holy Spirit" ignite a meeting; in St. Louis in 1895 he "could almost see the light playing about over the great audience, and in a dozen places they were shouting." But such moments were rare, and there was a listless petulance about his revivals that had not been present previously.[78]

Jones's effectiveness had diminished even in Nashville. "What can I do in this great city?" a despairing Jones asked in 1895. "I have worked and preached and prayed and have done almost nothing. . . . God never made a man that feared his enemies less than I do, but listen: God never made a man that leaned more on the aid and sympathies of his friends than I do. All I want, brothers, is your hearts." Again in 1900 Jones felt his words falling on closed ears and cold hearts. Embittered, he turned on the ministers. "I have never talked to such a heartless lot of people as your pastors are. If they had sat on this platform as corpses they could not have appeared more impotent and helpless than they have." A defeated Jones wrote the *Atlanta Journal* that he doubted he "spread much Christianity" in Nashville because "people don't listen to preachers anymore."[79]

One reason Jones's popularity had plummeted in the "Athens of the South" was that Nashville had changed. By 1900 it was a thriving publishing, manufacturing, and educational center. Its eighty thousand citizens enjoyed good city services, and many were affluent enough to afford automobiles, telephones, electricity, and indoor plumbing. The area around the Union Gospel Tabernacle on Fifth Street had deteriorated as wealthy Nashvillians moved to the suburbs, and there was some reluctance to go into the area at night to attend the Jones meetings. Many of the evangelist's ministerial supporters had left the city for other pastorates, and Methodist ministers were less enthusiastic in their support after Bishop Atticus Haygood forced Jones out of the regular ministry in 1893. Jones's campaign for the "Tabernacle Ticket" headed by Thomas Ryman in 1898 alienated those who did not believe religion and politics should mix. Also, his decision to oppose the Tennessee centennial after Nashville leaders voted to allow the sale of alcohol offended the city's sizable civic ego.[80]

The evangelist's abrasive authoritarianism also rankled. In 1902 Jones told ministers that he would label every one of them "a billy goat and a coward" if they refused to sign a petition endorsing the prohibitionist candidates for criminal judge and attorney general. "There may be preachers in this town who will sweat great drops when they sign it," Jones snarled, "but let them sweat." This coercion caused angry murmuring about Jones's despotic "domination of the priesthood." Though Jones claimed that the outcome of the election was "wrapped up," a rainstorm kept the drys at home and both reform candidates lost. It was the last revival Jones conducted in the city.[81]

In the spring of 1900, Jones confessed he had gotten but "meagre results" during the last decade. He blamed "a Worldly Godless Church and frequently an indifferent ministry who criticized me more than prayed for me and set around while I have tried to do my work." What America needed was a genuine "Holy Ghost revival. I have not seen one on this continent in ten years [and] we have got to have one." Three years later Jones hotly denied that he was a "back number," pointing out that he was still popular at Chautauquas. There may not have been enough spiritual power left in the country to fuel a camp meeting, but it did not take much to run a Chautauqua—"just enough to make a fellow behave."[82]

Some of Jones's personal characteristics—qualities that had made him seem refreshingly unique in the first years of fame—had begun to seem merely offensive. From the beginning of his celebrity Jones had been a braggart. "He has fallen into one form of egotism which is to be deplored," a Baptist editor wrote in 1886. "It gives him the appearance of self-righteousness, when as a fact we believe he is a devout and humble man." There were those who found his bragging "as ingratiating as the prattle about self of a bright innocent child." But as Jones became famous and spoke more of his abilities than God's power, such self-glorification seemed un-Christlike.[83]

Jones boasts of personal wealth—he claimed in 1895 to have made $750,000 by the power of his tongue—angered preachers who were struggling to get by on a fraction of his annual income. Jones's contention that he "never made a charge for holding a meeting in his life" did not convince those who had read of bountiful "love offerings" collected at the end of each revival. "It is a very easy matter," a Methodist minister sniffed, "for a man to give himself no concern about finance who gets more for one month's *evangelizing* than any man out of a large majority of our preachers gets for a year of hard labor and hard-living."[84]

Others objected to the evangelist's capitalizing on his celebrity. "No man who sells his dignity and his honesty for a cheap advertisement is fit even to sweep the synagogue," an incensed correspondent from Chattanooga wrote. "You are a howling fetish." When clerical support for his campaigns decreased, Jones took a more active part in the collections to cover daily expenses, a practice some did not find raised the level of reverence. "Pull out your pocketbook," Jones ordered his audiences. "If you haven't any money, put in a lock of hair. If you can't do that, spit in the hat—do something, don't let it pass you. You can run a negro and a wheelbarrow for seventy-five cents a day, but it costs something to run a locomotive—I'm a locomotive."[85]

Jones's inability to pass up a punchline also gave offense. "He loves the laugh of the crowd, and sometimes says improper things in order to excite it," the editor of the *Baltimore Baptist* wrote in 1886. Jones's levity "trivialized" religion, one Atlanta reporter charged during the 1896 revival. "Let me tell you, sister, . . . if you don't stop that dancin' and card playin' you'll go to hell sure," the reporter quoted the evangelist as saying. This announcement, heard by people who professed belief in "the good-old-fashioned hell of fire and brimstone and the bottomless pit that never dies" was greeted with "titters," the reporter noted with disgust. If these people truly believed their immortal souls were in peril, they would have sat "frozen and transfixed with horror." The *Looking Glass* reporter ended, "All this bears the evident stamp of insincerity. Its tendency is to decrease respect for sacred things and to dissipate the reverence that is essential to true belief." [86]

As crowds grew accustomed to his conversational condemnations and barnyard slang, Jones used more vulgarity to shock. Former supporters fell away. D. C. Kelley, who had praised Jones as the forerunner of "practical Christianity" in 1886, kept his Elm Street Methodist Church out of the Nashville revival of 1894. " 'Hog' has become one of his milder terms," a critic wrote in 1902. "Jones grows in his language worse and worse, coarser and coarser, from year to year." But his popularity only increases, until "today [he] draws larger crowds to hear him than any man on the platform. We may well ask, What has happened to the American people?" [87]

Changes in the American church also undermined Jones's career as an evangelist. The upheavals of the Gilded Age had destroyed the "great evangelical consensus," ending the unanimity needed for successful union revivals. A greater emphasis on Christian nurture undercut interest in costly revivals that provoked a conversion crisis. "Must Conversion be a Special and Conscious Experience?" the *Congregationalist* asked in 1895. Certainly not. For those "trained in infancy in Christian households, taught that they have been dedicated to God and belong to him," conversion often was so gradual as to be virtually imperceptible.[88]

The "practical Christianity" of action over emotion that Jones himself had promoted dampened the ardor of revivals. "Behold what rapid strides the Church is now making, yet her members do not have the jerks," a minister wrote defending the dearth of religious emotion. "They do not go into trances, as aforetime, they do not jump and scream, but they do build churches, colleges, hospitals, and asylums." Guilt became less popular; Christianity in the 1890s was "characterized by a less vivid sense of personal sinfulness and of the inherent evil of sin than was common formerly." In such an atmosphere, revivalism seemed old-fashioned, embarrassingly out of touch with the modern age.[89]

Even some who endorsed revivalism began to question the excesses of evangelists, wondering if they had not substituted "sound for sense and manipulation for power." The tendency of roving revivalists to ridicule settled pastors rankled, and some churchmen concluded that the itinerant evangelist was "rapidly becoming a source of danger to the cause of Christ." While evangelists had served a purpose when there was a frontier to follow, now most who attended revival meetings were already church members. If a real cussing, kicking sinner happened to fall under conviction and be converted, it was unlikely that he would wind up in church on the following Sunday listening to the unsanctified drone the minister had been made out to be. People would be saved to the sticking point through the patient toil of the settled pastor and by religious education, the *New York Times* decided in 1896, "not by fireworks or hurrah methods. . . . The day of the professional evangelist has passed, at least in modern cities and under modern social conditions."[90]

By late 1903 there were signs of renewed interest in revivalism. Though the "deterioration of moral fibre" continued, the *Advocate* noted that there was evidence of "rebellion against materialism." After putting himself in the hands of an Atlanta osteopath, Jones felt his health returning, and rejoiced that he could resume his evangelistic work. "I would rather preach the Gospel for $1 per day than stand on the lecture platform at $200 a night; but revivals take five times as much strength," he explained. However, age and abuse had thinned his voice, and he often restricted himself to one sermon a day, turning the bulk of the work over to George Stuart or Walt Holcomb. "Those who heard Sam Jones fifteen years ago look with surprise upon his face," a Houston reporter wrote. "His eye has lost the fire of old, his voice has been pounded on the anvil of debate and abused in open air addresses and shouted in halls of mighty size until the music of the fibre is lost." But so earnest was the evangelist that the listener "forgets all that when he begins to speak."[91]

The Welsh revival of 1905 sparked even more interest, and soon evangelism and Sam Jones were again ascending. The evangelist rejoiced to recognize such an outpouring of "pentecostal power" that "it made him think that the good old times were back again." From a pulpit in Knoxville in 1905, Jones confessed, "I thank God that there are more than one hundred cities greatly touched by His divine spirit." His children were, for the moment, more settled and sane. In the spring of 1904, Paul seemed to have put tragedy behind him and married Alya O'Neil, and Laura married her second (and third) husband, B. C. Sloan. That fall, Mary remarried. Sam Jones, who had been distracted by family troubles since Annie's elopement in 1889, had a temporary respite. He seemed infused with the old power; his health had returned and much of the old anger had been burned away by adversity.[92]

"The meetings throughout were marked by manifestations of the miraculous," an *Atlanta Journal* reporter who accompanied Jones to Memphis in 1905 wrote. "At one service a stillness that rivalled the movement of the stars, at another time by waves of emotion that swept through the audience like a tidal wave, and again by a wave of conviction that seemed to wash us up against the judgment throne." Jones considered the Memphis revival his most successful meeting in a decade. "The better day has come," he exulted, "and in cities and in country places all over America the old time power is manifest among men." Asked to account for his renewed power, Jones simply said: "If we suffer with Him, we shall reign with Him." People often said in those days, " 'Mr. Jones, you preach better, we believe, you are closer to God than ever before.' I don't know about the preaching," he answered, "but I have suffered, and I know I am closer to God than ever before." He would soon be closer yet.[93]

Though you have made me see troubles, many and bitter,

you will restore my life again; from the depths

of the earth you will again bring me up.

—Psalm 71:20

For the preacher's merit or demerit,

It were wished the flaws were fewer,

.   .   .   .

But the main thing is, does it hold good measure?

Heaven will soon set right all other matters.

—Robert Browning

 # Conclusion

After Sam Jones's death, George Winton, the newly appointed editor of the *Nashville Christian Advocate*, candidly discussed the evangelist's rise, decline, and resurrection. Beginning about 1883 and continuing for ten years, Jones had extraordinary success; his meetings "were probably the greatest in the history of religion in America," Winton wrote. His popularity then

> waned a good deal. This was due in part to conditions and in part to the man himself. There was during the late nineties a decided reaction

against sensational evangelism. The success of Jones and of a few others had brought into existence a large crop of cheap imitators. . . . The reaction which they caused coincided with the development of certain limitations which Mr. Jones had from the beginning exhibited. He allowed himself—unconsciously, perhaps, yet none the less truly—to become the victim of his facility in public utterance, especially of his wit and humor, and to fall into the habit of entertaining instead of teaching or moving his audiences. An air of self-satisfaction at his own popularity, coupled with the habit of rather roughly castigating other ministers, especially the regular pastors, indulged in humorously at first, became later an outstanding defect. . . .

[But] ripening experiences of life, considerable ill health, the death of his brother, a very real love for his fellowmen worked their effects in him with the years, and of late he had been preaching again with the old-time tenderness and power. . . . On the whole, [Sam Jones] carried himself through the vicissitudes, the excitements, the temptations, the exhaustions, the emotionalism, the mental and physical dissipations incident to the career of a popular evangelist about as creditably as a man well could. He plucked many a brand from the burning, and in thousands of hearts and homes all over the country his name is as ointment poured forth."[1]

Though his sudden death on October 15, 1906, shocked many, it would not have surprised Jones. For twenty years he had been saying, "I am a dying man." In 1886 Jones appealed to his Chicago audience not to buy pirated versions of his sermons. "I say this because I don't believe I will hold up at this work more than two or three years longer [and] the small royalty paid on these sermons may take care of my wife and children." In St. Louis in 1895 he struck the same mournful note. "I don't know how much longer I shall be able to preach. I am a broken-down, worked-out man in middle age." And in 1903 he wrote despondently, "I carry scars from a hundred-thousand battlefields. It is one thing to fight with fists and pistols and quite another to stand and fight the sins of men, and to oppose the prejudices of the gang and the cowardice of those in your own ranks."[2]

Jones loved to speak of his own death. "I don't know where, or when, or how I will die," he would intone. "I may fall in the pulpit; I can't tell." He hoped he would die as his father had, imparting inspiration to the children gathered around his deathbed.

And then, when the doctors have turned their backs upon me and said my case had swung beyond where *materia medica* reaches, I would spend my last moments talking to her who has been such a friend to me and who has helped me in all my life. And then, when the last moments came, I would wade down gently into the river of death, and when the river should come up to my shoulders I would reach back and kiss my wife and children good-by and go home to God as happy as a school boy ever went home from school.[3]

These constant predictions of imminent death are reminiscent of the ancient lady who died after having "enjoyed ill-health all her life." It is easy to dismiss Jones's gloominess, forgetting that besides battling his own body, Jones had to contend with threats from antiprohibitionists. These he shrugged off: "If I live until one of those cowardly scoundrels shoot me, I will make old Methusaleh look like a plumb baby by the side of me." It was those who suffered from "delusional insanity" who made Jones shudder, like German-born J. F. W. Risse, who came to Roselawn in 1898 to kill Jones for ruining "his character and his family." "The only fear I have ever entertained is that some fanatic, believing himself ordained by the Lord, will unceremoniously take my life," Jones would say. "I would leave any city on the shortest notice to get away from such a crank, for they are really dangerous."[4]

However, apprehension did not prevent this incorrigibly gregarious man from talking to strangers on the street, and admitting to all who asked that Sam Jones was his "forgiven name." One such exercise of hospitality almost killed him. On April 20, 1905, en route to deliver a lecture at Tuskegee Institute, Jones stopped to spend the night in Montgomery, Alabama. A man named Sam Windham who claimed to be a Methodist minister known as the "Drummer Evangelist" asked if Jones would come to his hotel room and look over some reading material to see if it was suitable for "a young preacher." When Jones entered the room, Windham locked the door, put the key in his pocket, and informed the evangelist: "I am a bigger man than you are and we will settle some things here in this room—at the sacrifice of your life or mine, if need be."[5]

"Sit down, neighbor, and let's talk over our plans," the unflappable evangelist suggested.

Relieved at Jones's apparent acquiescence, Windham confided: "I have my orders from God. You are to drop everything, go with me to Dothan tomorrow and marry me to my wife, and then begin meetings there, and from there we come to Montgomery. And it all depends on your following the program. But our first duty will be to preach Jeff Davis to hell!"

Pleasantly Jones answered: "There will be no trouble, my friend, in carrying out a right program, if you get your orders from God. I have been trying to get mine from headquarters for years also. Maybe this way of going by myself don't work, nohow. You remember the Savior sent his apostles in pairs, two and two. And so, you and I will make a pair, won't we?"

At this point, a reporter who had seen Jones go to Windham's room knocked on the door and said Jones was wanted on the phone. Lulled into believing his fantastic plans would be carried out, Windham unlocked the door and let the evangelist escape. Jones did not return to the room after his phone call, but he did not go to the police. It was clear to him that Windham was unbalanced; indeed, the man had spent years as an inmate in the Alabama asylum. When Windham followed Jones to the train depot that afternoon, however, an alert friend of the evangelist forcibly prevented Windham from boarding the train and reported him to the police. The former mental patient was detained in jail until his brother could collect him. Upon his arrival in Hartford, Alabama, Windham's former wife, captivated by his unorthodox wooing, remarried him.[6]

Threats, depression, a longing for rest, and a talent for emotional manipulation prompted Jones to preach frequently on death. Over and over, he reminded his audiences that no one knows the day of their death. "This meeting has come along to prepare some of you brothers for your coffin and your winding sheet. The spade that will dig your grave is in the hardware store tonight; the flowers that will cover your bier are growing in the greenhouse now." Every one of his revivals had been God's last plea to some sinner. "Brother, we've warned you," Jones said to "white faces" in Toledo, Ohio. "We've called you and some day when the tidal wave of God's wrath overtakes you you'll call for the rocks and hills to hide you," but you will be "swept suddenly into the presence of God."[7]

Death was on his mind when he preached in Oklahoma. "Men of Oklahoma City, look out," he warned. "Before my voice has died out in your ears, there will be deaths following this meeting that will shock this city and state and maybe this nation." Perhaps he would die. "I don't know when I shall die or where I may go down, whether in a railroad wreck or in a storm at sea. I might drop dead with heart failure; I don't know how I shall die, but I prefer to die easily." A reporter from the *Daily Oklahoman* wrote that "at times men shuddered, as Jones declared the fearful truths of the text. Sighs, tears and emotions were given free vent. Everyone felt that God had come closer and given a more earnest call to repentence."[8]

Jones's own anguish was close to the surface. The "old thirst" had been tormenting him for months, and his strategy of fighting saloons so he would not go into them was beginning to fail him. "It seems that this has been the hardest year of my life," he had said the month before. "At times it seemed that my grip on God was loosened, and then I went to him in great distress and poured out my soul in earnest prayer, and God came into my room and lifted the burden from my heart and gave me assurance of victory." At the men-only meeting in Oklahoma City Jones confided, "I've been [on] the ropes, boys, and now I suffer the words that no preacher ever was called upon to utter: Boys, after thirty years of sobriety, I say I shall never feel safe from a drunkard's grave until my poor wife shall kiss my lips in cold death."[9]

Jones had not felt well throughout the Oklahoma City revival. On Saturday night, October 13, he suffered a severe chill and was confined to his hotel room, but Sunday morning found him in the hotel lobby "chatting with friends." At lunchtime he suddenly felt much worse. Heavy rains had come through the roof of the unfinished department store he was using as a tabernacle, and he decided to head home. So abrupt was his departure that several hundred people were sitting in the First Methodist Church waiting for the final service as Sam, Laura, their daughters Annie and Julia, Walt Holcomb, and Thomas Dunham boarded the train. A big family reunion was planned for Tuesday to celebrate Jones's fifty-ninth birthday.[10]

Getting on the train, Jones noticed a "sick man and his tired wife" and gave the conductor money to have them moved to a pullman car where they could lie down. That night, Jones went to their berth and sat up with the consumptive so his wife could rest. "I am wondering if you have enough money to get home," Jones gently prodded. "Sometime, when we are traveling we run short of funds." Tearfully the wife confessed that their money had been exhausted in the West seeking a cure. They had only enough money to get to Memphis, not enough to get home. "Well, I'll buy the tickets to get you home and give you money for your meals," Jones said. "Don't let that worry you. Good night."[11]

Sam Jones died on that train early the next morning, not a word between his last joke and his last gasp. Seized by six violent stomach spasms around five o'clock, Jones asked Julia to bring the cup of hot water he drank each morning upon arising, a habit doctors recommended to those troubled with digestive problems, as it would "wash away all the stomach, liver and bowel poisons before breakfast." Jones took a few sips, laughed at his infirmity, then was stricken beyond speech. As his wife and daughters watched in horror, his face became white and as peaceful as a baby "falling asleep on its mother's breast."[12]

The next stop was Little Rock, Arkansas. Jones's body was taken off the train and embalmed, and telegrams were sent informing the family and the press of the evangelist's death. One telegram went to Colonel Thomas of the L and N railroad; Thomas responded by sending a special train to bring the body home. On that train, with doglike devotion, Thomas Dunham "stood at the head of the casket, and without eating or sleeping, gazed upon it every moment" from the time the train left Little Rock until the body was temporarily interred in an Atlanta cemetery three days later.[13]

As news of the evangelist's death spread, crowds gathered at the depots along the line to see the train draped in black with its life-sized picture of Jones bolted to the front: two thousand at Marietta, three thousand at Cartersville. "Glory to God!" one leading citizen of Jones's hometown shouted. "He has quit fighting the devils and gone to playing with the angels." Memorial services were held in twenty cities. In Atlanta thirty thousand people came to view the body as it lay in state in the rotunda of the capitol, surrounded by an honor guard of children from the Orphan Home.[14]

Eulogists vied with each other to praise the dead evangelist. Tom Watson called Jones "the greatest Georgian this generation has known, the greatest in some respects that any generation has known. . . . Brilliant, witty, wise, eloquent, profound in his knowledge of the human heart," Watson wrote, "no man ever faced an audience who could so easily master it." William Jennings Bryan, resting between runs for the presidency, praised Jones as a man with "a great mind, directed by a great heart; and eloquent tongue enlisted on the side of humanity, a marvellous energy employed for the improvement of society."[15]

"He said more quotable things than any man of his generation," his friend John Akin, senator-elect from Georgia, claimed. "He had a genius for proverb making." Even the *New York Times* conceded Jones's importance: "At one time he was the most widely known of all the itinerant preachers [and] he was often termed the most sensational preacher this country ever knew." Jones would have enjoyed the mawkish hucksterism that accompanied his death—the sudden resurrection of old books which were advertised under the headline "Being Dead Yet Speaketh," the hawking of copies of his last sermon with its now portentous title: "Sudden Death."[16]

Mrs. J. J. Ansley, president of the Georgia chapter of the Women's Christian Temperance Union, suggested a monument be raised to the prophet of prohibition; it would show "his manly figure standing upon a shaft which pierced the clouds, his right hand holding a two-edged sword pointing at the liquor traffic, his left raised in blessing over orphan children." Instead, Laura Jones buried her husband beside the railroad track in Cartersville, beneath a simple obelisk erected to remind railroad friends "of his life and works as they passed to and fro upon the line." On the monument is this verse: "They that turn many to righteousness shall shine in the stars forever."[17]

Given the extent of his fame in 1906, it is surprising that Sam Jones went so quickly from death to obscurity. Historians of American revivalism have tended to treat Sam Jones as a sideshow between the main acts of Dwight Moody and Billy Sunday. Though Jones's country-bumpkin style was a novelty, it was hardly original. William McLoughlin regards the evangelist's career as just one more attempt to revive an exhausted form, illustrating "the basic inability, or unwillingness, of most evangelical Protestants in America to meet squarely the challenge of the new urban-industrial society." Bernard Weisberger abruptly ended his account of American revivalism with Moody, dismissing his successors as idiosyncratic entertainers. "Once," Weisberger writes wistfully, "the salvation of the soul had been a miracle, recorded for certain only in God's book of life. Now, it was a nightly crowd performance, registered on cards . . . and the heirs of Edwards were colorful storytellers, for the most part, and utter strangers to the theological dictionaries."[18]

The revival had become more mechanized and less theological, but that did not make it any less important to Americans, a people untroubled by innovation and not fond of theological speculation. The revival was still the place people came to hear the old myths and ancient truths, to be challenged and convicted and converted and comforted, a place where tradition was honored and change made. Evangelists have ever been unorthodox and disorderly, disdainful of the ecclesiastical establishment and "settled" pastors, mavericks given to spectacle, experts at manipulating emotion. They are God's peculiar people. It was after all Charles Grandison Finney, viewed by McLoughlin and Weisberger as the pinnacle of American evangelism, who boasted that he had never read his church's creed, who noted the twistings and groans of his congregation with satisfaction, who did not hesitate to use methods that were condemned by his contemporaries as sensational, and who systematically described the techniques he used to obtain results. If the Almighty became a marginal component in revivals and human agency replaced the Divine, it had begun to happen long before Sam Jones set foot on a tabernacle platform.

There is continuity between revivalism before and after the Civil War, but there were changes also. The Gilded Age was the adolescence of American religion, alternately energetic and apathetic, iconoclastic yet afraid of the erosion of authority, puritanically rigid yet preoccupied with the flesh, materialistic but contemptuous of wealth. In this constellation of innovation and tradition, the revival continued to play an important role, with the revivalist both a prophet, calling the nation to repentance and judgment, and a priest, celebrating, praising, and anointing.

And Sam Jones was in the midst of it all, for ten years the country's most talked about evangelist, for many years more one of the people who shaped the future and interpreted the past of the nation. Though Jones eclipsed Moody for a time, Moody was more revered as a revivalist and had a greater influence on revival methodology. Jones was not an important political figure, but his endorsement was coveted and his weekly column in the *Atlanta Journal* gave him a voice in politics. He was not the most important prohibitionist of the day, but prohibition was an integral part of his ministry and he did much to influence public opinion against alcohol. Henry Grady is more closely identified with the idea of the "New South," but Jones helped northerners see their southern siblings as repentant rebels, and he helped the South reshape its present and its image of the past.

Though Jones belittled denominational distinctions, he was the most famous Methodist of the day, and his career illuminates a pivotal controversy in the Methodist church over professional evangelists, holiness advocates, and political prohibitionists. The clown of the conservative evangelicals, his war on worldliness and heresy illustrated a widening chasm between "called" conservatives and the liberal seminary graduates who had begun to occupy city pastorates, editorial posts, and ecclesiastical positions. Jones's opinions on society and the economy illuminate the attitude of the folks who would now proclaim themselves "the Moral Majority," and his city evangelism represented one of the ways the church coped with the vast influx of foreigners into the country and country folk into the city. His slide into racism is the tragic story of the erosion of the moderate position among southern white conservatives.

Like the movie mogul who boasted he did not have to analyze the public mind because he had it, Sam Jones is a study of the nobility and baseness, the generosity and meanspiritedness, of an age. Sam Jones did not *deflect* history as much as he *reflected* history. Though he had a minor role in many plays, one with so many character parts is an important study for anyone seeking to understand the history of revivalism, the South, the prohibition movement, Methodist history, and American history as a whole.

Sam Jones was affable and abrasive, irreverent and pious, meek and wild, a strange mixture of salt and sentimentality. Reading his sermons today, one is struck by their tart astringency, the sentences as lean as the man who fashioned them. With his unembellished candor and contrived coarseness, Sam Jones seems to belong more to the present than to the past with its flushed and florid preachers. In another sense, it is fitting that he outlived the nineteenth century by only six years, as he fit so perfectly into the company of the outlandish individuals who dominated that "most picturesque generation in our history." Scornful of caution, fulsomely sentimental, and unabashedly vulgar, Jones was the incarnation of an impulsive, eccentric age.[19]

Notes

Chapter 1: That Memorable Meeting

1. *San Francisco Chronicle*, March 4, 1889, 3; *Southern Evangelist*, August 11, 1887, 1; *St. Joseph Daily Herald*, October 2, 1885, 4.

2. *Savannah Morning News*, May 27, 1901, 3; *Nashville Daily American*, March 23, 1885, 1; clipping from *Rochester Chronicle*, October 16, 1906, Samuel Porter Jones Papers, University of Georgia, Athens.

3. *Chicago Tribune*, March 28, 1886, 9; *St. Louis Republic*, March 4, 1895, 3.

4. *Nashville Daily American*, March 23, 1885, 1; May 11, 1885, 1. Though Jones's comments seem exaggerated, Nashville was a pretty raw place at this time. See William Waller, ed., *Nashville in the 1890's* (Nashville: Vanderbilt University Press, 1970).

5. Stanley F. Horn, *The Decisive Battle of Nashville* (Baton Rouge: Louisiana State University Press, 1956), 19–32; Laura M. Jones, *The Life and Sayings of Sam P. Jones* (Atlanta: Franklin Turner, 1907), 142–44.

6. Laura M. Jones, *Life and Sayings*, 142–44.

7. *Nashville Daily American*, May 11, 1885, 1.

8. Laura M. Jones, *Life and Sayings*, 107.

9. *Knoxville Daily Chronicle*, April 14, 1885, cited in Herman Daniel Champion, "A Rhetorical Analysis of Selected Sermons by Sam Jones During His Emergence as a National Figure, 1872–1885" (Ph.D. dissertation, Louisiana State University, 1980), 174; *Nashville Banner*, March 25, 1885, 4.

10. *Nashville Banner*, March 23, 1885; Harold Ivan Smith, "An Analysis of the Evangelistic Work of Samuel Porter Jones in Nashville, 1885–1906" (thesis, Scarritt College for Christian Workers, 1971), 6; *Nashville Banner*, March 25, 1885, 4; O. P. Fitzgerald, *John B. McFerrin: A Biography* (Nashville: Publishing House of the Methodist Episcopal Church, South, 1888), 43; *Nashville Banner*, March 25, 1885, 4.

11. Carl Zibert, *Yesterday's Nashville* (Miami: E. A. Seeman, 1976), 26–27; *Daily Union* quoted in Laura M. Jones, *Life and Sayings*, 135.

12. *Nashville Banner*, March 30, 1885, 4; *Baltimore American*, May 19, 1886, 4; *Nashville Banner*, April 27, 1885, 3.

13. *Nashville Banner*, March 28, 1885, 2; *Toledo Bee*, March 10, 1899, 5; *Nashville Banner*, March 29, 1885, 7; *Nashville Banner*, March 28, 1885, 3.

14. *Wesleyan Christian Advocate*, February 21, 1883, 4; W. F. Glenn, "Revivals: What Hinders?" *Wesleyan Christian Advocate*, August 15, 1883, 4; *Wesleyan Christian Advocate*, September 12, 1883, 5.

15. *Nashville Christian Advocate*, February 2, 1884, 4; April 4, 1885, 1; and May 2, 1885, 9.

16. *Nashville Daily American*, May 12, 1885, 12; and May 12, 1885, 4.

17. Ibid., May 12, 1885, 4; *Nashville Banner*, May 12, 1885, 4.

18. *Nashville Banner*, May 27, 1890, 4; Sam Jones, *Sam Jones' Sermons* (Chicago: Rhodes and McClure, 1890), 1:34; *Nashville Daily American*, May 15, 1885, 2; and May 14, 1885, 5.

19. *Nashville Daily American*, May 14, 1885, 5.

20. Theodore M. Smith, "Biographical Sketch of Rev. Sam P. Jones," in *Sermons by Rev. Sam P. Jones*, by Sam Jones (Chicago: L. B. Clayton, 1886), xvii; *Nashville Daily Union*, May 12, 1885, 4, cited in Champion, "Rhetorical Analysis," 189.

21. *Nashville Daily American*, May 14, 1885, 5.

22. Louise Davis, " 'Steamboatin' Tom Ryman and His Gift to Nashville," *Tennessean Magazine*, January 27, 1974, 4; Paul Hemphill, *The Nashville Sound: Bright Lights and Country Music* (New York: Simon and Schuster, 1970), 103.

23. Hugh Morton in *History of the Tennessee Conference*, by Cullen T. Carter (Nashville: Methodist Publishing House, 1948), 230.

24. Hemphill, *Nashville Sound*, 103; Louise Davis, "When Captain Tom 'Got Religion,' " *Tennessean Magazine*, February 3, 1974, 14.

25. Walt Holcomb, *Sam Jones* (Nashville: Methodist Publishing House, 1947), 64.

26. *Nashville Daily Union*, May 14, 1885, 2; *Nashville Daily American*, May 16, 1885, 3; *Nashville Christian Advocate*, May 23, 1885, 1.

27. *Nashville Daily American*, May 19, 1885, 3.

28. Quoted in Champion, "Rhetorical Analysis," 193; *Nashville Daily American*, May 12, 1885, 7; and May 19, 1885, 3.

29. *Nashville Daily American*, May 19, 1885, 3.

30. Ibid.

31. Ibid.

32. Tom Watson, paraphrased in Laura M. Jones, *Life and Sayings*, 82; clipping from *Rome News-Tribune*, January 30, 1972, Sam P. Jones Papers, Sam P. Jones Museum, Cartersville, Ga.; *Nashville Daily American*, May 21, 1885, 3.

33. *Nashville Daily American*, May 17, 1885, 7; *Nashville Daily Union*, cited in Champion, "Rhetorical Analysis," 181; *Nashville Daily American*, May 18, 1885, 5.

34. *Nashville Daily American*, May 31, 1885, 2.

35. *Nashville Daily American*, May 22, 1885, 5; *Nashville Christian Advocate*, June 6, 1885, 17.

36. Laura M. Jones, *Life and Sayings*, 155; *Nashville Daily American*, May 21, 1885, 3; *Knoxville Daily Journal*, May 21, 1892, 1; Sam P. Jones, *Anecdotes and Illustrations* (Chicago: Rhodes and McClure, 1896), 259.

37. *Nashville Daily American*, May 28, 1885, 3.

38. Ibid.

39. Ibid., May 31, 1885, 2.

40. Ibid.

41. *Nashville Daily Union*, May 30, 1885, 2, cited in Champion, "Rhetorical Analysis," 250.

42. *Wesleyan Christian Advocate*, July 15, 1885, 5; *Nashville Daily American*, May 31, 1885, 2; Henry Malcolm Chalfant, *These Agitators and Their Ideas* (Nashville: Cokesbury Press, 1931), 192.

43. *Nashville Christian Advocate*, May 4, 1886, 1; *Wesleyan Christian Advo-*

cate, February 21, 1883, 4; *Journal of the Tennessee Conference of the Methodist Episcopal Church, South*, 1885 and 1886; *Nashville Banner*, May 13, 1885, 3.

44. *St. Louis Globe-Democrat*, March 14, 1895, 2; *Nashville Daily Union*, May 29, 1885, cited in Champion, "Rhetorical Analysis," 250; Sam Jones to Laura Jones, May 28, 1885, Jones Papers, University of Georgia; *Nashville Daily American*, May 31, 1885, 2.

45. Sam Jones to Laura Jones, May 28, 1885, Jones Papers, University of Georgia.

46. *Baltimore Sun*, May 13, 1886, 5; William Leftwich, ed., *Hot Shots: Sermons and Sayings by the Rev. Sam P. Jones* (Nashville: Southern Methodist Publishing House, 1885), 200.

47. *Nashville Christian Advocate*, June 20, 1885, 20; *Atlanta Georgian*, October 15, 1906, 1.

Chapter 2: Born and Born Again

1. Laura M. Jones, *Life and Sayings*, 33–34. Oak Bowery is near Opelika, Ala.

2. Obituary of Samuel Gamble Jones, *Wesleyan Christian Advocate*, April 24, 1895, 4; *Knoxville Daily Journal*, May 23, 1892, 4.

3. Laura M. Jones, *Life and Sayings*, 45–47.

4. Ibid., 35–36.

5. Ibid., 38, 35.

6. Sam P. Jones, *Sam Jones' Own Book: A Series of Sermons Collected and Edited Under the Author's Own Supervision* (Cincinnati: Jennings and Pye, 1886), 135; *Cartersville Standard-Express*, September 12, 1873, 5.

7. Holcomb, *Sam Jones*, 39.

8. Mrs. E. J. Fullilove to Sam Jones, August 16, 1886, Jones Papers, University of Georgia.

9. Jones, *Sermons by Rev. Sam P. Jones*, xiii. Thornton was a well-known orator of the day.

10. Sam P. Jones, *Living Words; or, Sam Jones' Own Book, Containing Sermons and Sayings of Sam P. Jones and Sam Small in Toronto* (Toronto: William Briggs, 1886), 11; undated clipping on "Character and Characters," Jones Papers, University of Georgia; *Baltimore Sun*, May 20, 1886, 5.

11. *Atlanta Journal*, June 22, 1901, 6; July 13, 1895, 7; and August 11, 1894, 7; Laura M. Jones, *Life and Sayings*, 49.

12. Laura M. Jones, *Life and Sayings*, 49; *St. Louis Globe-Democrat*, March 24, 1895, 2; *Savannah Press*, May 28, 1901, 2; J. W. Lee, "Sam Jones and His Work," unidentified article in the Sam P. Jones Papers, Archives of the State of Georgia, Atlanta.

13. Michael P. Johnson, *Toward a Patriarchal Republic: The Secession of Georgia* (Baton Rouge: Louisiana State University Press, 1977), 50; Joseph H. Parks, *Joseph E. Brown of Georgia* (Baton Rouge: Louisiana State University Press, 1977), 116–17. Though there were seven or eight slaveholders in Cass County who owned more than fifty slaves, according to the 1860 slave census, most slaveowners owned fewer than five, with the average around eight slaves per owner.

14. Johnson, *Toward a Patriarchal Republic*, 118; Lucien Lamar Knight, *Georgia's Bi-Centennial Memoirs and Memories* (Atlanta: Privately printed, 1932), 2:293–94; quoted in Frances Letcher Mitchell, *Georgia: Land and People* (Atlanta: Franklin, 1893), 272.

15. Robert Harris Jones letter accepting command of 22d Georgia Regiment, September 1861, in "A Very Personal Glimpse of the Civil War Era from 1849–1863," ed. Dorothy Jones Morgan (N.p.: Privately printed, 1990).

16. *Rome Courier*, September 13, 1861, "Flag Presentation at Silver Creek," and Roster of the Confederate Soldiers of Georgia, 22d Regiment Georgia Volunteer Infantry, Confederate States of America, both in "Very Personal Glimpse," ed. Morgan.

17. There is no male Skinner listed in the white census for Cass County in 1860, suggesting that the "J. Skinner" listed was Jane Skinner and the slaves an inheritance. John Jones's military record is found in the *Compiled Records of Confederate Soldiers from Georgia, 22nd Infantry, HE–K*, National Archives, Roll 343. Microfilm copy in the Archives of the State of Georgia.

18. Robert Harris Jones to Lucinthia Jones, November 17, 1861, in "Very Personal Glimpse," ed. Morgan; James M. McPherson, *Battle Cry of Freedom: The Civil War Era* (New York: Oxford University Press, 1988), 470; Robert Harris Jones to Lucinthia Jones, July 4, 1862, in "Very Personal Glimpse," ed. Morgan; Marlin Teat, "The Fireside Defenders," *Northwest Georgia Historical and Genealogical Quarterly* 19 (Spring 1987), reprinted in "Very Personal Glimpse," ed. Morgan.

19. *Cartersville Courant American*, October 21, 1897; "In Memory of Col. Jones," in "Very Personal Glimpse," ed. Morgan; *Cartersville Courant*, August 20, 1885, 3; unsigned handwritten eulogy for Captain Wesley F. Jones, in "Very Personal Glimpse," ed. Morgan.

20. Quoted in McPherson, *Battle Cry of Freedom*, 539–40; Robert Harris Jones to Lucinthia Jones, November 15, 1862, and "Tri-Weekly Courier from the 22nd Georgia, October 3, 1862," in "Very Personal Glimpse," ed. Morgan.

21. Teat, "The Fireside Defenders"; *Rome Courier*, September 13, 1861, in "Very Personal Glimpse," ed. Morgan.

22. "Civil War Service Records of the Jones Brothers," in "Very Personal Glimpse," ed. Morgan; Court Martial General Order No. 66, Headquarters, Department for Northern Virginia for May 25, 1863, *Compiled Records*, Roll 343; Bell Irvin Wiley, *The Life of Johnny Reb: The Common Soldier of the Confederacy* (New York: Bobbs-Merrill, 1943), 231; Lucinthia Jones to Robert Harris Jones, n.d., in "Very Personal Glimpse," ed. Morgan. Spelling in correspondence is often erratic; throughout this book the original spelling is preserved without comment.

23. Quoted in C. Mildred Thompson, *Reconstruction in Georgia: Economic, Social, Political, 1865–1872* (Savannah: Beehive Press, 1972), 28; *Compiled Records*, Roll 343; Mills Lane, ed., *"War Is Hell!": William T. Sherman's Personal Narrative of His March Through Georgia* (Savannah: Beehive Press, 1974), 59, and *The People of Georgia: An Illustrated Social History* (Savannah: Beehive Press, 1975), 217–18.

24. Laura M. Jones, *Life and Sayings*, 45.

25. Bill Arp in the *Atlanta Constitution*, September 27, 1885, 2.

26. Laura M. Jones, *Life and Sayings*, 45.

27. Ibid., 25; *Compiled Records*, Roll 343. Laura had recorded meeting her future husband in January 1864, but that was before Sherman's invasion and thus before Sam left Cartersville. They must have met in January 1865.

28. Clarence Poe, ed., *True Tales of the South at War: How Soldiers Fought and Families Lived, 1861–1865* (Chapel Hill: University of North Carolina Press, 1961), 74; Lucy Josephine Cunyus, *The History of Bartow County, Formerly Cass County* (Easley, S.C.: Tribune, 1933), 24, 244; *Cartersville Standard Express*, March 27, 1873, 3.

29. Thompson, *Reconstruction in Georgia*, 116; J. O. Dobbins, quoted in Alan Conway, *Reconstruction in Georgia* (Minneapolis: University of Minnesota Press, 1966), 122, 116–17; Laura M. Jones, *Life and Sayings*, 25. See also Page Smith, *Trial by Fire: A People's History of the Civil War and Reconstruction* (New York: McGraw-Hill, 1982), 652.

30. *San Francisco Daily Examiner*, March 9, 1889, 3; Clark Howell, *History of Georgia* (Atlanta: S. J. Clarke, 1926), 2:555; *Columbia Herald*, August 7, 1891, 1, clipping in Jones Papers, University of Georgia. Evans had a long and varied career. He served for twenty-five years as a Methodist preacher and was a successful businessman, a failed politician, and editor of the twelve-volume *Confederate Military History*. Evans's contention that one should join the church even in the absence of a conversion experience was acceptable to the Methodist church, which, unlike the Baptist, required only acceptance of Christ as the Son of God, willingness to submit to church law, and a "desire to flee from the wrath to come" (*Doctrine and Discipline of the Methodist Episcopal Church, South* [Nashville: Southern Methodist Publishing House, 1883], 119).

31. Wilbur J. Cash, *The Mind of the South* (New York: Vintage Books, 1941), 132.

32. This information is drawn from John Talmadge's biography, *Rebecca Latimer Felton: Nine Stormy Decades* (Athens: University of Georgia Press, 1960). On Mrs. Felton's racial radicalism, see Joel Williamson, *The Crucible of Race: Black and White Relations in the American South Since Emancipation* (New York: Oxford University Press, 1984), 124–35.

33. *Columbia Herald*, August 7, 1891, 1, clipping in Jones Papers, University of Georgia; *Atlanta Journal*, April 27, 1901, 1.

34. *Atlanta Journal*, April 27, 1901, 1; *Atlanta Constitution*, September 11, 1885, 8; interview with the Reverend Candler Budd, May 13, 1976, Atlanta; *Holston Methodist*, April 18, 1885, 8.

35. *Atlanta Journal*, September 28, 1885, 2; Charles Jones, quoted in Laura M. Jones, *Life and Sayings*, 41; Rebecca Latimer Felton, quoted in Laura M. Jones, *Life and Sayings*, 49.

36. Theodore Smith, quoted in Jones, *Sermons by Rev. Sam P. Jones*, xiii; Jones, *Sam Jones' Own Book*, 13.

37. See "The Making of Radical Reconstruction," in *Reconstruction: America's Unfinished Revolution, 1863–1877*, by Eric Foner (New York: Harper and Row, 1989), 228–80.

38. Valedictory Address, Jones Collection, Emory University. A fascinating

study on the intersection of the individual psyche and historical events is Erik H. Erickson, *Life History and the Historical Moment* (New York: W. W. Norton, 1975).

39. Thompson, *Reconstruction in Georgia*, 361–62, 364; *Atlanta Journal*, September 9, 1906. For the history of the Klan, see Allen W. Trelease, *White Terror: The Ku Klux Klan Conspiracy and Southern Reconstruction* (New York: Harper and Row, 1971). For Jones's relationship with Dixon, see Thomas Dixon to Sam Jones, n.d., Jones Collection, Emory University, and *Atlanta Journal*, February 6, 1904.

40. Valedictory Address, Jones Collection, Emory University; *San Francisco Daily Examiner*, March 24, 1889, 2; Joe Johnson, Jr., "Sam Jones: A Sketch," *Atlanta Journal*, December 9, 1893, 3.

41. Holcomb, *Sam Jones*, 42–43; Sam Jones, *Thunderbolts* (Nashville: Jones and Haynes, 1895), 20.

42. Sam Jones to Laura McElwain, February 5, 1868; August 24, 1868; and n.d., all in Jones Collection, Emory University.

43. Sam Jones to Laura McElwain, August 24, 1868; and May 26, 1868, both in Jones Collection, Emory University.

44. Laura M. Jones, *Life and Sayings*, 47, 25.

45. Ibid., 26; Theodore Smith, quoted in Jones, *Sermons by Rev. Sam P. Jones*, xii; Sam Jones to Laura McElwain, August 24, 1868, Jones Collection, Emory University; *Atlanta Journal*, June 5, 1987, 10; Holcomb, *Popular Lectures*, 85.

46. Sam Jones to Laura McElwain, February 13, 1870, Jones Collection, Emory University; the Reverend P. H. Brewster, *Cartersville Courant American*, September 24, 1896, 4; interview with Candler Budd, May 13, 1976, Atlanta.

47. *San Francisco Daily Examiner*, March 24, 1889, 2; *Chicago Daily Inter-Ocean*, February 28, 1885, 5; *St. Joseph Daily Herald*, October 1, 1885, 4; *St. Louis Globe-Democrat*, March 20, 1895, 2.

48. Annie Jones Pyron, ed., *Sam Jones' Revival Sermons* (New York: Fleming H. Revell, 1912), 151–52.

49. Laura M. Jones, *Life and Sayings*, 27; Jones, *Anecdotes and Illustrations* (Chicago: Rhodes and McClure, 1896), 190–91; *Wheeling Daily Intelligencer*, August 21, 1893, 2.

50. Jones often said that Beulah was the only child who ever saw him intoxicated, but unless he stayed away from home and his infant daughter, Mary, during this last spree, that could not be true.

51. Last Will and Testament of John J. Jones, August 20, 1872, Will Record A, Bartow County, Ga., 1836–85; Laura M. Jones, *Life and Sayings*, 53–54; Jones, *Sam Jones' Own Book*, 15.

52. A. W. Houchins, "Sam Jones," *Independent*, September 24, 1885, 5.

53. H.P.M., "Rev. Sam Jones in Cincinnati," *Zion's Herald*, February 24, 1886, 2; Laura M. Jones, *Life and Sayings*, 56.

54. J. C. Pollock, *Moody* (New York: Macmillan, 1963), 14; *Baltimore Sun*, May 17, 1886, 5; *St. Louis Globe-Democrat*, March 13, 1895, 2.

55. Jones, *Sam Jones' Own Book*, 134; Leftwich, *Hot Shots*, 55; *Wesleyan Christian Advocate*, May 23, 1892, 4.

56. Leftwich, *Hot Shots*, 20; *St. Louis Globe-Democrat*, March 13, 1895, 2.

57. *St. Louis Globe-Democrat*, March 13, 1895, 2.

58. Ibid., March 5, 1895, 3.

59. *Chicago Tribune*, April 5, 1886, 1.

60. *Knoxville Journal and Tribune*, May 29, 1905, 3; Jones, *Sam Jones' Own Book*, 15–16.

61. *Boston Daily Globe*, January 22, 1887, 3; Jones, *Sam Jones' Own Book*, 22.

62. Pyron, *Sam Jones' Revival Sermons*, 60–61.

63. *St. Louis Globe-Democrat*, March 20, 1895, 2.

64. *St. Joseph Daily Herald*, October 1, 1885, 2; *Nashville Banner*, May 20, 1890, 4; *Louisville Courier-Journal*, May 1, 1899, 8; *Indianapolis Journal*, June 21, 1886, 1; *New York Times*, September 10, 1899, 22; Laura M. Jones, *Life and Sayings*, 450.

65. *Holston Methodist*, April 14, 1882, 2; *Boston Daily Globe*, January 19, 1887, 2; Jones, *Sam Jones' Own Book*, 15–16; *Chicago Tribune*, April 5, 1886, 1.

66. Jones, *Sam Jones' Own Book*, 16–17.

67. "Autobiographical Sketch," in *Living Words*, by Jones, 17; Holcomb, *Sam Jones*, 52.

68. Laura M. Jones, *Life and Sayings*, 450; Holcomb, *Sam Jones*, 51–52.

Chapter 3: Shepherd and Sheepdog

1. Jones, *Sam Jones' Own Book*, 18; Statistical Report for the Year Ending November 31, 1872, Rome District, in *Minutes of the North Georgia Conference*, Methodist Episcopal Church, South, 6th Session, Atlanta, November 27–December 4, 1872 (Macon, Ga.: J. W. Burke, 1873).

2. Laura M. Jones, *Life and Sayings*, 65; interview with Mrs. R. D. Crowe, June 17, 1961, cited in Vernon Damon Vaughn, "A Critical Study of the Preaching of Samuel Porter Jones" (Th.D. dissertation, New Orleans Baptist Seminary, 1962); Jones, "Autobiographical Sketch," in *Living Words*, 19.

3. Quoted in Frederick A. Norwood, *The Story of American Methodism: A History of the United Methodists and Their Relations* (Nashville: Abingdon Press, 1974), 258.

4. Sydney E. Ahlstrom, *A Religious History of the American People* (New Haven, Conn.: Yale University Press, 1972), 2:717; E. Merton Coulter, *The South During Reconstruction*, vol. 2 of *A History of the South*, ed. Wendell Holmes Stephenson and E. Merton Coulter (Baton Rouge: Louisiana State University Press, 1947), 332; quoted in Victor Loefflath-Ehly, "Religion as the Principal Component of World-Maintenance in the American South From the 1830's to 1900 with Special Emphasis on the Clergy and Their Sermons: A Case Study in the Dialectic of Religion and Culture" (Ph.D. dissertation, Florida State University, 1978), 133–34.

5. James H. Moorhead, *American Apocalypse: Yankee Protestants and the Civil War, 1860–1869* (New Haven, Conn.: Yale University Press, 1978), 199; quoted in Ralph Morrow, "The Methodist Episcopal Church, South, and Reconstruction, 1865–1885" (Ph.D. dissertation, Indiana University, 1954), 88.

6. Charles Ferguson, *Organizing to Beat the Devil: Methodists and the Making of*

America (New York: Doubleday, 1971), 157; quoted in Charles T. Thrift, "Rebuilding the Southern Church," in *History of American Methodism*, ed. Emory Stevens Burke, vol. 2 (Nashville: Abingdon Press, 1964), 268.

7. Quoted in William Warren Sweet, *The Methodists* (Nashville: Abingdon-Cokesbury Press, 1933), 342; *Wesleyan Christian Advocate*, October 18, 1879, 5; *Wesleyan Christian Advocate*, May 17, 1879, 5.

8. Holcomb, *Sam Jones*, 55; Jones, *Living Words*, 340.

9. *Cartersville Tribune News*, January 21, 1926, 1, in newspaper clippings, Jones Papers, University of Georgia; undated clipping, Jones Papers, University of Georgia.

10. *St. Joseph Daily Herald*, October 13, 1885, 2; *St. Louis Globe-Democrat*, March 25, 1895, 2; *Nashville Banner*, January 1, 1900.

11. Jones, *Sam Jones' Own Book*, 21; unidentified clipping, Jones Collection, Emory University.

12. Jones, *Sam Jones' Own Book*, 20; Jones, *Sermons by Rev. Sam P. Jones*, 226–43; Charles Haddon Spurgeon, *Sermons of Rev. C. H. Spurgeon* (New York: Funk and Wagnalls, n.d.), 5:112–28; Jones, *Sermons by Rev. Sam P. Jones*, 348, 336–57; Craig Skinner, *The Lamplighter and Son* (Nashville: Boardman Press, 1984), 247–48.

13. Ernest W. Bacon, *Spurgeon: Heir of the Puritans* (Grand Rapids, Mich.: Baker Book House, 1967), 75.

14. Spurgeon, *Sermons*, 5:331; *San Francisco Daily Examiner*, March 27, 1889, 3; *Savannah Press*, May 13, 1901, 4; *Boston Daily Globe*, January 17, 1887, 2.

15. Spurgeon, *Sermons*, 5:206; Holcomb, *Sam Jones*, 156; *St. Louis Republican*, December 7, 1885, 6; Leftwich, *Sermons and Sayings*, 90, 91.

16. *Nashville Daily American*, May 28, 1885, 3; Spurgeon, *Sermons*, 5:386; Jones, *Sermons by Rev. Sam P. Jones*, 37; Jones, *Sam Jones' Own Book*, 40; quoted in William G. McLoughlin, *Modern Revivalism: Charles Grandison Finney to Billy Graham* (New York: Ronald Press, 1959), 294.

17. Spurgeon, *Sermons*, 5:349; *St. Louis Republic*, March 4, 1895, 3.

18. *Boston Daily Globe*, January 18, 1887, 2.

19. Bacon, *Spurgeon*, 80, 111.

20. *Atlanta Journal*, March 9, 1897, 5; *St. Joseph Daily Herald*, October 13, 1885, 2; *Nashville Daily American*, May 28, 1885.

21. *Indianapolis Journal*, June 17, 1886, 2; *Atlanta Journal*, May 10, 1897; *Boston Daily Globe*, January 21, 1897, 8.

22. *Dallas Morning News*, May 27, 1893, 6; clipping on the lecture "Character and Characters," Jones Papers, University of Georgia; Jones, *Sermons by Rev. Sam P. Jones*, 245; *Baltimore Sun*, May 22, 1886, 5; *Augusta Chronicle*, May 12, 1897, 5.

23. Holcomb McLain Stroup, Sr., "My Personal Knowledge of the Late Samuel Porter Jones," *Atlanta Constitution*, November 13, 1975.

24. *Baltimore Sun*, May 22, 1886; *St. Louis Globe-Democrat*, March 4, 1895, 4; *Boston Daily Globe*, January 17, 1887, 2; *St. Louis Republican*, November 26, 1885, 5; Jones, *Anecdotes and Illustrations*, 62.

25. "Rev. Sam P. Jones," *Cartersville Directory*, 1883–84. The story of the little boy in Texas was a favorite of my former minister, Bishop Robert Goodrich.

26. Jones, *Sam Jones' Own Book*, 20, *Living Words*, 36, *Sam Jones' Own Book*, 37; J. W. Lee, in *Atlanta Georgian*, October 16, 1906, 1.

27. *Southern Evangelist*, April 21, 1887, 1; *Atlanta Journal*, March 15, 1902, 1; Bill Arp, in *Atlanta Constitution*, September 27, 1885, 2.

28. Holcomb, *Sam Jones*, 36; Leftwich, *Hot Shots*, 86.

29. Laura M. Jones, *Life and Sayings*, 69–70. This information is drawn from the Statistical Reports contained in the *North Georgia Conference Minutes*, 1873–75. The man got well and proved true to his word.

30. Leftwich, *Hot Shots*, 73; Jones, *Living Words*, 22–23; Holcomb, *Sam Jones*, 74; Jones, *Sam Jones' Own Book*, 23.

31. Laura M. Jones, *Life and Sayings*, 73; Jones, *Sermons by Rev. Sam P. Jones*, 65.

32. Laura M. Jones, *Life and Sayings*, 73; Jones, *Living Words*, 22–23; Holcomb, *Sam Jones*, 74; Jones, *Sam Jones' Own Book*, 23.

33. Bernard A. Weisberger, *They Gathered at the River: The Story of the Great Revivalists and Their Impact upon Religion in America* (Boston: Little, Brown, 1958), 110; Ahlstrom, *Religious History*, 1:557.

34. Jones, *Living Words*, 23; Leftwich, *Hot Shots*, 66; *Baltimore Sun*, July 19, 1898, 7.

35. Holcomb, *Sam Jones*, 57; Statistical Report, *Minutes of the North Georgia Conference*, 1876, 9; Laura M. Jones, *Life and Sayings*, 69.

36. *St. Louis Globe-Democrat*, March 22, 1895, 2; *Chicago Tribune*, March 5, 1886, 3.

37. *Chicago Tribune*, March 5, 1886, 3; Laura M. Jones, *Life and Sayings*, 74.

38. Jones, *Sermons by Rev. Sam P. Jones*, 325, 324.

39. Interview with B. C. Kerr, May 24, 1981, Atlanta. Kerr, himself a Methodist minister, was the son of a Methodist minister in north Georgia who was very close to LaPrade. Though this story is found nowhere else, its veracity is confirmed in two newspaper accounts Jones gave about his drinking. In 1893 he said that he had not had a drink for eighteen years, and in 1895 he stated that he had not touched liquor for twenty years. Both of these accounts would date Jones's last drink in 1875, three years after his conversion and entrance into the ministry. See *St. Louis Globe-Democrat*, March 24, 1895, 2, and *Nashville Banner*, February 12, 1893, 6.

40. Clipping in letter to Sam Jones from S. E. Harness (Memphis), February 19, 1893, Jones Papers, University of Georgia; *St. Louis Globe-Democrat*, March 24, 1895, 2; *Nashville Banner*, February 12, 1893, 6.

41. *Times-Star* (no city designated), clipping in Jones Papers, University of Georgia; *Louisville Courier-Journal*, May 12, 1899, 6; F. W. Houchins, "Sam Jones," *Independent*, September 24, 1885, 5; *St. Louis Globe-Democrat*, November 28, 1885, 10.

42. *St. Joseph Daily Herald*, September 29, 1885, 3; *Nashville Daily American*, May 19, 1885, 3.

43. G. G. Smith, in *Nashville Christian Advocate*, January 24, 1895, 48; and July 27, 1899, 3; *Wesleyan Christian Advocate*, September 8, 1897, 3; Simon Peter Richardson, *The Lights and Shadows of Itinerant Life* (Nashville: Publishing House of the Methodist Episcopal Church, South, 1901), 110; D. J. Weems, "Reminiscences," *Wesleyan Christian Advocate*, July 30, 1895, 11.

44. D. J. Weems, "Reminiscences," *Wesleyan Christian Advocate*, July 30, 1895, 11; Richardson, *Lights and Shadows*, 132, 216, 132; Charles Henry Smith, *Bill Arp's Scrap Book: Humor and Philosophy* (Atlanta: Jas. P. Harrison, 1884), 232.

45. *Wesleyan Christian Advocate*, September 8, 1897, 3; "Autobiographical Sketch," in *Living Words*, by Jones, 29; Jones, *Sam Jones' Own Book*, 29.

46. Laura M. Jones, *Life and Sayings*, 87. This story was included in *A Treasury of American Anecdotes*, ed. B. A. Botkin (New York: Bonanza Books, 1967), 129.

47. Laura M. Jones, *Life and Sayings*, 82–83.

48. Ibid., 87; *Wesleyan Christian Advocate*, August 3, 1878, 5, September 8, 1878, 5, and September 21, 1878, 5.

49. Richardson, *Lights and Shadows*, 238.

50. R. W. J., "The Proper Way to Discuss Infidelity," *Wesleyan Christian Advocate*, March 8, 1882, 4.

51. Laura M. Jones, *Life and Sayings*, 437; Jones, *Anecdotes and Illustrations*, 50; *Knoxville Daily Journal*, May 25, 1892, 7.

52. *San Francisco Daily Examiner*, March 11, 1889, 2.

53. Richardson, *Lights and Shadows*, 238; *Madisonian*, April 19, 1879, 3; and April 12, 1897, 3; Laura M. Jones, *Life and Sayings*, 87; *Wesleyan Christian Advocate*, February 28, 1880, 5; J. B. Johnstone (Gainesville, Fla.) to Sam Jones, August 16, 1880, Jones Papers, University of Georgia.

54. Sam Jones to Laura Jones, February 29, 1880, Jones Papers, University of Georgia; Sam Jones to Laura Jones, n.d., Jones Collection, Emory University; Sam Jones to Laura Jones, September 2, 1884, Jones Papers, Jones Museum; Sam Jones to Laura Jones, March 24, 1881, Jones Collection, Emory University.

55. Jones, *Sam Jones' Own Book*, 31. These figures come from *Minutes of the North Georgia Conference*, 1872–81.

56. *Augusta Chronicle*, May 15, 1894, 5; and April 14, 1892, 7.

57. *Baltimore American*, May 3, 1886, 4; *Boston Daily Globe*, January 19, 1887, 2.

58. *Boston Daily Globe*, January 20, 1887, 2; *Missouri Republican*, December 3, 1885, 5.

59. George R. Stuart, *Famous Stories of Sam P. Jones* (New York: Fleming H. Revell, 1908), 60.

60. Laura M. Jones, *Life and Sayings*, 188, 73, 61.

61. *Boston Daily Globe*, January 22, 1887, 3; Stuart, *Famous Stories*, 133.

62. *Boston Daily Globe*, January 20, 1887, 2; *Chicago Tribune*, April 5, 1886, 2.

63. Jones, *Sam Jones' Own Book*, 37; *St. Louis Globe-Democrat*, March 22, 1895, 2; *Nashville Daily American*, May 31, 1885, 2.

Chapter 4: The Holy Terror

1. Jones, *Sam Jones' Own Book*, 470–71.
2. J. W. O. McKibben, "Institutional Care and Placing Out of Dependent Children as Conducted by the North Georgia Conference" (thesis, Candler School of

Theology, Emory University, 1921), 1–9, 21; Report on Orphans' Home, in *Minutes of the North Georgia Conference*, 1876, 11.

3. Laura M. Jones, *Life and Sayings*, 93, 95 (quoting an article in the *Nashville Christian Advocate*), 96.

4. Ibid., 97; contract between Sam Jones and L. M. Meriwether, n.d.; and G. H. Johnson to Sam Jones, June 24, 1881, both in Jones Papers, University of Georgia.

5. *St. Louis Globe-Democrat*, March 4, 1895, 4; G. H. Johnson to Sam Jones (quoting an earlier letter from Sam Jones), July 4, 1881, Jones Papers, University of Georgia.

6. Sam Jones, in *Wesleyan Christian Advocate*, January 7, 1882, 5.

7. Holcomb, *Sam Jones*, 7; *New York Times*, November 28, 1896, 9; Laura M. Jones, *Life and Sayings*, 97 (quoting an unidentified Atlanta paper).

8. Holcomb, *Sam Jones*, 83; Jones, *Anecdotes and Illustrations*, 216.

9. Stuart, *Famous Stories*, 123.

10. *Atlanta Journal*, May 16, 1903, 8; *Nashville Christian Advocate*, June 4, 1887, 9; *Boston Daily Globe*, January 18, 1887, 2; *Minutes of the North Georgia Conference*, 1885, 16; Laura M. Jones, *Life and Sayings*, 27.

11. Laura M. Jones, *Life and Sayings*, 97.

12. Ibid., 100.

13. Ibid., 103; *Memphis Daily Appeal*, January 4, 1884, 1.

14. Laura M. Jones, *Life and Sayings*, 101–2.

15. Ibid., 113–14.

16. Ibid., 110–11.

17. *St. Louis Globe-Democrat*, November 28, 1885, 10; M. J. Cofer to Sam Jones, July 31, 1882; J. A. Bunnen to Sam Jones, June 10, 1884; and J. A. Bunnen to Sam Jones, July 23, 1884, all in Jones Papers, University of Georgia.

18. Holcomb, *Sam Jones*, 248; Jones, *Sermons by Rev. Sam P. Jones*, 493.

19. *Waco Daily Examiner*, October 5, 1884, 3.

20. Sam Jones, *Hot Shots; or, Sermons and Sayings*, ed. W. M. Leftwich (Nashville: Publishing House of the Methodist Episcopal Church, South, 1912), 238.

21. Maximilian Rudwin, *The Devil in Legend and Literature* (New York: AMS Press, 1970), 51; Edward Langton, *Satan: A Portrait* (London: Skettington and Son, 1945), 104–5; 1 Peter 5; *Baltimore Sun*, July 19, 1890, 7; and May 7, 1900, 7.

22. *Nashville American*, February 8, 1897, 1–2; *Boston Daily Globe*, January 26, 1887, 2; *Nashville Banner*, June 2, 1892, 3; *Atlanta Constitution*, October 22, 1906, 5; *Baltimore Sun*, May 12, 1886, 7; *Augusta Chronicle*, May 18, 1897, 5.

23. *Cincinnati Commercial Gazette*, February 6, 1886, 3; *St. Louis Globe-Democrat*, March 23, 1895, 2.

24. *St. Louis Globe-Democrat*, March 22, 1895, 2; Laura M. Jones, *Life and Sayings*, 424.

25. *Baltimore American*, May 10, 1886, 4; *St. Louis Globe-Democrat*, March 7, 1895, 2.

26. *St. Louis Globe-Democrat*, March 6, 1895, 2; and March 6, 1895, 2; *Knoxville Daily Journal*, May 24, 1892, 1.

27. *San Francisco Daily Examiner*, March 27, 1889, 3; William J. McGuire of Yale University, cited in William Thomas, *An Assessment of Mass Meetings as a*

Method of Evangelism: Case Study of Eurofest '75 and the Billy Graham Crusade in Brussels (Amsterdam: Rodopi, 1977), 76; *Holston Methodist*, December 26, 1885, 1; Jones, *Sermons by Rev. Sam P. Jones*, 270.

28. Howard Louis Milkman, "Thomas DeWitt Talmage: An Evangelical Nineteenth Century Voice on Technology, Urbanization, and Labor-Management Conflicts" (Ph.D. dissertation, New York University, 1971), 243, 181–82; Jones, *Sermons by Rev. Sam P. Jones*, xviii.

29. William B. Mitchell (Oxford, Miss.) to Sam Jones, December 27, 1884, Jones Papers, University of Georgia; undated clipping, Jones Collection, Emory University; *Cartersville Weekly Tribune News*, February 23, 1950, cited in Raymond Charles Rensi, "Sam Jones: Southern Evangelist" (Ph.D. dissertation, University of Georgia, 1971); Laura M. Jones, *Life and Sayings*, 125.

30. Undated clipping, Susan Melvina Hawkins scrapbook, 1843–1913, Tennessee State Archives, Nashville; *Cartersville American*, January 20, 1885, 11; Jones, *Sermons by Rev. Sam P. Jones*, xviii.

31. *Boston Daily Globe*, January 20, 1887, 3; J. T. Gibson (Decatur, Ga.) to Sam Jones, February 4, 1885, 4; J. H. Bryson (Huntsville, Ala.) to Sam Jones, March 7, 1885, both in Jones Papers, University of Georgia.

32. Flakewhite's article in the *Christian Observer*, quoted in the *Nashville Christian Advocate*, April 4, 1885, 4; J. H. Bryson to Sam Jones, March 7, 1885, Jones Papers, University of Georgia.

33. Charles Jones to Sam Jones, September 5, 1882; May 23, 1880; and April 20, 1881; Charles Jones (Stilesboro, Ga.) to John T. Stocks, January 4, 1898; Joe Jones to Sam Jones, n.d., all in Jones Papers, University of Georgia.

34. Alex Bealer, in *Atlanta Journal*, October 15, 1905; Joe Jones to Sam Jones, July 10, 1889, Jones Collection, Emory University.

35. Laura Jones to Sam Jones, March 29, 1885, Jones Papers, Jones Museum; *Atlanta Constitution*, October 24, 1888, 1.

36. Joe Jones to Sam Jones, July 10, 1889, Jones Papers, Jones Museum; *Louisville Courier-Journal*, May 8, 1899, 5; Joe Jones (Stotts City, Mo.) to Sam Jones, August 17, 1898, Jones Papers, University of Georgia; *Cartersville News and Courant*, December 11, 1902, 1; Alex Bealer, in *Atlanta Journal*, October 15, 1905.

37. Joseph Mendels, *Concepts of Depression* (New York: John Wiley and Sons, 1970), 27; unsigned letter to Sam Jones, February 14, 1900, Jones Papers, University of Georgia; George Winokur, Paula J. Clayton, and Theodore Reich, *Manic Depressive Illness* (St. Louis: C. W. Mosby, 1969), 68–71; Annie Pyron Jones diary, September 21, 1892, in the possession of Louise Cade, Atlanta; Joe Jones (Stotts City, Mo.) to Sam Jones, August 17, 1898, Jones Papers, University of Georgia. The diagnosis of bipolar disorder or manic depressive illness was suggested to me by Dr. Don Turner, Atlanta psychiatrist, after a review of the emotional history of the family (interview, October 16, 1985, Atlanta). It was confirmed by Dr. Don Manning, a psychiatrist who specializes in bipolar disorder, in an interview on July 18, 1991, Atlanta.

38. Laura Jones to Sam Jones, April 22, 1884; February 17, 1885; and March 2, 1886, all in Jones Papers, University of Georgia.

39. Sam Jones to Mary Jones, October 24, 1886, Jones Papers, University of

Georgia; Bill Arp, in *Atlanta Constitution*, September 27, 1885, 2; Jones, *Thunderbolts*, 339; *St. Louis Globe-Democrat*, March 5, 1895, 3.

40. A. W. Lamar to Sam Jones, October 23, 1884; and William Leftwich to Sam Jones, both in the possession of Howell Jones, Atlanta.

41. Drs. P. C. Williams and Cary Thomas to Laura Jones, May 31, 1886, Jones Papers, University of Georgia; *Louisville Times*, March 28, 1901.

42. Holcomb, *Sam Jones*, 115; *St. Louis Globe-Democrat*, March 15, 1897; Holcomb, *Sam Jones*, 147.

43. Laura Jones to Sam Jones, March 29, 1890; and May 15, 1888, both in Jones Papers, University of Georgia; *Atlanta Constitution*, October 6, 1912.

44. *Louisville Courier-Journal*, May 1, 1899, 8; clipping from *Columbia Herald*, August 7, 1891, Jones Papers, University of Georgia.

45. *Southern Evangelist*, January 6, 1887; *Nashville Christian Advocate*, September 26, 1885, 16. The reader should be warned that Jones's calculations of his converts were often inflated.

46. Laura M. Jones, *Life and Sayings*, 202–3; *Nashville Christian Advocate*, August 8, 1885, 9. At the St. Louis revival reporters were present from Minneapolis, Minn.; Wheeling, W. Va.; Leavenworth, Kans.; Indianapolis, Ind.; and Springfield, Mass. During the Chicago meeting reporters from the *Cincinnati Tribune* and the *St. Louis Globe-Democrat* were present.

47. Holcomb, *Sam Jones*, 89; *St. Louis Republican*, December 19, 1885, 5; *Minneapolis Evening Journal*, June 24, 1886; clipping from unidentified newspaper in Ottowa, Ill., June 28, 1896, Jones Collection, Emory University; *Nashville American*, March 21, 1898, 8.

48. *Augusta Chronicle*, April 7, 1892, 5.

49. *San Francisco Daily Examiner*, January 6, 1889, 2.

50. *Daily Alta Californian*, quoted in *Wesleyan Christian Advocate*, April 10, 1889.

51. Holcomb, *Sam Jones*, 65–66.

52. *Baltimore Sun*, May 17, 1886, 3; *Baltimore American*, May 10, 1886, 4.

53. Laura M. Jones, *Life and Sayings*, 89.

54. Jones, *Sam Jones' Own Book*, 206; *Atlanta Journal*, August 16, 1902, 1; *Moberly Daily Monitor*, November 30, 1888.

55. *Toledo Bee*, March 25, 1899, 2; Bill Nye, in *Augusta Chronicle*, May 13, 1894, 16.

56. *Toledo Bee*, March 13, 1899, 8; Jones, *Thunderbolts*, 367; *Vicksburg Post*, October 18, 1906, Jones Papers, University of Georgia.

57. *Cincinnati Enquirer*, February 20, 1886, 17; *Independent*, January 27, 1887; and November 11, 1886, 14.

58. Undated clipping, Jones Collection, Emory University; Laura M. Jones, *Life and Sayings*, 159–60.

59. McLoughlin, *Modern Revivalism*, 240; quoted in Winthrop S. Hudson, *Revivalism in America* (New York: Charles Scribner's Sons, 1965), 230; *Waco Day*, September 8, 1884, 1; *Atlanta Journal*, March 8, 1897, 5; "Whatsoever a Man Soweth" (unpublished sermon), Jones Papers, University of Georgia; William G. McLoughlin, *Billy Sunday Was His Real Name* (Chicago: University of Chicago Press, 1955), 171.

60. D. C. Kelley, "Rev. Sam. P. Jones," *Southern Bivouac* 6 (January 1886): 500; quoted in Smith, "Analysis," 79.

61. Joseph Ditzler, *Central Methodist*, October 1895, 8, Jones Papers, Archives of the State of Georgia; J.A.H. to Sam Jones, n.d. (in which he enclosed "The Mountebank in the Pulpit" by Marion F. Ham), Jones Collection, Emory University; undated clipping, Jones Collection, Emory University; W. E. Barton, quoted in *Boston Daily Globe*, January 26, 1897, 3; undated clipping from *Rochester Herald*, Jones Papers, University of Georgia; *St. Louis Republic*, August 8, 1894, 1; *Dallas Weekly Herald*, September 3, 1885.

62. Stuart, *Famous Stories*, 250; *Louisville Courier-Journal*, May 2, 1899, 4; "Mrs. C." to Sam Jones, November 14, 1886, Jones Papers, University of Georgia; *Atlanta Journal*, October 16, 1906, 1; Sam Jones, *Good News: A Collection of Sermons by Sam Jones and Sam Small* (New York: J. S. Ogilvie, 1886), 137.

63. Laura M. Jones, *Life and Sayings*, 231; Jones, *Sam Jones' Own Book*, 466; *Atlanta Constitution*, March 11, 1886, 4.

64. Undated clipping, Jones Collection, Emory University; Laura M. Jones, *Life and Sayings*, 457; *San Francisco Daily Examiner*, March 24, 1889; Sam P. Jones, "Whatsoever a Man Soweth" (unpublished sermon), Jones Papers, University of Georgia.

65. *Baltimore Sun*, quoting from *Baltimore Baptist*, May 28, 1886, 5; Kelley, "Rev. Sam. P. Jones," 502.

66. *New York Times*, quoted in McLoughlin, *Billy Sunday*, xx; *Atlanta Constitution*, October 17, 1906, 6; *Boston Daily Globe*, January 17, 1887, 2; *Atlanta Journal*, September 15, 1900, 5.

67. *Knoxville Tribune*, June 4, 1905; *Dallas Morning News*, June 2, 1893, 1.

68. Interview with Walt Holcomb, in Vaughn, "Critical Study," 36; *San Francisco Daily Examiner*, March 11, 1889, 2.

69. Clipping in Flournoy Rivers scrapbook, 41, Sam Jones File, Tennessee State Archives, Nashville.

70. *Memphis Commercial Appeal*, October 16, 1886, 3; E. Brooks Holifield, "The Southern Heritage and the Minister's Image," lecture delivered during Minister's Week, 1976, Candler School of Theology, Emory University, Atlanta; Robert S. Michaelsen, "The Protestant Ministry in Historical Perspective," in *Ministry in Historical Perspectives*, ed. H. Richard Niebuhr and Daniel D. Williams (New York: Harper and Row, 1956), 283; *Toledo Bee*, March 12, 1899, 4; and March 15, 1899, 8.

71. Interview with Dr. R. G. Lee, May 24, 1961, St. Louis, Mo., in Vaughn, "Critical Study," 25; *Pensacola Daily News*, November 9, 1890; interview with W. C. Kenson, June 17, 1961, in Vaughn, "Critical Study," 64.

72. Quoted in C. F. Wimberly, *Modern Apostles of Faith* (Nashville: Cokesbury Press, 1930), 111; *New York Times*, March 3, 1886, 2.

73. *St. Joseph Daily Herald*, September 30, 1885, 3.

74. *Missouri Republican*, November 24, 1885, 10; Laura M. Jones, *Life and Sayings*, 161–62.

75. *St. Joseph Daily Herald*, October 3, 1885, 2; *Baltimore Sun*, May 29, 1886, 5; *Baltimore American*, May 8, 1886, 2; *Holston Methodist*, April 4, 1885, 2.

76. Thomas M. Lindsay, "Revivals," *Contemporary Review* 88 (1905): 361.

77. *Nashville Christian Advocate*, October 29, 1905, 1.

78. W. W. Pinson, *George R. Stuart: Life and Work* (Nashville: Cokesbury Press, 1927), 94; George Stuart, *Methodist Evangelism* (Nashville: Publishing House of the Methodist Episcopal Church, South, 1923), 131.

79. Jones, *Sermons by Rev. Sam P. Jones*, 53; *St. Louis Globe-Democrat*, August 7, 1894, 5.

80. Dr. R. W. Park to Sam Jones, October 7, 1884, Jones Papers, University of Georgia; 1 John 3:7.

81. *Nashville Banner*, May 13, 1885, 2; *Baltimore Sun*, May 17, 1886, 3; and May 24, 1886, 5.

82. *Chicago Tribune*, March 1, 1886, 2; *Boston Herald*, January 5, 1897, 1.

83. *St. Louis Globe-Democrat*, March 17, 1895, 6; *Southern Evangelist*, February 10, 1887, 3; *Independent*, June 10, 1886, 14; Robert V. Orr to Sam Jones, July 3, 1888, Jones Papers, University of Georgia.

84. Flournoy Rivers scrapbook, 40–41, Jones File, Tennessee State Archives.

85. *Independent*, September 16, 1895, 1.

86. Kelley, "Rev. Sam. P. Jones," 504; "Editor's Outlook," *Chautauquan*, March 1886, 417.

Chapter 5: Priest of the New South

1. Haywood Jefferson Pearce, Jr., *Benjamin H. Hill, Secession, and Reconstruction* (Chicago: University of Chicago Press, 1920), 174.

2. *Atlanta Journal*, October 6, 1894, 1.

3. Pearce, *Hill*, 212, 239.

4. Paul M. Gaston, *The New South Creed: A Study in Southern Mythmaking* (New York: Alfred A. Knopf, 1970), 48; Holcomb, *Sam Jones*, 38.

5. Raymond Blalock Nixon, *Henry W. Grady, Spokesman of the New South* (New York: Alfred A. Knopf, 1943), 7; Holcomb, *Sam Jones*, 22; quoted in Nixon, *Grady*, 8. See also Harold E. Davis, "Henry W. Grady, Master of the Atlanta Ring, 1880–1886," *Georgia Historical Quarterly* 69 (Spring 1985): 1–38.

6. Nixon, *Grady*, 8–11; Holcomb, *Sam Jones*, 21, 15; T. W. Reed, quoted in Nixon, *Grady*, 8.

7. Nixon, *Grady*, 180; *Atlanta Journal*, January 30, 1904.

8. Quoted in Joel Chandler Harris, *Life of Henry W. Grady* (New York: Cassell, 1890), 89; quoted in Williamson, *The Crucible of Race*, 135; *Atlanta Journal*, June 1, 1900; and September 1, 1900, 7. Nineteenth-century southerners did not capitalize *Negro*, using it in contrast to *white* rather than to *Caucasian*.

9. Quoted in Harris, *Life of Grady*, 100–101; *San Francisco Daily Examiner*, March 24, 1889, 2; quoted in Harris, *Life of Grady*, 303; *Atlanta Journal*, September 1, 1900. See also Claude H. Nolen, *The Negro's Image in the South: The Anatomy of White Supremacy* (Lexington: University of Kentucky Press, 1967), and Robert Moats Miller, "Southern White Protestantism and the Negro, 1865–1965," in *The Negro in the South Since 1865: Selected Essays in American Negro History*, ed. Charles E. Wynes (New York: Harper and Row, 1968).

10. McColloch, "Theology and Practices of Methodism," ed. Burke, *History of Methodism*, 2:638.

11. Quoted in Harris, *Life of Grady*, 100–101; *San Francisco Daily Examiner*, March 24, 1889, 2; quoted in Hunter Dickinson Farish, *The Circuit Rider Dismounts: A Social History of Southern Methodism, 1865–1900* (Richmond: Dietz Press, 1938), 219–20. See also David M. Reimers, *White Protestants and the Negro* (New York: Oxford University Press, 1965).

12. *Nashville Banner*, June 13, 1892.

13. Sam Jones, "A Medley of Philosophy, Facts, and Fun" (lecture notes), Jones Collection, Emory University; Cal M. McWilliams (Ft. Smith, Ark.) to Sam Jones, July 3, 1893, Jones Papers, University of Georgia; *Charlotte Observer*, April 13, 1947, clipping in Jones Papers, Jones Museum.

14. Quoted in Harris, *Life of Grady*, 97; *Knoxville Daily Journal*, May 27, 1892, 4; Stuart, *Famous Stories*, 226–27; *Knoxville Daily Journal*, March 29, 1885, 1.

15. Quoted in Harris, *Life of Grady*, 99; quoted in Nixon, *Grady*, 347; Jones, *Thunderbolts*, 483.

16. Williamson, *The Crucible of Race*, 340; I. A. Newby, *Jim Crow's Defense: Anti-Negro Thought in America, 1900–1930* (Baton Rouge: Louisiana State University Press, 1965), 50; Moorhead, *American Apocalypse*, 215–16; quoted in Harris, *Life of Grady*, 90.

17. Williamson, *The Crucible of Race*, 335; Charles Crowe, "Racial Massacre in Atlanta: September 22, 1906," *Journal of Negro History* 53 (April 1969): 160.

18. *St. Joseph Daily Herald*, September 29, 1885, 3; and October 7, 1885, 4.

19. *Cincinnati Commercial Gazette*, January 24, 1886, 3; and February 13, 1886, 3.

20. *Western Appeal: An Organ in the Interest of the Colored People of the Northwest*, April 30, 1887, 1.

21. Quoted in Harris, *Life of Grady*, 137; Grady speech printed in *Atlanta Journal and Constitution*, December 21, 1986, 11; *Chicago Tribune*, March 23, 1886, 1; *Boston Daily Globe*, January 18, 1887, 7.

22. Paul Buck, *The Road to Reunion, 1865–1900* (Boston: Little, Brown, 1937), 208–9; Gaston, *The New South Creed*, 179; Rollin G. Osterweis, *The Myth of the Lost Cause, 1865–1900* (Hamden, Conn.: Archon Books, 1973), 30–31.

23. C. Vann Woodward, *Origins of the New South: 1877–1917*, vol. 9 of *A History of the South*, ed. Wendell Holmes Stephenson and E. Merton Coulter (Baton Rouge: Louisiana State University Press, 1951), 158; quoted in Dow Kirkpatrick, "Early Efforts at Reunion," in *History of Methodism*, ed. Burke, 2:669, 694.

24. Farish, *The Circuit Rider Dismounts*, 138, 158; "The Negro Problem: An Impartial View," *Nashville Christian Advocate*, April 8, 1899, 1; "Lynch Law," *Nashville Christian Advocate*, August 6, 1903, 2.

25. *Baltimore American*, May 2, 1886, 5; Obituary for Samuel White Small, *Atlanta Constitution*, November 22, 1931, 10.

26. *Cincinnati Commercial Gazette*, February 20, 1886; Pearce, *Hill*, 274–77; *Missouri Republican*, October 18, 1885; Frank Small, in *Minneapolis Evening Journal*, June 24, 1886, 2.

27. Jones, *Sam Jones' Own Book*, 531; *Cartersville Courant*, September 24, 1885, 3; *Cartersville American*, December 1, 1897, 2.

28. *Nashville Christian Advocate*, June 20, 1885, 1; *San Francisco Daily Examiner*, March 21, 1889; *Chicago Tribune*, April 5, 1886, 2; *St. Louis Daily Herald*, October 8, 1885, 3.

29. *Chicago Tribune*, April 6, 1886, 4; *Los Angeles Daily Herald*, January 22, 1889, 4; *Nashville Christian Advocate*, February 6, 1886, 16; *Chicago Commercial Gazette*, January 12, 1886, 8; *Chicago Tribune*, March 5, 1886, 5; *Independent*, February 17, 1887, 14.

30. *Toledo Bee*, March 18, 1899, 2; *Baltimore Sun*, May 3, 1886, 1; *St. Louis Republic*, March 4, 1895, 3; *Dallas Morning News*, May 28, 1893, 4; and May 27, 1893, 11.

31. *Dallas Morning News*, May 21, 1893, 11.

32. Weisberger, *They Gathered*, 232; *San Francisco Daily Examiner*, March 21, 1889.

33. Quoted in Gaston, *The New South Creed*, 182; "Sam Jones is Comin'," Jones Papers, University of Georgia.

34. R. Kelso Carter to Sam Jones, October 16, 1896, Jones Papers, University of Georgia.

35. *Minneapolis Evening Journal*, June 24, 1886, 1; Joseph Hillman (Round Lake, N.Y.) to Sam Jones, May 15, 1886, Jones Papers, University of Georgia.

36. Father Phelan, quoted in *New York Times*, November 30, 1885; *St. Louis Republican*, December 10, 1885, 6; and December 17, 1885, 6.

37. John Higham, *Strangers in the Land: Patterns of American Nativism, 1860–1925* (New York: Atheneum, 1974), 92; *Wesleyan Christian Advocate*, March 23, 1899; Holcomb, *Sam Jones*, 24; *Atlanta Journal*, July 30, 1898. In 1897, during a revival in Savannah, Jones spoke out against the American Protective Association (*Savannah Press*, May 23, 1901). However, it may be that by inflaming prohibition sentiment, Jones contributed to the growth of the APA. A history of Augusta, Georgia, insinuates that Jones's call for virtuous country folk to clean up the iniquitous city appealed to prejudice against foreigners. "It was probably no coincidence that the Augusta Branch of the American Protective Association was organized at the time of the Sam Jones revival" (Edward J. Cashin, *The Story of Augusta* [Augusta, Ga.: Richmond Board of Education, 1980], 183).

38. *New York Times*, November 30, 1885; *St. Louis Republican*, December 10, 1885, 6; and December 17, 1885, 6; *Holston Methodist*, January 16, 1886, 2.

39. Unnamed Chicago paper quoted in *Independent*, March 4, 1886; *Independent*, March 4, 1886; Holcomb, *Sam Jones*, 91; Jones, *Thunderbolts*, 448.

40. *Chicago Tribune*, March 1, 1886, 1.

41. Atticus Haygood to Sam Jones, March 25, 1885, Jones Papers, University of Georgia; *Chicago Daily Inter-Ocean*, April 5, 1886, 4.

42. *San Francisco Daily Examiner*, March 27, 1889, 2; *Boston Herald*, January 5, 1897; *Nashville Banner*, April 2, 1895, 1; *Boston Daily Globe*, January 16, 1897, 5. Moody followed Jones to Nashville, Memphis, and Mobile, and twice to Chicago. Jones followed Moody to St. Louis in 1885, on his California campaign of 1889, and to Atlanta in 1895. Both Moody and Jones conducted a revival in Boston in the winter of 1897.

43. Stephen Longstreet, *Chicago: 1860–1919* (New York: David McKay, 1973), 135; Lane, *The People of Georgia*, 251; *Milledgeville Federal Union*, quoted in

James Michael Russell, *Atlanta, 1847–1890: City Building in the Old South and the New* (Baton Rouge: Louisiana State University Press, 1988), 11; Franklin Garrett, quoted in *Atlanta Constitution*, September 7, 1991.

44. Williamson, *The Crucible of Race*, 57; *Atlanta Journal*, October 11, 1902.

45. Grady, quoted in Harris, *Life of Grady*, 87; Wykoop Hellenbeck, *New York at the Cotton States and International Exposition* (Albany, N.Y.: Crawford, 1896), 83.

46. Quoted in *New York Times*, November 28, 1896, 9. It may be that the idea for the Cotton States and International Exposition originated at the party celebrating the Joneses' twenty-fifth anniversary. Jones had just returned from a revival near Waco, Tex., and was favorably impressed with an exposition held in that city, the exposition that was the inspiration for the Atlanta fair. Among those at the anniversary party were W. A. and R. A. Hemphill of the *Atlanta Constitution*, T. J. Kelly, advertising manager of that paper, Hoke Smith, editor of the *Atlanta Journal*, and former governor William J. Northen, all supporters of the Cotton States and International Exposition.

47. *Atlanta Constitution*, January 6, 1895, 3.

48. James F. Findlay, Jr., *Dwight L. Moody: American Evangelist, 1837–1899* (Chicago: University of Chicago Press, 1969), 401; *Wesleyan Christian Advocate*, October 2, 1895, 1.

49. *Atlanta Constitution*, December 15, 1895, 32. Some of the Atlantans involved with the National Christian Conference were William J. Northen, former governor and head of the Georgia Immigration and Investment Bureau, and Walter B. Hill, an Atlanta attorney soon to be elected president of the University of Georgia.

50. *Atlanta Journal*, December 23, 1895, 5; *Minutes of the Evangelical Ministers' Association*, December 23, 1895; Walker Lews, quoted in *Atlanta Journal*, March 14, 1896, 2.

51. *Atlanta Journal*, November 30, 1895, 8.

52. Gaston, *The New South Creed*, 202–7; Woodward, *Origins*, 291–320; *Atlanta Journal*, January 24, 1898; March 5, 1904; and May 31, 1897.

53. Undated clipping from *Boston Daily Globe*, Jones Papers, University of Georgia.

54. *Atlanta Constitution*, December 16, 1895, 7; February 1, 1896; and March 3, 1896, 7; *Atlanta Journal*, March 28, 1896, 7.

55. *Atlanta Journal*, March 28, 1896, 7; *Atlanta Constitution*, March 5, 1896, 8; and March 24, 1896, 7.

56. *Looking Glass*, March 14, 1896, 5; *Atlanta Constitution*, March 11, 1896, 3; and March 15, 1896, 22.

57. *Atlanta Constitution*, October 7, 1885; March 13, 1896, 7; March 15, 1896, 22; and March 27, 1896, 9.

58. Ibid., March 27, 1896, 5; *Looking Glass*, February 29, 1896, 16.

59. *Looking Glass*, February 29, 1896; *Atlanta Journal*, March 9, 1897.

60. Mrs. J. J. Ansley, *History of the Georgia Women's Christian Temperance Union from Its Organization, 1883 to 1907* (Columbus, Ga.: Gilbert, 1914), 148; *Atlanta Constitution*, December 16, 1895, 7.

61. Stuart, *Famous Stories*, 46; *Atlanta Journal*, April 9, 1904; and April 18, 1903.

62. *Louisville Courier-Journal*, May 2, 1899, 4; *Dallas Morning News*, June 1, 1893, 3; *Indianapolis Journal*, June 14, 1886, 2.

63. Ray Ginger, *The Bending Cross* (New Brunswick, N.J.: Rutgers University Press, 1949), 99, 180.

64. *Atlanta Constitution*, March 19, 1896, 7. See also Mercer Griffen Evans, "The History of the Organized Labor Movement in Georgia" (Ph.D. dissertation, University of Chicago, 1929).

65. *Atlanta Constitution*, March 19, 1896, 7.

66. *Atlanta Journal*, September 28, 1893, 7; *Nashville Banner*, April 20, 1895, 6; *Atlanta Journal*, October 27, 1894, 3. Jones's views were common. See Aaron I. Abell, *The Urban Impact on American Protestantism* (Cambridge, Mass.: Harvard University Press, 1943).

67. *Atlanta Constitution*, March 30, 1896, 5; March 29, 1896, 16; March 30, 1896, 5; and April 17, 1896, 7.

68. The five churches for which church registers are available were First and Central Presbyterian, First and Second Baptist, and Central Congregational. Because individual church records have been lost, an analysis of the Methodist churches was made from the *Minutes of the North Georgia Conference*, 1891–1902. Between the years 1891 and 1895, Grace Methodist averaged 42.8 accessions per year; 104 entered the church in 1896, and the average for the next five years dropped to 33.2. The figures for Trinity Methodist are as follows: 1891–95, an average of 43 accessions per year, 107 in 1896, and an average of 31.6 from 1897 to 1901. The information about the social class to which Jones appealed was arrived at by correlating professional status as listed in the *Atlanta City Directory* with church membership records.

During the revival of 1897, the *Constitution* listed the names of contributors who had given twenty-five dollars to repair the tabernacle for the Jones revival. Correlating this list with the *Atlanta City Directory* indicates that Jones was supported by prominent businessmen and professionals, such as George W. Muse of Muse's Department Store and Howard Palmer, an attorney with Palmer and Read.

69. *Atlanta Journal*, January 18, 1897, 9; *Atlanta Constitution*, January 18, 1897; *Atlanta Journal*, March 9, 1897; *Wesleyan Christian Advocate*, April 14, 1897, 4. The figure of 150,000 does not allow for repeaters and was arrived at by simply multiplying the audience of 15,000 a day by 10.

70. *Atlanta Constitution*, March 8, 1897, 5; and March 17, 1897, 5; *Looking Glass*, March 26, 1897.

71. *Atlanta Constitution*, March 1, 1897, 1.

72. Ibid.; and March 9, 1897, 4.

73. *Looking Glass*, March 13, 1897, 9; and February 27, 1897, 4.

74. *Minutes of the Evangelical Ministers' Association*, Record Book 3, July 3, 1899; September 5, 1898; and September 4, 1899.

75. *Atlanta Journal*, June 2, 1906, 10.

76. Ibid., November 5, 1917, quoted in Franklin M. Garrett, *Atlanta and Environs: A Chronicle of Its People and Events* (Athens: University of Georgia Press, 1954), 2:711.

Chapter 6: That Old-Time Religion

1. Josiah Strong, *Our Country: Its Possible Future and Its Present Crisis* (New York: American Home Missionary Society, 1885), 130.

2. *Independent*, December 17, 1885; quoted in Martin E. Marty, *Righteous Empire: The Protestant Experience in America* (New York: Dial Press, 1970), 184.

3. Henry Demorest Lloyd, quoted in Ray Ginger, *Age of Excess: The United States from 1877 to 1914* (New York: Macmillan, 1965), 32; Henry Nash Smith, ed., *Popular Culture and Industrialism, 1865–1900* (Garden City, N.Y.: Doubleday, Anchor Books, 1967), 84; Longstreet, *Chicago*, 135. See also John Tipple, "The Robber Baron in the Gilded Age: Entrepreneur or Iconoclast?" in *The Gilded Age: A Reappraisal*, ed. H. Wayne Morgan (Syracuse, N.Y.: Syracuse University Press, 1963).

4. Robert Wiebe, *The Search for Order, 1877–1920* (New York: Hill and Wang, 1967); quoted in Henry F. May, *Protestant Churches and Industrial America* (New York: Harper and Brothers, 1949), 91; *Southern Evangelist*, March 24, 1887, 2; quoted in May, *Protestant Churches*, 60. See also David A. Wells, "Recent Economic Changes," in *The Nation Transformed: The Creation of an Industrial Society*, ed. Sigmund Diamond (New York: G. Braziller, 1963), 63.

5. Isaiah 32:2; Edwin S. Gaustad, *Historical Atlas of Religion in America* (New York: Harper and Row, 1962), 52. On evangelism in Roman Catholicism, see Jay P. Dolan, *Catholic Revivalism: The American Experience, 1830–1900* (Notre Dame, Ind.: University of Notre Dame Press, 1978).

6. Abell, *Urban Impact*, 88–123; quoted in Norwood, *American Methodism*, 254. On the YMCA see C. Howard Hopkins, *History of the Y.M.C.A. in North America* (New York: Abingdon Press, 1951). On the Salvation Army see Edward H. McKinley, *Marching to Glory: The History of the Salvation Army in the United States of America, 1880–1980* (New York: Harper and Row, 1980).

7. Arthur M. Schlesinger, Sr., *A Critical Period in American Religion, 1875–1900* (Philadelphia: Fortress Press, 1967), 531–32; quoted in Paul Allen Carter, *The Spiritual Crisis of the Gilded Age* (DeKalb: Northern Illinois University Press, 1971), 140; quoted in May, *Protestant Churches*, 93.

8. Quoted in May, *Protestant Churches*, 93; quoted in Sidney Mead, *The Lively Experiment: The Shaping of Christianity in America* (New York: Harper and Row, 1963), 160.

9. *Daily Christian Advocate*, August 17, 1890, 4. On nativism, see Higham, *Strangers in the Land*.

10. On the beginnings of the fundamentalist movement, see George M. Marsden, *Fundamentalism and American Culture: The Shaping of Twentieth-Century Evangelicalism, 1870–1925* (New York: Oxford University Press, 1980).

11. W. F. Glenn, quoted in *Wesleyan Christian Advocate*, September 12, 1883, 5; DeWitt Talmage, quoted in Weisberger, *They Gathered*, 164; Dwight Moody, quoted in McLoughlin, *Modern Revivalism*, 275.

12. H. L. Fair, "Southern Methodists on Education and Race, 1900–1920" (Ph.D. dissertation, Vanderbilt University, 1971), 148–50; quoted in Francis Butler Simkins, *The South, Old and New: A History, 1820–1947* (New York: Alfred A. Knopf, 1947), 317.

13. Richard Hofstader, quoted in P. A. Carter, *Spiritual Crisis*, 13, 10; Osterweis, *Myth*, 119. See also Cash, *The Mind of the South*, 140–42.

14. O. P. Fitzgerald, quoted in Farish, *The Circuit Rider Dismounts*, 105; *Wesleyan Christian Advocate*, November 27, 1895, 3.

15. Carl Oblinger, *Religious Nemesis: Social Bases for the Holiness Schism in Late Nineteenth-Century Methodism: The Illinois Case, 1869–1889*, Institute for the Study of American Religion, Monograph Series, no. 1, 1973, 10–18; Robert S. Michaelsen, "The Protestant Ministry in America: 1850 to the Present," in *The Ministry in Historical Perspectives*, ed. H. Richard Niebuhr and Daniel D. Williams (New York: Harper and Row, 1956), 277; *Homiletic Review* 7 (October 1882): 30–31; and 7 (November 1882): 125.

16. Andrew Landale Drummond, *The Story of American Protestantism* (Boston: Beacon Press, 1951), 309; W. E. Garrison, quoted in Drummond, *Story of Protestantism*, 310. See also Martin E. Marty, *Pilgrims in Their Own Land: Five Hundred Years of Religion in America* (New York: Little, Brown, 1984).

17. Cash, *The Mind of the South*, 137.

18. Interview with Nida Lipscomb, May 31, 1975, Cartersville, Ga.; interview with Bishop Bevel Jones, July 16, 1976, Atlanta; *Portland Evening Telegram*, July 19, 1899, clipping in "Get There and Stay There" (lecture folder), Jones Collection, Emory University.

19. William McLoughlin, *Revivals, Awakenings, and Reform: An Essay on Religious and Social Change, 1607–1977* (Chicago: University of Chicago Press, 1978), 6; *New Orleans Christian Advocate*, August 16, 1885; Holcomb, *Popular Lectures*, 16.

20. Holcomb, *Popular Lectures*, 15; Stuart, *Famous Stories*, 137.

21. *St. Louis Globe-Democrat*, March 13, 1895, 2.

22. "Get There and Stay There" (lecture folder), Jones Collection, Emory University; Holcomb, *Popular Lectures*, 25, 29–30.

23. *Atlanta Journal*, February 17, 1900; unidentified clipping, Jones Papers, Archives of the State of Georgia.

24. On Ingersoll see Orvin Prentiss Larson, *American Infidel: Robert G. Ingersoll* (New York: Citadel Press, 1962).

25. Quoted in Larson, *American Infidel*, 131; *Boston Reveler*, quoted in Larson, *American Infidel*, 131; James Redpath, quoted in Larson, *American Infidel*, 173; Larson, *American Infidel*, 139. These similarities between Ingersoll and Jones were suggested in a tape by Walt Holcomb, in the possession of Louise Holcomb Cade.

26. Interview with Robert G. Ingersoll, published in *Truth Seeker* (New York), September 5, 1885, in *The Works of Robert G. Ingersoll*, ed. C. P. Farrell (New York: Ingersoll, 1900), 256; *St. Louis Globe-Democrat*, March 24, 1895, 2; and March 25, 1895, 2.

27. Leftwich, *Hot Shots*, 9; *Nashville Banner*, May 4, 1888, 2; quoted in Loefflath-Ehly, "World-Maintenance," 175; *St. Louis Globe-Democrat*, March 25, 1895, 2.

28. Leftwich, *Hot Shots*, 10–11.

29. *Los Angeles Times*, January 14, 1889, 1; *Boston Daily Globe*, January 28, 1897, 17; *Atlanta Constitution*, January 30, 1897, 4; *Louisville Courier-Journal*, May 20, 1899, 3.

30. *Chicago Tribune*, March 3, 1886, 3.

31. Mrs. J. J. Ansley, "Sam Jones: The Prophet," in *Epworth Era*, clipping in Jones Papers, Archives of the State of Georgia; *Atlanta Journal*, July 21, 1899.

32. Ahlstrom, *Religious History*, 2:286; Marsden, *Fundamentalism and American Culture*, 103, 118–20; George W. Dollar, *The History of Fundamentalism* (Greenville, S.C.: Bob Jones University Press, 1973), 78–81.

33. Nancy Ammerman, *Bible Believers: Fundamentalists in the Modern World* (New Brunswick, N.J.: Rutgers University Press, 1987), 98–99; "Sam Jones Holds Forth at City Hall," Jones Collection, Emory University. Prefundamentalists, who were mainly Presbyterians and Baptists, strongly defended an intellectual faith and a learned clergy.

34. *Dallas Morning News*, May 30, 1893, 2.

35. *St. Louis Globe-Democrat*, March 19, 1895, 2. Not all prefundamentalists believed in an angry God: Dwight Moody preached a God of love and compassion.

36. *St. Louis Globe-Democrat*, March 16, 1895, 2; *Toledo Bee*, March 14, 1899, 2.

37. *Boston Daily Globe*, January 18, 1887, 2; *St. Joseph Daily Herald*, October 1, 1885, 44; *Boston Daily Globe*, January 18, 1887, 2.

38. *San Francisco Daily Examiner*, March 24, 1889, 2; *Atlanta Journal*, October 16, 1906, 3.

39. Ammerman, *Bible Believers*, 42; *St. Louis Globe-Democrat*, March 6, 1895, 2; *San Francisco Daily Examiner*, March 4, 1889, 2.

40. *San Francisco Daily Examiner*, March 24, 1889, 2; Sam Jones, *Quit Your Meanness* (Chicago: Cranston and Stowe, 1889), 422; Marsden, *Fundamentalism and American Culture*, 20; Jones, *Sermons and Sayings*, 93; *St. Louis Globe-Democrat*, March 11, 1895; *Atlanta Journal*, February 10, 1890; undated clipping from the *Baltimore American*, Jones Collection, Emory University.

41. Quoted in Marsden, *Fundamentalism and American Culture*, 101; *Nashville Tennessee Magazine*, December 7, 1947, 25; *St. Louis Globe-Democrat*, March 13, 1895, 2.

42. Ahlstom, *Religious History*, 2:284; *Toledo Daily Blade*, February 21, 1888, Jones Papers, University of Georgia; *Minneapolis Evening Journal*, June 29, 1886, 1; Laura M. Jones, *Life and Sayings*, 424.

43. Jones, *Living Words*, 33; Laura M. Jones, *Life and Sayings*, 213–14; *St. Louis Globe-Democrat*, March 13, 1895, 2; *Nashville Banner*, June 4, 1892, 3.

44. *Atlanta Journal*, April 20, 1895; Holcomb, *Popular Lectures*, 17; *Toledo Bee*, March 8, 1899, 3; *Nashville American*, March 5, 1900, 5; and April 26, 1897, 7.

45. *Atlanta Journal*, June 7, 1903; Jones, *Sam Jones' Own Book*, 92; *Baltimore American*, May 3, 1886, 4; Marsden, *Fundamentalism and American Culture*, 277–87, 50; *Boston Daily Globe*, January 18, 1887, 2. On the importance of millennialism in fundamentalism, see Marsden, *Fundamentalism and American Culture*, 277–87.

46. *Southern Evangelist*, January 27, 1887, 2; *Atlanta Journal*, June 7, 1903.

47. Bishop Charles Galloway, quoted in Chalfant, *Agitators*, 94; *Wesleyan Christian Advocate*, June 17, 1885, 1; undated clipping, Jones Papers, Archives of the State of Georgia; *Boston Daily Globe*, February 1, 1897, 7.

48. Quoted in Vaughn, "Critical Study," 143; quoted in Holcomb, *Sam Jones*, 8.

49. *Boston Daily Globe*, January 20, 1887, 3; *San Francisco Sunday Examiner*, January 15, 1889, 9; *Nashville Banner*, June 2, 1892, 6; *Dallas Morning News*, June 1, 1893, 3. On the Salvation Army see McKinley, *Marching to Glory*. Jones was assisted by Salvation Army officers in Minneapolis (1887), Dallas (1893), and Cartersville (1905).

50. *Toledo Bee*, March 13, 1899, 2; *Boston Daily Globe*, February 2, 1897, 2; *Atlanta Journal*, March 22, 1897, 5; *Baltimore Sun*, May 26, 1886; *Atlanta Journal*, April 11, 1896, 4.

51. Hopkins, *History of the Y.M.C.A.*, 148–63; *Missouri Republican*, October 12, 1885, 4; *Nashville Banner*, October 23, 1885.

52. *Savannah Morning News*, May 14, 1901, 7; Holcomb, *Sam Jones*, 143; *Nashville Banner*, May 27, 1890, 4; *Atlanta Journal*, October 19, 1906; *Atlanta Georgian*, October 18, 1906; untitled newspaper clipping, February 11, 1894, Jones Collection, Emory University.

53. *Dallas Morning News*, June 1, 1893, 3; *Chicago Tribune*, March 23, 1886, 3.

54. *St. Louis Globe-Democrat*, August 8, 1894, 1; *Chicago Tribune*, March 1, 1886, 2.

55. *Boston Daily Globe*, January 18, 1897, 7; *St. Louis Republic*, March 14, 1895, 5.

56. *Chicago Tribune*, March 2, 1886, 2. On the Social Gospelers see C. Howard Hopkins, *The Rise of the Social Gospel in American Protestantism, 1865–1915* (New Haven, Conn.: Yale University Press, 1940).

57. *Baltimore American*, November 19, 1900; *Atlanta Journal*, April 23, 1899.

58. "A Medley of Philosophy, Facts, and Fun" (lecture folder), Jones Collection, Emory University; *Atlanta Journal*, December 21, 1898.

59. *Atlanta Journal*, November 27, 1897; and January 8, 1898; *Baltimore American*, May 3, 1886, 4; *Atlanta Journal*, January 16, 1897.

60. Woodward, *Origins*, 233; *Nashville Banner*, October 19, 1885, 2; *Atlanta Journal*, April 16, 1898; *Nashville Banner*, October 22, 1885, 2.

61. *Nashville Daily American*, March 28, 1885; *Toledo Bee*, March 15, 1899. See also Richard Hofstadter, *Social Darwinism in American Thought, 1860–1915* (Philadelphia: University of Pennsylvania Press, 1945).

62. *Atlanta Journal*, August 28, 1897, 11; *Boston Daily Globe*, February 2, 1897, 3.

63. *Boston Daily Globe*, January 22, 1897, 4; and January 18, 1887, 2; *Atlanta Journal*, January 20, 1900, 4.

Chapter 7: Be Ye Therefore Holy

1. Quoted in Francis P. Weisenberger, *Ordeal of Faith: The Crisis of Churchgoing America, 1865–1900* (New York: Philosophical Library, 1959), 251; Edwin L. Godkin, quoted in Morrow, "Methodist Church and Reconstruction," 5; *Nashville Banner*, June 6, 1887, 2.

2. John Wesley, *A Plain Account of Christian Perfection* (London: Epworth Press, 1952), 107–8, 45, 33; John Wesley, *Journal of John Wesley* (London: J. M. Dent, 1907), 6:740.

3. Smith, "Theology of Methodism," in *History of Methodism*, ed. Burke, 2:609–11. On Phoebe Palmer see Charles Edward White, *The Beauty of Holiness: Phoebe Palmer as Theologian, Revivalist, Feminist, and Humanitarian* (Grand Rapids, Mich.: Francis Asbury Press, 1986).

4. Vinson Synan, *The Holiness-Pentecostal Movement in the United States* (Grand Rapids, Mich.: William B. Eerdmans, 1971), 37. On the holiness movement before the Civil War, see Timothy L. Smith, *Revivalism and Social Reform in Mid–Nineteenth Century America* (New York: Abingdon Press, 1957). See also Charles Edwin Jones, *Perfectionist Persuasion: The Holiness Movement and American Methodism, 1867–1936* (Metuchen, N.J.: Scarecrow Press, 1974).

5. Merrill Elmer Gaddis, "Christian Perfectionism in America" (Ph.D. dissertation, University of Chicago, 1929), 339; *Wesleyan Christian Advocate*, March 8, 1893, 2. On the socioeconomic origins of holiness, see Anton T. Boisen, "Economic Distress and Religious Experience: A Study of the Holy Rollers," *Psychiatry* 2 (May 1939): 185–94, and Oblinger, *Religious Nemesis*.

6. *Nashville Christian Advocate*, March 22, 1890, 5; *Wesleyan Christian Advocate*, August 5, 1891, 1; *Nashville Christian Advocate*, February 16, 1893, 8.

7. Melvin Easterday Dieter, *The Holiness Revival of the Nineteenth Century* (Metuchen, N.J.: Scarecrow Press, 1980), 205; *Wesleyan Christian Advocate*, February 10, 1886, 2.

8. Quoted in Ferguson, *Organizing*, 92; *Nashville Christian Advocate*, January 19, 1884, 1.

9. Synan, *Holiness-Pentecostal Movement*, 35; quoted in Thrift, "Rebuilding the Southern Church," in *History of Methodism*, ed. Burke, 2:325; *Wesleyan Christian Advocate*, October 4, 1879, 7; *Nashville Christian Advocate*, May 17, 1884, 5. See also Charles Johnson, *The Frontier Camp Meeting: Religion's Harvest Time* (Dallas: Southern Methodist University Press, 1955).

10. McColloch, "Theology and Practices of Methodism," in *History of Methodism*, ed. Burke, 2:638.

11. Thrift, "Rebuilding the Southern Church," 326; S. A. Steel to Sam Jones, February 20, 1893, Jones Papers, University of Georgia; *Nashville Banner*, May 27, 1890, 4.

12. Quoted in Ferguson, *Organizing*, 282; *Wesleyan Christian Advocate*, April 5, 1879, 5; January 24, 1880; and March 5, 1881.

13. *Zion's Outlook*, June 20, 1901, 13; and June 13, 1901, 17.

14. *Wesleyan Christian Advocate*, August 19, 1882, 5.

15. *Atlanta Journal*, January 12, 1901; *Boston Daily Globe*, January 19, 1887, 2; *Nashville Banner*, October 12, 1888, 3; *Nashville American*, March 5, 1900, 5.

16. *St. Louis Globe-Democrat*, November 27, 1885, 10; *Baltimore Sun*, May 29, 1886, 5; *Zion's Outlook*, June 13, 1901, 17.

17. Beniah Pendleton to Sam Jones, March 20, 1897, Jones Papers, University of Georgia; *Living Water*, May 16, 1918, 2–3.

18. *Atlanta Journal*, February 25, 1905; *Living Water*, May 16, 1918, 2.

19. Jones, *Sermons by Rev. Sam P. Jones*, 422; *Zion's Herald*, August 4, 1886, 1.

20. *Baltimore Sun*, May 29, 1886, 5; Jones, *Sermons by Rev. Sam P. Jones*, 422.

21. *Minneapolis Evening Journal*, May 2, 1887, 2; *Dallas Morning News*, May 31, 1893, 3.

22. *Baltimore American*, May 5, 1886, 4.

23. *Atlanta Constitution*, July 12, 1885, 13; *Wesleyan Christian Advocate*, November 12, 1883; Synan, *Holiness-Pentecostal Movement*, 39; *Wesleyan Christian Advocate*, August 19, 1882, 5; *Atlanta Constitution*, July 12, 1885, 14.

24. A. J. Jarrell to George Jarrell, December 29, 1892, Charles Jarrell Collection, Emory University, Atlanta.

25. *Atlanta Constitution*, July 9, 1885, 3.

26. *Atlanta Constitution*, July 12, 1885, 13; July 14, 1885, 4; and July 17, 1885, 2; *Wesleyan Christian Advocate*, August 12, 1885, 1.

27. Warren Akin Candler to Sam Jones, March 29, 1884, Warren Akin Candler Collection, Emory University, Atlanta.

28. Alfred M. Pierce, *Giant Against the Sky: The Life of Bishop Warren Akin Candler* (Nashville: Abingdon and Cokesbury Press, 1958), 46–47; Warren Akin Candler to A. J. Jarrell, November 5, 1885; and November 8, 1885, both in Jarrell Collection.

29. Charles Jarrell to George Jarrell, July 25, 1885, Jarrell Collection.

30. *New York Times*, April 18, 1888, 6; *Baltimore Sun*, May 29, 1886, 5; *Wesleyan Christian Advocate*, September 23, 1885, 1.

31. *St. Paul Dispatch*, June 25, 1886, 1; *Nashville Banner*, June 2, 1892, 6.

32. *Baltimore Sun*, May 11, 1886, 5.

33. *Wesleyan Christian Advocate*, July 22, 1882, 1; *Nashville Christian Advocate*, September 15, 1888, 9; *Nashville Banner*, February 9, 1897, 2; *St. Paul Dispatch*, June 25, 1886, 1; *Toledo Bee*, March 13, 1899, 2; *Boston Daily Globe*, January 27, 1897, 5.

34. *Wesleyan Christian Advocate*, July 28, 1897, 2; quoted in John Leland Peters, *Christian Perfection and American Methodism* (Nashville: Abingdon Press, 1956), 168–69.

35. *Wesleyan Christian Advocate*, October 28, 1885, 1; *St. Paul Dispatch*, June 25, 1886, 1; *Baltimore Sun*, May 29, 1886, 5.

36. A. J. Jarrell, "Christian Perfection," manuscript, Jarrell Collection; *Wesleyan Christian Advocate*, August 9, 1885, 5.

37. *Toledo Bee*, March 13, 1899, 2; *Boston Daily Globe*, January 27, 1897, 5.

38. A. J. Jarrell to George Jarrell, March 20, 1894; and October 16, 1894, both in Jarrell Collection; *Nashville Christian Advocate*, September 17, 1896, 3.

39. L. A. Jarrell to George Jarrell, November 6, 1896, Jarrell Collection.

40. Synan, *Holiness-Pentecostal Movement*, 37; Robert Lloyd Lunsford, "A Historical Background of the Holiness Movement" (thesis, Marion College, 1940). See also Elmer T. Clark, *The Small Sects in America* (Nashville: Abingdon Press, 1937), 51–84.

41. *Wesleyan Christian Advocate*, December 3, 1881, 6; *Nashville Christian Advocate*, October 22, 1896, 5.

42. *Wesleyan Christian Advocate*, September 9, 1885, 5; Smith, "Theology of Methodism," 624; H. C. Morrison, *Open Letters to the Bishops, Ministers, and Members of the Methodist Episcopal Church, South* (Louisville, Ky.: Pentecostal, n.d.), 51–52; *Nashville Christian Advocate*, November 22, 1890, 14; and November 29, 1890, 2. Morrison, a local preacher, was temporarily expelled from the Methodist Episcopal Church, South, in 1896 for "insubordination." He had con-

ducted a holiness revival in a city park in Dublin, Tex., over the protest of the pastor appointed there. On Morrison, later a bishop in the church, see Percival A. Wesche, *Henry Clay Morrison, Crusader Saint* (Wilmore, Ky.: Asbury Theological Seminary, 1963), 140.

43. Joseph E. Campbell, *The Pentecostal Holiness Church, 1898–1948: Its Background and History* (Franklin Springs, Ga.: Publishing House of the Pentecostal Holiness Church, 1951), 18–72; James K. Mathews, *Set Apart to Serve: The Meaning and Role of the Episcopacy in the Wesleyan Tradition* (Nashville: Abingdon Press, 1985), 160.

44. Obituary of David Campbell Kelley, *Journal of the Tennessee Conference*, 1909, 61–62; B. F. Haynes, *Tempest-Tossed on Methodist Seas* (Kansas City, Mo.: Nazarene Publishing House, 1914), 135–39. See also B. F. Haynes, *Facts, Faith, and Fire; or, Chapter on the Situation* (Nashville: B. F. Haynes, 1900). For an extensive discussion of the Kelley-Hargrove case, see T. A. Kerley, *Conference Rights: Governing Principles of the Methodist Episcopal Church, South* (Nashville: Publishing House of the Methodist Episcopal Church, South, 1898), 243–308.

45. *Nashville Christian Advocate*, June 9, 1898; August 10, 1905, 4; and November 22, 1890, 15. For the divisions in American Methodism, see Clark, *Small Sects*, 60–61.

46. Haynes, *Tempest-Tossed*, 135–39.

47. *Nashville Christian Advocate*, November 15, 1890, 3.

48. Ibid., August 23, 1894, 1; and March 5, 1896, 4.

49. *Indianapolis Journal*, June 17, 1886, 1.

50. Smith, "Theology of Methodism," 620; Farish, *The Circuit Rider Dismounts*, 73; Stuart, *Methodist Evangelism*, 121.

51. *Nashville Christian Advocate*, May 22, 1886, 16; *Baltimore Sun*, May 11, 1886, 3.

52. *Baltimore American*, May 9, 1886, 5; *Baltimore Sun*, May 11, 1886, 3.

53. *Baltimore Sun*, May 17, 1886, 3.

54. *Holston Methodist*, June 4, 1887, 2; *Nashville Christian Advocate*, February 16, 1893, 10; April 26, 1894, 9; and December 21, 1893, 8.

55. *Homiletic Review* 30 (July 25, 1895): 121; *Nashville Christian Advocate*, January 14, 1891, 4.

56. *Nashville Christian Advocate*, January 24, 1891, 1; *Wesleyan Christian Advocate*, February 24, 1892, 2; *Waco Day*, September 8, 1884, 1.

57. *Homiletic Review* 30 (July 25, 1895): 121; *Wesleyan Christian Advocate*, December 17, 1881, 5; *Chautauquan* 4 (June 1884): 239–40; *Nashville Christian Advocate*, September 12, 1895, 1.

58. *New Orleans Christian Advocate*, January 21, 1892, 1; *Wesleyan Christian Advocate*, March 27, 1895, 6.

59. *Arkansas Methodist*, quoted in *Wesleyan Christian Advocate*, March 20, 1895, 1; *Nashville Christian Advocate*, December 8, 1892, 5. On the question of the effectiveness of revivalism, see Samuel W. Dike, "A Study of New England Revivals," *American Journal of Sociology* 15 (November 1909): 261–78; Loefferts A. Loetscher, "Presbyterianism and Revivals in Philadelphia Since 1878," *Pennsylvania Magazine of History and Biography* 68 (1944); Glenn Firebaugh, "How Effective Are City-wide Crusades? A Scientific Survey Estimates the Effects of

the 1976 Billy Graham Crusade in Seattle," *Christianity Today*, March 27, 1981, 24–29; and Thomas, *Mass Meetings*.

60. *New York Christian Advocate*, October 5, 1899, 24; *Nashville Christian Advocate*, April 7, 1891, 5; P. H. Lotz, quoted in Ralph Lightsey, "The Relationship of the Professional Evangelist to the Parish Minister" (thesis, Candler School of Theology, Emory University, 1951), 76.

61. *Nashville Christian Advocate*, January 11, 1890, 3; *Michigan Christian Advocate*, quoted in *Nashville Christian Advocate*, May 16, 1889, 9.

62. Pinson, *George R. Stuart*, 80–82.

63. Simon Peter Richardson to Sam Jones, April 23, 1890; November 4, 1890; and November 17, 1890, all in Jones Papers, University of Georgia.

64. Thomas G. Whitten (Moberly, Mo.) to Sam Jones, November 24, 1890, Jones Papers, University of Georgia; *Tennessee Methodist*, July 16, 1891, 2; untitled clipping from Columbus, Ind., December 7, 1892, Jones Papers, University of Georgia.

65. Kerley, *Conference Rights*, 206, 173; Mathews, *Set Apart to Serve*, 159–65.

66. *Atlanta Journal*, December 11, 1893; Elam Franklin Dempsey, *Atticus Greene Haygood* (Nashville: Parthenon Press, 1940), 190, 157, 150.

67. Dempsey, *Atticus Greene Haygood*, 369.

68. *Nashville Christian Advocate*, May 31, 1890, 8; and January 5, 1893, 10; Dempsey, *Atticus Greene Haygood*, 419; W. B. Palmore (editor of the *St. Louis Christian Advocate*) to Sam Jones, December 1897, Jones Papers, University of Georgia.

69. Atticus Haygood to William Leftwich, February 11, 1886, Jones Papers, University of Georgia.

70. *Nashville Christian Advocate*, January 25, 1894, 3.

71. *Atlanta Journal*, December 11, 1893; draft for article in *Nashville Christian Advocate*, January 25, 1894, Jones Papers, University of Georgia.

72. *Nashville Christian Advocate*, January 11, 1894, 9.

73. *Atlanta Journal*, December 11, 1893.

74. *Nashville Christian Advocate*, January 25, 1894, 3; and February 1, 1894, 9.

75. Draft for article in *Nashville Christian Advocate*, January 25, 1894, Jones Papers, University of Georgia.

76. *Nashville Christian Advocate*, January 11, 1894, 9; February 1, 1894, 9; and February 22, 1894, 3.

77. Ibid., May 5, 1894, 1–2.

78. Isaiah Reid of the Iowa Holiness Association, quoted in Smith, "Theology of Methodism," 625; *Nashville Christian Advocate*, May 5, 1894, 1–2.

79. *Nashville Christian Advocate*, May 10, 1894, 2.

80. Synan, *Holiness-Pentecostal Movement*, 53–54; *Wesleyan Christian Advocate*, October 12, 1898, 15; *Louisville Courier-Journal*, May 2, 1899, 4; Sermons and Lectures, "The Truth and Nothing but the Truth," Jones Papers, University of Georgia.

81. Haynes, *Tempest-Tossed*, 153; "Sam Jones Mad," undated clipping from *Tennessee Methodist*, Jones Papers, University of Georgia.

82. J. A. Timmerman to Sam Jones, May 24, 1895, Jones Papers, University of Georgia.

83. W. Dunbar (Augusta, Ga.) to Sam Jones, August 10, 1895, Jones Papers, University of Georgia.

84. Sam Jones to W. B. Stradley, September 6, 1895; W. M. McIntosh (New Albany, Miss.) to Sam Jones, July 29, 1895, both in Jones Papers, University of Georgia.

85. *Nashville Christian Advocate*, October 24, 1895, 8; Sam Jones to W. B. Stradley, September 6, 1895, Jones Papers, University of Georgia. *Tennessee Methodist* was sold to J. O. McClurkan of Nashville, who changed the name to the *American Outlook* (1897), then to *Zion's Outlook* (1898).

86. *Daily Advocate*, May 23, 1898, 7. The *Daily Advocate* is published during general conference.

87. Ibid.

88. *Nashville Christian Advocate*, May 28, 1898, 1; *Daily Advocate*, May 23, 1895, 7.

89. Quoted in C. F. Wimberley, *A Biographical Sketch of Henry Clay Morrison, D.D.: The Man and His Ministry* (Chicago: Fleming H. Revell, 1922), 103.

Chapter 8: Apostle of Prohibition

1. Farish, *The Circuit Rider Dismounts*, 4.

2. On the northern Methodist church see Donald G. Jones, *The Sectional Crisis and Northern Methodism: A Study in Piety, Political Ethics, and Civil Religion* (New York: Scarecrow Press, 1979).

3. Quoted in Frederick A. Norwood, ed., *Source Book on American Methodism* (Nashville: Abingdon Press, 1983), 331–32; quoted in Farish, *The Circuit Rider Dismounts*, 148–49.

4. Quoted in Farish, *The Circuit Rider Dismounts*, 97.

5. Ibid., 104.

6. William McLoughlin, "Jones Versus Jones," *American Heritage* 12 (April 1961): 58; Kelley, "Rev. Sam. P. Jones," 503. See also James Benson Sellers, *The Prohibition Movement in Alabama, 1702–1943* (Chapel Hill: University of North Carolina Press, 1943), and Joseph Rowntree and Arthur Sherwell, *The Temperance Problem and Social Reform* (New York: Tuslove Hanson and Comba, 1900).

7. Leftwich, *Hot Shots*, 29; Laura M. Jones, *Life and Sayings*, 437.

8. Joseph Gusfield, *Symbolic Crusade: Status Politics and the American Temperance Movement* (Urbana: University of Illinois Press, 1963), 101; E. M. Jellineck, "Recent Trends in Alcohol and Alcohol Consumption," *Quarterly Journal of Studies on Alcohol* 8 (July 1947): 1–43; *Atlanta Journal*, March 4, 1899, 4; Norman H. Clark, *Deliver Us from Evil: An Interpretation of American Prohibition* (New York: W. W. Norton, 1976), 55; *Augusta Chronicle*, April 10, 1892, 5; and May 12, 1897, 5.

9. Jones, *Sam Jones' Own Book*, 280; *Atlanta Journal*, March 4, 1899; Leftwich, *Hot Shots*, 281; *Atlanta Journal*, May 28, 1902; and January 22, 1905.

10. Brian Harrison, *Drink and the Victorians: The Temperance Question in England, 1865–1872* (Pittsburgh: University of Pittsburgh Press, 1971), 50; James H. Timberlake, *Prohibition and the Progressive Movement, 1900–1920* (Cambridge,

Mass.: Harvard University Press, 1963), 68–77; quoted in Mark Edward Lender and James Kirby Martin, *Drinking in America: A History* (New York: Free Press, 1982), 108.

11. Jones, *Sermons by Rev. Sam P. Jones*, 119; *Augusta Chronicle*, April 6, 1892, 5; *Milledgeville Union and Recorder*, February 16, 1886.

12. *St. Louis Globe-Democrat*, March 23, 1895, 2; *Toledo Bee*, March 13, 1899, 2; *Missouri Republican*, November 29, 1885, 4; Leftwich, *Hot Shots*, 244.

13. Farish, *The Circuit Rider Dismounts*, 310; Proverbs 31:6; Matthew 15:11; Daniel J. Whitener, *Prohibition in North Carolina, 1715–1945* (Chapel Hill: University of North Carolina Press, 1946), 73; *Savannah Morning News*, May 14, 1901, 7.

14. *Baltimore American*, May 10, 1886, 4; *San Francisco Daily Examiner*, March 25, 1889, 4; Colossians 2:21; Joshua 6:18; 1 Corinthians 6:1–10; Jones, *Sam Jones' Own Book*, 248; 1 Timothy 2:23; Philippians 3:13; "Sermons and Lectures" (undated "Temperance Speech" delivered in Dalton, Ga.), Jones Papers, University of Georgia.

15. *Boston Daily Globe*, February 2, 1897, 10; *Savannah Morning News*, May 26, 1901; Jones, *Sam Jones' Own Book*, 280; *Atlanta Journal*, November 3, 1885, 4.

16. *Boston Daily Globe*, January 22, 1887, 4; Lecture scrapbook, "Get There and Stay There," undated clipping, Jones Collection, Emory University; *Baltimore American*, May 10, 1886, 4; *Knoxville Journal and Tribune*, May 28, 1905, 3.

17. Harrison, *Drink and the Victorians*, 1–65, 71–72; Lender and Martin, *Drinking in America*, 34; Ruth Bordin, *Women and Temperance: The Quest for Power and Liberty, 1873–1900* (Philadelphia: Temple University Press, 1981), xiv.

18. Harrison, *Drink and the Victorians*, 79–84.

19. Quoted in Jack S. Blocker, Jr., *Retreat from Reform: The Prohibition Movement in the United States, 1890–1913* (Westport, Conn.: Greenwood Press, 1976), 47–48. For the history of the Prohibition party, see also D. Leigh Colvin, *Prohibition in the United States: A History of the Prohibition Party of the Prohibition Movement* (New York: George H. Doran, 1926).

20. Bordin, *Women and Temperance*, 11–12.

21. Ibid., 22–30, 137.

22. Ahlstrom, *A Religious History*, 2:388; Peter H. Odegard, *Pressure Politics: The Story of the Anti-Saloon League* (New York: Columbia University Press, 1928), 22, 79; Larry Engelmann, *Intemperance: The Lost War Against Liquor* (New York: Free Press, 1979), 11; Sean Dennis Cashman, *Prohibition: The Lie of the Land* (New York: Free Press, 1981), 7; Odegard, *Pressure Politics*, 87.

23. Odegard, *Pressure Politics*, 38, 181, 60, 39–50; Engelmann, *Intemperance*, 4–5; quoted in Martin E. Marty, *Righteous Empire: The Protestant Experience in America* (New York: Dial Press, 1970), 214.

24. Timberlake, *Prohibition*, 19; Ahlstrom, *Religious History*, 2:388–89; Odegard, *Pressure Politics*, 17; Cashman, *Prohibition*, 7; Virginius Dabney, *Dry Messiah: The Life of Bishop James Cannon* (New York: A. A. Knopf, 1949), 35; C. C. Pearson and J. Edwin Hendricks, *Liquor and Anti-Liquor in Virginia, 1619–1919* (Durham, N.C.: Duke University Press, 1965), 183. The states that went dry between 1907 and 1914 were Georgia, Arizona, Colorado, Mississippi, North Carolina, Oklahoma, Oregon, Tennessee, Virginia, West Virginia, and Washington.

25. Quoted in *Charlotte Observer*, January 4, 1948, 8; John Temple Graves, "The Fight Against Alcohol: Georgia Pioneers of the Prohibition Crusade," *Cosmopolitan* 45 (1908): 84–86.

26. Samuel S. Hill, ed., *Religion in the Southern States: A Historical Study* (Macon, Ga.: Mercer University Press, 1983), 408–9; Francis P. Weisenberger, *Triumph of Faith: Contributions of the Church to American Life, 1865–1900* (Richmond, Va.: William Byrd Press, 1962), 155; Pearson and Hendricks, *Liquor and Anti-Liquor*, 201.

27. *Wesleyan Christian Advocate*, September 12, 1883; *St. Louis Globe-Democrat*, March 21, 1895.

28. Unidentified clipping dated Cartersville, Ga., 1888, Jones Collection, Emory University.

29. John Haggai, "Viewpoint," *Haggai News and Third World Report*, May–June 1982, clipping in Jones Papers, Jones Museum.

30. Sam Jones, *Rifle Shots at the King's Enemies and I'll Say Another Thing* (London: T. Wooner, 1887), 15; Scrapbook, Letters to the Editor, February 3, 1902, Jones Papers, University of Georgia; John Marshall Barker, *The Saloon Problem and Social Reform* (reprint, New York: Arno Press, 1970), 7; *Atlanta Journal*, February 28, 1904, 4.

31. *Atlanta Journal*, March 28, 1903, 4. See also E. Merton Coulter, "The Athens Dispensary," *Georgia Historical Quarterly* 50 (1966): 14–36.

32. *Rome Morning Tribune*, quoted in *Atlanta Journal*, April 23, 1904.

33. *St. Louis Globe-Democrat*, August 7, 1894, 5; Jones, *Sam Jones' Own Book*, 290; *New York Times*, March 3, 1886, 2; *Atlanta Journal* article by Medora Field Perkerson, dated 1928, clipping in Jones Papers, Jones Museum. A blind tiger was a clandestine spot where liquor could be purchased after hours or in dry areas.

34. Peter Findlay Dunne, *Mr. Dooley at His Best* (New York: Archon Books, 1969), 262; quoted in Colvin, *Prohibition*, 189; *Southern Evangelist*, November 3, 1887; *Atlanta Journal*, November 3, 1900, 11.

35. *St. Louis Globe-Democrat*, August 7, 1894, 5; *Atlanta Journal*, March 1, 1902, 1.

36. Jones, *Rifle Shots*, 145; *Nashville Christian Advocate*, March 1, 1906, 17; Ahlstrom, *Religious History*, 2:389; Pearson and Hendricks, *Liquor and Anti-Liquor*, 242.

37. *Augusta Chronicle*, May 23, 1892, 2; Blocker, *Retreat from Reform*, 174; James W. Bodley to Sam Jones, June 6, 1904; and June 7, 1904, both in Jones Papers, University of Georgia.

38. James W. Bodley to Sam Jones, June 7, 1904, Jones Papers, University of Georgia; *Atlanta Journal*, June 25, 1904, 9; untitled clipping dated Cartersville, Ga., June 24, 1904, Jones Collection, Emory University.

39. *Nashville Banner*, June 4, 1887, 1; *Atlanta Journal*, June 2, 1894, 8; Scrapbook, "Letters to the Editor," October 21 (no year), Jones Collection, Emory University; Jones, *Rifle Shots*, 152.

40. Weisenberger, *Triumph of Faith*, 125; Schlesinger, *Critical Period*, 13.

41. *Atlanta Journal*, April 18, 1896; *St. Louis Globe-Democrat*, March 11, 1895, 5.

42. *Nashville Christian Advocate*, April 9, 1899, 4.

43. *Louisville Courier-Journal*, May 2, 1899, 4; May 5, 1899, 5; and May 14, 1899, 17.

44. Ibid., May 8, 1899.

45. *Louisville Times*, May 6, 1899, 4; and May 5, 1899, 4.

46. Ibid., May 6, 1899, 4; *Louisville Courier-Journal*, May 10, 1899, 2.

47. *Atlanta Journal*, August 21, 1893, 5; *Chicago Daily Inter-Ocean*, March 29, 1886; *St. Louis Globe-Democrat*, March 25, 1895, 2; reminiscence of Jim Peters of the State Board of Education, given by John Prickett, interview, August 30, 1978, Atlanta.

48. McLoughlin, "Jones Versus Jones," 59; McLoughlin, *Modern Revivalism*, 318–25.

49. McLoughlin, "Jones Versus Jones," 86; *Toledo Bee*, March 18, 1899, 7; and March 15, 1899, 1.

50. *Toledo Bee*, April 21, 1899; March 15, 1899; and March 27, 1899, 2.

51. Ibid., March 13, 1899, 2; and March 5, 1899, 3.

52. Ibid., March 4, 1899, 3; March 4, 1899, 1; March 27, 1899, 1; and March 6, 1899, 1.

53. Ibid., March 6, 1899, 1; and March 7, 1899, 5.

54. Ibid., March 8, 1899, 3; March 20, 1899, 5; and March 13, 1899, 2.

55. Ibid., March 11, 1899, 7; and March 13, 1899, 2.

56. Ibid., March 15, 1899, 2; March 18, 1899, 7; March 11, 1899, 7; and March 20, 1899, 5.

57. Ibid., March 8, 1899, 3; March 22, 1899, 2; March 23, 1899, 4; March 10, 1899, 5; and March 12, 1899, 4.

58. Laura M. Jones, *Life and Sayings*, 285; *Toledo Bee*, March 23, 1899, 4; March 11, 1899, 7; and March 23, 1899, 4; Laura M. Jones, *Life and Sayings*, 285; McLoughlin, "Jones Versus Jones," 89; Brand Whitlock, *Forty Years of It* (1914; reprint, New York: Greenwood Press, 1968), 113.

59. Untitled clipping, n.d., Jones Collection, Emory University; *Atlanta Journal*, July 7, 1894, 4; and August 16, 1902. William McLoughlin suggests that the confrontation between the Joneses "dramatized the irreconcilable conflict between the evangelicals, who felt that reform must begin with the individual, and the social gospelers, who believed that it must begin with society" ("Jones Versus Jones," 56).

60. McLoughlin, "Jones Versus Jones," 59; clipping from lecture "Shams and the Genuine," n.d., Jones Collection, Emory University. Joseph Gusfield discusses the trend toward coercion in his chapter "Coercive Reform and Cultural Conflict," in *Symbolic Crusade*, 87–110. For the social purpose of the saloon, see Perry R. Davis, *The Saloon: Public Drinking in Chicago and Boston, 1880–1920* (Urbana: University of Illinois Press, 1983), 94–113.

61. *Atlanta Journal*, March 27, 1899; quoted in Chalfant, *Agitators*, 188; quoted in McLoughlin, *Modern Revivalism*, 312; Jones, *Rifle Shots*, 166; *Chicago Tribune*, March 15, 1886, 6.

62. *Atlanta Journal*, March 27, 1899; Jones, *Thunderbolts*, 109, 114; St. Joseph *Daily Herald*, October 1, 1885, 4.

63. Jones, *Sam Jones' Own Book*, 248.

64. Timberlake, *Prohibition*, 43; Clark, *Deliver Us from Evil*, 146–49. For the social and economic results of prohibition, see Clark Warburton, *The Economic Results of Prohibition* (New York: Columbia University Press, 1932); and Jellineck, "Recent Trends," 1–42.

65. Timberlake, *Prohibition*, 43.

66. N. H. Clark, *Deliver Us from Evil*, 13, 65–67, 3; Chalfant, *Agitators*, 188.

67. Bordin, *Women and Temperance*, 6; Clark, *Deliver Us from Evil*, 4, 116–17.

68. M. B. Chapman, pastor of the Trinity Methodist Episcopal Church, South, quoted in *Baltimore Sun*, February 10, 1896, 6; Marty, *Righteous Empire*, 214.

69. *San Francisco Daily Examiner*, March 24, 1889, 2. On Social Darwinism see Robert Bannister, *Social Darwinism: Science and Myth in Anglo-American Social Thought* (Philadelphia: Temple University Press, 1979).

70. Quoted in John Hammond Moore, "The Negro and Prohibition in Atlanta, 1885–1887," *South Atlantic Quarterly* 69 (1970): 41.

71. *Nashville Christian Advocate*, January 14, 1904, 3.

72. Ibid., August 8, 1905, 1; Samuel W. Small, *Pleas for Prohibition* (Atlanta: N.p., 1890), 129; Sellers, *Prohibition in Alabama*, 46–50; quoted in Andrew Sinclair, "The Psychology of Prohibition," in *Recent America: Conflicting Interpretations of the Great Issues*, ed. Sidney Fine (New York: Macmillan, 1967), 142. Both Norman Clark and Joseph Gusfield see little connection between racial fears and prohibition (see Gusfield, *Symbolic Crusade*, 105, and N. H. Clark, *Deliver Us from Evil*, 111).

73. Quoted in Whitener, *Prohibition in North Carolina*, 65; quoted in Leonard Scott Blakey, *The Sale of Liquor in the South: The History of the Development of a Normal Social Restraint in Southern Commonwealths* (New York: AMS Press, 1912), 26.

74. *Atlanta Constitution*, September 4, 1885; Moore, "The Negro and Prohibition," 38–57.

75. *Atlanta Journal*, June 1, 1900; *Atlanta Constitution*, February 21, 1886, 5.

76. *Nashville Banner*, April 10, 1895; and February 12, 1893; Holcomb, *Sam Jones*, 21.

Chapter 9: Poli-ticks

1. *Atlanta Journal*, August 11, 1906, 7; and September 22, 1900; clipping from *Winona Assembly Record* (Winona, Ind.), July 26, 1900, Jones Papers, Emory University.

2. Arthur S. Link, "The Progressive Movement in the South, 1870–1914," *North Carolina Historical Review* 23 (1946): 173; Alex Matthews Arnett, *The Populist Movement in Georgia: A View of the "Agrarian Crusade" in the Light of Solid-South Politics* (1922; reprint, New York: AMS Press, 1967), 16–20, 156–60.

3. See also Robert Saunders, "Southern Populists and the Negro, 1893–1895," *Journal of Negro History* 54 (July 1969): 240–61.

4. David B. Parker, *Alias Bill Arp: Charles Henry Smith and the South's "Goodly*

Heritage" (Athens: University of Georgia Press, 1991), 32; untitled clipping, "Letters to Editors," Jones Papers, Emory University; *Atlanta Journal*, March 27, 1893.

5. *Boston Daily Globe*, January 20, 1897; *Atlanta Journal*, September 19, 1896.

6. *Atlanta Journal*, September 22, 1894, 7.

7. James K. Hines to Sam Jones, August 8, 1896, Jones Collection, University of Georgia; *Atlanta Journal*, September 26, 1896.

8. *Atlanta Journal*, September 9, 1896, 17; Russell Korobkin, "The Politics of Disfranchisement in Georgia," *Georgia Historical Quarterly* 74 (Spring 1990): 20–58; *Augusta Chronicle*, May 12, 1898, 5.

9. Korobkin, "Politics of Disfranchisement," 35; *Atlanta Journal*, September 9, 1896, 17.

10. *Atlanta Journal*, September 19, 1896; and September 9, 1896, 17.

11. Quoted in Barton Shaw, "The Wool-Hat Boys: A History of the Populist Party in Georgia, 1892 to 1910" (Ph.D. dissertation, Emory University, 1979), 193–96, 230–31.

12. *Atlanta Journal*, September 26, 1896, 1.

13. Wynes, *Negro in the South*, 53–55; Dewey Grantham, "Georgia Politics and the Disfranchisement of the Negro," *Georgia Historical Quarterly* 42 (March 1948): 3; Korobkin, "Politics of Disfranchisement," 32; *Cartersville Courant-American*, February 24, 1898, 1; *Atlanta Journal*, September 26, 1896; *Atlanta Constitution*, November 3, 1885, 4.

14. *Atlanta Journal*, February 19, 1898, 1.

15. Ibid., February 21, 1898, 1.

16. *Atlanta Constitution*, February 20, 1898.

17. *Nashville Banner*, May 24, 1888, 2; Jones, *Sam Jones' Sermons*, 49; *Atlanta Journal*, November 3, 1885, 4; Jones, *Thunderbolts*, 443; *Atlanta Constitution*, February 22, 1898, 5.

18. Seab Wright to Sam Jones, n.d.; clipping from John I. Fullerwood to Sam Jones, February 25, 1898; clipping from *Advance-Courier* (Cedartown, Ga.), February 25, 1898, all in Jones Papers, University of Georgia.

19. Unidentified clipping, lecture scrapbook, "Manhood and Money," Jones Papers, University of Georgia.

20. *Atlanta Journal*, October 6, 1894, 1.

21. Ibid., January 18, 1897, 9; November 27, 1897, 2; and January 16, 1897.

22. Clipping from *Pilot*, "The Question of Taxation," n.d., Jones Collection, Emory University; *Atlanta Journal*, September 7, 1901; *Knoxville Journal and Tribune*, May 27, 1905, 5.

23. Woodward, *Origins*, 39, 60–64; *Atlanta Journal*, February 21, 1898, 1.

24. *Atlanta Journal*, February 21, 1898, 1; and February 24, 1898, 1.

25. George R. Stuart (Chattanooga, Tenn.) to Sam Jones, February 19, 1898; T. G. Ryman to Sam Jones, February 19, 1898; and J. W. Thomas to Sam Jones, February 20, 1898, all in Jones Papers, University of Georgia.

26. *Atlanta Journal*, February 24, 1898, 1.

27. Ibid., November 28, 1898.

28. Ibid., February 26, 1898.

29. Ibid., July 30, 1898; and July 16, 1898. See also Kenneth M. MacKen-

zie, *The Robe and the Sword: The Methodist Church and the Rise of American Imperialism* (Washington, D.C.: Public Affairs Press, 1961).

30. *Atlanta Journal*, July 30, 1898; "Irreligion," in "Get There and Stay There" (lecture folder), Jones Collection, Emory University; *Atlanta Journal*, January 13, 1899.

31. Newby, *Jim Crow's Defense*, 52–53, 3; quoted in Rayford W. Logan, *The Negro in American Life and Thought: The Nadir, 1877–1901* (New York: Dial Press, 1954), 90–91.

32. Newby, *Jim Crow's Defense*, ix; Clarence Bacote, "Negro Proscriptions, Protests, and Proposed Solutions in Georgia, 1880–1908," *Journal of Southern History* 25 (November 1959): 489–98.

33. Kenneth Stampp, "Triumph of the Conservatives," in *Blacks in White America Since 1865: Images and Interpretations*, ed. Robert C. Twombley (New York: David McKay 1971), 40–57; *Atlanta Constitution*, January 3, 1898, 4.

34. Newby, *Jim Crow's Defense*, ix–x, 53.

35. *Atlanta Constitution*, July 21, 1892; Shaw, "Wool-Hat Boys," 67–68.

36. Vernon Lane Wharton, "The Elimination of the Negro as an Active Factor in Politics," in *Blacks in White America*, ed. Twombly, 66.

37. John Dittmer, *Black Georgia in the Progressive Era, 1900–1920* (Urbana: University of Illinois Press, 1977), 169–70; August Meier, "Booker T. Washington: An Interpretation," in *Blacks in White America*, ed. Twombly, 81–121. See also Eugene J. Watts, "Black Political Progress in Atlanta: 1865–1895," *Journal of Negro History* 49 (July 1974): 268–86; Grantham, "Georgia Politics"; Moore, "The Negro and Prohibition."

38. Arnold H. Taylor, *Travail and Triumph: Black Life and Culture in the South Since the Civil War* (Westport, Conn.: Greenwood Press, 1976), 96–97.

39. Ray Stannard Baker, *Following the Color Line: An Account of Negro Citizenship in the American Democracy* (1908; reprint, New York: Harper and Row, 1964), 53; quoted in Frenise A. Logan, *The Negro in North Carolina, 1876–1894* (Chapel Hill: University of North Carolina Press, 1964), 139; quoted in Leon F. Litwach, "The Ordeal of Black Freedom," in *The Southern Enigma: Essays on Race, Class, and Folk Culture*, ed. Walter J. Fraser, Jr., and Winfred B. Moore (Westport, Conn.: Greenwood Press, 1983), 14. Ray Stannard Baker agreed with Du Bois. He wrote: "The Negro that the South fears and dislikes is the educated, property-owning Negro who is beginning to demand rights, to take his place among men as a citizen" (*Following the Color Line*, 245.

40. Quoted in Howard N. Rabinowitz, *Race Relations in the Urban South, 1865–1890* (New York: Oxford University Press, 1978), 225; Williamson, *The Crucible of Race*, 111, 118; *Nashville Christian Advocate*, October 17, 1895, 1.

41. Quoted in Williams, *The Crucible of Race*, 118; quoted in Charles Crowe, "Racial Violence and Social Reform: Origins of the Atlanta Riot of 1906," *Journal of Negro History* 53 (July 1968): 242, 246.

42. Crowe, "Racial Massacre," 169; Baker, *Following the Color Line*, 5; Williamson, *The Crucible of Race*, 309, 180; Crowe, "Racial Violence," 249.

43. Williamson, *The Crucible of Race*, 185; Bacote, "Negro Proscriptions," 478–80; Charles Daniel (editor of the *Atlanta Evening News*), quoted in Crowe, "Racial Violence," 252; Parker, *Alias Bill Arp*, 128.

44. Ralph E. Reed, Jr., "Emory College and the Sledd Affair of 1902: A Case Study in Southern Honor and Racial Attitudes," *Georgia Historical Quarterly* 72 (Fall 1988): 469; Mark K. Bauman, "A Famous Atlantan Speaks Out Against Lynching: Bishop Warren Akin Candler and Social Justice," *Atlanta Historical Bulletin* 20 (Spring 1976): 28–29.

45. *Nashville Christian Advocate*, October 17, 1895, 1; *Atlanta Constitution*, September 24, 1906, 3.

46. Jones, *Thunderbolts*, 139; *Atlanta Journal*, July 11, 1903.

47. *Cartersville Courant American*, April 27, 1899, 1; R. E. Reed, "Emory College," 468. On the lynching of Sam Hose, see Bauman, "Famous Atlantan," and Taylor, *Travail and Triumph*, 42.

48. *Atlanta Journal*, April 29, 1899; May 6, 1899; and August 19, 1899, 17.

49. *Atlanta Journal*, April 29, 1899; and May 6, 1899.

50. Dittmer, *Black Georgia*, 175–78; Bacote, "Negro Proscriptions," 489–91.

51. *Atlanta Journal*, September 22, 1894, 1; November 7, 1896; and March 8, 1897, 7.

52. *Dallas Morning News*, May 30, 1893, 2; *Atlanta Constitution*, July 21, 1892.

53. *St. Louis Globe-Democrat*, March 25, 1890, 2; *New York Times*, August 26, 1895, 9; *Knoxville Daily Journal*, May 23, 1892, 1; *Dallas Morning News*, February 3, 1900.

54. Clarence A. Bacote, "Georgia's Reaction to the Negro Policy of Theodore Roosevelt," *Atlanta History Bulletin* 21 (Spring 1977): 72–73.

55. Unidentified clipping dated September 16, 1904, Jones Collection, Emory University; *Atlanta Journal*, January 17, 1903; *Houston Daily Post*, February 3, 1903, 7.

56. *Atlanta Journal*, January 10, 1903; *Houston Daily Post*, February 2, 1903; Bacote, "Georgia's Reaction," 87–89.

57. Laura M. Jones, *Life and Sayings*, 339.

58. *Atlanta Constitution*, May 30, 1906, 5. On the governor's race of 1906, see Crowe, "Racial Violence," 243–56, and Dittmer, *Black Georgia*, 95–99.

59. *Atlanta Constitution*, May 25, 1906, 6; July 17, 1906; and May 26, 1906; Dittmer, *Black Georgia*, 98; Korobkin, "Politics of Disfranchisement," 50. Georgia restricted voting through five qualifications. The voter must (1) be a war veteran; (2) be known for "good character"; (3) show evidence of literacy, to be tested through reading, writing, or questions on the Constitution; (4) own property of forty acres or property worth $500; (5) pay the poll tax at least six months before the election. These qualifications dramatically reduced black voting. Whereas 28.3 percent of blacks were registered in 1904, by 1910 the number was 4.3 percent (Dittmer, *Black Georgia*, 102).

60. *Atlanta Constitution*, July 10, 1904, 4; and July 10, 1906; *Atlanta Journal*, June 5, 1906, 8; and August 1, 1906, 8; Korobkin, "Politics of Disfranchisement," 50.

61. "Correspondence, March 1–October 15, 1906," untitled letter, n.d., Jones Papers, University of Georgia; *Atlanta Journal*, June 1, 1900.

62. *Atlanta Journal*, March 24, 1906, 6; *St. Joseph Daily Herald*, October 1, 1885, 4.

63. *Atlanta Journal*, March 24, 1906, 6.

64. Williamson, *The Crucible of Race*, 210. See also Crowe, "Racial Violence," 237–39.

65. John W. White, "Prohibition: The New Task and Opportunity of the South," *South Atlantic Quarterly* 7 (1908): 136.

66. Crowe, "Racial Massacre," 168. See also Gerald L. Mixon, "The Atlanta Riot of 1906" (Ph.D. dissertation, Auburn University, 1989).

67. Williamson, *The Crucible of Race*, 222; quoted in Crowe, "Racial Violence," 253–56.

68. Williamson, *The Crucible of Race*, 220–23; Crowe, "Racial Violence." Crowe stated that Sam Jones and his bevy of followers in Atlanta contributed to the climate of racial hatred by continuing to inflame the link between prohibition and race. "By September [1906] virtually the whole city pulpit had preached enthusiastically on the topic and the Reverend Sam P. Jones promised to conduct in mid-month a major revival for a full week with the 'liquor traffic' as the central theme" (235). Jones's revival was in Cartersville, and though doubtless some people visiting the revival or reading of it in the paper were inflamed by Jones's denunciations of "Decatur Street dives," Jones had been preaching prohibition since 1872. Jones is held even more accountable by Joel Williamson in *The Crucible of Race*. Williamson drew on Crowe's research to conclude that "during the summer, the Reverend Jones preached sermon after sermon attacking the Decatur Street dives, depicting all manner of debaucheries there and rousing his audience to frenzies" (209). Jones was not in Atlanta in any official capacity after March 19, 1906, when he spoke at the close of the Tabernacle Bible Conference (*Atlanta Constitution*, October 16, 1906, 3). Though Jones was culpable insofar as he linked race and repression to prohibition, he did not play the immediate role in inciting riot of which he is accused by Crowe and Williamson.

69. Quoted in Graves, "The Fight Against Alcohol," 89; *Atlanta Constitution*, September 24, 1906, 7.

70. *Atlanta Journal*, September 27, 1906; *Atlanta Constitution*, September 24, 1906.

Chapter 10: Heart Trouble

1. *St. Louis Republic*, March 11, 1895, 8; untitled 1928 article by Medora Field Perkerson, Jones Papers, Jones Museum.

2. *Holston Methodist*, April 4, 1885, 2; *St. Joseph Daily Herald*, September 29, 1885, 2; Stuart, *Famous Stories*, 262.

3. *New York Times*, March 10, 1888.

4. *Chattanooga Daily Times*, December 26, 1895, 2.

5. *Atlanta Journal*, May 10, 1897; *St. Louis Globe-Democrat*, March 13, 1895, 2.

6. *Wesleyan Christian Advocate*, March 25, 1891, 4; *Nashville Banner*, June 2, 1893, 6.

7. Interview with Howell Jones, November 15, 1992, Atlanta.

8. Interview with Louise Holcomb Cade, December 11, 1975, Atlanta; interview with Dorothy Ann Roth, June 5, 1991, Cartersville, Ga.

9. *Cartersville Courant-American*, November 20, 1890, 1.

10. Ibid., February 5, 1891, 1; and November 20, 1890, 1.

11. Ibid., November 20, 1890, 1.

12. Ibid., February 5, 1891, 1.

13. Ibid., January 8, 1891, 1.

14. *Atlanta Constitution*, February 9, 1891, 1.

15. Ibid., February 4, 1891, 1.

16. *Atlanta Journal*, February 5, 1891, 1; and February 7, 1891, 9; *Atlanta Constitution*, February 5, 1891, 1.

17. *Cartersville Courant-American*, February 12, 1891, 1; *Atlanta Journal*, February 7, 1891, 9.

18. Bartow County, Letters of Administration, Guardians, Testamentary, 1902–23.

19. *Atlanta Journal*, June 25, 1892; and June 12, 1892; *Daily Oklahoman*, October 9, 1906, 6.

20. Paul Jones to Laura and Sam Jones, November 24, 1897, Jones Papers, University of Georgia.

21. *Baltimore Sun*, May 20, 1886, 5; clipping, "Get There and Stay There," Jones Papers, University of Georgia; *Nashville Banner*, March 24, 1902.

22. Interview with Paul Jones, Jr., February 7, 1976, Atlanta; *Atlanta Journal*, March 6, 1987; interview with Florine Dillard, June 26, 1976, Cartersville, Ga.; Sam Jones to Laura Jones, May 1, 1906, Jones Papers, University of Georgia. Atlantans will recognize the name of Paul Jones, Jr., who was for many years the film critic for the *Atlanta Constitution*. Laura married three times during her father's life. She married David Flournoy on December 31, 1902, and B. C. Sloan on March 24, 1904, and again on March 31, 1905.

23. Interview with Paul Jones, Jr., February 7, 1976, Atlanta; Sam Jones to Julia Jones, November 1903, Jones Papers, Archives of the State of Georgia; and April 12, 1905, Jones Museum, Cartersville; personal interview with Dorothy Ann Roth, June 5, 1991, Cartersville, Ga.

24. *Nashville Christian Advocate*, February 4, 1904, 7; interview with Dorothy Ann Roth, June 5, 1991, Cartersville, Ga.; interview with Howell Jones, November 15, 1992, Atlanta.

25. *Louisville Courier-Journal*, May 8, 1889, 5; *Nashville American*, March 21, 1898, 8; *Atlanta Journal*, March 6, 1898; September 9, 1901; and September 13, 1901. The papers give no names, but it seems likely that the two daughters were Annie and Mary. Julia was still very young, and Laura was so perpetually unrepentant that it is unlikely that Jones would have thought he could pressure her into confession.

26. *Atlanta Journal*, January 4, 1896; Silvano Arieti, *American Handbook of Psychiatry* (New York: Basic Books, 1959), 1:428.

27. *Daily Oklahoman*, October 16, 1906, 3.

28. William Manchester, the superb biographer of Winston Churchill, notes the same phenomenon in his subject. Churchill's depressions, which he called the "Black Dog," were much less pronounced when he was in a protracted struggle with enemies in parliament or abroad. "Nothing," Manchester writes, "could match the

satisfaction of directing his hostility outward, toward a great antagonist, a figure worthy of massive enmity" (*The Last Lion, Winston Spencer Churchill, Visions of Glory: 1874–1932* (Boston: Little, Brown, 1988), 24.

29. *Cartersville News and Courant*, January 1, 1903, 1; *Atlanta Journal*, May 7, 1892; Ron Fieve, *Mood Swings: The Third Revolution in Psychiatry* (New York: Morrow, 1975), 101.

30. Sam Jones to Laura Jones, July 14, 1899, Jones Papers, Archives of the State of Georgia.

31. Pyron, *Sam Jones' Revival Sermons*, 28.

32. Fieve, *Mood Swings*, 3.

33. *Independent*, September 24, 1885, 5; record pages of the Sam P. Jones family Bible, Jones Papers, Archives of the State of Georgia; *Cartersville News*, January 31, 1907, 3; interview with Howell Jones, December 18, 1992, Atlanta.

34. *Cartersville News*, January 20, 1926; Fieve, *Mood Swings*, 13; interview with Paul Jones, Jr., May 6, 1978, Atlanta; interview with Howell Jones, December 18, 1992, Atlanta; interview with Paul Jones, Jr., May 6, 1978, Atlanta. At the time of her mother's death, Laura was listed as Laura Schroeder of Miami.

35. Laura Jones (New Orleans) to Laura Jones, December 10, 1925; Laura Mays (Marietta, Ga.) to Julia Holcomb, n.d., both in the possession of Howell Jones, Atlanta.

36. Interview with Paul Jones, Jr., May 6, 1878, Atlanta; *Cartersville Courant-American*, December 17, 1896, 5; *Savannah Morning News*, May 18, 1901, 10; *Atlanta Journal*, December 17, 1926, 18.

37. Paul Jones to Mrs. Sam Jones, July 12, 1921, Jones Papers, University of Georgia. Paul married Alice (Alya) O'Neill on April 27, 1904. One child, Porter, was born to that marriage. He married Leila Booker on June 2, 1910, and their children were Katherine Adeline Jones (b. April 1, 1911), Paul H. Jones, Jr. (b. October 22, 1913), Howell Madison Jones (b. January 30, 1916), and Ann Cordelia Jones (b. August 1, 1917).

38. Paul Jones to Mrs. Sam Jones, July 12, 1921, Jones Papers, University of Georgia.

39. Eulogy for Paul Jones, December 1926, in the possession of Howell Jones, Atlanta.

40. *Cartersville Courant-American*, January 1, 1891, 4.

41. Winokur, Clayton, and Reich, *Manic Depressive Illness*, 73–75; Annie Jones diary, July 5, 1891; and July 9, 1891.

42. Annie Jones diary, October 13, 1891; March 5, 1892; April 15, 1892; April 25, 1892; and July 18, 1892; Winokur, Clayton, and Reich, *Manic Depressive Illness*, 64; Annie Jones diary, October 15, 1892; and January 17, 1893.

43. Will Graham to Sam Jones, March 29, 1895, Jones Papers, University of Georgia; Annie Jones diary, June 20, 1895.

44. Annie Jones diary, July 30, 1895; interview with Dorothy Ann Roth, June 5, 1991, Cartersville, Ga.; Annie Jones diary, October 19, 1895; February 13, 1896; and October 13, 1900; undated letter, in Annie Jones diary.

45. Interview with Paul Jones, Jr., May 6, 1978, Atlanta; interview with Howell Jones, December 18, 1992, Atlanta; clipping from unnamed Cartersville newspaper, May 24, 1924, Jones Papers, Jones Museum.

46. *Atlanta Journal*, June 25, 1892, 8; Mendels, *Concepts of Depression*, 11.

47. Robert M. Goldenson, *The Encyclopedia of Human Behavior: Psychology, Psychiatry, and Mental Health* (Garden City, N.Y.: Doubleday, 1970), 2:586; J. H. Bryson (Huntsville, Ala.) to Sam Jones, March 7, 1885, Jones Papers, University of Georgia; *Alabama Advocate*, quoted in *Nashville Christian Advocate*, March 14, 1891, 2; *Cartersville Courant-American*, November 19, 1991, 1; Mrs. Sam P. Jones diary, February 13, 1891, Jones Papers, Archives of the State of Georgia.

48. Annie Jones diary, October 15, 1900; *Atlanta Journal*, May 28, 1902; Norman S. Endler, *Holiday of Darkness: A Psychologist's Personal Journey Out of His Depression* (New York: John Wiley and Sons, 1982), 125. Jones recovered quickly and campaigned for Dupont Guerry with Sam Small, Thomas Watson, and Seaborn Wright.

49. *Boston Daily Globe*, January 27, 1897, 5; *St. Louis Globe-Democrat*, March 4, 1895, 4; Russ Daniel (Atlanta, Tex.) to Sam Jones, March 30, 1890, Jones Papers, University of Georgia; *Atlanta Journal*, March 10, 1897, 5.

50. *Baltimore Sun*, July 20, 1898, 10.

51. *Atlanta Journal*, July 10, 1899, 4; July 15, 1899, 4; and September 30, 1899, 4.

52. Ibid., July 10, 1899, 4. While it is unlikely that Jones could drink and conceal it, it is possible that he took opium for his stomach ulcers because opium was a common remedy for stomach disorders.

53. Ibid., October 12, 1899, 10; and October 7, 1899; Sam Jones to Laura Jones, July 9, 1899, Jones Papers, University of Georgia.

54. *Atlanta Journal*, September 15, 1903, 6.

55. *Atlanta Journal*, September 18, 1903, 1; and September 19, 1903, 1; *New York Times*, September 15, 1903, 3; and September 18, 1903, 1.

56. *Atlanta Georgian*, October 18, 1906, 5.

57. Interview with Dorothy Ann Roth, June 5, 1991, Cartersville; *Atlanta Journal*, October 16, 1897, 5.

58. *Cartersville American*, January 12, 1893, 1.

59. *Nashville Banner*, October 6, 1888, 7; and October 16, 1888, 1.

60. Sam Jones to Laura Jones, July 25, 1888, and October 14, 1880; H. B. Jones to Sam Jones, March 26, 1890; document of payment dated July 20, 1891, all in Jones Papers, University of Georgia. Mrs. Henry Ward Beecher and J. B. Hawthorne, pastor of the First Baptist Church in Atlanta, were among the religious celebrities featured in patent-medicine advertisements.

61. Quoted in Rufus B. Spain, *At Ease in Zion: A Social History of Southern Baptists, 1865–1900* (Nashville: Vanderbilt University Press, 1961), 203–4; Weisenberger, *Triumph of Faith*, 157.

62. *Nashville Christian Advocate*, April 23, 1896; quoted in Robert Joseph Clarke, *The Story of Tobacco in America* (New York: A. A. Knopf, 1949), 169–71.

63. Clarke, *Tobacco in America*, 169; clipping in the *Chicago Herald*, n.d., Jones Collection, Emory University; *Chicago Daily Inter-Ocean*, February 28, 1886, 5; Oscar Todhunter to Sam Jones, March 29, 1886, Jones Papers, University of Georgia.

64. *Chicago Tribune*, March 24, 1886, 3; *New York Times*, April 11, 1886, 6; *Zion's Herald*, April 7, 1886, 108.

65. *Chicago Daily Inter-Ocean*, April 3, 1886, 4; and March 31, 1886, 12; Oscar Todhunter to Sam Jones, March 29, 1886, Jones Papers, University of Georgia; *Chicago Tribune*, April 4, 1886, 4.

66. Sam Small to Sam Jones, August 20, 1886; Albert Janson to Sam Jones, February 1, 1888, both in Jones Papers, University of Georgia; *Dallas Morning News*, May 28, 1893, 4; clipping from *Church News* (Lewistown, Pa.), January 1900, Jones Papers, University of Georgia.

67. *Los Angeles Times*, January 27, 1889, 4; *Minneapolis Evening Journal*, June 24, 1886, 1; clipping from *Toronto World*, n.d., Jones Papers, University of Georgia.

68. *San Francisco Daily Examiner*, March 27, 1889, 3; *Minneapolis Evening Journal*, June 24, 1886, 1; *Nashville Banner*, April 9, 1895, 2.

69. *St. Joseph Daily Herald*, October 11, 1885; *Minneapolis Evening Journal*, June 24, 1886, 1; *St. Joseph Daily Herald*, October 11, 1885, 4.

70. *Cartersville News and Courant*, December 11, 1902, 1.

71. *Atlanta Constitution*, June 16, 1906.

72. *Atlanta Journal*, August 31, 1886.

73. Quoted in Theodore Morrison, *Chautauqua: A Center for Education, Religion, and the Arts in America* (Chicago: University of Chicago Press, 1974), 231.

74. *Lyceumite*, October 15, 1906, Jones Papers, University of Georgia; Sam Jones, quoted in Gay MacLauren, *Morally We Roll Along* (Boston: Little, Brown, 1938), 78; *Baltimore Sun*, May 15, 1886; Holcomb, *Sam Jones*, 21; *St. Louis Globe-Democrat*, March 13, 1895, 2.

75. Quoted in Morrison, *Chautauqua*, 27.

76. *Bartow Herald*, October 3, 1928, Jones Papers, Jones Museum.

77. Newspaper clipping from Austin, Tex., January 16 (no year), Jones Collection, Emory University; Holcomb, *Sam Jones*, 149; Laura M. Jones, *Life and Sayings*, 302; *Atlanta Journal*, July 21, 1906. Jones's fees for lectures—$250 per night for weeknights and cities, $125 for Saturdays and small towns—was moderate. The highest-paid lecturers received between $300 and $500.

78. *Knoxville Daily Journal*, May 18, 1892, 1; *Nashville Banner*, April 9, 1895, 2.

79. *Nashville Banner*, April 10, 1895, 10; *Nashville American*, March 22, 1900, 3; *Atlanta Journal*, March 24, 1900, 17.

80. Smith, "Analysis," 113–36, 142–45.

81. *Nashville Banner*, April 1, 1902; April 3, 1902, 2; and April 8, 1902.

82. *Atlanta Journal*, April 14, 1900, 13; *Nashville Banner*, January 1, 1900.

83. *Baltimore Baptist*, May 28, 1886, 5; *New Orleans Christian Advocate*, January 16, 1890, 4.

84. *Nashville Christian Advocate*, September 12, 1895; Holcomb, *Sam Jones*, 111; T. Cameron, "Evangelists, and Their Methods," *New Orleans Christian Advocate*, November 12, 1891.

85. Anonymous (Chattanooga, Tenn.) to Sam Jones, December 16, 1899, Jones Papers, University of Georgia; *Augusta Chronicle*, May 17, 1897, 2.

86. *Baltimore Baptist*, quoted in *Baltimore Sun*, May 28, 1886, 5; *Looking Glass*, April 4, 1896.

87. *St. Louis Globe-Democrat*, March 10, 1895; Smith, "Analysis," 142; Calvin

Dill Wilson, "The Phenomenon of Sam Jones," *Critic* 40 (April 1902): 356–57.

88. Ahlstrom, *Religious History*, 2:297; Findlay, *Dwight L. Moody*, 394.

89. A. M. Robinson, "Revivals—Then and Now," *Nashville Christian Advocate*, July 14, 1904, 3.

90. G. B. Winton, "Rev. Sam P. Jones," *Nashville Christian Advocate*, October 19, 1906, 11; William Harrison, "Evangelists and Pastors," *Southern Methodist Review* (March 1888): 105; P. H. Lotz, quoted in Lightsey, "Relationship," 17; *New York Times*, October 13, 1896, 9; and October 11, 1896, 12.

91. *Nashville Christian Advocate*, October 19, 1903, 1; untitled newspaper clipping, May 1904, Jones Collection, Emory University; Herman B. Teeter, "Sam Jones: Methodism's Greatest Evangelist," *Together* 9 (October 1965): 43; *Houston Daily Post*, February 2, 1903.

92. *Atlanta Journal*, April 20, 1905; *Knoxville Journal and Tribune*, June 4, 1905; and May 25, 1905.

93. *Atlanta Journal*, April 20, 1905, 7; *Knoxville Journal and Tribune*, June 5, 1905.

Conclusion

1. Winton, "Rev. Sam P. Jones," 10–11.

2. Holcomb, *Sam Jones*, 137; *Chicago Tribune*, March 20, 1886, 5; *St. Louis Republic*, March 25, 1895, 8; *Atlanta Journal*, September 18, 1903, 1.

3. Holcomb, *Sam Jones*, 138; "Sudden Death" (last sermon preached by Sam Jones), Jones Collection, Emory University.

4. Laura M. Jones, *Life and Sayings*, 271; *Atlanta Constitution*, October 21, 1906.

5. Jones's encounter with Windham was carried in papers throughout the South, with predictable variations in content (see *Memphis Commercial Appeal*, April 21, 1905, 3; and *Montgomery Advertiser*, April 21, 1905, 1). I have taken my version from the *Atlanta Journal*, April 21, 1906, 5, an interview with Jones on his arrival back in Georgia.

6. *Atlanta Journal*, April 26, 1905, 5.

7. *Toledo Bee*, March 6, 1899, 3.

8. *Daily Oklahoman*, October 12, 1906.

9. Ibid., October 6, 1906, 1.

10. Holcomb, *Sam Jones*, 25.

11. Ibid.

12. Clipping from the *Atlanta Evening News*, n.d., Jones Papers, University of Georgia; *Wesleyan Christian Advocate*, April 25, 1919, 19; *Atlanta Georgian*, October 18, 1906, 1.

13. Laura M. Jones, *Life and Sayings*, 346.

14. Ibid., 452, 358.

15. Watson, quoted in Chalfant, *Agitators*, 186; and in "Sam Jones: The Scourging Evangelist," *Literary Digest* 33 (1906): 722; Bryan, quoted in Laura M. Jones, *Life and Sayings*, 452.

16. Laura M. Jones, *Life and Sayings*, 452; *New York Times*, October 16, 1906; *Nashville Christian Advocate*, November 30, 1906.

17. *Epworth Era*, June 27, 1907; Cunyus, *History of Bartow County*, 292; Laura M. Jones, *Life and Sayings*, 452.

18. McLoughlin, *Modern Revivalism*, 283; Weisberger, *They Gathered*, 272.

19. *Nashville Christian Advocate*, quoted in *Nashville American*, May 24, 1890; Vernon L. Parrington, *Main Currents in American Thought: On Interpretation of American Literature from the Beginnings to 1920* (New York: Harcourt Brace, 1930), 11.

Bibliography

Primary Sources

MANUSCRIPT COLLECTIONS

Bartow County, Ga. Letters of Administration, Guardians, Testamentary. Record Book C, 1902–23.

Bartow County Scrapbook. Archives of the State of Georgia, Atlanta.

Candler, Warren Akin. Collection. Emory University, Atlanta.

Cobb, Pharaoh Lee. Diary. Tennessee State Archives, Nashville.

Hawkins, Susan Melvina. Scrapbook, 1834–1913. Tennessee State Archives, Nashville.

Jarrell, Charles. Collection. Emory University, Atlanta.

Jones, Annie Pyron. Diary. In the possession of Louise Cade, Atlanta.

Jones, John J. Will. Will Record A, Bartow County, Ga., 1872.

Jones, Laura. Will. Will Record C, Bartow County, Ga., 1926.

Jones, Sam P. Collection. Emory University, Atlanta.

———. Papers. Archives of the State of Georgia, Atlanta.

———. Papers. In the possession of Lucy Cunyus Mulcahy, Atlanta.

———. Papers. Sam P. Jones Museum, Cartersville, Ga.

———. Papers. University of Georgia, Athens.

———. Will. Will Record B, Bartow County, Ga., 1885–1922.

McGill, Ralph Emerson. Collection. Emory University, Atlanta.

Ransom, J. J. Papers. Tennessee State Archives, Nashville.

Rivers, Flournoy. Scrapbook, 1896–1950. Tennessee State Archives, Nashville.

Thomas Ryman Line. Papers. Tennessee State Archives, Nashville.

UNPUBLISHED PRIMARY SOURCES

Bartow County, Ga. Court of Ordinary Wills. Records, 1906. Microfilm. Archives of the State of Georgia, Atlanta.

Bartow County, Ga. Tax Digest, 1880–1906. Microfilm. Archives of the State of Georgia, Atlanta.

Bartow County Bank. Directory, 1883–84: Cherokee, Ga.; Cartersville, Ga. Sam P. Jones Museum, Cartersville, Ga.

Bridges, Luther B. "Trinity Methodist Episcopal Church, South: A Compilation of Her History, 1854–1935." Pamphlet. Trinity United Methodist Church, Atlanta.

Cass County, Ga. Census, 1860. Microfilm. Archives of the State of Georgia, Atlanta.

Central Congregational Church. Records. Central Congregational Church, Atlanta.

Central Presbyterian Church. Records. Central Presbyterian Church, Atlanta.

Compiled Records of Confederate Soldiers from Georgia, 22d Infantry. Microfilm. Archives of the State of Georgia, Atlanta.

Dellinger, S. E. "History of the Second Ponce de Leon Baptist Church and Its Antecedents, 1854–1969." Pamphlet. Second Ponce de Leon Baptist Church, Atlanta.

Ellis, J. B. "History of Liberty Methodist Church, Shady Dale Circuit, Jasper County." Special Collections, Pitts Theology Library, Emory University, Atlanta.

Evangelical Ministers' Association. Minutes. Atlanta, 1894–1902. Christian Council, Atlanta.

First Baptist Church. Records. First Baptist Church, Atlanta.

First Presbyterian Church. Records. First Presbyterian Church, Atlanta.

Garrett, Franklin. "Atlanta Obituaries." Microfilm. Archives of the State of Georgia, Atlanta.

Godly, Margaret. "The Centennial Story of Trinity Methodist Church, 'Mother Church of Savannah Methodism,' 1848–1948." Special Collections, Pitts Theology Library, Emory University, Atlanta.

Liberty Methodist Church, Monticello, Ga. Records. Special Collections, Pitts Theology Library, Emory University, Atlanta.

Mansfield Methodist Church, Newborn Charge of the North Georgia Conference. Records. Special Collections, Pitts Theology Library, Emory University, Atlanta.

Monticello Methodist Church. Records. Microfilm. Archives of the State of Georgia, Atlanta.

Morgan, Dorothy Jones, ed. "A Very Personal Glimpse of the Civil War Era from 1849–1863." Privately printed, 1990.

Murphy, W. Y. "A History of the Newborn Methodist Church of North Georgia." 1954. Special Collections, Pitts Theology Library, Emory University, Atlanta.

Newborn Methodist Church. Records. Special Collections, Pitts Theology Library, Emory University, Atlanta.

Second Baptist Church. Records. Second Baptist Church, Atlanta.

Second Ponce de Leon Baptist Church. Records. Second Ponce de Leon Baptist Church, Atlanta.

PUBLISHED PRIMARY SOURCES

Atlanta City Directory for 1897. Atlanta: Bullock and Saunders, 1897.

Bureau of the Census. Religious Bodies. Vol. 2, Separate Denominations. Washington, D.C.: U.S. Government Printing Office, 1929.

Doctrine and Discipline of the Methodist Episcopal Church, South. Nashville: Southern Methodist Publishing House, 1883.

Dore, Gustave, ed. Sam Jones' Late Sermons as Delivered by the Great Preacher. Chicago: Rhodes and McClure, 1907.

Flood, Theodore. "Sam Jones." Chautauquan 6 (March 1886): 417.

Gaustad, Edwin S. *Historical Atlas of Religion in America*. New York: Harper and
Row, 1962.
Haynes, B. F. *Facts, Faith, and Fire, or, Chapters on the Situation*. Nashville:
B. F. Haynes, 1900.
———— . *Tempest-Tossed on Methodist Seas*. Kansas City, Mo.: Nazarene
Publishing House, 1914.
Holcomb, Brent H. *Marriage and Death Notices from the Southern Christian
Advocate*. Vol. 1, *1837–1860*. Easley, S.C.: Southern Historical Press, 1979.
———— . *Marriage and Death Notices from the Southern Christian Advocate*.
Vol. 2, *1860–1867*. Easley, S.C.: Southern Historical Press, 1980.
Holcomb, Walt. "Rev. Sam P. Jones: A Tribute." *Talent: A Magazine of Public
Speaking* 17 (November 1906): 5–6.
———— . *Sam Jones*. Nashville: Methodist Publishing House, 1947.
———— , ed. *Best Loved Sermons of Sam Jones*. Nashville: Parthenon
Press, 1950.
———— , ed. *Popular Lectures of Sam P. Jones*. Chicago: Fleming H.
Revell, 1950.
Holt, Ivan L., ed. *Sam Jones*. Vol. 4, *Great Pulpit Masters*. New York:
Fleming H. Revell, 1950.
Jones, Laura M. *The Life and Sayings of Sam P. Jones*. Atlanta: Franklin
Turner, 1907.
Jones, Sam P. *Anecdotes and Illustrations*. Chicago: Rhodes and McClure, 1896.
———— . "Come, Ye Weary and Heavy Laden." *Sword of the Lord*, August 14,
1959, 1, 6–7.
———— . "Decision of Destiny." *Sword of the Lord*, May 18, 1956, 1, 8–9.
———— . "The Downward Pull of Sin." *Sword of the Lord*, February 8, 1957, 1,
8–10.
———— . *Good News: A Collection of Sermons by Sam Jones and Sam Small*. New
York: J. S. Ogilvie, 1886.
———— . *Lightning Flashes and Thunderbolts*. Louisville, Ky.: Pentecostal, 1912.
———— . *Living Words; or, Sam Jones' Own Book, Containing Sermons and
Sayings of Sam P. Jones and Sam Small in Toronto*. Toronto: William
Briggs, 1886.
———— . *The Prodigal Son: A Sermon to Men and Other Sermons*. Cartersville,
Ga.: Thomas Dunham, Special Agent, 1885.
———— . *Quit Your Meanness*. Chicago: Cranston and Stowe, 1889.
———— . *Rifle Shots at the King's Enemies* and *I'll Say Another Thing*. London:
T. Woolner, 1887.
———— . *Sam Jones' Own Book: A Series of Sermons Collected and Edited Under
the Author's Own Supervision*. Cincinnati: Jennings and Pye, 1886.
———— . *Sam Jones' Sermons*. Vol. 1. Chicago: Rhodes and McClure, 1890.
———— . *Sam Jones' Sermons*. Vol. 2. Chicago: Rhodes and McClure, 1896.
———— . *Sermons by Rev. Sam P. Jones as Stenographically Reported and
Delivered in St. Louis, Cincinnati, Chicago, Baltimore, Atlanta, Nashville, Waco
and Other Cities*. Chicago: L. B. Clayton, 1886.
———— . *Thunderbolts*. Nashville: Jones and Haynes, 1895.

Journal of Conventions: Diocese of Georgia, 1891–1902.

Kelley, D. C. "Rev. Sam P. Jones." *Southern Bivouac* 6 (January 1886): 500–504.

Kerley, T. A. *Conference Rights: Governing Principles of the Methodist Episcopal Church, South, Found in the History, Legislation, and Administration of the Church, with Suggestions to Hurtful Tendencies Thereby Detected and Needed Changes.* Nashville: Publishing House of the Methodist Episcopal Church, South, 1898.

Leftwich, William, ed. *Hot Shots; or, Sermons and Sayings by the Rev. Sam. P. Jones.* Nashville: Southern Methodist Publishing House, 1885.

———. *Sermons and Sayings by Rev. Sam. P. Jones, of Georgia.* Cincinnati Music Hall Series. Cincinnati: Cranston and Stowe, 1886.

Minutes of the General Association of the Presbyterian Church of the United States of America, Atlanta Synod. 1891–1902.

Minutes of the Georgia Baptist Convention, Atlanta Association. 1891–1902.

Minutes of the Georgia Synod of the Presbyterian Church of the United States of America, Augusta Synod. 1881–1900.

Minutes of the North Georgia Conference, Methodist Episcopal Church, South. 1871–1906.

Minutes of the North Mississippi Conference, Methodist Episcopal Church South. 1879–89.

Minutes of the Tennessee Conference, Methodist Episcopal Church, South. 1884–85.

Pyron, Annie Jones, ed. *Sam Jones' Revival Sermons.* Vol. 4 of *Great Pulpit Masters.* New York: Fleming H. Revell, 1912.

Record of the Stone Mountain Association (Baptist). 1891–1902.

Richardson, Simon Peter. *The Lights and Shadows of Itinerant Life.* Nashville: Publishing House of the Methodist Episcopal Church, South, 1901.

Small, Samuel W. *From Press to Pulpit.* Chicago: F. H. Revell, 1886.

———. *Pleas for Prohibition.* Atlanta: N.p., 1890.

Spurgeon, Charles Haddon. *Sermons of Rev. C. H. Spurgeon.* Vol. 5. New York: Funk and Wagnalls, n.d.

Strong, Josiah. *Our Country: Its Possible Future and Its Present Crisis.* New York: American Home Missionary Society, 1885.

Stuart, George R. *Famous Stories of Sam P. Jones.* New York: Fleming H. Revell, 1908.

———. *Methodist Evangelism.* Nashville: Publishing House of the Methodist Episcopal Church, South, 1923.

———. "Sam Jones, The Preacher." *Methodist Quarterly Review* 69 (1920): 1419–37.

———. *What Every Methodist Should Know.* Nashville: Cokesbury Press, 1935.

Tigert, John T., ed. *The Doctrine and Discipline of the Methodist Episcopal Church, South.* Nashville: Publishing House of the Methodist Episcopal Church, South, 1894.

Wagner, Charles L. "Reminiscences of Sam Jones." *Talent* 17 (November 1906): 7–8.

Wesley, John. *Journal of John Wesley.* Vol. 6. London: J. M. Dent, 1907.
———. *A Plain Account of Christian Perfection.* 1743. Reprint. London: Epworth Press, 1952.
Willard, Frances. *Women and Temperance; or, The Work and the Workers of the Women's Christian Temperance Union.* New York: Arno Press, 1972.
Wilson, Calvin Dill. "The Phenomenon of Sam Jones." *Critic* 40 (April 1902): 356–57.

PERSONAL INTERVIEWS

Budd, Candler. May 13, 1976, Atlanta.
Cade, Mrs. Louis (granddaughter of Sam Jones). December 11, 1975, Atlanta.
Flynt, Mrs. Francis. October 13, 1985, Atlanta.
Jones, Bevel. July 16, 1976, Atlanta.
Jones, Howell. December 18, 1992, Atlanta.
Jones, Paul, Jr. (grandson of Sam Jones). February 7, 1976, Atlanta.
Kerr, B. C. May 24, 1981, Atlanta.
Lipscomb, Nida. May 31, 1975, Cartersville, Ga.
Mulcahy, Lucy Cunyus (great-grandniece of Sam Jones). March 11, 1975, Atlanta.
Prickett, John. August 30, 1978, Atlanta.
Roth, Dorothy Ann. June 5, 1991, Cartersville, Ga.
Turner, Don. October 16, 1985, Atlanta.

RELIGIOUS PERIODICALS

Baltimore Baptist. 1885, 1886, 1895, 1896.
Central Baptist (St. Louis, Mo.). 1885, 1894, 1895.
Christian Advocate (New York). 1898–1900.
Daily Christian Advocate. 1886, 1890, 1894, 1898.
Holston Methodist. 1885–88.
Homiletic Review. 1882–98.
Independent. 1885–1906.
Living Water. 1903–6.
Methodist Review. 1887–96.
Nashville Christian Advocate. 1878–1906.
Presbyterian Quarterly. 1887–88.
Quarterly Review. 1891–96.
Southern Evangelist. 1887.
Southern Methodist Review. 1888–91.
St. Louis Evangelist (Presbyterian). 1885, 1895.
Tennessee Methodist. 1891–93.
Wesleyan Christian Advocate. 1872–1906.
Zion's Outlook. 1900–1902.

Atlanta Constitution. 1879, 1885, 1886, 1889, 1896, 1897, 1926, 1975.
Atlanta Georgian. 1906.
Atlanta Independent. 1906.
Atlanta Journal. 1884–1906.
Augusta Chronicle. 1892, 1894, 1897.
Baltimore American. 1885–86.
Baltimore Sun. 1886, 1892, 1898, 1900.
Birmingham Age Herald. 1926.
Boston Daily Globe. 1887, 1897.
Boston Evening Transcript. 1887.
Brunswick Times-Call (Georgia). 1901.
Calhoun Times (Georgia). 1881.
Calhoun Times and Gordon County News (Georgia). 1906.
Carroll County Times (Georgia). 1880.
Carrollton Times-Georgian (Georgia). 1880.
Cartersville American (Georgia). 1882, 1884.
Cartersville Courant (Georgia). 1885.
Cartersville Courant-American (Georgia). 1896, 1898, 1899.
Cartersville Express (Georgia). 1877.
Cartersville Free Press (Georgia). 1880–81.
Cartersville News (Georgia). 1906.
Cartersville News-Courant (Georgia). 1902.
Cartersville Standard and Express (Georgia). 1871–73.
Cartersville Tribune (Georgia). 1941.
Charlotte Observer (North Carolina). 1949.
Chattanooga Daily Times. 1889.
Chautauquan, 1885–1906.
Chicago Daily Inter-Ocean. 1886.
Chicago Tribune. 1886.
Cincinnati Commercial Gazette. 1886.
Columbus Daily Enquirer-Sun (Georgia). 1884.
Columbus Enquirer (Georgia). 1881.
Daily Oklahoman, 1906.
Dallas Morning News (Texas). 1893, 1900, 1906.
Dallas New Era (Georgia). 1883.
Dalton Argus (Georgia). 1889.
Dalton Citizen (Georgia). July 1889.
Dublin Enquirer-Dispatch (Georgia). 1901–2.
Houston Chronicle. 1906.
Houston Daily Post. 1903.
Huntsville Gazette (Alabama). 1884.
Hustler of Rome (Georgia). 1897.
Indianapolis Journal. 1886.
Knoxville Daily Journal. 1885, 1892.

Knoxville Journal and Tribune. 1905.

Looking Glass (Atlanta). 1896–97.

Los Angeles Times. 1889.

Louisville Courier-Journal (Kentucky). 1899.

Louisville Times (Kentucky). 1899.

Macon Telegraph and Messenger. 1881, 1884.

Madisonian (Madison, Ga.). 1879.

Memphis Commercial Appeal. 1886.

Memphis Daily Appeal. 1884.

Meriwether Vindicator (Georgia). 1884.

Milledgeville Union and Recorder (Georgia). 1881, 1882, 1884, 1886.

Milwaukee Journal. 1896.

Minneapolis Evening Journal. 1886–87.

Minneapolis Tribune, 1887.

Moberly Daily Monitor (Missouri). 1889–90.

Mobile Daily Register. 1901.

Montgomery Daily Advertiser. 1892.

Nashville American. 1897, 1898, 1900.

Nashville American Outlook. 1897.

Nashville Banner. 1885, 1887, 1888, 1890–93, 1895, 1897, 1900.

Nashville Daily American. 1885, 1887, 1897.

New York Times. 1885–1906.

North Georgia Citizen (Dalton). July 1889.

Rockmart Journal (Georgia). 1972.

San Francisco Chronicle. 1889.

San Francisco Daily Examiner. 1889.

Savannah Morning News. 1883, 1901.

Savannah Press. 1901.

Sparta Ishmaelite (Georgia). 1884.

St. Joseph Daily Herald (Missouri). 1885.

St. Louis Globe-Democrat. 1885, 1894, 1895.

St. Louis Missouri Republican. 1885.

St. Louis Republic. 1894–95.

St. Louis Republican. 1885.

St. Paul Dispatch. 1886.

Tifton Gazette (Georgia). 1902.

Toledo Bee. 1899.

Waco Daily Examiner (Texas). 1884.

Waco Day (Texas). 1884.

Waycross Herald (Georgia). 1901.

Weekly Cartersville Express (Georgia). 1867.

Western Appeal: An Organ in the Interest of the Colored People of the Northwest (St. Paul). 1887.

Western Watchman (St. Louis). 1885.

Wheeling Daily Intelligencer (West Virginia). 1893.

Secondary Sources

UNPUBLISHED SECONDARY SOURCES

Champion, Herman Daniel. "A Rhetorical Analysis of Selected Sermons by Sam Jones During His Emergence as a National Figure, 1872–1885." Ph.D. dissertation, Louisiana State University, 1980.

Evans, Mercer Griffen. "The History of the Organized Labor Movement in Georgia." Ph.D. dissertation, University of Chicago, 1929.

Fair, H. L. "Southern Methodists on Education and Race, 1900–1920." Ph.D. dissertation, Vanderbilt University, 1971.

Gaddis, Merrill Elmer. "Christian Perfectionism in America." Ph.D. dissertation, University of Chicago, 1929.

Henderson, Jerry E. "The Ryman Auditorium: Its Years as a Religious Center of Nashville and the South." Address to the Tennessee Historical Society, December 12, 1967.

Holifield, E. Brooks. "The Southern Heritage and the Minister's Image." Lecture delivered during Minister's Week, 1976, Candler School of Theology, Emory University, Atlanta.

Lightsey, Ralph. "The Relationship of the Professional Evangelist to the Parish Minister." Thesis, Candler School of Theology, Emory University, 1951.

Loefflath-Ehly, Victor. "Religion as the Principal Component of World-Maintenance in the American South from the 1830's to 1900 with Special Emphasis on the Clergy and Their Sermons: A Case Study in the Dialectic of Religion and Culture." Ph.D. dissertation, Florida State University, 1978.

Lunsford, Robert Lloyd. "A Historical Background of the Holiness Movement." Thesis, Marion College, 1940.

McKibben, J. W. O. "Institutional Care and Placing Out of Dependent Children as Conducted by the North Georgia Conference." Thesis, Candler School of Theology, Emory University, 1921.

Milkman, Howard Louis. "Thomas DeWitt Talmage: An Evangelical Nineteenth Century Voice on Technology, Urbanization, and Labor-Management Conflicts." Ph.D. dissertation, New York University, 1971.

Mixon, Gerald L. "The Atlanta Riot of 1906." Ph.D. dissertation, Auburn University, 1989.

Morrow, Ralph. "The Methodist Episcopal Church, South, and Reconstruction, 1865–1885." Ph.D. dissertation, Indiana University, 1954.

Rensi, Raymond Charles. "Sam Jones: Southern Evangelist." Ph.D. dissertation, University of Georgia, 1971.

Shaw, Barton. "The Wool-Hat Boys: A History of the Populist Party in Georgia, 1892 to 1910." Ph.D. dissertation, Emory University, 1979.

Smith, Harold Ivan. "An Analysis of the Evangelistic Work of Samuel Porter Jones in Nashville, 1885–1906." Thesis, Scarritt College for Christian Workers, 1971.

Vaughn, Damon Vernon. "A Critical Study of the Preaching of Samuel Porter Jones." Th.D. dissertation, New Orleans Baptist Theological Seminary, 1962.

BOOKS

Abell, Aaron I. *The Urban Impact on American Protestantism*. Cambridge, Mass.: Harvard University Press, 1943.

Ahlstrom, Sydney E. *A Religious History of the American People*. New Haven, Conn.: Yale University Press, 1972.

Alexander, Gross. *History of the Methodist Episcopal Church, South*. New York: N.p., 1894.

American Psychiatric Association. *Diagnostic and Statistical Manual of Mental Disorders*. New York: N.p., 1980.

Ammerman, Nancy Tatom. *Bible Believers: Fundamentalists in the Modern World*. New Brunswick, N.J.: Rutgers University Press, 1987.

Ansley, Mrs. J. J. *History of the Georgia Women's Christian Temperance Union from Its Organization, 1883 to 1907*. Columbus, Ga.: Gilbert, 1914.

Arieti, Silvano. *American Handbook of Psychiatry*. Vol. 1. New York: Basic Books, 1959.

Arnett, Alex Mathews. *The Populist Movement in Georgia: A View of the "Agrarian Crusade" in the Light of Solid-South Politics*. 1922. Reprint. New York: AMS Press, 1967.

Bacon, Ernest W. *Spurgeon: Heir of the Puritans*. Grand Rapids, Mich.: Baker Book House, 1967.

Bailey, T. J. *Prohibition in Mississippi; or, Anti-Liquor Legislation from Territorial Days, with Its Results in the Counties*. Jackson, Miss.: Privately printed, 1917.

Baker, Ray Stannard. *Following the Color Line: An Account of Negro Citizenship in the American Democracy*. 1908. Reprint. New York: Harper and Row, 1964.

Bannister, Robert. *Social Darwinism: Science and Myth in Anglo-American Social Thought*. Philadelphia: Temple University Press, 1979.

Barker, John Marshall. *The Saloon Problem and Social Reform*. Reprint. New York: Arno Press, 1970.

Beardsley, Frank Grenville. *Religious Progress Through Religious Revivals*. New York: American Tract Society, 1943.

Bell, Marion L. *Crusade in the City: Revivalism in Nineteenth-Century Philadelphia*. Lewisburg, Pa.: Bucknell University Press, 1977.

Blakey, Leonard Stott. *The Sale of Liquor in the South: The History of the Development of a Normal Social Restraint in Southern Commonwealths*. New York: Columbia University Press, 1912.

Blocker, Jack S., Jr. *Alcohol, Reform, and Society: The Liquor Issue in Social Context*. Westport, Conn.: Greenwood Press, 1979.

——— . *Retreat from Reform: The Prohibition Movement in the United States, 1890–1913*. Westport, Conn.: Greenwood Press, 1976.

Boardman, Tom W., Jr. *America and the Gilded Age: 1876–1900*. New York: Henry Z. Walck, 1972.

Bode, Frederick A. *Protestantism and the New South: North Carolina Baptists and Methodists in Political Crisis, 1894–1903*. Charlottesville: University Press of Virginia, 1975.

Bordin, Ruth. *Women and Temperance: The Quest for Power and Liberty, 1873–1900*. Philadelphia: Temple University Press, 1981.

Botkin, B. A., ed. *A Treasury of American Anecdotes*. New York: Bonanza Books, 1967.

Buck, Paul. *The Road to Reunion, 1865–1900*. Boston: Little, Brown, 1937.

Burke, Emory Stevens, ed. *The History of American Methodism*. Vols. 2 and 3. Nashville: Abingdon Press, 1964.

Campbell, Joseph E. *The Pentecostal Holiness Church, 1898–1948: Its Background and History*. Franklin Springs, Ga.: Publishing House of the Pentecostal Holiness Church, 1951.

Carter, Cullen T. *History of the Tennessee Conference*. Nashville: Methodist Publishing House, 1948.

Carter, Paul Allen. *The Spiritual Crisis of the Gilded Age*. DeKalb: Northern Illinois University Press, 1971.

Cash, Wilbur J. *The Mind of the South*. New York: Vintage Books, 1941.

Cashin, Edward J. *The Story of Augusta*. Augusta, Ga.: Richmond Board of Education, 1980.

Cashman, Sean Dennis. *Prohibition: The Lie of the Land*. New York: Free Press, 1981.

Chalfant, Henry Malcolm. *These Agitators and Their Ideas*. Nashville: Cokesbury Press, 1931.

Chapman, J. Wilbur. *Present-Day Evangelism*. New York: Baker and Taylor, 1903.

Clark, Elmer T. *The Small Sects in America*. Nashville: Abingdon Press, 1937.

Clark, Norman H. *Deliver Us from Evil: An Interpretation of American Prohibition*. New York: W. W. Norton, 1976.

Clarke, Robert Joseph. *The Story of Tobacco in America*. New York: A. A. Knopf, 1949.

Clebsch, William A. *From Sacred to Profane America: The Role of Religion in American History*. New York: Harper and Row, 1968.

Colvin, D. Leigh. *Prohibition in the United States: A History of the Prohibition Party of the Prohibition Movement*. New York: George H. Doran, 1926.

Conn, Walter E., ed. *Conversion: Perspectives on Personal and Social Transformation*. New York: Alba House, 1978.

Conway, Alan. *Reconstruction in Georgia*. Minneapolis: University of Minnesota Press, 1966.

Coulter, E. Merton. *The South During Reconstructon*. Vol. 2 of *A History of the South*, edited by Wendell Holmes Stephenson and E. Merton Coulter. Baton Rouge: Louisiana State University Press, 1947.

Cunyus, Lucy Josephine. *The History of Bartow County, Formerly Cass County*. Easley, S.C.: Tribune, 1933.

Dabney, Virginius. *Dry Messiah: The Life of Bishop Cannon*. New York: A. A. Knopf, 1949.

Davis, Perry R. *The Saloon: Public Drinking in Chicago and Boston, 1880–1920*. Urbana: University of Illinois Press, 1983.

Dempsey, Elam Franklin. *Atticus Greene Haygood*. Nashville: Parthenon Press, 1940.

Diamond, Sigmund. *The Psychology of the Methodist Revival: An Empirical and Descriptive Study*. London: Oxford University Press, 1962.

————, ed. *The Nation Transformed: The Creation of an Industrial Society.* New York: G. Braziller, 1963.

Dieter, Melvin Easterday. *The Holiness Revival of the Nineteenth Century.* Metuchen, N.J.: Scarecrow Press, 1980.

Dittmer, John. *Black Georgia in the Progressive Era, 1900–1920.* Urbana: University of Illinois Press, 1977.

Dolan, Jay P. *Catholic Revivalism: The American Experience, 1830–1900.* Notre Dame, Ind.: University of Notre Dame Press, 1978.

Dollar, George W. *The History of Fundamentalism.* Greenville, S.C.: Bob Jones University Press, 1973.

Drummond, Andrew Landale. *The Story of American Protestantism.* Boston: Beacon Press, 1951.

Dunne, Peter Findlay. *Mr. Dooley at His Best.* New York: C. Scribner's Sons, 1938.

————. *Mr. Dooley in Peace and in War.* Boston: Small, Maynard, 1899.

Eighmy, John Lee. *Churches in Cultural Captivity: A History of the Social Attitudes of Southern Baptists.* Knoxville: University of Tennessee Press, 1972.

Endler, Norman S. *Holiday of Darkness: A Psychologist's Personal Journey Out of His Depression.* New York: John Wiley and Sons, 1982.

Engelmann, Larry. *Intemperance: The Lost War Against Liquor.* New York: Free Press, 1979.

Erickson, Erik H. *Life History and the Historical Moment.* New York: W. W. Norton, 1975.

Ezell, John Samuel. *The South Since 1865.* New York: Macmillan, 1963.

Farish, Hunter Dickinson. *The Circuit Rider Dismounts: A Social History of Southern Methodism, 1865–1900.* Richmond: Dietz Press, 1938.

Farrell, C. P., ed. *The Works of Robert G. Ingersoll.* New York: Ingersoll, 1900.

Felton, Mrs. William H. *My Memoirs of Georgia Politics.* Atlanta: Index, 1911.

Ferguson, Charles. *Organizing to Beat the Devil: Methodists and the Making of America.* New York: Doubleday, 1971.

Fieve, Ronald. *Mood Swings: The Third Revolution in Psychiatry.* New York: Morrow, 1975.

Findlay, James F., Jr. *Dwight L. Moody: American Evangelist, 1837–1899.* Chicago: University of Chicago Press, 1969.

Fine, Sidney, ed. *Recent America: Conflicting Interpretations of the Great Issues.* New York: Macmillan, 1967.

Finney, Charles Grandison. *Lectures on Revivals of Religion.* New York: Deavitt, Lord, 1835.

Fitzgerald, O. P. *John B. McFerrin: A Biography.* Nashville: Publishing House of the Methodist Episcopal Church, South, 1888.

Flynn, Charles L. *White Land, Black Labor: Caste and Class in Late Nineteenth-Century Georgia.* Baton Rouge: Louisiana State University Press, 1983.

Foner, Eric. *Reconstruction: America's Unfinished Revolution, 1863–1877.* New York: Harper and Row, 1989.

Fraser, Walter J., Jr., and Winfred B. Moore, Jr., eds. *The Southern Enigma:*

Essays on Race, Class, and Folk Culture. Westport, Conn.: Greenwood Press, 1983.

Furnas, J. C. *The Life and Times of the Late Demon Rum.* New York: G. P. Putnam's Sons, 1965.

Garrett, Franklin M. *Atlanta and Environs: A Chronicle of Its People and Events.* Vol. 2. Athens: University of Georgia Press, 1954.

Gaston, Paul M. *The New South Creed: A Study in Southern Mythmaking.* New York: Alfred A. Knopf, 1970.

Gaustad, Edwin Scott. *A Religious History of America.* New York: Harper and Row, 1966.

————. *Religion in America: History and Historiography.* American Historical Society Pamphlets, no. 260. Washington, D.C.: American Historical Association, 1966.

Ginger, Ray. *Age of Excess: The United States from 1877 to 1914.* New York: Macmillan, 1965.

————. *The Bending Cross.* New Brunswick, N.J.: Rutgers University Press, 1949.

Goldenson, Robert M. *The Encyclopedia of Human Behavior: Psychology, Psychiatry, and Mental Health.* Garden City, N.Y.: Doubleday, 1970.

Gusfield, Joseph R. *Symbolic Crusade: Status Politics and the American Temperance Movement.* Urbana: University of Illinois Press, 1963.

Hammond, John L. *The Politics of Benevolence: Revival Religion and American Voting Behavior.* Norwood, N.J.: Ablex, 1979.

Harris, Joel Chandler. *Life of Henry W. Grady.* New York: Cassell, 1890.

Harrison, Brian. *Drink and the Victorians: The Temperance Question in England, 1865–1872.* Pittsburgh: University of Pittsburgh Press, 1971.

Hellenbeck, Wycoop. *New York at the Cotton States and International Exposition.* Albany, N.Y.: Crawford, 1896.

Hemphill, Paul. *The Nashville Sound: Bright Lights and Country Music.* New York: Simon and Schuster, 1970.

Higham, John. *Strangers in the Land: Patterns of American Nativism, 1860–1925.* New York: Atheneum, 1974.

Hill, Samuel S., ed. *Religion in the Southern States: A Historical Study.* Macon, Ga.: Mercer University Press, 1983.

Hofstader, Richard. *Social Darwinism in American Thought, 1860–1915.* Philadelphia: University of Pennsylvania Press, 1945.

Hopkins, C. Howard. *History of the Y.M.C.A. in North America.* New York: Abingdon Press, 1951.

————. *The Rise of the Social Gospel in American Protestantism, 1865–1915.* New Haven, Conn.: Yale University Press, 1940.

Horn, Stanley. *The Decisive Battle of Nashville.* Baton Rouge: Louisiana State University Press, 1956.

Howell, Clark. *History of Georgia.* Vol. 2. Atlanta: S. J. Clarke, 1926.

Hudson, Winthrop S. *Religion in America.* New York: Charles Scribner's Sons, 1965.

Hurlburt, Jesse L. *The Story of Chautauqua.* New York: G. P. Putnam's Sons, 1921.

Isaac, Paul E. *Prohibition and Politics: Turbulent Decades in Tennessee, 1885–1920*. Knoxville: University of Tennessee Press, 1965.

Johnson, Charles. *The Frontier Camp Meeting: Religion's Harvest Time*. Dallas: SMU Press, 1955.

Johnson, Michael P. *Toward a Patriarchal Republic: The Secession of Georgia*. Baton Rouge: Louisiana State University Press, 1977.

Jones, Charles Edwin. *Perfectionist Persuasion: The Holiness Movement and American Methodism, 1867–1936*. Metuchen, N.J.: Scarecrow Press, 1974.

Jones, Donald G. *The Sectional Crisis and Northern Methodism: A Study in Piety, Political Ethics, and Civil Religion*. New York: Scarecrow Press, 1979.

Knight, Lucien Lamar. *Georgia's Bi-Centennial Memoirs and Memories*. Vol. 2. Atlanta: Privately printed, 1932.

Lane, Mills. *The People of Georgia: An Illustrated Social History*. Savannah: Beehive Press, 1975.

————, ed. *War Is Hell! William T. Sherman's Personal Narrative of His March Through Georgia*. Savannah: Beehive Press, 1974.

Langton, Edward. *Satan: A Portrait*. London: Skettington and Son, 1945.

Larson, Orvin Prentiss. *American Infidel: Robert G. Ingersoll*. New York: Citadel Press, 1962.

Lawrence, Harold, ed. *Methodist Preachers in Georgia, 1783–1900*. Tignall, Ga.: Boyd, 1984.

Lender, Mark Edward, and James Kirby Martin. *Drinking in America: A History*. New York: Free Press, 1982.

Logan, Frenise A. *The Negro in North Carolina, 1876–1894*. Chapel Hill: University of North Carolina Press, 1964.

Logan, Rayford W. *The Negro in American Life and Thought: The Nadir, 1877–1901*. New York: Dial Press, 1954.

Longstreet, Stephen. *Chicago: 1860–1919*. New York: David McKay, 1973.

MacKenzie, Kenneth M. *The Robe and the Sword: The Methodist Church and the Rise of American Imperialism*. Washington, D.C.: Public Affairs Press, 1961.

McKinley, Edward H. *Marching to Glory: The History of the Salvation Army in the United States of America, 1880–1980*. San Francisco: Harper and Row, 1980.

MacLauren, Gay. *Morally We Roll Along*. Boston: Little, Brown, 1938.

McLoughlin, William G. *Billy Sunday Was His Real Name*. Chicago: University of Chicago Press, 1955.

————. *Modern Revivalism: Charles Grandison Finney to Billy Graham*. New York: Ronald Press, 1959.

————. *Revivals, Awakenings, and Reform: An Essay on Religion and Social Change, 1607–1977*. Chicago: University of Chicago Press, 1978.

McPherson, James M. *Battle Cry of Freedom: The Civil War Era*. New York: Oxford University Press, 1988.

Mann, Harold W. *Atticus Greene Haygood: Methodist Bishop, Editor, and Educator*. Athens: University of Georgia Press, 1965.

Marsden, George M. *Fundamentalism and American Culture: The Shaping of Twentieth Century Evangelicalism, 1870–1925*. New York: Oxford University Press, 1980.

Marty, Martin E. *Pilgrims in Their Own Land: Five Hundred Years of Religion in America*. Boston: Little, Brown, 1984.

———. *Righteous Empire: The Protestant Experience in America*. New York: Dial Press, 1970.

Mathews, James K. *Set Apart to Serve: The Meaning and Role of the Episcopacy in the Wesleyan Tradition*. Nashville: Abingdon Press, 1985.

May, Henry F. *Protestant Churches and Industrial America*. New York: Harper and Brothers, 1949.

Mead, Sidney. *The Lively Experiment: The Shaping of Christianity in America*. New York: Harper and Row, 1963.

Mendels, Joseph. *Concepts of Depression*. New York: John Wiley and Sons, 1970.

Mitchell, Frances Letcher. *Georgia: Land and People*. Atlanta: Franklin, 1893.

Moberg, David O. *The Church as a Social Institution: The Sociology of American Religion*. Englewood Cliffs, N.J.: Prentice-Hall, 1962.

Moorhead, James H. *American Apocalypse: Yankee Protestants and the Civil War, 1860–1869*. New Haven, Conn.: Yale University Press, 1978.

Morgan, H. Wayne, ed. *The Gilded Age: A Reappraisal*. Syracuse, N.Y.: Syracuse University Press, 1963.

Morrison, H. C. *Open Letter to the Bishops, Ministers, and Members of the Methodist Episcopal Church, South*. Louisville, Ky.: Pentecostal, n.d.

Morrison, Theodore. *Chautauqua: A Center for Education, Religion, and the Arts in America*. Chicago: University of Chicago Press, 1974.

Newby, I. A. *Jim Crow's Defense: Anti-Negro Thought in America, 1900–1930*. Baton Rouge: Louisiana State University Press, 1965.

Newton, J. C. C. *The New South and the Methodist Episcopal Church, South*. Baltimore: King Brothers, 1887.

Niebuhr, H. Richard, and Daniel D. Williams. *The Ministry in Historical Perspectives*. New York: Harper and Row, 1956.

Nixon, Raymond Blalock. *Henry W. Grady, Spokesman of the New South*. New York: Alfred A. Knopf, 1943.

Nolen, Claude H. *The Negro's Image in the South: The Anatomy of White Supremacy*. Lexington: University of Kentucky Press, 1967.

Norwood, Frederick A. *The Story of American Methodism: A History of the United Methodists and Their Relations*. Nashville: Abingdon Press, 1974.

Oblinger, Carl. *Religious Nemesis: Social Bases for the Holiness Schism in Late Nineteenth-Century Methodism: The Illinois Case, 1869–1889*. Institute for the Study of American Religion, Monograph Series, no. 1, 1973.

Odegard, Peter H. *Pressure Politics: The Story of the Anti-Saloon League*. New York: Columbia University Press, 1928.

Osterweis, Rollin G. *The Myth of the Lost Cause, 1865–1900*. Hamden, Conn.: Archon Books, 1973.

Parks, David B. *Alias Bill Arp: Charles Henry Smith and the South's "Goodly Heritage."* Athens: University of Georgia Press, 1990.

Parks, Joseph H. *Joseph E. Brown of Georgia*. Baton Rouge: Louisiana State University Press, 1977.

Parrington, Vernon Louis. *The Main Currents in American Thought: An*

Interpretation of American Literature from the Beginnings to 1920. New York: Harcourt, Brace, 1930.

Pearce, Haywood Jefferson, Jr. *Benjamin H. Hill, Secession, and Reconstruction*. Chicago: University of Chicago Press, 1920.

Pearson, C. C., and Hendricks, J. Edwin. *Liquor and Anti-Liquor in Virginia, 1619–1919*. Durham, N.C.: Duke University Press, 1965.

Peters, John Leland. *Christian Perfection and American Methodism*. Nashville: Abingdon Press, 1956.

Pierce, Alfred M. *Giant Against the Sky: The Life of Bishop Warren Akin Candler*. Nashville: Abingdon and Cokesbury Press, 1958.

————. *A History of Methodism in Georgia: February 5, 1736–June 24, 1955*. Atlanta: North Georgia Conference Historical Society, 1956.

Pinson, W. W. *George R. Stuart: Life and Work*. Nashville: Cokesbury Press, 1927.

Poe, Clarence, ed. *True Tales of the South at War: How Soldiers Fought and Families Lived, 1861–1865*. Chapel Hill: University of North Carolina Press, 1961.

Pollack, J. C. *Moody*. New York: Macmillan, 1963.

Rabinowitz, Howard N. *Race Relations in the Urban South, 1865–1890*. New York: Oxford University Press, 1978.

Reimers, David M. *White Protestantism and the Negro*. New York: Oxford University Press, 1965.

Richardson, Harry V. *Dark Salvation: The Story of Methodism as It Developed Among Blacks in America*. Garden City, N.Y.: Doubleday, 1976.

Rowntree, Joseph, and Arthur Sherwell. *The Temperance Problem and Social Reform*. New York: Tuslove Hanson and Comba, 1900.

Rudwin, Maximilian. *The Devil in Legend and Literature*. New York: AMS Press, 1970.

Ruether, Rosemary Radford, and Rosemary Skinner Keller, eds. *Women and Religion in America*. Vol. 1, *The Nineteenth Century*. San Francisco: Harper and Row, 1981.

Russell, James Michael. *Atlanta, 1847–1890: City Building in the Old South and the New*. Baton Rouge: Louisiana State University Press, 1988.

Schlesinger, Arthur M., Sr. *A Critical Period in American Religion, 1875–1900*. Philadelphia: Fortress Press, 1967.

Sellers, James Benson. *The Prohibition Movement in Alabama, 1702–1943*. Chapel Hill: University of North Carolina Press, 1943.

Simkins, Francis Butler. *The South, Old and New: A History, 1820–1947*. New York: Alfred A. Knopf, 1947.

Sizer, Sandra S. *Gospel Hymns and Social Religion: The Rhetoric of Nineteenth-Century Revivalism*. Philadelphia: Temple University Press, 1978.

Smith, Charles Henry. *Bill Arp's Scrap Book: Humor and Philosophy*. Atlanta: Jas. P. Harrison, 1884.

Smith, Henry Nash, ed. *Popular Culture and Industrialism, 1865–1890*. Garden City, N.Y.: Doubleday, Anchor Books, 1967.

Smith, Page. *Trial by Fire: A People's History of the Civil War and Reconstruction*. New York: McGraw Hill, 1982.

Smith, Timothy L. *Revivalism and Social Reform in Mid–Nineteenth Century America*. New York: Abingdon Press, 1957.

Spain, Rufus B. *At Ease in Zion: A Social History of Southern Baptists, 1865–1900*. Nashville: Vanderbilt University Press, 1961.

Sweet, William Warren. *Methodism in American History*. New York: Abingdon Press, 1961.

———. *The Methodists*. Nashville: Abingdon–Cokesbury Press, 1933.

———. *Revivalism in America: Its Origin, Growth, and Decline*. New York: Scribners, 1944.

Synan, Vinson. *The Holiness-Pentecostal Movement in the United States*. Grand Rapids, Mich.: William B. Eerdmans, 1971.

Talmadge, John E. *Rebecca Latimer Felton: Nine Stormy Decades*. Athens: University of Georgia Press, 1960.

Taylor, Arnold H. *Travail and Triumph: Black Life and Culture in the South Since the Civil War*. Westport, Conn.: Greenwood Press, 1976.

Thomas, William. *An Assessment of Mass Meetings as a Method of Evangelism: Case Study of Eurofest '75 and the Billy Graham Crusade in Brussels*. Amsterdam: Rodopi, 1977.

Thompson, C. Mildred. *Reconstruction in Georgia: Economic, Social, Political, 1865–1872*. Savannah: Beehive Press, 1972.

Timberlake, James H. *Prohibition and the Progressive Movement, 1900–1920*. Cambridge, Mass.: Harvard University Press, 1963.

Trealease, Allen W. *White Terror: The Ku Klux Klan Conspiracy and Southern Reconstruction*. New York: Harper and Row, 1971.

Twombly, Robert C. *Blacks in White America Since 1865: Images and Interpretation*. New York: David McKay, 1971.

Tyrell, Ian R. *Sobering Up: From Temperance to Prohibition in Antebellum America, 1800–1860*. Westport, Conn.: Greenwood Press, 1979.

Waller, William, ed. *Nashville in the 1890's*. Nashville: Vanderbilt University Press, 1970.

Warburton, Clark. *The Economic Results of Prohibition*. New York: Columbia University Press, 1932.

Weisberger, Bernard A. *They Gathered at the River: The Story of the Great Revivalists and Their Impact upon Religion in America*. Boston: Little, Brown, 1958.

Weisenberger, Francis P. *Ordeal of Faith: The Crisis of Churchgoing America, 1865–1900*. New York: Philosophical Library, 1959.

———. *Triumph of Faith: Contributions of the Church to American Life, 1865–1900*. Richmond, Va.: William Byrd Press, 1962.

Wells, David F., and John D. Woodbridge, eds. *The Evangelicals: What They Believe, Who They Are, Where They Are Changing*. Nashville: Abingdon Press, 1975.

Wesche, Percival A. *Henry Clay Morrison, Crusader Saint*. Wilmore, Ky.: Asbury Theological Seminary, 1963.

White, Charles Edward. *The Beauty of Holiness: Phoebe Palmer as Theologian, Revivalist, Feminist, and Humanitarian*. Grand Rapids, Mich.: Francis Asbury Press, 1986.

Whitener, Daniel J. *Prohibition in North Carolina, 1715–1945.* Chapel Hill: University of North Carolina Press, 1946.

Whitlock, Brand. *Forty Years of It.* 1914. Reprint. New York: Greenwood Press, 1968.

Wiebe, Robert. *The Search for Order, 1877–1920.* New York: Hill and Wang, 1967.

Wiley, Bell Irvin. *The Life of Johnny Reb: The Common Soldier of the Confederacy.* New York: Bobbs-Merrill, 1943.

Willard, Frances. *Women and Temperance; or, The Work and the Workers of the Women's Christian Temperance Union.* 1883. Reprint. New York: Arno Press, 1972.

Williamson, Joel. *The Crucible of Race: Black-White Relations in the American South Since Emancipation.* New York: Oxford University Press, 1984.

Wilson, Charles Reagan. *Baptized in Blood: The Religion of the Lost Cause, 1865–1920.* Athens: University of Georgia Press, 1980.

Wimberly, C. F. *A Biographical Sketch of Henry Clay Morrison, D.D.: The Man and His Ministry.* Chicago: Fleming H. Revell, 1923.

Winokur, George, Paula J. Clayton, and Theodore Reich. *Manic Depressive Illness.* St. Louis: C. W. Mosby, 1969.

Woodward, C. Vann. *Origins of the New South: 1877–1917.* Vol. 9 of *A History of the South,* edited by Wendell Holmes Stephenson and E. Merton Coulter. Baton Rouge: Louisiana State University Press, 1951.

———. *The Strange Career of Jim Crow.* New York: Oxford University Press, 1974.

Wynes, Charles E., ed. *The Negro in the South Since 1865: Selected Essays in American Negro History.* New York: Harper and Row, 1968.

Zibert, Carl. *Yesterday's Nashville.* Miami: E. A. Seeman. 1976.

ARTICLES

Bacote, Clarence A. "Georgia's Reaction to the Negro Policy of Theodore Roosevelt." *Atlanta History Bulletin* 21 (Spring 1977): 72–94.

———. "The Negro in Atlanta Politics." *Phylan: The Atlanta University Review* 16, no. 4 (1955): 333–68.

———. "Negro Proscriptions, Protests, and Proposed Solutions in Georgia, 1880–1908." *Journal of Southern History* 25 (November 1959): 471–98.

Bauman, Mark K. "A Famous Atlantan Speaks Out Against Lynching: Bishop Warren Akin Candler and Social Justice." *Atlanta Historical Bulletin* 20 (Spring 1976): 24–31.

Boisen, Anton T. "Economic Distress and Religious Experience: A Study of the Holy Rollers." *Psychiatry* 2 (May 1939): 185–94.

Cadman, S. Parkes. "Famous Revivalists of the United States." *Chautauquan* 20 (January 1895): 441–49.

Cannon, J. F. "Evangelism: Its Place and Promotion." *Presbyterian Quarterly* 1 (October 1888): 462–65.

Coulter, E. M. "The Athens Dispensary." *Georgia Historical Quarterly* 50 (1966): 14–36.

Crowe, Charles. "Racial Massacre in Atlanta: September 22, 1906." *Journal of Negro History* 54 (April 1969): 150–75.

———. "Racial Violence and Social Reform: Origins of the Atlanta Riot of 1906." *Journal of Negro History* 53 (July 1968): 234–56.

Curry, Daniel. "City Evangelization." *Methodist Review* 69 (March 1887): 289–95.

———. "Evangelists and Revivals." *Methodist Review* 69 (March 1887): 284–88.

Davis, Harold E. "Henry W. Grady, Master of the Atlanta Ring, 1880–1886." *Georgia Historical Quarterly* 69 (Spring 1985): 1–38.

Davis, Louise. "Ryman Fans 'Rally Round.'" *Tennessean Magazine*, February 24, 1974, 14.

———. "Steamboatin' Tom Ryman and His Gift to Nashville." *Tennessean Magazine*, January 27, 1974, 4–9.

———. "When Captain Tom 'Got Religion.'" *Tennessean Magazine*, February 3, 1974, 11–14.

Dike, Samuel W. "A Study of New England Revivals." *American Journal of Sociology* 15 (November 1909): 261–78.

Figh, Margaret Gillis. "Life in Nineteenth Century Georgia as Reflected in Bill Arp's Works." *Georgia Historical Quarterly* 35 (March 1951): 16–21.

Firebaugh, Glenn. "How Effective Are City-wide Crusades? A Scientific Survey Estimates the Effects of the 1976 Billy Graham Crusade in Seattle." *Christianity Today*, March 27, 1981, 24–29.

Grantham, Dewey. "Georgia Politics and the Disfranchisement of the Negro." *Georgia Historical Quarterly* 42 (March 1948): 1–21.

Graves, John Temple. "The Fight Against Alcohol: Georgia Pioneers of the Prohibition Crusade." *Cosmopolitan* 45 (1908): 83–90.

Harrison, W. P. "Evangelists and Pastors." *Southern Methodist Review* 4 (March 1888): 105–8.

———. "The Modern Evangelist." *Quarterly Review* 20 (July 1891): 424–27.

Helm, Benjamin. "Evangelism: Its Place and Promotion." *Presbyterian Quarterly* 1 (April 1888): 130–44.

Henderson, Jerry E. "Nashville's Ryman Auditorium." *Tennessee Historical Quarterly* 28 (Winter 1966): 360–70.

Jackson, Stephen. "Preacher's Mansion May Be Restored." *Atlanta Constitution Magazine*, July 14, 1974, 7–8.

Jellineck, E. M. "Recent Trends in Alcohol and Alcohol Consumption." *Quarterly Journal of Studies on Alcohol* 8 (July 1947): 1–43.

Korobkin, Russell. "The Politics of Disfranchisement in Georgia." *Georgia Historical Quarterly* 74 (Spring 1990): 20–58.

Lindsay, Thomas M. "Revivals." *Contemporary Review* 88 (1905): 344–62.

Link, Arthur S. "The Progressive Movement in the South, 1870–1914." *North Carolina Historical Review* 23 (1946): 172–95.

Loetscher, Loefferts A. "Presbyterianism and Revivals in Philadelphia Since 1875." *Pennsylvania Magazine of History and Biography* 68 (1944): 172–95.

McGlywn, Edward. "Evangelizing Methods." *Homiletic Review* 13 (February 1887): 170–71.

McLoughlin, William G. "Jones Versus Jones." *American Heritage* 12 (April 1961): 56–59, 84–89.

Metcalf, Arthur. "Evangelism: Its Defects." *Homiletic Review* 35 (March 1898): 279–83.

Millard, Nelson. "The Manliness of Religion." *Homiletic Review* 7 (October 1882): 30–31.

Moore, John Hammond. "Jim Crow in Georgia." *South Atlantic Quarterly* 66 (Fall 1967): 554–65.

———. "The Negro and Prohibition in Atlanta, 1885–1887." *South Atlantic Quarterly* 69 (1970): 38–57.

Moore, Vandi Osment. "The Sam Jones Story." *North Georgia Quarterly* 4 (Spring 1990): 47–53.

O'Donell, Red. "Ryman's Gospel Tabernacle." *Nashville Banner*, February 8, 1974, 39.

Parker, Charles A. "The Camp Meeting on the Frontier and the Methodist Religious Resort in the East: Before 1900." *Methodist History* 17 (March 1980): 179–92.

Peck, J. O. "Revival Methods." *Homiletic Review* 9 (April 1885): 351–53.

———, William Brodbeck, and H. W. Bolton. "The Revival: A Symposium." *Methodist Review* 75 (March–April 1893): 240–53.

Peck, Thomas E. "Revivals of Religion." *Presbyterian Quarterly* 2 (January 1888): 399–415.

Pierson, Arthur R. "Modern Evangelistic Movements: Their Influence on the Organic Life of the Church." *Homiletic Review* 24 (July 1892): 15–19.

Porter, Curt. "Chautauqua: Monteagle and the Industrial Assemblies." *Tennessee Historical Quarterly* 22 (December 1963): 343–60.

Reed, George E. "Evangelistic Methods." *Homiletic Review* 16 (August 1888): 180–82.

Reed, Ralph E., Jr. "Emory College and the Sledd Affair of 1902: A Case Study in Southern Honor and Racial Attitudes." *Georgia Historical Quarterly* 72 (Fall 1988): 463–92.

Saunders, Robert. "Southern Populists and the Negro, 1893–1895." *Journal of Negro History* 54 (July 1969): 240–61.

Sizer, Sandra. "Politics and Apolitical Religion: The Great Urban Revivals of the Late Nineteenth Century." *Church History* 48 (March 1979): 81–98.

Stevens, Abel. "Methodist Preaching: Old and New Style." *Homiletic Review* 9 (June 1885): 477–84.

Teeter, Herman B. "Sam Jones: Methodism's Greatest Evangelist." *Together* 9 (October 1965): 42–45.

Turley, Briane. "A Wheel Within a Wheel: Southern Methodism and the Georgia Holiness Association." *Georgia Historical Quarterly* 75 (Summer 1991): 295–320.

Watts, Eugene J. "Black Political Progress in Atlanta: 1868–1895." *Journal of Negro History* 59 (July 1974): 268–86.

Wheeler, David H. "Changes in Methodist Preaching." *Homiletic Review* 7 (March 1883): 340–42.

White, John E. "Prohibition: The New Task and Opportunity of the South." *South Atlantic Quarterly* 7 (1908): 130–42.

Wilkinson, William C. "The Question of 'Evangelists.'" *Homiletic Review* 14 (November 1887): 430–32.

Wilson, Richard L. "Sam Jones: An Apostle of the New South." *Georgia Historical Quarterly* 51 (Winter 1973): 459–74.

Witherspoon, T. D. "Nineteenth Century Evangelism." *Presbyterian Quarterly* 1 (October 1887): 280–96.

Wylie, A. McElroy. "Sensationalism and the Pulpit." *Homiletic Review* 21 (April 1891): 221–27.

Index

Ministerial duties of Sam Jones:
  as Agent for an orphan home: 57–60,
    151, 154, 156, 216
  as Circuit preacher, 37–56; DeSoto,
    48–49; Monticello, 53, 54;
    Newbern, 51, 52, 54; Van Wert,
    37, 38, 39, 44, 45, 46, 53
Moody, Dwight L., 32, 61, 72, 75, 82,
  94, 98–99, 100, 101, 102, 112, 115,
  152, 242, 243
Moon, Lottie, 113
Moral Majority: comparison of Sam
  Jones's views with, 243
Morrison, H. C., 147–48
Music in revivals, 66, 92, 94–95, 98

New South. *See under* Southern history
Nye, Bill, 74

Ochs, Julius, 81
Old South. *See under* Southern history
O'Neill, Alya, 219, 234
Orphan Home (Decatur, GA): Sam
  Jones as agent of, 57–60, 151, 154,
  156, 216
Owens, Webb, 24

Palmer, Phoebe, 135
Parks, W. A., 138, 139–40, 142
Pentecostal movement, 146–47, 234
People's Party, 189, 192
Phelan ("Father"), 96–97
Pierce, George, 5, 142
Pierce, Lovick, 137, 167
Populism, 51, 188–93, 197, 206,
  229–30
Prefundamentalism, 122–27, 243
Progressive: Sam Jones's reputation as
  a, *x*, 125, 164, 180–81, 193. *See
  also* Ecumenicism
Prohibition, 165–82:
  Anti-Saloon League, 169–70,
    174–75
  Laws to suppress the use of alcohol,
    166, 172–75, 183

as a Moral issue, 167, 170–71
  Politics and, 148, 194–95, 243
  Prohibition party, 148, 174–75
  Temperance vs. abstinence, 7–8,
    166–69, 171–73
  Women's Christian Temperance
    Union, 70, 105, 169, 226
Protestant sects: bickering among, 109,
  118, 125, 134, 242
Proudfit, Alexander, 114
Pyron, Rouhs, 221

Racial issues:
  Alcohol: use among blacks, 184–85,
    205–6
  Changing (inconsistent) views of Sam
    Jones on, 4, 28, 86–91, 185,
    195–202, 205, 243
  Education of blacks, 86–87, 204
  Erosion of Northern liberalism, 89
  Membership of blacks in Methodist
    churches, 39, 107
  Riots and lynchings, 28, 90, 109,
    190, 199–200, 206–7, 211
  Sam Jones vs. Theodore Roosevelt,
    202–3
  Voting, 89, 90, 189, 204, 205
Regeneration: views of Sam Jones on,
  141, 144–45, 158
Revivals:
  Failure of other revivalists in
    Atlanta, 100–101, 108, 109
  Failure of, to generate new church
    members, 4, 14, 107–8, 151–53
  Featuring Sam Jones (by location):
    Atlanta, 102–10; Baltimore, 69,
    94, 150; Boston, 91; Brooklyn,
    65–66; Chicago, 71–72, 91, 94,
    97, 98, 100, 226, 237;
    Cincinnati, 90, 128; Corinth, 62;
    Huntsville, 66; Knoxville, 151;
    Memphis, 61–62, 63, 65, 67–68,
    69, 78, 234–35; Milledgville
    (GA), 79; Nashville, 1–15, 61, 69,
    230–31, 233; Northern and
    Midwestern tour, 61, 70, 90–91,

Revivals: Featuring Sam Jones (*cont'd*)
94, 96; Oklahoma City, 239–40;
Omaha, 128; Palestine (TX), 212;
St. Joseph, 79, 90, 104, 128; St.
Louis, 79, 95–98, 120, 230, 237;
Waco, 58, 63, 65; Welsh, 234.
See also Chautauquas
Fluctuations of interest in, 14, 72,
113–14, 116–17, 233–35
Meetings restricted to specific
groups, 11, 73–74, 81–82, 88,
103, 106, 214
Use of music in, 66, 92, 94–95, 98
Reynolds, Joseph A., 136
Richardson, Simon Peter, 49–51, 52,
151, 154, 212
Risse, J. F. W., 238–39
Robbins, John B., 156, 157
Roosevelt, Theodore, 202–3
Roselawn, 12, 238
Ryman, Thomas, 6–7, 194, 231

Salvation: Sam Jones's views on way to
attain, 2, 7, 41–42, 54–56, 80–83,
123–25
Salvation Army, 128
Sam Jones Female College, 129
Sanctification, 138–47, 158
Sankey, Ira, 66, 94, 95, 98
Sawyer, John, 159
Scriptures: Sam Jones's views on
literality of, 52–53, 115–16, 118–19,
122, 124–25
Sin, 2, 5, 7, 41–46, 54–56, 80–83,
123–25, 146
Slater, John F., 155
Slaton, William, 18, 104
Sledd, Andrew, 199–200
Sloan, B. C., 210, 234
Small, Annie, 93
Small, Paul, 110
Small, Samuel White, 92–94, 95,
97–98, 109, 170, 197, 225, 226–27
Smith, Hoke, 193–94, 204, 205, 206,
224
Social Darwinism, 132, 165, 195–96

Social Gospelers, 127–28, 130–32
Southern history (*see also* Economic
issues; Racial issues; Revivals;
Women's Roles and Rights):
Agriculture, 86, 101–2, 112
Atlanta (*see also under* Revivals): as
embodiment of the New South, 98,
101–2; modernization of, 99–104;
race riot in, 90; social and
political wars in, 104–5, 108; visit
of Booker T. Washington to,
99–100
New South, 84–92, 101–2, 155,
163–65, 201, 231, 243
Old South, 4, 5, 85, 91, 111, 163,
201
Reconstruction, 84–85, 89
Spencer, Herbert, 132
Spurgeon, Charles, 40–42, 44
Stanton, Frank F., 219–20
Steel, S. A., 61, 138
Stein, Orth, 103, 109
Stocks, Annie (Sam Jones's sister), 19,
67, 68, 209, 220–21, 240
Stocks, Porter (Sam Jones's nephew),
67, 213
Stradley, William, 159–60
Stuart, George, 81, 95, 103, 150,
153–54, 160, 170, 194, 234
Sumner, William Graham, 132
Sunday, Billy, 75, 77, 109–10, 242
Swing, David, 125

Talmage, Dewitt, 65–66, 115
Taylor, Bob, 230
Thomas, John W., Jr., 106, 194,
240–41
Thorne, William H., 196–97
Tigert, J. J., 162
Tigert, J. M., 149
Tillett, Wilbur F., 129, 156
Tobacco, 226–28
Torrey, R. A., 108, 109
Tucker, Emma, 105
Tulip Street Methodist Church
(Nashville), 4, 13, 14

Turner, M. D., 142–43
Turner, William L., 210

Uncle Ben (sexton), 62

Vincent, John H., 229

Wadsworth, W. W., 52
Washington, Booker T., 99–100, 197, 202–3
Watson, George, 138, 143–44
Watson, Thomas E., 51, 189–91, 241
Weisberger, Bernard, 242
Wesley, John, 49, 82, 124, 134–36, 142, 144–47, 152
Wesleyan Methodism, 49, 82, 124, 134–36, 142, 144–47, 152
White, John E., 205

Willard, Frances, 169
Williams, John Sharp, 195–96
Winchell, Alexander, 115–16
Windham, Sam ("Drummer Evangelist"), 238–39
Wingfield, A. R., 150
Winton, George, 236–37
Wofford, W. T., 25
Women's Christian Temperance Union, 70, 105, 169, 226
Women's roles and rights, x, 105, 126, 145, 147, 213–14
Woodward, James, 207
Word (mayor of Palestine, TX), 212
Wright, Seaborn, 189, 191, 192

YMCA, 113, 128–29